AFRICAN AMERIC

GEORGIA LOWCOUNTRY

Race in the Atlantic World, 1700–1900

AFRICAN AMERICAN LIFE IN THE GEORGIA LOWCOUNTRY

The Atlantic World and the Gullah Geechee

Edited by Philip Morgan

ॐ

Published in association with the Georgia Humanities Council

THE UNIVERSITY OF GEORGIA PRESS

ATHENS AND LONDON

Paperback edition, 2011
© 2010 by the University of Georgia Press
Athens, Georgia 30602
www.ugapress.org
Set in Garamond Premier Pro by Copperline Book Services
Printed and bound by Thomson-Shore, Inc.

The paper in this book meets the guidelines for
permanence and durability of the Committee on
Production Guidelines for Book Longevity of the
Council on Library Resources.

Printed in the United States of America

11   12   13   14   15   P   5   4   3   2   1

The Library of Congress has cataloged the hardcover
edition of this book as follows:
African American life in the Georgia lowcountry : the Atlantic
world and the Gullah Geechee / edited by Philip Morgan.
xi, 311 p., [46] p. of plates : ill., maps ; 25 cm. —
(Race in the Atlantic world, 1700–1900)
Includes bibliographical references and index.
ISBN-13: 978-0-8203-3064-8 (hardcover : alk. paper)
ISBN-10: 0-8203-3064-7 (hardcover : alk. paper)
1. African Americans—Georgia—Atlantic Coast—History.
2. African Americans—Georgia—Atlantic Coast—Social conditions.
3. African Americans—Georgia—Atlantic Coast—Religion.   4. Gullahs—
Georgia—Atlantic Coast—History.   5. Atlantic Coast (Ga.)—History.
6. Atlantic Coast (Ga.)—Social conditions.   7. Atlantic Coast (Ga.)—
Religious life and customs.   I. Morgan, Philip D., 1949–
F295.N4A376 2010
305.896′073075—dc22   2009022714

Paperback ISBN-13: 978-0-8203-4307-5
ISBN-10: 0-8203-4307-2

British Library Cataloging-in-Publication Data available

Grateful acknowledgment is made to the Georgia Historical Society
for its special assistance with the illustrations used in this volume.

Dedicated to the African Americans who lived and
worked on Ossabaw Island and to their descendants
in Pin Point and elsewhere who continue
to foster their rich heritage

Contents

Foreword

How do you share an island without destroying it? That challenge became the starting point for a symposium on African American life in the Georgia lowcountry that took place in Savannah in early 2008. Thirty years prior to that event, the state of Georgia acquired Ossabaw Island as its first heritage preserve. By the terms of the preserve, most of the twenty-six-thousand-acre island is to revert to a state of nature and to be used only for "natural, scientific, and cultural study, research, and education." Since that time, scientists, artists, and teachers as well as Boy Scouts, students, and environmentalists have come to explore, observe, and learn more of the third-largest island off the coast. The fact that only a few dozen people can visit on any one day poses a Hobson's choice. How can Ossabaw be shared without generating crowds of people that would destroy the setting whose beauty and isolation make it so transforming an experience?

In pursuit of the overarching goal, the Ossabaw Island Education Alliance held a roundtable discussion during the summer of 2005 to discuss ways to tell the story of African Americans from their arrival on the island in the eighteenth century until the twentieth century. The tabby cabins, built during the 1840s and continuously inhabited until the 1980s, served as the focal point for this conversation. The state archaeologist has called them "one of Georgia's most significant archaeological and historical sites."

The historians and anthropologists who participated in the roundtable discussion recommended that the alliance begin by focusing its attention on the role of African Americans on the entire coast of Georgia. They felt that most writers, when speaking of the lowcountry, begin with a passing nod to the stretch from Georgetown to Cumberland Island and then focus their attention on South Carolina. The Georgia lowcountry has been relatively neglected. And yet the experience of African Americans, both urban and rural, was an important one, not only for the ways that this experience replicated the traditions, culture, and patterns in Carolina but for how it possessed its own unique identity. That identity had to do with the place of Georgia in the larger Black Atlantic, religious survivals along the coast, the evolution of communities like Pin Point, and the unfolding of events like General Sherman's Special Field Order No. 15 on the barrier islands. Given the comparative lack of attention to this subject, it seemed a propitious moment to hold a symposium to consider black life on the Georgia coast and the interaction of culture with environment and economics for over two hundred years. It also seemed a good moment to place this story within the larger context of the Atlantic world, the world of West Africa, the Caribbean, and Europe.

As the director of the Ossabaw Island Education Alliance, I found willing sponsors in the Ossabaw Island Foundation, the Georgia Historical Society, Armstrong Atlantic State University, Georgia Southern University, Savannah State University, and the University of Georgia Press. Ten scholars, including three winners of the Bancroft Prize, accepted the invitation to present original research. The response of those asked to underwrite the symposium was equally encouraging: the Wormsloe Foundation, the Hodge Foundation, the Georgia Humanities Council, Colonial Oil/ Enmark, and Brasseler USA all contributed funds. The University of Georgia Press committed early in the planning process to publish the papers as a book in their new series, Race in the Atlantic World, 1700–1900.

On February 27–29, 2008, a symposium took place in Savannah, Georgia, under the title "The Atlantic World and African Life and Culture in the Georgia Lowcountry: 18th to the 20th Century." In seeking an audience for this event, the alliance pursued dual goals: on the one hand to attract academics and scholars throughout the country and, on the other, to reach out to the general public. The response showed the growing interest in the topic. More than 450 people attended from eighteen states and three countries. Especially gratifying was the considerable turnout of the African American community in Savannah. The mayor of Savannah, a former dean at Savannah State University, proclaimed to the audience he was Gullah on his mother's side and Geechee on his father's side. The symposium included visits to the tabby cabins on Ossabaw Island, a tour of African American sites in Savannah, and workshops for teachers.

The symposium has had a further consequence. It sped efforts to tell the story of the African Americans on Ossabaw Island and how their descendants formed a community on the mainland, Pin Point, where values and traditions extending back into the eighteenth century found an echo. The Ossabaw Island Foundation is grateful for the energy, enthusiasm, and wisdom of Bo Bowens, owner of Bandy's Bait Shop, and Bill Haynes, retired architect, in spearheading the attempt to recover the memories of that community at a time when so much of its history has been lost. Mr. Bowens, who spent his earliest years in a tabby cabin on Ossabaw, passed away in May 2008.

Paul Pressly
Director
Ossabaw Island Education Alliance

AFRICAN AMERICAN LIFE IN THE
GEORGIA LOWCOUNTRY

Philip Morgan

Introduction

MYSTERY and exoticism shroud the lowcountry of Georgia and South Carolina. The landscape is seductive: the noble live oak, the swaying palmetto, and the lofty pine inspire; the rich hues of tangled swampland give way to sweeping vistas of dense, tall grass savannas; stretches of salt marsh alternate with majestic sandy beaches; ubiquitous Spanish moss, hanging from trees in long festoons, adds an eerie, otherworldly dimension to the scene. A volatile subtropical climate heightens the contrasts: "in the spring a paradise, in the summer a hell, and in the autumn a hospital" was one early adage. Eden-like during parts of the year, oppressively hot and humid at other times, subject to devastating hurricanes at periodic intervals, the lowcountry climate both ravishes and ravages in about equal measure. Lowcountry topography contributes to the exoticism. The vast majority of the lowcountry's tidal shoreline consists of barrier islands, isolated places, the stuff of legends, each a world of its own, but also connected to the mainland via waterways that interlace the region. Remote and yet interconnected, the lowcountry is an unusual place.[1]

Equally mysterious are the Gullah-Geechee people who bore the imprint of, even as they shaped, the distinctive lowcountry landscape. In the eighteenth century, they formed a black majority in the region's population, the only such majority in North America. *Gullah* (probably deriving from Angola, or possibly the Gola of the Windward Coast, or perhaps a combination of the two) is generally the term applied to those blacks living in the South Carolina section of the lowcountry; *Geechee* (which some have attributed to the Kissi of Upper Guinea, but more likely traceable to a shortened form of the Muskogean name for a prominent Georgia river, the Ogeechee) refers to those living south of the Savannah River. Gullah-Geechee culture draws much inspiration from African traditions — whether in language, material culture, foodways, dancing, music, or religion. Particularly intriguing — and baffling — are the tales of flying Africans that gain a sympathetic hearing from Timothy Powell in this volume.[2]

A pertinent question immediately arises: are the Gullah-Geechee people to be considered, in Erskine Clarke's words, "a largely marginal group in American society and consequently an attraction for tourists seeking an exotic and fading culture" or "a part of a broad American experience and a window into the very character of American history"? It is to be hoped that Gullah-Geechee culture is resilient and not merely a tourist attraction, but perhaps the answer is yes to at least parts of both questions. On the one hand, Gullah-Geechees clearly are marginal to the larger story of black people in North America. As one title of a book about the Gullah notes, they were "a peculiar people," and, as Emory Campbell reflects in the concluding essay in this volume, once he left the sea islands, people had trouble identifying him: was he from the Caribbean, from Africa, or from some other exotic locale? Few could imagine that he was from a part of the United States.[3] In the eighteenth century, the center of gravity of black life in North America was the tobacco coast of the Chesapeake region; in the following century, it became the cotton South; and in the twentieth century, with migration, it was the urban North and Midwest. In all these periods, the lowcountry was peripheral, marginal to those mainstreams. The signature crops of the lowcountry — rice, indigo, and sea island cotton — also made it exceptional, unusual by North American standards. The task system, by which lowcountry slave labor was organized — and in which individual slaves were largely left to their own devices, provided they completed their assigned jobs — also diverged from the sunup-to-sundown, collectively driven gang labor experienced by most American slaves. Gullah-Geechee culture is strikingly, excitingly, and mysteriously different, an exotic phenomenon.

At the same time, however, the lowcountry has some claims on being a significant part — in some instances, a central component — of the black experience in North America. Sullivan's Island has been rightly labeled the "Ellis Island" of black North America; it is only appropriate that in 2008 the Toni Morrison Society and National Park Service dedicated a suitable memorial, "a bench by the road," to honor those who survived and those who died during the Middle Passage, the brutal transatlantic journey from Africa. Over half (56 percent) of the 388,000 Africans forcibly landed in North America over the course of the slave trade arrived in the lowcountry. From the perspective of the forced migration of Africans, the lowcountry was the preeminent, not a peripheral, destination. Not surprisingly, too, the lowcountry was the site, as Michael Gomez notes, "of the largest gathering of African Muslims in early North America." The lowcountry has other claims to fame. It was a place where the archaeology of the African diaspora took root, and our understanding of key items of black material culture — their self-made colonoware, for example — has come to light. It was also the home of the first separate black Baptist church. It was one of the earliest, if not the earliest, to describe itself as "African." It was a hub from which satellite Baptist churches radiated throughout the Black Atlantic, reaching out to Nova Scotia, Sierra Leone, and Jamaica. Lowcountry Georgia, and Savannah in particular, was thus a precocious place where blacks chose to identify themselves and their institutions as "African." The lowcountry was also a place of infamy. The plantation may symbolize elegant living, but it was a site of extraordinary exploitation — and no region in the United States had a harsher form of slavery than the lowcountry. A tidewater rice plantation was "a huge hydraulic machine," a feat of early modern social engineering, making enormous demands of its labor force, and uprooting thousands of Africans to feed its insatiable desire for yet more labor. Former South Carolina slave Ben Horry, looking back on slavery on a rice plantation, spoke of "them dark days." Peter Wood has suggested the terms "slave labor camp" or even "gulag" as synonyms for "plantation."[4]

Issues of marginality and centrality frame my opening essay, which is intended as a general introduction to black life in the Georgia lowcountry in roughly its first century. While pointing out that the Georgian experience was often out of step with developments in other parts of North America, I offer a number of ways for thinking about this singular colonial and early national experience as a microcosm of broader forces sweeping the Atlantic world — for example, its precocious antislavery character; its notable borderlands status, giving rise to complex and intricate relations between Native Americans and blacks, which were more wide-ranging in the Lower South than in other parts of British North America; its participation in a greater plantation world, with connections throughout the circum-Caribbean; its ties to Africa, which were deep and extensive; and finally its exemplification of the many ironies of the black experience during the Revolutionary era. Early Georgia, I suggest, offers a special perspective on at least five larger Atlantic stories.

While I touch on the era of the American Revolution, Betty Wood probes the period in depth. She finds that the American Revolution had mixed results for lowcountry black women, a group that has been far too invisible in most history books. The Revolution, she finds, expanded the opportunities for freedom, most notably by facilitating escape from slavery. Slave women ran away at much greater rates during the Revolutionary War than ever before — since escaping to British lines offered a real chance at freedom — and families, not just solitaries, now fled. Furthermore, urban women, working in close proximity to whites and dominating the public markets, were also important disseminators of news, vital during wartime. The free women of color who organized an "Ethiopian Ball" in Charleston to which they invited only officers of the British Army and slave women, symbolized the breaching of racial and gendered boundaries that wartime facilitated. At the same time, however, the war brought much disruption and hardship for women of color. The Revolutionary War in the Lower South was especially violent, descending often into savagery; black women were notably vulnerable, and they suffered deprivations more than most. Many of those who escaped experienced even harsher slavery in the Caribbean. The aftermath of the war also launched an expansion of slavery in the lowcountry, as planters sought to replenish depleted labor forces first from other parts of the South and then from Africa, and as they reasserted their power, repressing maroon communities and developing new crops such as sea island cotton. As always, slave women bore the brunt of field labor associated with renewed staple production.

The American Revolutionary era is also the setting for Vincent Carretta's exploration of five black authors who published accounts of their lives. Only one of the five is known definitively to have been born in the lowcountry (another, Olaudah Equiano, might have been), but the region left its mark on all of them. For one thing, the lowcountry is usually considered the most inhospitable place in North America for evangelical Christianity. Nevertheless, all five were exposed to it in some degree. Even Boston

King, who was converted outside the lowcountry, nevertheless had a father who was a lay preacher. Evangelical Christianity in its early phases tended to be radical, although George Whitefield made his accommodations with slavery, as did the Countess of Huntingdon, who plays an important role in Carretta's story. She even requested her agents in Savannah to purchase a "woman-slave" who was to be named "SELINA after me."[5] Two of the black authors had significant contacts with Native Americans when in the Lower South — John Marrant lived with the Cherokees for two years (and would later preach to the Micmacs); David George lived as a slave among the Creeks — and a third, Equiano, with Misquito Indians in Central America. Why does the lowcountry play such a disproportionate role in the development of early black autobiography, Carretta rightly asks? In addition to the answer he gives, perhaps the particularly traumatic nature of the American Revolutionary experience in that region played a role. More blacks fled the lowcountry than other parts of North America. Naturally, some of them ended up in Britain where they published their life histories. If the British Army and Navy had spent more time in the Chesapeake, perhaps we would have more life histories from ex-slaves from that region. In the same way that the chaos of the Revolutionary War in the Lower South permitted some black men to organize separate churches, so it facilitated opportunities for some to evacuate the region and then publicize their stories. Whatever the answer, as Carretta notes, some "Sons of the lowcountry put themselves up for adoption," and an important black diaspora moved eastward as well as westward.

Some prominent Muslims, the coincidences of whose stories are striking — most notably the two Bilalis (Salih of St. Simons and Mohammed of Sapelo) born about the same time but a thousand miles apart in Africa, both taken to the Bahamas, albeit separately, and then relocated to adjoining islands in Georgia, where they became prominent drivers — naturally attract notice, but Michael Gomez puts such singular individuals into a wider context. Some Muslims, their names dotting the runaway slave advertisements in South Carolina and Georgia newspapers, fled inland, where Native Americans sometimes provided sanctuary and at other times acted as captors. Some Muslims were North Africans, but the majority hailed from West Africa. Naming patterns are one important clue to Muslim identities; particularly notable are those slave parents, with seemingly no Muslim associations — such as Nelson and Venus — who nevertheless gave their child a Muslim name, in their case, Hammett. Some lowcountry slaves held devoutly to their Muslim faith, evidenced by their resort to ritual ablutions, prayer mats and beads, dietary regulations, and reading of the Qur'ān. There are even hints of conversion to Islam in the lowcountry. White masters often favored Muslim slaves, appointing them to privileged positions, and attempting—sometimes successfully—to gain their support in buttressing the slave system. Muslim slaves are emblematic of the status differentiation that was possible under slavery.

Alongside the divide between Muslim and non-Muslim slaves, there arose, as Erskine Clarke points out, an even more pervasive gulf—between the worlds of Christianity and conjuring, between preacher and "Obey-Man" (obeah practitioner), between piety and magic, between the book and the charm. His essay probes two paired contests: one in the lowcountry between a fugitive slave conjuror and a driver who was a Baptist lay leader; and the other in West Africa between a white Presbyterian missionary, originally from the lowcountry, and a "fetish priest." The contrast between the two places provides intelligent commentaries upon one another. The lowcountry debts to Africa become clear, as in the ways in which charms mimic fetishes, but accommodations and loss are also evident. The African dream tradition is incorporated into African American Christianity. Secrecy, not openness, characterizes the world of conjuring under slavery. Lowcountry witchcraft was a much more attenuated phenomenon than its West African counterpart. What was retained, what was transformed, and what was jettisoned come into sharper relief as a result of this sensitive comparative treatment.

Archaeologists in the lowcountry have found a few objects—pierced coins, which may have been worn as amulets, and pots marked with incised crosses—that perhaps had religious significance, but for the most part their findings have illuminated material, not spiritual, life. (For African Americans, this distinction between sacred and profane was far more blurred than for modern scholars.) Without archaeology, for example, we would never have known that slaves created their own earthenware pottery, but apparently Gullah peoples created bowls and pots far more readily than Geechees. Perhaps this difference was more a function of chronology than anything else: most Georgian plantations that have been excavated are from the nineteenth century, when colonoware had been replaced by ironware. Viewed in a circum-Caribbean context, however, pottery making varied in scope and scale from place to place, so perhaps Georgian slaves never fully developed the vernacular tradition of pottery making.

A distinctive housing form — tabby construction, made from oyster-shell building material — was unique to the lowcountry; it may owe something to Spanish precedents, although Theresa Singleton suggests it might also have Caribbean analogues. Despite the widespread use of tabby, wattle-and-daub was the most common type of slave housing; it probably owed something to African, European, and Native American origins. Archaeology has also demonstrated that Gullah-Geechee peoples obtained a large amount of their protein from wild resources; even remnants of guns and musket balls have been found among slave settlements. In pottery, housing, and diet, then, archaeologists have added considerably to our understanding of lowcountry black life.

Just as some of the first archaeological studies of Georgia plantations explored status differences among planters, overseers, and slaves, so Jacqueline Jones emphasizes that, although Gullah-Geechee culture was undoubtedly distinctive, it shared much with the values espoused by whites. She singles out the entrepreneurial tendencies exhibited by blacks even under slavery, and then their commitment to schooling and political participation once freed. Her larger point is that one cannot understand black life without an understanding of the broader social, economic, and political context. A history of the black experience must always encompass that of whites, since their lives were deeply connected and inextricably interwoven. She investigates, in particular, how Savannah's white leaders co-opted the white laboring classes, especially Irish immigrants, who lived cheek by jowl and often colluded with their fellow black workers. The war seriously strained the success of the white supremacist policies of Savannah's elites. During Reconstruction, as Jones notes, the elites repaired their relations with poor whites "by casting the postwar challenge in terms of continued resistance to all Yankees and by intimidating would-be black voters, preventing black men and women from achieving any measure of equality with whites in the workplace and before the law."

In the same way that Jones introduces us to new black leaders such as Aaron A. Bradley and James Simms, who presented a challenge not just to elite whites but to traditional black churchmen at war's end, Allison Dorsey highlights a number of defiant characters — such as Mustapha Shaw and John Timmons — who thought themselves entitled to land, resisted its seizure by a resurgent white landowning class, and yet found themselves in struggles with other blacks, as tensions arose between outsiders who secured land and local freedmen who were not so fortunate. The context for this development goes back to General Rufus Saxton's Port Royal Experiment, begun in 1861, in which the islanders gained access to individual plots of land, but even more pertinent was General William Sherman's Special Field Order No. 15 of January 16, 1865, which reserved abandoned rice fields within thirty miles of the sea for "the negroes now made free by the acts of war." The assertiveness of black leaders such as Shaw and Timmons in seeking land is matched by the name blacks on postwar Ossabaw Island gave their Baptist church: Hinder Me Not. This expression of defiance, of wanting to be left on their own, suggests how much blacks sought autonomy. If landownership was not possible — and for locals on Ossabaw Island, the bitter reality was that it was not — they took solace in "the connection to home place" to work, family, and religious faith. They focused on building an autonomous community life.

Another form of consolation was to honor the role of the ancestors, which explains the importance of the flying Africans' story in the oral traditions of African American communities of coastal Georgia. Apparently, the inspiration for the story was a real-life event that took place around the turn of the century. It involved a group of Ibo (also known as Igbo) slaves brought illegally into Georgia; transported in an overcrowded coasting schooner, they rebelled. Some of them, it was claimed, drowned themselves in the expectation they would return to Africa. One story was that they turned into buzzards, took wing, and flew back across the Atlantic. In this way, the weak escaped the powerful clutches of the strong. Other versions were not connected to a drowning. Priscilla McCullough located the story in the fields as slaves worked; they formed a circle, moved round faster and faster, singing and shouting, till they rose up in the air before flying back home. Timothy Powell interprets the story from the perspective of Kongo cosmology — a worthwhile exercise since so many Africans in the lowcountry came from West Central Africa — noting that the line separating the world of the dead from that of the living was between land and water. He also brings the story into the modern day, by exploring the ways in which Toni Morrison the novelist and Cornelia Bailey the memoirist have reflected on the relevance of the tale.

Finally, Emory Campbell returns us to the mystery at the heart of Gullah-Geechee culture. He itemizes its various aspects — the foods, particularly the importance of rice, as in the classic hoppin' John dish (and the notable presence of many African plants such as okra, red peas, sorghum, and benne); head carrying and sweet grass baskets; a religious emphasis on seeking and dream visions, including his wry admission of a belief in God "with Dr. Buzzard as backup"; a commitment to extended family; and above all the grammatically distinctive constructions, melodious lilt, and rapid-fire delivery of a speaker of the Gullah language — but he also notes that there are still legitimate questions about precise origins, about how to allocate the debts to Africa, to Europe, and to Native Americans. Furthermore, he tells a tale of masking and deception, as a way of warding off the denigration of outsiders. Only in his lifetime has Gullah-Geechee culture begun the journey in public estimation from inferiority to respect. Only recently has it begun to come out into the open, revealing some of its secrets.

Emory Campbell is one of many notable lowcountry characters introduced to us in these pages. He is a living link to some extraordinary African Americans who populate this volume's essays: Fenda Lawrence, the African slave trader, who arrived in Georgia from Senegambia intending to settle as a free woman; David Margate, the black preacher who saw slaves as God's chosen people and thought God would deliver them from bondage, much as he freed the children of Israel from the Egyptian yoke; Betty, the slave woman belonging to James Laurens, who took advantage of her situation as a self-hired slave in Charleston during the American Revolutionary War to present her "list of grievances" (perhaps she had heard of the Declaration of Independence's bill of indictment, and decided to personalize it); John Marrant, who dared to interrupt a sermon by the famous evangelist George Whitefield in Charleston by playing a tune on his French horn, only to be struck speechless and senseless and thereby gain his salvation; the imposing, Arabic-speaking Muslim "S'Quash" who came into Charleston in one of the last legal transatlantic slavers, became a head man on a North Carolina plantation, and stood aloof from other slaves; Sam, the Baptist lay preacher who, despite being a slave, owned, among other things, a tidy sum of money, a small herd of cattle, and a horse; Okra, the African, who built an almost square, tiny hut, with basket-weave, mud walls and flat, palmetto roof, and no windows, to remind himself of his African home (akin to the photographic images of the house built by Tahro, an African from the Congo, brought to Edgefield, South Carolina, on the slave ship *Wanderer* in 1858); Jackson B. Sheftall, the butcher in Savannah, who made a killing during the Civil War supplying the Confederate authorities with meat; Abalod Shigg of Ossabaw Island, who in 1867 showed himself well versed in the Constitution as he delivered an impassioned assertion of black landowning and citizenship rights; and finally Sapelo Island's chronicler and champion, Cornelia Bailey, who flew to Sierra Leone "on the wings of man" where she immediately felt at home. The aggregate black experience emerges only from individual lives such as these.[6]

But this distinctive black experience also arises from encounters with a special place, one that an early observer aptly described as having "an oppressive beauty." The lowcountry blends land and water, island and mainland, town and country. Consider, for instance, the tiny port of Darien on the Altamaha, which runs as a thread in the tapestry of the essays in this volume. Named after the failed Scottish colony on the Isthmus of Panama, it is first encountered as the place from which in 1738 a group of Highland Scots famously denounced slavery. Its antislavery credentials persisted, for on the eve of the American Revolution a committee of its patriots also pledged themselves to bring about the end of slavery. In 1811, a group of slaves made their own antislavery statement: they escaped Darien, making for Spanish Florida. Later in the nineteenth century, Sambo Swift, enslaved in Darien, "right in the epicenter of the Muslim world in coastal Georgia," as Michael Gomez puts it, was able to reach Mecca, Indiana, a region that would later attract a number of adherents to the Moorish Science Temple. In 1866, Tunis Campbell, the son of a free black blacksmith in New Jersey, who came to the lowcountry in 1863 and two years later became the civilian agent of the Freedmen's Bureau in Savannah, bought the Belleville Plantation in Darien, and encouraged freedmen to relocate there as part of what Allison Dorsey describes as his "black separatist vision." As she notes, this decision was intriguing, because in June 1863 Major Robert Gould Shaw, commander of the legendary all-black Massachusetts Fifty-fourth had overseen the torching of what one observer described as a "beautiful, flourishing, and striving town." Did Campbell know of Darien's antislavery origins? Was he envisioning a phoenixlike rebirth from the ashes? Finally, there are the "haunting portraits" of some black residents of Darien — most notably Wallace Quarterman, Priscilla McCullough, and William Rogers — who the fieldworkers of the Savannah Unit of the Federal Writers' Project interviewed in the 1930s. All three provide some of the most telling testimonies about "the story of the flying Africans," which "seemed to be a familiar one," noted the interviewers.[7]

It is appropriate to conclude this introduction on a note of enchantment. As with the intriguing stories of slaves taking flight for Africa, there is much we will never understand about lowcountry black life. Many blacks encountered Native Americans in the Lower South, but the character of their relations is still largely unplumbed. The lack of black female voices in the historical record makes their rescue from the condescension of history problematic. Even with black male autobiographies, there is often a white amanuensis filtering the message, making it difficult to recover the authentic black voice. It is impossible to provide anything other than the most approximate count of Muslim slaves in the lowcountry. The bush arbor, or "hush arbor" as it was often known, was the crucible out of which poured much of the energy and vigor of African American Christianity, but what precisely occurred in these out-of-the-way places is still enveloped in secrecy. Quite why one slave household on a plantation exhibited evidence of hunting and others did not is hard to explain. The balance between fraternization and hostility among blacks and lower-class whites in mid-nineteenth-century Savannah will always be hard to weigh. The mentality of freedmen and women as they exited slavery — the mix of anger and exhilaration, the pull of old loyalties and new attachments, the urge to leave and the desire to stay — will never be easy to recapture. The ring shout tapped into powerful ecstatic forces, but its origins and functions are still difficult to fathom. The past is never dead, but it is never easily recovered.

Indeed, inevitably much will remain unknowable. After witnessing a slave funeral in Liberty County, Georgia, the Presbyterian minister Charles Colcock Jones, an insightful informant, thought he had been present at an unfathomable event, where "the living had come to commune with silence and the dead." After his many years of ministering to lowcountry blacks, Jones tellingly expressed his futility. "Persons live and die in the midst of Negroes and know comparatively little of their real character," he reflected, "The Negroes are a distinct class in community, and keep themselves very much *to themselves*. They are one thing before the whites, and another before their own color." There is no need to endorse Jones's peevishness and racial condescension, but his recognition that concealment and masking were central to lowcountry black life is insightful and is echoed in Emory Campbell's concluding essay. We hope that all the essays in this volume contribute to lifting the veil of secrecy — however slightly — but, like Jones, we are under no illusions that we can ever fully penetrate the mysteries of lowcountry black life. In all humility, therefore, we offer these essays as a small token of our appreciation for the endurance — and enigma — of Gullah-Geechee culture.[8]

NOTES

1. Johann David Schoepf, *Travels in the Confederation [1783–1784]*, trans. and ed. Alfred J. Morrison, 2 vols. (Philadelphia, W. J. Campbell, 1911), ii, 172. For evocative readings of the lowcountry landscape, I am indebted to, among others, William S. McFeely, *Sapelo's People: A Long Walk into Freedom* (New York: W. W. Norton, 1994) and Erskine Clarke, *Dwelling Place: A Plantation Epic* (New Haven, Conn.: Yale University Press, 2005). See also John R. Gillis, *Islands of the Mind: How the Human Imagination Created the Atlantic World* (New York: Palgrave Macmillan, 2004).

2. Althea Sumpter, "Geechee and Gullah Culture," http://www.georgiaencyclo pedia.org (accessed April 1, 2009).

3. Margaret Washington Creel, *"A Peculiar People": Slave Religion and Community Among the Gullahs* (New York: New York University Press, 1988).

4. Peter H. Wood, *Black Majority: Negroes in Colonial South Carolina from 1670 through the Stono Rebellion* (New York: Knopf, 1974), xiv; Felicia R. Lee, "Beach of Memory at Slavery's Gateway," *New York Times*, July 28, 2008; http://wilson.library. emory.edu:9090/tast/index.faces, estimates page; James Sidbury, *Becoming African in America: Race and Nation in the Early Black Atlantic* (New York, 2007), 67–73; Mart A. Stewart, *"What Nature Suffers to Groe": Life, Labor, and Landscape on the Georgia Coast, 1680–1920* (Athens: University of Georgia Press, 1996), 98; William Dusinberre, *Them Dark Days: Slavery in the American Rice Swamps* (New York: Oxford University Press, 1996); Peter H. Wood, "Slave Labor Camps in Early America: Overcoming Denial and Discovering the Gulag," in Carla Gardiner Pestana and Sharon V. Salinger, eds., *Inequality in Early America* (Hanover, N.H.: University Press of New England, 1999), 222–38.

5. Boyd Stanley Schlenther, *Queen of the Methodists: The Countess of Huntingdon and the Eighteenth-Century Crisis of Faith and Society* (Durham, U.K.: Durham Academic Press, 1997), 91.

6. Charles Town or Charlestown became Charleston at the end of the American Revolution.

7. Walter Edgar, *South Carolina: A History* (Columbia: University of South Carolina Press, 1998), 6; Buddy Sullivan, *Early Days on the Georgia Tidewater: The Story of McIntosh County and Sapelo* (Darien, Ga.: McIntosh County Board of Commissioners, 1990), 312; Savannah Unit, Georgia Writers' Project, Works Project Administration, *Drums and Shadows: Survival Studies among the Georgia Coastal Negroes* (1940; repr. Athens: University of Georgia Press, 1986), 146–57.

8. Clarke, *Dwelling Place*, 165, 229.

Philip Morgan

Lowcountry Georgia and the Early Modern Atlantic World, 1733–ca. 1820

ARLY GEORGIA does not bulk large in popular and scholarly consciousness. The "runt of the mainland American colonies," a "fledgling province," the youngest of the thirteen original states, it seems marginal. A utopian experiment in its initial guise, it was exceptional, sui generis. The first and only British colony to reject slavery, it also became the only place where colonists formally claimed that the institution was indispensable, "the one thing needful" to ensure progress. Lying between Spanish Florida and British South Carolina, with French Louisiana to the west and the polyglot Caribbean to the southeast — and surrounded by major Native American nations — it was meant to be, and long remained, a buffer zone. Indeed, it seems a place subject to much buffeting, more acted upon than actor in some ways. Georgia was somewhat laggard during the American Revolution, halfhearted in its commitment to nonimportation, the only colony of the thirteen not to send delegates to the First Continental Congress, and the first place the British invaded when they adopted their southern strategy in 1778. Georgia, the British thought, represented the softest underbelly of the Patriot movement. For some time thereafter, Georgia remained out of step with most of the other thirteen states that became the United States. Until recently, it was thought to be the place where the last slave ship reached the South. In many respects, then, Georgia can be portrayed as something of an isolated backwater, on the fringes, a peripheral place.[1]

Precisely because of its unusualness, however, Georgia occupies something of a center ground. It straddles a number of shared historiographies. An exemplar, Georgia is a microcosm of broader forces at work in the Atlantic world. The first set of larger forces worth exploring — befitting Georgia's beginnings — are those associated with antislavery. In some ways, Georgia is not quite the anomaly it appears, from a wide-ranging, pan-Atlantic, antislavery perspective, although its trajectory might be said to reverse the usual pattern. A second, special vantage point is Georgia's borderlands status. It truly was on the margins, and is therefore the perfect place to explore a marchland, a contested border region, a place of entangled histories. It was also a zone of imperial rivalry, in which profound international influences were at play. Thus, there is no better site than lowcountry Georgia to tell significant stories about multiracial and multiethnic encounters. A third narrative that Georgia can illumine is that of a greater plantation world, whether more specifically a greater lowcountry or an extended Caribbean. Georgia's story can be profitably told with larger reference to developments elsewhere in the plantation orbit. Fourth, Africa contributed significantly to early Georgia, so considerations of a larger African diaspora must be taken into account to comprehend fully its development. Finally, while in the discussion of these four themes I take the story into the Revolutionary era, I want to touch on Georgia from the perspective of the Revolutionary Atlantic, because of the many contradictions that bedeviled the region during that period. In these ways, and in what can be only a quick and impressionistic sketch, early Georgia offers a special perspective on at least five larger Atlantic stories.[2]

An Atlantic approach should broaden horizons, by calling attention to wider perspectives and transnational comparisons. The aim is to look across national boundaries and language areas, and put specialized work within a larger framework of a loosely connected but increasingly cohesive Atlantic world. As people, commodities, and cultural values moved around the Atlantic basin, profound transformations in all spheres of life occurred on the lands bordering on or connected to the ocean. Events in one place had repercussions in others. The great virtue of thinking in Atlantic terms is that it encourages broad perspectives, transnational orientations, and expanded horizons at the same time that it offers a chance for overcoming national and other parochialisms. Connections and contrasts can help overcome myopia and myriad details.

ANTISLAVERY

Genuine antislavery principles are usually thought to have been confined to the late eighteenth century. The extent of that moral revolution is captured in David Brion Davis's words that, for thousands of years, people "thought of sin as a kind of slavery," but then in the late eighteenth century, they began "to think of slavery as sin." Increasingly, however, scholars have uncovered antislavery impulses that had an older lineage than previously imagined. It transpires that the enslavement of Africans had long been considered a moral wrong. In 1573, a Spanish jurist asserted the natural right of enslaved Africans to liberty. As early as the 1580s, a New World Jesuit priest declared all slaveholders sinners. A century later, the papacy condemned the enslavement and sale of Africans. By the early eighteenth century, decades before the abolitionist movement developed, individual moralists, admittedly isolated for the most part and certainly part of no movement, nevertheless expressed an unease, or what one scholar has termed a degree of "managed discomfort," about slavery. Before 1730, almost fifty English poems have been discovered to touch on slavery, most portraying the institution as evil, with few condoning it.[3]

Such evidence puts Georgia's antislavery into perspective, although still there is no doubt of the colony's initial distinctiveness. "Of all the French, British, Dutch, Spanish, and Portuguese colonies in the New World," one historian notes, "only Georgia . . . attempted to avoid the stain" of black slavery. For a while at least, it was the "only free-soil region in the Western Hemisphere." True, the Georgia trustees opposed slavery more for what it did to whites than what it did to slaves. James Oglethorpe perhaps derived his opposition to slavery from his attack on the practice of naval impressment; his pamphlet "The Sailors Advocate," published anonymously in 1728, equated a pressed seaman with a slave and asked how a man could be expected to fight for liberty while experiencing "the pangs of slavery." For the most part, the trustees followed a pragmatic rather than a principled opposition to the institution. They aimed at the redemption of the English poor, and they believed that slavery would depress wages, stigmatize labor, and promote idleness among the people they targeted. The Georgia experiment represented a repudiation of plantation slavery particularly as it had developed in its neighbor to the north, a society deemed dominated by greedy plutocrats and troublesome slaves. Furthermore, the envisaged economic staples of Georgia — silk, wines, and olives — would be best cultivated by free labor, or so it was imagined. Finally, and perhaps most tellingly, the trustees thought slavery highly dangerous in a frontier setting, especially with the Spaniards offering a beacon of liberty to fugitive slaves if only they could reach St. Augustine. Strategic considerations of imperial defense were a, probably *the*, key reason for keeping slaves out of Georgia. The province's intended role as a protective barrier was similar to that envisaged for Jamaica in the 1650s and the Carolinas in the 1660s. Ironically, of course, by promising to close the southern escape hatch to freedom, Georgia strengthened slavery in South Carolina.[4]

In fact, the Georgia experiment was a mix of backward- and forward-looking impulses. In part, the trustees revived the scheme of the sixteenth-century West Country promoters, who had proposed Virginia as a colonial workhouse to redeem England's idle poor. Ever since Virginia's establishment, colonies had been seen as asylums for the down-and-out. Furthermore, since the founding of the Carolinas, New Jersey, and Pennsylvania, the idea of a religious refuge — another goal of the Georgia trustees — was commonplace. At the same time, however, Georgia represented a break with the past. As one scholar has noted, it was "a preview of the later doctrines of 'systematic colonization' advocated by Edward Gibbon Wakefield and others for the settlement of Australia and New Zealand." In contrast to such places as Jamaica and South Carolina, the trustees intended Georgia as "a regular Colony," orderly, methodical, disciplined, and, of course, free.[5]

As much as expediency governed the prohibition of slavery, principle played a part. In the late 1730s and early 1740s, as the pressure to allow slavery intensified, some impassioned opponents of the institution occasionally invoked morality. Oglethorpe thus condemned slavery as an "abominable and destructive custom," and expressed a precocious sympathy for Africans when he opposed slave importations because they would, he said, "occasion the misery of thousands in Africa." The most famous denunciation of slavery in the province came from the eighteen Highland Scots who signed the petition from Darien describing slavery as "shocking to human Nature," a natural rights' claim that would, in Davis's words, "reverberate through the anti-slavery movement and culminate in Lincoln's Second Inaugural Address." Another Scot, Isaac Gibbs, expressed outrage at slavery, describing it as "Inhumane and Abominable." The Reverend Johann Martin Bolzius of Ebenezer, the religious leader of the Salzburg settlers, thought slavery sinful and the slave trade unjust, and he expressed concern for Africans. Admittedly, these invocations of broad moral principles were rare, but, in fact, similar isolated pronouncements could be multiplied around the Atlantic world.[6]

Once slavery was legalized on January 1, 1751, oppositional voices were muted, if not completely silenced. Henry Ellis, a slave-trading captain who defended the traffic before becoming, in the words of a contemporary, a "humane governor" of Georgia from 1756 to 1760, regularly commiserated over the "hard and forlorn fate" of slaves in the colony; but, according to his recollections, his proposal that mulattoes should be freed to form an intermediate class between whites and blacks and that other slaves should be freed at age thirty never found favor. Another unlikely humanitarian was Ellis's friend, William Knox, at one time provost-marshal of Georgia, briefly its London agent, and substantial plantation owner, who in 1768, when resident back in England, disapproved of the cruel treatment of slaves. After all, he added, they were the king's subjects — a rather astonishing claim. As such, he maintained, they deserved the "impartial dispensation of the laws"; indeed, they had "legal rights." Admittedly, Knox made this claim more to assert Parliament's sovereign authority to legislate for the colonies than to ensure humane treatment of the enslaved, but the notion of slaves as subjects possessing legal rights was, to say the least, surprising.[7]

Even on the eve of the American Revolution, ambivalence characterized expressions of antislavery. Thus, in 1775, a committee of Georgia Patriots from Darien, echoing the earlier petition from the same place, declared that they were motivated only by "a general philanthropy for all mankind" to proclaim their "disapprobation and abhorrence of the unnatural practice of Slavery in America, . . . a practice founded in injustice and cruelty." They pledged themselves "to use our utmost endeavors for the manumission of our Slaves in this Colony." While seemingly altruistic, the Darien Resolutions expressed more concern for whites than for blacks. Slavery, according to the inhabitants of Darien, was "highly dangerous to our liberties (as well as lives), debasing part of our fellow-creatures below men, and corrupting the virtue and morals of the rest." A "stinging indictment of slavery," one scholar notes, yet the Darien Resolution was primarily aimed at rallying support for the Patriot cause (and, alarmed by a recent slave uprising, perhaps even a cynical attempt to keep slaves from going over to the British); of course, its vision of a new system under which slaves would be freed on a "safe and equitable footing for the masters and themselves" was a pipe dream. In the following year, Oglethorpe, like Knox now resident in England, revealed how his antislavery had become more principled than pragmatic. He then explained to Granville Sharpe, the famous English abolitionist, that the trustees had refused to condone chattel slavery because it was a "horrid crime," opposed by "the Gospel, as well as the fundamental law of England," and he predicted that its sins would invite divine retribution. This is a post-hoc rationalization, for there is no evidence that the trustees had opposed slavery religiously or legally, but his recollections betray the shift in the moral climate.[8]

As Georgia deepened its commitment to slavery in the years of the early republic, those who raised doubts about the institution were marginalized. Some of Georgia's leading men detested the transatlantic slave trade — in 1798 the state legislature banned it, citing the "principles of benevolence and humanity" — but they also passionately defended their right to import Africans. Urged to set an example by acting against slavery, newcomer to Georgia, Nathanael Greene, the Revolutionary War hero, spurned such a course, although he admitted that "nothing could be said in [slavery's] defense." In 1797, when John E. Smith, editor of the *Augusta Chronicle*, condemned the inhumanity of slave trade and castigated masters for their "satanic depravity," for acting, as he put it, like "savages," he stirred up a hornet's nest. He quickly issued a clarification three weeks later: no, he was not advocating abolition, he hastened to say, merely arguing for humanity and against excessive cruelty. Even more intriguing is the stinging critique of slavery issued in 1804 by Judge Jabez Bowen, a recent immigrant from Rhode Island. Apparently influenced by events in Haiti, Bowen convened a grand jury in Chatham County and issued his charge that Georgia legislators had "silenced the cries of oppression and the voice of truth." The abolition of slavery was necessary, he believed, before "civil warfare" began. He proposed immediate emancipation of all female slaves at age ten and all male slaves at age twenty-one. The grand jury accused Bowen of fomenting insurrection; he was arrested, and he escaped trial only by hastily leaving the state, never to return.[9]

The story of antislavery in Georgia is mixed, then, when placed in an Atlantic context. An early precociousness — albeit certainly not radical — soon gave way to an almost complete elimination of doubts or anxieties about slavery. As the antislavery movement intensified throughout the late-eighteenth-century Atlantic world, Georgia was increasingly out of step, and the attempt by its primary founder to rewrite the reasons for its antislavery ban seem hollow. Furthermore, by then, Georgia was an outpost of rabid proslavery sentiment. The province's embryonic antislavery credentials were firmly a thing of the past.[10]

BORDERLANDS

A similar trajectory from fluidity to eventual rigidity applies to Georgia as a borderland region. As a contested zone lying between empires, Georgia, in some ways, was a place of flexible and inclusive intercultural frontiers. A measure of mutual acculturation — ethnic and racial mixing — and cohabitation took place. Perhaps the most bizarre example is Christian Gottlieb Prieber's "Kingdom of Paradise," the Christian utopia he planned among the Cherokees in the late 1730s, a place where Indians, runaway slaves, and other fugitives could coexist without private property, monogamous marriage, or racial distinctions. Captured by Creeks, put in a Frederica guardhouse, he died in 1743 of a fever. One hesitates to use the term "middle ground" to describe such a situation, because it has become such a cliché, but a measure of in-between-ness, negotiation, and compromise characterized early Georgia. That flexibility gradually disappeared over time. At the same time, as Claudio Saunt notes, to Native Americans, "Middle grounds and borderlands were simply homelands." He continues pointedly, "Narratives that foreground negotiation, compromise, and boundary crossing between races and cultures perhaps reflect more the emancipatory fantasies of twenty-first-century scholars than the lives of eighteenth-century Indians, whose nations were invaded and reduced, if not destroyed." With that caveat in mind, it is worth probing the entangled, triangular relationships that developed between whites, Indians, and blacks on the Georgia borderlands.[11]

When Georgia was established, there were about eleven thousand Creeks in the colony's interior. Long exposed to European contact and diseases, they were astute traders, aggressive warriors, and readily absorbed refugees into their loose federation of towns. Creek political and social arrangements were highly decentralized, with groups often fragmenting and coalescing: the band of two hundred Yamacraws and their elderly headman Tomochichi, perhaps the son of a Yamasee father and Creek mother,

who greeted Oglethorpe when he arrived in Georgia, were one such splin-
ter group. Creeks dominated the region between southern Appalachia and
the sea, strategically situated between three rival European forces. Taking
advantage of their location through aggressive military and diplomatic policies, they enhanced their power and their numbers. In 1760, their population stood at thirteen thousand, over twice the size of Georgia's white
population and almost four times the size of the black population. On the
eve of the Revolution, the white population had outgrown the Creeks, but
not by much — eighteen thousand to fourteen thousand — while the black
population had grown the fastest and stood at fifteen thousand. In short,
the three groups were in rough numerical parity — fertile soil for a measure
of negotiation and compromise.[12]

Military concerns were a key feature of Georgia as an intercultural
frontier. From the first, Oglethorpe needed allies. He even formed two
companies of Indian militia from among the Yamacraws, and commissioned two of their leaders as captains. Furthermore, in his first treaty with
the so-called Lower Creeks in 1733, he supplied the chiefs with a laced coat,
hat, and shirt, and the warriors with guns in return for a pledge to return any runaway slaves to the closest garrison for various rewards. From
the colony's inception, then, Georgia's rulers sought Indian cooperation
and attempted to minimize collusion among Indians and black slaves.
Georgians offered material incentives for Indian assistance in bolstering
Georgia's defensive position as a buffer zone between the British mainland
and Spanish Florida. Those incentives rose to try and ensure that Creeks
largely cooperated with whites in maintaining the slave system. Under the
terms of a 1763 treaty with Georgia, Creeks received a bounty of about 40
percent of their annual deerskin production for every runaway slave they
returned; eleven years later, the bounty increased to 60 percent for fugitives
returned directly to Savannah. One reason for the increase was the belief
that Creeks sold many captured fugitives in Spanish Louisiana. The idea
was to get them to return the slaves to Georgia. In general, then, Georgians
were desperate to ensure that Creek country did not become an asylum
for fugitive slaves. To some degree, Creeks became auxiliaries policing the
frontier.[13]

The War of Jenkins's Ear, which began in 1739, provides a window
onto the intercultural frontier. Oglethorpe hoped to recruit two thousand
Cherokee and Creek warriors, but in reality secured the assistance of only
a few hundred. Despite their small numbers, they played an important

role as scouts and raiders, although considerable tensions arose when the English tried to incorporate Indians into their conventional forces and Indians preferred to engage in guerrilla raids. When Indian auxiliaries presented Oglethorpe with the severed head of a Spanish-allied Yamasee, he called them "barbarous Dogs." Oglethorpe not only recruited Indians but also black pioneers to build and fortify defenses along Georgia's southern edge. He requested that South Carolina supply eight hundred black slaves to construct the necessary entrenchments and fortifications. South Carolina's Assembly thought four hundred more feasible and apparently felt confident enough about their loyalty, despite Oglethorpe's request for 160 white guards, to allow "all Negroes employed or carried from South Carolina during the Time of the Expedition" to have "liberty to pass and repass without interruption; or being subject to forfeiture." Thus, Georgia's leaders were quite willing to waive the ban against black slavery in a time of extremis; they also revealed the superior combat role they accorded Indians and the inferior laboring status they envisaged for blacks. Opposing Oglethorpe and his men were not just Spanish regulars but also about one hundred black militiamen, many of them former slaves from lowcountry South Carolina, and led by a Mandinga captain Francisco Menendez, from Gracia Real de Santa Teresa de Mose, a free black town established two miles north of St. Augustine. In the summer of 1740, a mixed expeditionary band of Spanish, Indians, and free blacks inflicted a significant defeat on the British invaders. Oglethorpe retreated. In 1741, the Spanish mounted an invasion force of one thousand regular troops, twenty-four black and mulatto officers, almost five hundred free blacks and colored militiamen from Cuba, and one hundred black militiamen from St. Augustine. Their defeat at the Battle of Bloody Marsh on St. Simons Island led to an uneasy stalemate. Part of the unease undoubtedly derived from the sight of colored soldiers whom the British described as "mulattoes of savage dispositions."[14]

Slavery was another important area of intercultural contact. When the trustees banned the importation and use of slaves in 1735, their prohibition applied only to blacks, not to Indians. Southern Indians had a long familiarity with slavery. Mary Musgrove (later Matthews and Bosomgrove), the half-Creek, half-English woman who became an interpreter and intermediary for Oglethorpe, held several Indians in bondage, using them as servants at her trading post. Indeed, when one of Tomichichi's Yamacraws accidentally killed one of her slaves, the Georgia authorities paid for a replacement. However much Indians brutalized their captive slaves, Indian slavery was distinct from chattel slavery among the English. Before exposure to Europeans, Creeks placed no great premium on personal property. They usually incorporated slaves into their lineages. In 1738, Lower Creek leaders made it clear which imperial power they favored: they preferred the Spanish, who "enslave no one as the English do." Creeks contrasted the iron chains and manacles they associated with English slavery to their looser, less rigid ropes by which they bound their captives. In 1756, a Creek leader warned his people that the English had "a Mind to make Slaves of them all, for [they] have already filled their nation with English Forts and great Guns, Negroes and Cattle."[15]

As African American slaves began to appear in greater numbers in Georgia from roughly mid-century onward, inevitably Indians began to encounter them on a routine basis. By the 1760s, a small number of Creeks began keeping black slaves. Still, because they disliked coercion and showed little interest in accumulating property, most Creeks allowed black, just like Indian, slaves considerable latitude. They adopted them formally into a Creek clan and, upon marriage, they gained their freedom. Creeks were quick to sell their dependents, however, if they remained unmarried. Such was the fate of David George, a black Virginian who ended up in Creek country and would later go to Nova Scotia and thereafter Sierra Leone; his Creek master traded him for rum, linen, and a gun. Never completely sure how they would be received, nevertheless, blacks continued to flee into Creek country, because, as a contemporary noted, "slaves" and "masters" could scarcely be distinguished there. Assimilation and incorporation were the norm. Thus, in 1769, a fugitive slave, described as a "new negroe fellow . . . of the Bumbo country," had managed to learn Muskogee while living among the Creeks. That a recent African immigrant could assimilate so quickly says much about him and Creek adoptive practices. Similarly, Ketch, an African American slave of John Galphin, the son of the great deerskin trader George Galphin, served as an interpreter in the deerskin trade. In his youth, he too picked up a Muskogean language, and Muskogees relied on him to convey their most important diplomatic speeches. After the Revolutionary War, in which he served as an officer's servant, Ketch fled servitude and went into the Creek nation, where he lived, so one contemporary noted, as an "Indian negro."[16]

By the late eighteenth century, a major division had emerged among the Creeks. On the one hand, the mestizo children born to white traders and their Indian wives had risen to power in many places. They were full members of their mothers' clans, yet comfortable with the economic practices of their fathers, and they brought into the heart of Creek society the plantation slavery Creeks had so long abhorred. Some of these wealthy mestizos owned numbers of black slaves who they treated little differently from white masters. Alexander McGillivray, the son of a Scots trader and a Creek woman of the Wind clan, personified this new elite. At his death in 1793, he owned sixty black slaves, three hundred cattle, and many horses. Some Creeks now needed locks and whips in order to keep their possessions and human chattel in order. Rather than welcoming fugitives, they now raided for slaves. On the other side of the divide were those Creeks who continued to adopt blacks into their clans and give them all the rights and obligations of other kin. In the 1780s and 1790s, African American fugitives could still be welcomed and treated as full-fledged participants in community life, if they could reach those Creek towns on the lower Chattahoochee and north-central Florida. Here, of course, was the genesis of the Seminoles.[17]

The complexity of Creek-black interactions is perhaps best captured in the realm of religion. Silver Bluff, located on the Savannah River, was a true borderlands settlement, where Creek hunters and Irish, Scottish, and English traders mixed with African American cowboys and packhorsemen. There, George Galphin had children with both Native American and African American women. This intense intercultural contact, as Joel Martin has suggested, may well have "encouraged a novel form of creativity among the African American population," leading in the early 1770s to the founding of Silver Bluff Baptist Church, the first separate African American church in North America. Famous African American preachers, most notably George Liele, but also Andrew Bryan, David George (who, as noted, was owned for a time by a Creek master), and Jesse Peter or Jesse Galphin began their careers there; one of the early preachers was Henry Francis, a man of Native American ancestry. In the 1790s, one Creek woman had in her household a black preacher who preached to his fellow blacks in the woods. That there were enough blacks in one Creek town to afford such practices is significant. That a mestizo master would complain that his black slaves were not working because of this preacher's activities also speaks to his having imbibed Anglo-American racial attitudes. Finally, that the Creek master of this black preacher protected him reveals a degree of household incorporation. Five years later, Creeks murdered a black slave because they suspected him of being a "wizard"— demonstrating that the spiritual power claimed by African Americans also could be dangerous. In 1812, a black preacher who we know only as Phil was said to be making his black slaves "crazy," complained an Upper Creek chief. In general, however, Creeks seem to have borrowed from, rather than repudiated, African American cultural influences; apparently Creeks contributed to African American religious creativity.[18]

In short, the borderlands formed an ever-shifting terrain that had to be navigated shrewdly. Slaves fleeing the lowcountry had to calculate the odds of freedom, and the odds kept changing. Prior to 1763, their best chances were with the Spanish who offered freedom to any slave professing a desire to convert to Catholicism. A few hundred probably made it and found sanctuary at Mose. Between 1763 and 1783, when East Florida was British, their best chances lay with the Creeks, and many hundreds fled there during that twenty-year period. Immediately after 1783, when Florida reverted to Spain, slaves again headed for St. Augustine. For example, Bacchus and Betty Camel and their seven children (including Bacchus Jr., age nine) exchanged a harsh master in Savannah for freedom in Spanish Florida. In 1785, Spanish soldiers encountered maroons near the St. John's River, apparently making their way to St. Augustine. The following year a six-feet-tall, thirty-year-old carpenter named Prince Witten, his wife Judy, and their children Polly and Glasgow escaped Georgia for sanctuary in St. Augustine. In 1788, a band of twenty-one slaves fled Georgia to the Spanish city. So concerned were slave owners at these escapes that they pressured Thomas Jefferson, then secretary of state, to have Spain abrogate its century-old sanctuary policy. In 1790, as part of a larger attempt to halt the spread of revolutionary ideas, the Spanish government ordered the governor of St. Augustine to desist from freeing fugitive slaves. This denial of sanctuary drove fugitive slaves once again into Creek country, where the chances of freedom were shrinking, unless they could reach the Seminoles. Even so, slaves still continued to run to Florida. In the mid-1790s, for example, a slave named Titus led twelve fugitives in a successful group escape from a Georgia plantation. In 1797, when he was about to be returned to Georgia, he escaped and made his way back to the Savannah River, where he set up a maroon band. As late as 1811, John escaped from Darien with several other slaves, was recaptured at St. Mary's, managed to break jail, and finally made it to Florida where he assumed the name John Spaniard. He escaped wearing "something in a small bag suspended by a string around his neck"— perhaps a charm bag. In the following year, with the war against Britain and Seminole resistance in Florida, the governor of Georgia reported that most "of our male slaves on the sea bord [*sic*] are restless and make many attempts to get off to Augustine, and many have succeeded." He mentioned the need for constant guards and patrols.[19]

About the time John Spaniard made it to Florida, that particular borderland became especially contentious. Spain's imperial weakness invited predators. North Florida swampland attracted rice planters, and its islands and pinelands supported sea island cotton, lumbering, and ranching. Much to the chagrin of slaveholders, fugitive slaves from Georgia continued to find a haven, particularly among the Seminoles. The continued import of Africans into Amelia Island was destabilizing to some white Georgians, and the Spanish imperial model of incorporating blacks and Indians into its military alarmed southern slave owners. Thus, in 1812, the ex-governor of Georgia mounted an expedition to rid the lowcountry of its problem neighbor. But black troops and Seminoles, many of whom were ex-slaves from the lowcountry, helped the Spanish defeat the invasion force. Meanwhile, the British began using Florida as a base for their guerrilla operations, and in 1815 they invaded Cumberland Island. Half of their troops were black, and they enticed about fifteen hundred to two thousand lowcountry slaves to join them. The island became "the scene of one of the most extraordinarily effective mass military emancipations ever seen in the United States." Almost 140 of Pierce Butler's slaves went over to the British; some men "said they must follow their daughters, others their wives," but all thought "their happy days had come." Two years later, Scottish and French adventurers, together with many ex-Haitian slaves and other free blacks, captured Amelia Island and for a time turned it into a privateering and smuggling center. Armed blacks, in short, were an especially notable presence on Georgia's borders in the second decade of the nineteenth century, outraging whites and inspiring blacks. Overlapping and ambiguous jurisdictions presented opportunities to lowcountry African Americans. Not until 1821 when Spain relinquished Florida did this southern escape hatch finally close, thereby removing the specter of black men in arms — at least for forty years or so.[20]

THE GREATER PLANTATION WORLD

As Georgians gradually defined their borders and made slavery fairly secure, their plantations thrived. South Carolina was a colony of a colony, but Georgia was a colony of a colony of a colony. In other words, Georgia can trace its larger affiliations not only to South Carolina, but to Barbados and indeed to other West Indian islands. Georgia was part of a Greater Carolina, while at the same time forming an extension of a Greater Caribbean. Now, admittedly, if Georgia's initial strategic role was reminiscent of the role of certain West Indian islands, other aspects of its founding were initially intended as a counter-model to the Caribbean. The Georgia trustees did not just prohibit slavery and try to inhibit the development of plantations; they even banned the consumption of rum, the Caribbean's signature product. But just as the hurricanes sweeping across the Atlantic bore down on the Caribbean and the mainland alike, so Georgia could hardly resist — and indeed embraced — Caribbean influences.

The links to the Caribbean were both small and large. News of an insurrection in Jamaica in the late 1730s served to argue against the introduction of slaves. Conversely, when Georgia opened the floodgates to slavery, the West Indian plantation system was an obvious model. A relatively small group of whites became immensely rich, leisured, and politically powerful by exploiting a large and growing population of enslaved Africans. There was always more space for yeoman whites in Georgia than on a Caribbean island, but still the oligarchic structures in both regions began to resemble one another. On the eve of the American Revolution, one historian calculates, just sixty planters, or 1 percent of the white population, owned half of the thirteen thousand slaves in the colony.

Crucial information about indigo cultivation came from the Caribbean. In the 1730s, the Georgia trustees hired botanists to tour the West Indies in search of plants. The first long staple "black-seed" cotton grown in Georgia in the 1780s came from the Bahamas; island cotton gins were prototypes for mainland imitators. In the early nineteenth century, Georgians imported the Otaheite and later the so-called ribbon variety of sugar cane, as well as hired experts with sugar-making experience, from Jamaica. The lowcountry's expansive forests provided much-needed lumber for the deforested West Indian islands, while Georgia's pinewoods, canebrakes, and savannas provided forage for the cattle needed to drive Caribbean sugar mills. When reflecting on Georgia's reconstituted slave code of 1765, Governor James Wright first mentioned Jamaica as a particularly influential model. A Scots merchant contingent in Georgia had strong connections to St. Kitts. As his son Jack set off for a visit to Jamaica in 1774, Lachlan McIntosh warned him of the dangers of "vicious and immoral company" — presumably the island's black and colored women. The examples could be multiplied. Suffice to say, the links between Georgia and the Caribbean were extensive. While lowcountry Georgia possessed the territorial extent of a mainland colony, it bore many of the features of a Caribbean island.[21]

The Caribbean was certainly an important source of slaves for Georgia. Immediately after chattel slavery was legalized, Georgia colonists lacked the capital to attract slave shipments direct from Africa, but they could afford smaller shipments from the Caribbean. The few hundred slaves imported in the 1750s came entirely from the Caribbean. In the 1760s, when ships direct from Africa began arriving in Georgia, as many slaves came via the West Indies (2,300 in that decade) as from Africa (another 2,300). One noticeable influx occurred in the mid-1760s, after the Seven Years' War. From 1764 to 1767, transshipments came from all over the Caribbean: 550 slaves from Jamaica, over 300 from St. Kitts, almost 200 from Grenada, 70 from Curaçao, 70 from Antigua, 50 from Barbados, and other small numbers from another seven islands. In 1768, a slave named Pedro ran away: perhaps he was one of those recently imported from Curaçao, because he was said to speak Papiamento, the Creole language spoken on the island. While in the early 1770s, African imports significantly outdistanced those from the Caribbean (by a ratio of 6:1), by the 1780s, as Georgia gradually recovered from the depredations of the Revolutionary War, it again drew heavily on Caribbean transshipments. Thus, in 1785, Alexander McGillivray, the mestizo trader, even purchased and shipped slaves from Jamaica in what he described as a "very small Vessell." He was not alone. In the 1780s, the ratio of slave imports from the Caribbean as compared to Africa was 1:2. That would change in the 1790s and early 1800s, as Africans flooded directly into the lowcountry. But, overall, a fifth of Georgia's slaves came via transshipments from the Caribbean, at least double the proportion that came from that region into South Carolina. Over two hundred vessels — almost twice the number from Africa — came into Georgia carrying slaves from the Caribbean.[22]

Intra-American slave movements were important to Georgia and complicate the issue of the African origins of its slaves. Transshipped Africans — those who arrived in one ship in the Caribbean, where they were sold and re-sorted, before eventually being put onto another ship destined for Georgia — were a more heterogeneous group than those who arrived direct from Africa and invariably arrived from a single coastal region of that continent. Africans purchased by Caribbean merchants for the Georgia market experienced an additional round of purchase and sale, of being sorted and re-sorted. As Greg O'Malley notes, "Slaves who recorded their stories of slavery often fixated on the auction block — on the experience of being purchased, of having a price for their worth publicly negotiated — as a defining moment. Slaves transshipped after the Middle Passage confronted this commoditization additional times." Viewed as no more than chattels, these newcomers likely shed their ethnic identities and embraced a new African identity, since they were thrown together with other Africans of diverse origins.[23]

Olaudah Equiano, the famous black abolitionist, provides a fascinating personal connection between the Caribbean and Georgia. In the mid-1760s, when in his early twenties, Equiano, then a slave sailor based in Montserrat, came to Savannah a number of times. On at least one occasion — in 1766 — he was a crew member on a vessel that acquired slaves in St. Eustatius for transshipment to Georgia. His tales of life in Savannah and environs are grim: near death from a fever and ague; beatings by a slave owner and his overseer, abuse and assault from a slave; fraudulent dealings by whites; a flogging from the town watch; desperate encounters with alligators; and kidnapping attempts. He had some occasional warmer memories: care from a white physician, hearing the celebrated evangelical preacher George Whitefield, the purchase of a suit of "Georgia superfine blue cloathes" to wear at the dance celebrating his freedom, friendship with a black man named Mosa (presumably a Muslim), and delivery of a funeral sermon for a black woman who had lost a young child. His parting comment in 1767 was not something the tourism board would want to broadcast: "I thus took a final leave of Georgia; for the treatment I had received in it disgusted me very much."[24]

Throughout the eighteenth century, but particularly in the early decades, an even greater flow of slaves into early Georgia came not from the Caribbean but from South Carolina. Thus, Georgia was part of a larger Carolina plantation world that, while it had Caribbean antecedents and parallels, had even greater mainland connections. The most obvious tie, of course, was the degree to which Carolina and Georgia shared the same signature crop, its iconic product. Lowcountry Georgia, like its neighbor to the north, became a "rice thumping country," as one contemporary put it. Georgia's rice industry was, at least in its earliest phases, essentially imitative. It was a literal extension of South Carolina's. Most of the Carolinian applicants for Georgia's land owned slaves who would have been familiar with lowcountry methods of rice production. Rice was grown elsewhere in the Atlantic world, but outside South Carolina and Georgia, Brazil was the only other part of the Americas that produced rice efficiently enough to justify shipping it to transatlantic markets — mainly Portugal in its case. Production in Brazil centered on its northeastern sector, the Amazonian delta region. But its rice exports never matched those of the lowcountry. Cacao and cotton were far more important crops in northeastern Brazil than was rice. The lowcountry, of course, was never a monoculture, developing first indigo and then sea island cotton as secondary staples, but compared to northeastern Brazil the lowcountry's dependence on rice is striking.[25]

Another distinctive feature of the lowcountry plantation world was its labor arrangement. Slaves largely worked by task rather than by gang in the lowcountry. Gang labor was much likelier in indigo, certain aspects of sea island cotton production, and even some parts of rice production; nevertheless, the basic task unit, the quarter-acre, became so ingrained in lowcountry life that ex-slaves in the twentieth century still thought in terms of it. The advantage of tasking from the slaves' point of view was that, if the daily work allotment could be completed early, the rest of the day was theirs, whereas gang labor was always sunup to sundown. The advantage from the masters' point of view was a saving on supervisory costs. The idea that task labor introduced a measure of freedom into slavery's oppression overlooks the ability of planters to intensify work requirements. The task system could not protect most slaves from almost ceaseless labor, even if its redeeming characteristic was the opportunity it gave laborers to gain time for their own affairs. Slaves preferred tasking because, at bottom, it involved their participation, even if hardly lightening their laboring load. An Atlantic perspective on tasking reveals that sea island cotton planters in the Bahamas employed the system, as did timber and naval stores producers in places as remote as Cape Fear in North Carolina, Honduras, and Suriname, as did Caribbean coffee planters. While few places generated such an extensive and deeply rooted task system as the lowcountry, the practice was present in many other places.[26]

One last distinctive feature of the lowcountry plantation world was its spatial organization, which in part was a combination of remoteness and interconnectedness. Plantations were spread out, often literally islands, highly isolated, but at the same time integrated by coasting schooner, flatboat, canoe, and eventually roads into a connected network. Field hands were left largely to their own devices and lived quite remote lives; other slaves such as boatmen and sailors were quite cosmopolitan and provided the linkage between plantation and port. Terrestrial and maritime worlds were quite separate even if interconnected. Another aspect of the distinctive spatial arrangement was its extensive character — plantations moved ever outward from a central core to outlying riverine territories. A shifting geography occurred, until all the best swamplands were taken. There was considerable geographic mobility, too, even if lowcountry slaves did not move great distances overland, as other slaves on the mainland did. Since planters often owned more than one plantation, management was often distant rather than direct. Finally, a core-periphery pattern was a major aspect of the lowcountry spatial arrangement. Savannah was never Charleston in terms of size and importance — in 1820, Savannah totaled only about seven thousand people (half of them slaves); Charleston was that size seventy years earlier, but the city nevertheless played some of the same roles. It was a place to which the big planters often retreated, so planting plans were often hatched in an urban place and then enacted in the countryside through various intermediaries, such as managers, overseers, and drivers. It was a place to which rural slaves resorted — whether to market their products, attend a dance or religious meeting, visit the local grog shops, and try to pass as free. The temporary absenteeism of planters, an important urban center, and the paradox of remoteness and connectedness constitute a distinctively lowcountry spatial phenomenon, even as it is a pattern that can be found in many Caribbean locales.[27]

In short, then, lowcountry Georgia both replicated the developmental patterns of South Carolina and formed part of an extended Caribbean. It also can be connected to a larger plantation world that stretched all the way from Maryland and Delaware (perhaps even parts of Rhode Island) all the way south at least to Bahia.

GREATER AFRICA

Just as Georgia was an extension of the Caribbean and Carolina, so it was of Africa. Transatlantic slave ships carried about 32,500 enslaved Africans to Georgia. From a broad pan-Atlantic perspective, this is an extremely small number, a minuscule fraction — 0.2 percent — of all the Africans conveyed to the Americas, now thought to total 12.5 million people. Georgia was a marginal market, peripheral to the transatlantic slave-delivery system. It also received slaves direct from Africa for a mere half-century — from 1766 to about 1820 — and there were many years, particularly during wartime, when Georgia received few or no Africans.[28]

Despite the small numbers, however, the compressed time period when Africans arrived meant that they were a significant presence on lowcountry Georgia plantations, at least for a time — how significant it is hard to say. During the 1760s and 1770s, Betty Wood estimates the ratio between African-born and native-born among Georgia fugitive slaves as at least 3:1. Since fugitives tended to be more creolized than slaves generally, Africans probably outnumbered Creoles by perhaps 4:1 on the eve of the Revolution.[29]

Where in Africa did they come from? The thrust of much recent Atlantic scholarship has been to assess the impact of specific ethnic or cultural groups deriving from identifiable regions of West or West Central Africa. It is common nowadays to assert with greater precision a particular Kongolese, Ibo, or Bambara influence on specific places in the Americas. What can be said of early Georgia? In the decade or so before the American Revolution, when Georgia imported about sixty-five hundred slaves directly from Africa, about four of every five were from Upper Guinea (that part of the African coast stretching from present-day Senegal to Liberia) — and, in eighteenth-century terms, primarily from Senegambia, but also from Sierra Leone and the Windward Coast. One reason for this predominance, it has been thought, was the preference of lowcountry Georgian planters for slaves from rice-growing areas in Africa. However, a full Atlantic perspective reveals that in the third quarter of the eighteenth century, Upper Guinea became a significant supplier generally to the Americas. Thus, Georgia was not alone in getting slaves disproportionately from Upper Guinea, even if it received relatively more than most. It is not wholly clear why this general rise in the importance of Upper Guinea happened. What is known is that, across the whole of Atlantic Africa in the third quarter of the eighteenth century, the loading times of vessels increased markedly. In response, more slave-trading vessels sought slaves in Upper Guinea — previously not a favored part of the African coast, despite its proximity to the Americas — than had previously been the case.[30]

Thus, while some Africans from Upper Guinea brought knowledge of rice growing into Georgia, and certain parallels can be detected particularly in the milling, winnowing, and cooking processes between the two regions, nevertheless this transfer happened despite, rather than because of, planter preferences. Furthermore, rice cultivation always involved a combination of methods and knowledge. Perhaps Africans contributed their hollow logs or trunks that regulated the flow of water between rivers and fields, but then again remember that Europeans knew much about draining and embanking wetlands, and they, too, employed hollow logs. Moreover, lowcountry planters soon adopted hanging floodgates, known only to European agriculture. In lowcountry rice cultivation, some slaves undoubtedly introduced a distinctively African sowing style, pressing a hole with the heel and covering the rice seed with the foot; they hand processed rice using an African-style mortar and pestle; and they fanned rice with African-style coiled baskets. As slaves planted, hulled, and winnowed — accompanied by their distinctive songs — they unquestionably incorporated African folkways into their routines. But these "survivals" do not amount to an entire agricultural complex. Rice cultivation in the lowcountry was, in fact, a hybrid; it was the result of many influences.[31]

Far more Africans arrived in Georgia after, than before, the Revolution, and they came from a much wider array of places. Between 1782 and 1820, at least twenty-two thousand Africans landed in Savannah. The period of greatest influx was the 1790s, when more than twelve thousand arrived. In the post-Revolutionary years, the coastal regions of Africa shifted markedly — yet another indication that planter preferences were hardly driving the trade. Sierra Leone was the primary region of origin, contributing one-third of all arrivals, but now only half of the Africans came from Upper Guinea. Two African regions that had been minor suppliers prior to the Revolution were now major contributors. Almost 30 percent of Africans who arrived in early national Georgia were from West Central Africa, and another fifth were from the Gold Coast. A more diverse set of Africans came into the region than was the case before the Revolution.[32]

Claims, therefore, that Georgia slaves had a West Central African — an Angolan or Kongo — foundation, like their Carolinian counterparts, seem inaccurate, although West Central Africans certainly became more numerous after the Revolution. While Senegambia is a more likely origin for Georgia's charter generation of Africans, nevertheless Mande-speaking Africans and Bambaras were probably always outnumbered by others. Overall, lowcountry Georgia received a progressively heterogeneous mix of Africans. There are some famous Muslim slaves. There were Kisi, Temne, and presumably Gola from Sierra Leone, although we know from some fugitive slaves in 1795 that Gola country meant in their case Angola. Certainly, Congos and Angolans were much more numerous around the turn of the century. Ibos were also present in early Georgia. In 1781, a fifty-six-year-old Ibo woman led an exodus from her plantation, and among her group were two of her daughters, a son, and a granddaughter; in 1803, an overseer of a plantation on Butler's Island noted that none of his slaves could converse with a group of recently purchased "Ibos" and "Angolas" — and yet there is not one known case of a slave vessel arriving from the Bight of Biafra.[33]

The broad contours of the horrifying Middle Passage to Georgia can be outlined. The size of slave complements varied considerably — ranging from one four-hundred-ton vessel that brought in 500 slaves from Sierra Leone to a thirty-two-ton sloop that landed just 35 slaves from the Gold Coast. The average number on a ship, however, was just 142 slaves, less than half the typical complement for the trade as a whole — yet another indication of the marginality of the Georgia slave trade. More small vessels arrived in Savannah than in other Atlantic ports. The average passage time was sixty-six days. Three insurrections occurred on the 118 known transatlantic slave voyages to Georgia, but all were successfully suppressed. The loss of human life on all the voyages averaged 13 percent, much higher than the norm for the period. For some reason, Georgia's slavers lost more Africans than was generally the case — at least in the late eighteenth and early nineteenth century. Most Africans spent some time in quarantine on Tybee Island before they were sold in Savannah. More ships came from London than from Liverpool, but Providence, Rhode Island, outnumbered both. Even though Georgia banned the transatlantic slave trade in 1798, fourteen known vessels landed over 2,000 Africans between 1801 and 1820. There were undoubtedly many more illicit landings. In 1858, the last known slave ship, the *Wanderer*, disembarked over 300 slaves on Jekyll Island.[34]

Did the lowcountry place a particular emphasis on the acquisition and evaluation of enslaved women? Allegedly, the higher value placed on female labor in the lowcountry is because it was a rice-growing region, since the cultivation of that crop in Africa was typically a female activity. In fact, however, the proportion of males from Upper Guinea was higher than that from all other African regions. Indeed, the male percentage in the Georgia slave trade was 72 percent — also quite a bit higher than normal. Males seem to have predominated among lowcountry Africans for two main reasons: first, the work demands of clearing swampland, digging ditches, and building embankments, which the shift to tidal rice agriculture demanded, put a premium on masculine labor. Second, and perhaps even more important, the high proportion of men and boys in slave trading vessels owed much to African suppliers. Apparently, women and children formed the majority of captives in wars and raids in Upper Guinea and seem to have been retained domestically because they were easier to control and would in the future reproduce. Thus, the local African demand for female slaves helps to explain why slaves exported from Upper Guinea were predominantly male. The prices for adult women in the lowcountry were roughly 80 percent of those of adult men. The idea that a higher value was placed on slave women vis-à-vis men in the lowcountry is a myth.[35]

The links between lowcountry Georgia and Africa were many. Women carried their babies strapped to their backs, and men toted heavy items on their heads, African style. Slaves might wake to the sound of a conch shell and sleep to the sound of rhythmic drumming. They cultivated African crops — from the tania, millet, sorghum, and okra to peppers, groundnuts, and sesame, or benne. They lived in huts of mud walls, rammed earth, and palmetto thatch and in compoundlike settlements. They made walking sticks embellished with reptile and human figures; utensils from gourds; drums and banjos; and quilts using strips, highly contrasting colors, and offbeat patterns. They paddled their canoes to the sound, as one traveler put it, of "their plaintive African songs." Their words, their intonations, their exclamations, their pronunciations, not to mention the grammatical and semantic structures underlying the Creole language they created, owed much to African languages. In 1785, thirty-year-old Betty, "with her country marks very conspicuous in her face" spoke "three different African languages," according to her master. Their dances, ways of walking, hairstyles, magical symbols, even their gestures all evoked homeland associations.[36]

Two unusual Africans suggest the range of personal connections spanning the Atlantic. None was more striking than Fenda Lawrence, who left the Gambia in May 1772 on board the *New Britannia*, a slaving vessel, in the company of 220 Africans. She was a free woman, formerly married to an English man, and a slave trader herself. She had an interest in five of the individuals on board ship: two women, each with a child, and one boy named James Lawrence, perhaps her son. At the request of the slave ship captain, she received a certificate from the government of Georgia permitting her to pass unmolested. She intended to settle in the colony. Unfortunately, nothing more is known about her. David Margate — or "David the

African," as he was known — a Methodist missionary, arrived in Georgia two years after Lawrence. He went to Bethesda, the orphanage about ten miles outside Savannah, whereupon he claimed to be a second Moses called to deliver his people from slavery — a view of Moses that would be popular among slaves into the nineteenth century. He managed to alienate whites who alleged, in addition to his insurrectionary potential, that he threatened to poison them, and blacks by trying to take another's wife as his own. Not surprisingly, David Margate lasted a short time in Georgia; he was shipped back to England to avoid a lynch mob.[37]

REVOLUTIONARY ATLANTIC

That David Margate just missed the American Revolution is ironic, but then again the Revolutionary era, as it played out in Georgia, was full of ironies. One was how quickly a revolution with noble ideals descended into savagery. In early 1776, Georgia's Patriot militia, dressed like Indians, and joined by about thirty Creeks, determined to set an example to fugitive slaves on Tybee Island who were trying to reach British ships. Although the so-called patriots captured some fugitives, they preferred to kill as many as possible as a way of terrorizing and deterring others. Predatory bands, both Patriot and Loyalist, marauded across the state, particularly across the border between Florida and Georgia. Few parts of lowcountry Georgia escaped brutalizing warfare; this was a civil war of unsurpassed internecine ferocity. In the fratricidal fight, slaves were often pawns, victims, and objects of plunder. By the end of the war, Patriots used captured slaves and those from sequestered Loyalist estates as bounties to encourage enlistments. It cannot be underestimated, then, how much the Revolutionary War was a traumatic event in African American life.[38]

A second paradox is that, "without meaning to do so," as Sylvia Frey notes, "the British Army . . . made the revolutionary war in Georgia a war about slavery." When the British invaded Georgia in late 1778, thousands of slaves saw the chance to gain liberty by fleeing to their lines. This exodus was a result of British conquest, but it was not something the British sought or encouraged. Depriving Patriot slaveholders of their most precious private property was not a way to win hearts and minds, nor could the British afford to alienate slaveholding loyalists. Unsurprisingly, then, the British proved unreliable liberators. They returned many slaves to their plantations, and they generally refused to arm them. Sometimes, when the

manpower crisis became acute, they did provide weapons — armed black
slaves helped save Savannah from the French, who, incidentally, had a company of free blacks from St. Domingue on their side — but arming slaves
or free blacks served only to terrify southern slaveholders, thereby making
matters worse. While largely depriving themselves of a potentially valuable
military resource, then, the British generally won no favors among the locals with their exceptions. Furthermore, continuing slave flight infuriated
whites, intensified their solidarity, and contributed to the eventual British
defeat.[39]

A third paradox concerns the actions of slaves. Although they primarily sought freedom from slavery, they often did so in the name of the king.
In February 1776, when the first few hundred slaves fled their Patriot masters and offered themselves to Sir James Wright, Georgia's last royal governor, they declared that "they were come for the King." Scipio Handley,
who escaped Charleston in 1775 and went to Barbados, volunteered for
the king's service as a member of the British invasion force of Savannah;
during the city's siege in 1779, he proved his loyalty to the king by taking
a musket ball in the leg while carrying grapeshot to the batteries. David
George set up a profitable business as a butcher in Savannah, while his wife
did laundry for British officers; he had a military pass certifying that he
was "a free Negro" and "a good subject to King George." In 1787, years after
the war ended, black maroons along the Savannah River, serving under
captains and calling themselves "King of England Soldiers," continued to
harass local planters. This royalism may have been purely strategic, but
it can be found among slaves throughout the Atlantic world — most famously, slaves in the great Haitian revolt rose up as defenders of king and
faith — and may owe something to African political ideology. Whatever
motivated them, thousands of slaves — perhaps as many as five thousand,
roughly one-third the prewar population — ran to the British. Such an
exodus has emboldened some historians to label it the largest slave uprising in American history. Surely, however, to justify that tag requires some
degree of collective action; while groups and sometimes whole plantations
fled, most slaves ran as individuals or at best as families. Mostly they were
trying to escape sheer chaos, and the British seemed to offer a chance at a
better life.[40]

Yet another paradox concerns the direction and fate of the black
diaspora that the Revolution spawned. To think of a black diaspora is, of
course, to conjure up an image of the slave trade, that westward-moving

torrent of human bodies from Africa to the Americas; but the Revolutionary War set in motion a reverse stream, one primarily eastward-moving, which in some cases went from the Americas back to Africa. Their fate was also paradoxical. The tragedy for most blacks who escaped Georgia during the American Revolution is that they ended up working on plantations in the Caribbean. Some exiles, however, were more fortunate. Thus, Scipio Handley, like other black loyalists, ended up in England, where, if he was poor, he was at least free. George Liele went with his wife and four children to Jamaica, where he was instrumental in forming a number of independent black Baptist churches. Brother Amos established a church at New Providence in the Bahamas. David George became a leader of the black community, first in Nova Scotia and later in Sierra Leone, where he erected the first independent black Baptist church in Africa. A Georgian black diaspora, then, radiated out across the Atlantic as a result of the Revolutionary War.[41]

So traumatic was the American Revolution in Georgia that, rather than challenge slavery, the Revolution in fact entrenched it. The vaunted war for liberty became a war to perpetuate slavery. Here is yet another irony. The nature of the war and its aftermath explains why antislavery principles had little chance in early national Georgia. It also accounts for the rarity of manumissions in postwar Georgia. In 1820, only 805 free blacks lived in the lowcountry, and slaves outnumbered them 32:1. The war even explains why in 1791 a group of white women petitioned for the life of a slave man who was to be executed for theft. Their primary reason was that the man's mother had been a loyal Patriot during the war. The loss of so many slaves during the war also explains why Georgians led the way in the reopening of the African slave trade after the Revolution ended, and why Georgians were so adamant in winning sanctions and protections for slavery in the Constitutional Convention and in the first federal Congress. It explains why the slave population doubled in the 1790s and almost doubled again in the 1800s, the largest percentage increase in population of any of the original states. The memory of so much anarchy and chaos, as well as their continuing sense of vulnerability from a formidable triangle of forces — Indians, Spaniards, and their own runaway slaves — also explains the hypersensitivity of Georgians to news from Saint Domingue. In 1799, one planter reported to Georgia governor James Jackson that French spies were "raising the Slaves" against their masters. Even as late as 1809, when a ship docked in Savannah with French refugees, once of St. Domingue but now forced out of Cuba, and of whom about fifty were enslaved or free people of color, city officials were quick to deny permission to land. They wanted no contamination. Access to free territory, not just in the new republic of Haiti but in the northern United States, also helps explain why Georgian slaves largely lost the chance to go to foreign ports on maritime vessels — something they had done before the Revolution. Arguably, too, the inability of lowcountry planters to vanquish their slaves' humanity — revealed most starkly during the Revolution through the wholesale exodus of their slaves — led them to try channeling that humanity in what, for them, were more acceptable directions. This shift helps account for their attempts to Christianize their slaves, one of the most notable developments in early national Georgia.[42]

And perhaps here is the final, biggest irony of all. As the masters' domination tightened and the irrevocable commitment to slavery hardened, the slaves' ability to mold their own culture within the interstices of the system deepened. Over time, by dint of hard-won struggles, slaves helped set the boundaries of the task. Over time, leaders — whether drivers, artisans, healers, conjurors, or preachers — emerged to oppose white hegemony. Over time, lowcountry slaves eked out a little space for themselves to develop a remarkable, if always limited, informal economy, which involved the right to some personal possessions and the right to market goods. Over time, hawkers, hucksters, and so-called Cake Wenches, who resorted to Savannah to sell their wares, would be accused of monopoly practices, price gouging, and worse crimes. Over time, slave families put down strong and extensive roots, even as they were always subject to separation. Over time, slave children grew up speaking Creole and learning animal tales. Over time, more slaves converted to Christianity than ever before — building, in fact, the largest independent black church in the South — even as a vibrant folk religion continued to flourish. Thus, in 1775, when a black preacher elicited criticism for presiding at a slave funeral where the slaves had "a dance for a fellow that was shot in the Woods," he justified himself by saying that "it was a custom among the Negroes to make mery [*sic*] for the dead." Similarly, when "Long Harry" ran away in 1788, his master noted "his remarkable conjurations of pigs feet [and] rattlesnakes teeth" with which he was said to "have performed miracles." Over time, as Erskine Clarke eloquently puts it, slaves also learned "the world of whites, with its straight roads leading to plantation houses and patriarchy, was not the only world or the only ways of understanding the landscape ... Trails provided avenues of escape, swamps offered the promise of hiding places, and the imagination of the settlements included the possibility of freedom from white oppression." By carving out some independence for themselves, by forcing masters to recognize their humanity, by creating an autonomous culture, slaves eased the torments of slavery.[43]

SLAVES SHAPED their destiny at the same time as they were victims of a brutal, dehumanizing system. By the early nineteenth century, the forces of unbridled domination and naked exploitation gathered strength: antislavery principles had been firmly squelched, borders were more secure than they had ever been; the state no longer needed African newcomers, the radical impulses of the Revolutionary era had been contained, and the state was poised to become a seedbed of the Cotton South. While prospects looked bleak, not even an oppressive regime could crush the slaves' unquenchable human spirit. Whatever the constraints, slaves contributed to the making of their history. Not only did they work for their masters, but they labored for themselves; not only did they engage in unrelenting toil for few benefits, but they derived personal satisfaction from their work; not only were their lives destroyed and disrupted, but they built and rebuilt family structures that sustained them; not only were they stripped of the opportunity to worship their own gods, but they established the earliest and most independent of black churches. Subject to grinding daily exploitation, caught in the grip of powerful forces, slaves nevertheless strove to create order in their lives, to preserve their humanity, to achieve dignity, and to sustain dreams of a better future.

NOTES

1. Betty Wood, *Women's Work, Men's Work: The Informal Slave Economies of Lowcountry Georgia* (Athens: University of Georgia Press, 1995), 7; Harold E. Davis, *The Fledgling Province: Social and Cultural Life in Colonial Georgia 1733–1776* (Chapel Hill: University of North Carolina Press, 1976); Betty Wood, *Slavery in Colonial Georgia, 1730–1775* (Athens: University of Georgia Press, 1984), 79; Erik Calonius, *The Wanderer: The Last American Slave Ship and the Conspiracy That Set Its Sail* (New York: St. Martin's Press, 2006); Sylvaine A. Diouf, *Dreams of Africa in Alabama: The Slave Ship Clotilda and the Story of the Last Africans Brought to America* (New York: Oxford University Press, 2007).

2. For a similar case, see Bradley G. Bond, ed., *French Colonial Louisiana and the Atlantic World* (Baton Rouge: Louisiana State University, 2005).

3. David Brion Davis, *The Problem of Slavery in Western Culture* (Ithaca, N.Y.:

Cornell University Press, 1966), 90; Christopher Leslie Brown, *Moral Capital: Foundations of British Abolitionism* (Chapel Hill: University of North Carolina Press, 2006), 33–77; John Richardson, *Slavery and Augustan Literature: Swift, Pope, Gay* (London: Routledge, Chapman & Hall, 2004), 30; James G. Basker, ed., *Amazing Grace: An Anthology of Poems about Slavery, 1660–1810* (New Haven, Conn.: Yale University Press, 2002), xxxi–61.

4. Davis, *Problem of Slavery*, 144; idem, *Inhuman Bondage: The Rise and Fall of Slavery in the New World* (New York: Oxford University Press, 2006), 136; Julie Anne Sweet, "The British Sailors' Advocate: James Oglethorpe's First Philanthropic Venture," *Georgia Historical Quarterly* (hereafter, *GHQ*) 91 (2007): 1–27, esp. 12.

5. Jack P. Greene, "Travails of an Infant Colony: The Search for Viability, Coherence, and Identity in Colonial Georgia," in *Imperatives, Behaviors and Identities: Essays in Early American Cultural History* (Charlottesville: University of Virginia Press, 1992), 113–42, esp. 117.

6. Ruth Scarborough, *Opposition to Slavery in Georgia prior to 1860* (Nashville: Cornell University Library, 1933), 1–75; Davis, *Problem of Slavery*, 144–50; Harvey H. Jackson, "The Darien Antislavery Petition of 1739 and the Georgia Plan," *William and Mary Quarterly* (hereafter, *WMQ*), 3rd Ser., 34 (1977): 618–31; Wood, *Slavery in Colonial Georgia*, 3–23, 30–31, 59–73; idem, "The Earl of Egmont and the Georgia Colony," in *Forty Years of Diversity: Essays on Colonial Georgia*, ed. Harvey H. Jackson and Phinizy Spalding (Athens: University of Georgia Press, 1984), 80–96; idem, "James Edward Oglethorpe, Race, and Slavery: A Reassessment," in *Oglethorpe in Perspective: Georgia's Founder after Two Hundred Years*, ed. Phinizy Spalding and Harvey H. Jackson (Tuscaloosa: University of Alabama Press, 1989), 66–79; George Fenwick Jones, *The Georgia Dutch: From the Rhine and Danube to the Savannah, 1733–1783* (Athens: University of Georgia Press, 1992), 266–74; Sir Keith Thomas, "James Edward Oglethorpe, Sometime Gentleman Commoner of Corpus," in *James Edward Oglethorpe: New Perspectives on His Life and Legacy*, ed. John C. Inscoe (Savannah, Ga.: Georgia Historical Society, 1997), 16–34, esp. 31–32; and Brown, *Moral Capital*, 79–87.

7. Edward J. Cashin, *Governor Henry Ellis and the Transformation of British North America* (Athens: University of Georgia, 1994), 115, 250n36; William Knox, *Three Tracts respecting the Conversion and Instruction of the Free Indians and Negro Slaves in the Colonies . . .* (London, 1768); Leland J. Bellot, *William Knox: The Life and Thought of an Eighteenth-Century Imperialist* (Austin: University of Texas, 1977); David Waldstreicher, *Runaway America: Benjamin Franklin, Slavery, and the American Revolution* (New York: Hill and Wang, 2004), 186–92; and Brown, *Moral Capital*, 226–7.

8. David Brion Davis, *The Problem of Slavery in the Age of Revolution, 1770–1823* (Ithaca, N.Y.: Cornell University Press, 1975), 280, 282; Harvey H. Jackson, "American Slavery, American Freedom and the Revolution in the Lower South: The Case of Lachlan McIntosh," *Southern Studies* 19 (Spring 1980): 82–93; Wood, *Slavery in Colonial Georgia*, 3–4, 201–4; Edward J. Cashin, *William Bartram and the American Revolution on the Southern Frontier* (Columbia: University of South Carolina

Press, 2000), 120–22; Phinizy Spalding, "James Oglethorpe and the American Revolution," *Journal of Imperial and Commonwealth History* 3 no. 3 (1975): 396–407; Brown, *Moral Capital*, 107, 187–88.

9. David Hugh Connolly Jr., "A Question of Honor: State Character and the Lower South's Defense of the African Slave Trade in Congress, 1789–1807" (PhD diss., Rice University, 2008), 2, 44 (my thanks to the author for allowing me to read his dissertation); Roger N. Parks, ed., *The Papers of General Nathanael Greene*, Vol. 13: *22 May 1783–13 June 1786* (Chapel Hill: University of North Carolina Press, 2005), 192; *Augusta Chronicle and Gazette of the State*, September 16, 1797; October 7, 1797; May 26, 1804; June 23, 1804; *Columbian Museum and Savannah Advertiser*, April 28, 1804; Jabez Bowen, *Gentlemen of the Grand Jury* (Providence, 1804); Walter G. Charlton, "A Judge and a Grand Jury," *Report of the Thirty First Annual Session of the Georgia Bar Association*, 1914 (Macon, 1914), 209–12; Scarborough, *Opposition to Slavery in Georgia*, 183–84, 243–45; Watson Woodson Jennison III, "Cultivating Race: Slavery and Expansion in Georgia, 1750–1860" (PhD diss., University of Virginia, 2005), 62–63, 77–81.

10. The antislavery strain, in muted fashion, persisted among some prominent lowcountry churchmen: Charles Colcock Jones thought slavery "a violation of all the laws of God and man," even as he came to terms with slaveholding; Thomas Smyth thought slavery an evil that ought to be removed "as soon as God in His providence should open the way": Erskine Clarke, *Dwelling Place: A Plantation Epic* (New Haven, Conn.: Yale University Press, 2005), 108, 117, 169.

11. Verner W. Crane, "A Lost Utopia of the First American Frontier," *Sewanee Review* 27 (1919): 48–61; Mellon Knox Jr., "Christian Prieber and the Jesuit Myth," *South Carolina Historical Magazine* 61 (1960): 75–81; idem, "Christian Prieber's Cherokee 'Kingdom of Paradise,'" *GHQ* 57 (1973): 319–31; George Fenwick Jones, *Georgia Dutch*, 65–67. More generally, see Richard White, *The Middle Ground: Indians, Empires, and Republics in the Great Lakes Region, 1650–1815* (New York: Cambridge University Press, 1991); Jeremy Adelman and Stephen Aron, "From Borderlands to Borders: Empires, Nation-States and the Peoples in between in North American History," *American Historical Review* 104 (1999): 814–41; Claudio Saunt, "'Our Indians': European Empires and the History of the Native-American South," in *The Atlantic in Global History, 1500–2000*, ed. Jorge Cañizares-Esguerra and Erik R. Seeman (Upper Saddle River, N.J.: Prentice Hall, 2007), 61–76; Julie Anne Sweet, *Negotiating for Georgia: British-Creek Relations in the Trustee Era, 1733–1752* (Athens: University of Georgia Press, 2005), 3–6; Lisa Ford, "Empire and Order on the Colonial Frontiers of Georgia and New South Wales," *Itinerario* 30, no. 3 (2006): 95–113.

12. Peter H. Wood, "The Changing Population of the Colonial South: An Overview by Race and Region, 1685–1790," in *Powhatan's Mantle: Indians in the Colonial Southeast*, rev. ed., ed. Gregory A. Waselkov, Peter H. Wood, and Tom Hatley (Lincoln: University of Nebraska Press, 2006), 57–132, esp. 81–87.

13. Sweet, *Negotiating for Georgia*, 33, 36, 38; Kathryn E. Holland Braund, "The Creek Indians, Blacks, and Slavery," *Journal of Southern History* (hereafter, *JSH*]

57, no. 4 (1991): 601–36, esp. 611–12; Martha Condrey Searcy, "The Introduction of African Slavery into the Creek Indian Nation," *GHQ* 66 (1982): 22–23, 24; see also James Taylor Carson, *Making an Atlantic World: Circles, Paths, and Stories from the Colonial South* (Knoxville: University of Tennessee Press, 2007), 91–92.

14. *South Carolina Journal of Commons House* 3:168–76; 5:199–200; John Tate Lanning, ed., *The St. Augustine Expedition of 1740: A Report to the South Carolina General Assembly* (Columbia: South Carolina Archives Department, 1954), 11–12, 17, 25, 62, 72, 73, 85, 93, 96–97, 98–99, 102, 114, 126, 129–30, 132, 148, 169, 173; Larry E. Ivers, *British Drums on the Southern Frontier: The Military Colonization of Georgia, 1733–1749* (Chapel Hill: University of North Carolina Press, 1974), 96, 102; Rodney M. Baine, "General James Oglethorpe and the Expedition against St. Augustine," *GHQ* 84 (2000): 197–229; Sweet, *Negotiating for Georgia*, 140–58; Shane Alan Runyon, "Borders and Rumors: The Georgia Frontier in the Atlantic World" (PhD diss., University of Florida, 2005), 215–16; Jane Landers, *Black Society in Spanish Florida* (Urbana: University of Illinois Press, 1999), 35–41.

15. Sweet, *Negotiating for Georgia*, 72, 76, 99; Rodney M. Baine, "Myths of Mary Musgrove," *GHQ* 76 (1992): 428–35; idem, "Indian Slavery in Colonial Georgia," *GHQ* 79 (1995): 418–24; Claudio Saunt, *A New Order of Things: Property, Power, and the Transformation of Creek Indians, 1733–1816* (New York: Cambridge University Press, 1999), 28–30, 38–46; Christina Snyder, "Conquered Enemies, Adopted Kin, and Owned People: The Creek Indians and Their Captives," *JSH* 73 (2007): 255–88.

16. Saunt, *New Order of Things*, 34–35, 50–63; Joel W. Martin, *Sacred Revolt: The Muskogees' Struggle for a New World* (Boston: Beacon Press, 1991), 71–72; Kathryn E. Holland Braund, *Deerskins and Duffels: The Creek Indian Trade with Anglo-America, 1685–1815* (Lincoln: University of Nebraska Press, 1993), 181–84; Snyder, "Conquered Enemies, Adopted Kin, and Owned People," 276–85.

17. Saunt, *New Order of Things*, 67–89, 100–101, 106, 109, 111–35; Snyder, "Conquered Enemies, Adopted Kin, and Owned People," 255–88; Patrick Riordan, "Seminole Genesis: Native Americans, African Americans, and Colonists on the Southern Frontier from Prehistory through the Colonial Era" (PhD diss., Florida State University, 1996).

18. Saunt, *New Order of Things*, 120–21; Martin, *Sacred Revolt*, 42, 73–76.

19. Landers, *Black Society*, 47–60, 77–79; Saunt, *New Order of Things*, 124–26, 244–45; for the larger context, see Julius S. Scott, "The Common Wind: Currents of Afro-American Communication in the Era of the Haitian Revolution" (PhD diss., Duke University, 1986).

20. Rembert W. Patrick, *Florida Fiasco: Rampant Rebels on the Georgia-Florida Border 1810–1815* (Athens: University of Georgia Press, 1954), esp. 31, 179–94, 214–15, 251, 285–89; Frank Lawrence Owsley Jr., *Struggle for the Gulf Borderlands: The Creek War and the Battle of New Orleans, 1812–1815* (Gainesville: University of Florida Press, 1981), 101–3, 135–36; Mary R. Bullard, *Black Liberation on Cumberland Island in 1815* (Deleon Springs, Fla.: M. R. Bullard, 1983); Roswell King to Pierce Butler, March 18, 1815, cited in Malcolm Bell Jr., *Major Butler's Legacy: Five Generations*

of a Slaveholding Family (Athens: University of Georgia Press, 1987), 182; Frank Lawrence Owsley Jr. and Gene A. Smith, *Filibusters and Expansionists: Jeffersonian Manifest Destiny, 1800–1821* (Tuscaloosa: University of Alabama Press, 1997), 77–79, 118–40; Landers, *Black Society*, 220–31, 237–46; Paul E. Hoffman, *Florida's Frontiers* (Bloomington: Indiana University Press, 2002), 242–81; James G. Cusick, *The Other War of 1812: The Patriot War and the American Invasion of Spanish East Florida* (Gainesville: University Press of Florida, 2003), esp. 5, 47–49, 185–86, 189, 205–9, 213–21, 231–37, 272–75, 298–99; Jon Latimer, *1812: War with America* (Cambridge, Mass.: Belknap Press, 2007), 393.

21. "An Impartial Inquiry into the State and Utility of the Province of Georgia" (London, 1741), in *Georgia Historical Collections*, 1:171; James C. Bonner, *A History of Agriculture, 1732–1860* (Athens: University of Georgia Press, 1964), 8; Joyce E. Chaplin, *An Anxious Pursuit: Agricultural Innovation and Modernity in the Lower South, 1730–1815* (Chapel Hill: University of North Carolina Press, 1993), 151–55; Mart A. Stewart, *"What Nature Suffers to Groe": Life, Labor, and Landscape on the Georgia Coast, 1680–1920* (Athens: University of Georgia Press, 1996), 116, 122–26; Governor James Wright to the Board of Trade, June 8, 1768, in *The Colonial Records of the State of Georgia*, vol. 28, ed. Allen D. Candler and Lucian L. Knight (Atlanta: C. P. Byrd, 1904–16), 255, as cited in Jennison, "Cultivating Race," 16; Ben Marsh, *Georgia's Frontier Women: Female Fortunes in a Southern Colony* (Athens: University of Georgia Press, 2007), 112, 117; Paul M. Pressly, "Scottish Merchants and the Shaping of Colonial Georgia," *GHQ* 91, no. 2 (2007): 135–68, esp. 138, 144–45, 156, 159–60.

22. *Georgia Gazette*, July 13, 1768; D. C. Corbitt, "Papers Relating to the Georgia-Florida Frontier, 1784–1800. Part II," *GHQ* 21 (1937): 75, as cited in Saunt, *New Order of Things*, 117; but here I am most indebted to Gregory E. O'Malley, "Final Passages: The British Inter-colonial Slave Trade, 1619–1807" (PhD diss., Johns Hopkins University, 2007). He estimates that 204 shipments of slaves came into Georgia from the Caribbean, bringing in 5,414 slaves. The 1790s was by far the high point of the slave trade into Georgia (when over 13,000 arrived in the state), and the ratio of Caribbean to African imports was at 1:12 its most lopsided. In the 1800s, the numbers dropped, and the ratio was 1:7.

23. Gregory E. O'Malley, "Beyond the Middle Passage: Quantifying Slave Migration from the Caribbean to North America, 1619–1867," *WMQ*, 3rd Ser., 66 (2009): 125–72, briefly explores these implications while providing the best numerical estimates of the scale of the intercolonial migration.

24. Olaudah Equiano, *The Interesting Narrative and Other Writings*, ed. Vincent Carretta (New York: Penguin Classics, 2003), 123–24, 127–30, 133–35, 138–41, 147, 157–61, 277n363; Vincent Carretta, *Equiano the African: Biography of a Self-Made Man* (Athens: University of Georgia Press, 2005), 108, 112, 121, 122, 127, 131–32.

25. In the 1750s, when the best estimate is that perhaps 350 slaves arrived from the Caribbean and none from Africa, the slave population of Georgia rose by about 3,500. Almost all of them must have been from South Carolina. Similarly, in the 1760s, when the growth rate of Georgia's slave population was about 6,000, seaborne

imports, many of whom must have died within a few years of arrival, numbered only about 4,500 — so probably half the increase came from South Carolina. More generally, see David R. Chesnut, *South Carolina's Expansion into Colonial Georgia, 1720–1765* (New York: Garland Publisher, 1989); Stewart, *"What Nature Suffers to Groe,"* 91–92; Wood, *Slavery in Colonial Georgia*, esp. 88–109; and, for the broader history of the signature crop, see Peter A. Coclanis, "Distant Thunder: The Creation of a World Market in Rice and the Transformations It Wrought," *American Historical Review* (hereafter, *AHR*) 98 (1993): 1050–78, and his "Rice" in www.georgiaencyclopedia.org.

26. Philip D. Morgan, *Slave Counterpoint: Black Culture in the Eighteenth-Century Chesapeake and Lowcountry* (Chapel Hill: University of North Carolina Press, 1998), 179–87; idem, "Task and Gang Systems: The Organization of Labor on New World Plantations," in *Work and Labor in Early America*, ed. Stephen Innes (Chapel Hill: University of North Carolina Press, 1988), 189–220; Peter A. Coclanis, "How the Low Country Was Taken to Task: Slave-Labor Organization in Coastal South Carolina and Georgia," in *Slavery, Secession, and Southern History*, ed. Robert Louis Paquette and Louis Ferleger (Charlottesville: University Press of Virginia, 2000), 59–78.

27. S. Max Edelson, *Plantation Enterprise in Colonial South Carolina* (Cambridge, Mass.: Harvard University Press, 2006), 7, 92–165. For Savannah's population, see Betty Wood, *Women's Work, Men's Work: The Informal Slave Economies of Lowcountry Georgia* (Athens: University of Georgia Press, 1995), 7, 81, 110, 131, 164, 181, 192n20, 211n6, 223n13, 224n28.

28. My thanks to David Eltis, for his help with the new transatlantic slave trade database (available at http://wilson.library.emory.edu:9090/tast/index.faces) and the estimate. Between 1766 and 1820, the estimate is that 28,717 Africans arrived in Georgia; making allowance for mortality in the Middle Passage accounts for the overall estimate. For a useful short overview of the Georgia slave trade, see Darold D. Wax, "'New Negroes Are Always in Demand': The Slave Trade in Eighteenth-Century Georgia," *GHQ* 68 (1984): 193–220.

29. Wood, *Slavery in Colonial Georgia*, 173.

30. David Eltis, Philip Morgan, and David Richardson, "Agency and Diaspora in Atlantic History: Reassessing the African Contribution to Rice Cultivation in the Americas," *AHR* 112 (2007): 1329–58.

31. Judith A. Carney, *Black Rice: The African Origins of Rice Cultivation in the Americas* (Cambridge, Mass.: Harvard University Press, 2001); Edelson, *Plantation Enterprise*, 53–91; Eltis, Morgan, and Richardson, "Agency and Diaspora in Atlantic History," *AHR* 112 (2007): 1329–58.

32. http://wilson.library.emory.edu:9090/tast/index.faces, searching by principal region of slave purchase; see also James McMillin, *The Final Victims: Foreign Slave Trade to North America, 1783–1810* (Columbia: University of South Carolina Press, 2004).

33. Ras Michael L. B. Brown, "Crossing Kalunga: West-Central Africans and their Cultural Influence in the South Carolina-Georgia Lowcountry" (unpublished

ms.); idem, "'Walk in the Feenda': West-Central Africans and the Forest in the South Carolina–Georgia Lowcountry," in *Central Africans and Cultural Transformations in the American Diaspora*, ed. Linda M. Heywood (Cambridge: Cambridge University Press, 2002), 289–318; Allan D. Austin, *African Muslims in Antebellum America: Transatlantic Stories and Spiritual Struggles* (New York: Routledge, 1997), 6, 85–113; Michael A. Gomez, *Exchanging Our Country Marks: The Transformation of African Identities in the Colonial and Antebellum South* (Chapel Hill: University of North Carolina Press, 1998), 69–70, 76–87, 118–20; *Georgia Gazette*, August 13, 1795; August 20, 1795; Mary Thomas, *Royal Georgia Gazette*, January 4, 1781; King to Butler, May 13, 1803, as cited in Bell, *Major Butler's Legacy*, 132.

34. The largest ship was the four-hundred-ton ship *Charleston*, which in 1795 disembarked five hundred Africans (ID no. 25054 in http://wilson.library.emory.edu:9090/tast/index.faces), and the smallest, the thirty-two-ton sloop *Diana* (ID no. 36583), which disembarked thirty-five Africans in 1793. There were sixteen ships registered in London, ten in Liverpool, and twenty in Providence. The story of the *Wanderer* is told in Calonius, *Wanderer*, and Diouf, *Dreams of Africa in Alabama*, 2, 74, 78–79, 83, 88–89, 110, 132, 140, 170.

35. Carney, *Black Rice*, 26–28, 49–55, 107–41; see http://wilson.library.emory.edu:9090/tast/index.face, exploring summary statistics for the 118 voyages to Georgia; Eltis, Morgan, and Richardson, "Agency and Diaspora in Atlantic History," 1349–53.

36. Morgan, *Slave Counterpoint*, 118–20, 141–42, 198–200, 242–44, 248–49, 420, 432, 450, 560–73, 575, 578–80, 582–87, 589, 593, 597–98, 603, 605, 617–18, 620, 622; Samuel Beecroft, *Gazette of the State of Georgia*, October 20, 1785, also cited in Tiwanna M. Simpson, "'She Has Her Country Marks Very Conspicuous in the Face': African Community and Culture in Early Georgia" (PhD diss., Ohio State University, 2002), 1.

37. Lillian Ashcraft-Eason, "'She Voluntarily Hath Come': A Gambian Woman Trader in Colonial Georgia in the Eighteenth Century," in *Identity in the Shadow of Slavery*, ed. Paul E. Lovejoy (London: Leicester University Press, 2000), 202–21; Boyd Stanley Schlenther, *Queen of the Methodists: The Countess of Huntingdon and the Eighteenth-Century Crisis of Faith and Society* (Durham, U.K.: Durham Academic Press, 1997), 91; Morgan, *Slave Counterpoint*, 424–45, 649–50; Sylvia R. Frey and Betty Wood, *Come Shouting to Zion: African American Protestantism in the American South and British Caribbean to 1830* (Chapel Hill: University of North Carolina Press, 1998), 112–14, 116; and Edward J. Cashin, *Beloved Bethesda: A History of George Whitefield's Home for Boys, 1740–2000* (Macon, Ga.: Mercer University Press, 2001), 117–18.

38. For different accounts of what happened on Tybee Island (for my purposes, intentions are more important than outcomes), see Peter H. Wood, "The Dream Deferred," in *In Resistance: Studies in African, Caribbean, and Afro-American History*, ed. Gary Y. Okihiro (Amherst: University of Massachusetts Press, 1986), 179–80; Cassandra Pybus, "Jefferson's Faulty Math: The Question of Slave Defections in the American Revolution," *WMQ*, 3d Ser., 62 (2005): 250–51; and Jim Piecuch,

PHILIP MORGAN

Three Peoples, One King: Loyalists, Indians, and Slaves in the Revolutionary South, 1775–1782 (Columbia: University of South Carolina Press, 2008), 84–85.

39. Sylvia R. Frey, *Water from the Rock: Black Resistance in a Revolutionary Age* (Princeton, N.J.: Princeton University Press, 1991), 81–107 (quote on 107); on the Chasseurs-Volontaires de Saint-Domingue, see Alexander Lawrence, *Storm over Savannah: The Story of Count d'Estaing and the Siege of the Town in 1779* (Athens: University of Georgia Press, 1951); Stewart R. King, *Blue Coat or Powdered Wig: Free People of Color in Pre-Revolutionary Saint Domingue* (Athens: University of Georgia Press., 2001), 65–69; John D. Garrigus, "Catalyst or Catastrophe? Saint Domingue's Free Men of Color and the Battle of Savannah, 1779–1782," *Revista/Review Interamericana* 22, no. 1–2 (1992): 109–25; idem, *Before Haiti: Race and Citizenship in French Saint-Domingue* (New York: Palgrave McMillan, 2006), 206–13, 224, 246.

40. Frey, *Water from the Rock*, 39, 66, 169–70; Piecuch, *Three Peoples, One King*, 169; Cassandra Pybus, *Epic Journeys of Freedom: Runaway Slaves of the American Revolution and Their Global Quest for Liberty* (Boston: Beacon Press, 2006), 40; Brendan McConville, *The King's Three Faces: The Rise and Fall of Royal America, 1688–1776* (Chapel Hill: University of North Carolina Press, 2006), 181; John Thornton, "'I Serve the King of the Kongo': African Political Ideology in the Haitian Revolution," *Journal of World History* 4 (1993), 181–214; David Patrick Geggus, "Slavery, War, and Revolution in the Greater Caribbean, 1789–1815" in *A Turbulent Time: The French Revolution and the Greater Caribbean*, ed. David Barry Gaspar and David Patrick Geggus (Bloomington: Indiana University Press, 1997), 7–9; idem, *Haitian Revolutionary Studies* (Bloomington: Indiana University Press, 2002), 12, 36, 66, 123, 129, 141–43, 266n33.

41. Mary Beth Norton, "The Fate of Some Black Loyalists of the American Revolution," *Journal of Negro History* 68 no. 4 (1973): 404; Pybus, *Epic Journeys of Freedom*, 37–40, 209, 210–12; Thomas J. Little, "George Liele and the Rise of Independent Black Baptist Churches in the Lower South and Jamaica," *Slavery and Abolition* 16, no. 2 (1995), 188–204; John W. Pulis, "Bridging Troubled Waters: Moses Baker, George Liele, and the African American Diaspora to Jamaica," in *Moving On: Black Loyalists in the Afro-Atlantic World*, ed. John W. Pulis (New York: Routledge, 1999), 183–222; Frey and Wood, *Come Shouting to Zion*, 130–32.

42. Betty Wood, *Gender, Race, and Rank in a Revolutionary Age: The Georgia Lowcountry, 1750–1820* (Athens: University of Georgia Press, 2000), 13; idem, "White Women, Black Slaves and the Law in Early National Georgia: The Sunbury Petition of 1791," *Historical Journal* 35 (1992): 611–22; Connolly, "Question of Honor," esp. 1–72; James Read to James Jackson, March 23, 1799, Jacob Read Papers, University of South Carolina; *Republican and Savannah Evening Ledger*, May 23, 1809; May 25, 1809; June 20, 1809; July 27, 1809; and Savannah City Council Minutes, May 22, 1809; May 26, 1809; August 7, 1809, as cited in Ashli White, "Revolution and Refuge: Saint Dominguan Exiles in the United States, 1791–1820" (unpublished manuscript), and my thanks to the author for allowing me to cite this example; W. Jeffrey Bolster, *Black Jacks: African American Seamen in the Age of Sail* (Cambridge, Mass.: Harvard University Press, 1997), 156; Jeffrey Robert Young, *Domesticating Slavery:*

The Master Class in Georgia and South Carolina, 1670–1837 (Chapel Hill: University of North Carolina Press, 1999), 113–14.

43. Timothy James Lockley, *Lines in the Sand: Race and Class in Lowcountry Georgia, 1750–1860* (Athens: University of Georgia Press, 2001), 57–97, 131–62; Wood, *Women's Work, Men's Work*, esp. 80–100, 142–48, 160–76; on families, see Morgan, *Slave Counterpoint*, 498–558, and for the later period, Daina Ramey Berry, *"Swing the Sickle for the Harvest Is Ripe": Gender and Slavery in Antebellum Georgia* (Urbana: University of Illinois Press, 2007), 52–103; Julia Floyd Smith, *Slavery and Rice Culture in Low Country Georgia, 1750–1860* (Knoxville: University of Tennessee Press, 1985), 141–65; Whittington B. Johnson, *Black Savannah, 1788–1864* (Fayetteville: University of Arkansas Press, 1996), 5, 7–35; Frey and Wood, *Come Shouting to Zion*, 116–17, 131, 159–60; Elizabeth Cosson to the Countess of Huntingdon, September 12, 1775, A3/4/7, Cheshunt Foundation, Westminster College, Cambridge; *Gazette of the State of Georgia*, October 9, 1788; Erskine Clark, *Dwelling Place: A Plantation Epic* (New Haven, Conn.: Yale University Press, 2005), 53.

Betty Wood

"High notions of their liberty"

Women of Color and the American
Revolution in Lowcountry Georgia and
South Carolina, 1765–1783

ALTHOUGH paling into insignificance when compared to that of New England and Virginia, in recent years a substantial historiography has built up that deals with many different facets of the American Revolution in lowcountry Georgia and South Carolina. Building upon the pioneering work of Benjamin Quarles, Sylvia Frey, Philip Morgan, and Robert Olwell among others have supplemented a previous scholarship that focused on those of European ancestry by drawing our attention to those who composed the majority of the lowcountry's population on the eve of the War of American Independence: people of West and West Central African ancestry.[1] However, this rich vein of historical research is marked by a glaring gender imbalance, in that thus far virtually no attention has been paid to African and African American women, be they enslaved or legally free. True, they make an appearance in the work of the scholars mentioned above, but as yet there is not a single book, and only a handful of essays, devoted entirely to them.[2]

Due to universal constraints upon literacy and, in the present context, particularly upon the ability to write, we lack the firsthand voices of the enslaved and legally free people of the eighteenth-century lowcountry.

However, they have left a great many historical footprints in various literary sources, ranging from newspapers and letters to army records, which enable us to accurately re-create their daily lives, their hopes, and their fears, as between the mid-1760s and 1775 the imperial crisis escalated into all-out war.

The year 1765 was decisive for lowcountry Georgia and South Carolina, as indeed it was for all of Britain's mainland and Caribbean colonies. Everywhere, news of the Stamp Act that the British House of Commons had passed caused an uproar. In Charleston and Savannah, the self-styled Patriots began to mobilize and plot their strategy to secure the overthrow of the hated Stamp Act.[3] Somewhat ironically given their heavy dependence upon racial slavery, they bitterly complained about their own enslavement by a tyrannical British ministry. Their rhetoric of English rights and liberties would not be lost upon the lowcountry's enslaved Africans and African Americans. In Georgia, however, and a sure sign that enslaved people would not be the beneficiaries of the Patriots' clamor for liberty and equality, the mid-1760s saw the opening of the transatlantic slave trade to Savannah.[4]

All that women like the young, Guinea-born Sally — who probably arrived on one of the first slave ships to dock in Savannah — could look forward to was a life of unremitting toil in Georgia's unhealthy rice swamps.[5] Exactly the same was true of many other enslaved women, who had spent longer or who had been born in the lowcountry: women like Hannah and her mother Dinah, who labored on one of the Lining family's South Carolina plantations,[6] and Betty, who worked in Charleston as a domestic servant for James Laurens and his family.[7] Phillis George, a legally free woman of color, who together with her husband David would migrate from Virginia to Georgia, might well have fretted about the security of her family's right to continuing freedom should the Georgia Patriots ever succeed in displacing the British.[8] For these women, indeed for all women of color in the lowcountry, whatever their legal status, their personal freedom, with all that it might entail, was a most precious commodity, a commodity that they both yearned and struggled for on a daily basis.

By the early 1770s, as the imperial crisis deepened, it began to appear to enslaved women and men that in the not-too-distant future, freedom from bondage might well be within their reach. Their hopes stemmed partly from two longstanding beliefs: first, that an external liberator, or liberators, would come to their assistance, and second, the growing conviction of many enslaved people that, sooner or later, the Christian God would grant them secular as well as spiritual freedom and, at the same time, punish those who had held them, and who continued to hold them, in bondage.

In the lowcountry, particularly following the settlement of Georgia in 1733, Spain offered freedom to any enslaved people who managed to make their way to St. Augustine; in 1739, this migration had been the principle aim of the unsuccessful Stono rebels.[9] Spanish defeat in the Seven Years' War, and the cession of large portions of Florida to the English, did not entirely eradicate the attractiveness of that region to runaways from the lowcountry.

As implausible as it might seem given Britain's long and deep involvement in the transatlantic slave trade, even before the onset of the imperial crisis enslaved people in both the Upper and the Lower South had some reason to believe that the British might prove to be their liberators. It was well known in the lowcountry of the late 1760s and early 1770s that, within the lifetimes of many blacks as well as whites, between 1735 and 1750, the Georgia trustees, under the leadership of James Oglethorpe, had struggled, albeit unsuccessfully, to keep Georgia free of black slavery.[10] Responsibility for the introduction of slavery, it could be argued, and believed, rested with avaricious local colonists rather than with the distant British.

The case for the British as liberators was strengthened during the early 1770s, as news of the test cases against slavery being mounted in the English and Scottish law courts — and particularly the monumental Somerset Case of 1772, which arguably ended slavery in England — quickly crossed the Atlantic and was soon being published in southern newspapers.[11] It proved impossible to hide this controversial information from enslaved people, information that only lent credence to their belief that the British, and more specifically the British king, would soon be coming to their aid. The monarch, who was increasingly being depicted by the Patriots as a tyrant, came to be regarded in a very different light by enslaved people.

In mid-1775, and highly reminiscent of events in Virginia in the early 1730s, when enslaved rebels had maintained that the British king had decreed that Christians could not be held in perpetual bondage by other Christians,[12] the rationale behind a planned insurrection in South Carolina was that because he had failed to implement this promise, "the old King [George II] . . . was now gone to Hell, & in Punishmt.," but that "the Young King [George III] . . . was about to alter the World, & set the Negroes Free."[13] The failure of this rebellion, together with the trial and execution of its leader, Jerry, did little to diminish enslaved peoples' faith in the British and, in particular, the British Crown.[14] Indeed, over the next few months and years, they would pay considerable heed to the declarations and promises made by the king's representatives in the southern mainland.

The notion of the British king and his proxies in the colonies, men like Lord Dunmore and General Henry Clinton, as their liberators coalesced with another theme that by 1775 had been present for many decades in the religious ideology of at least some enslaved people in the lowcountry: millenarianism, the belief that slaveholding was sinful and that, as with all sins, sooner or later the Christian God would wreak a terrible vengeance on those who continued to hold slaves.[15] This was a message of hope that enslaved people could and did take from their own interpretation of the Bible, particularly the Old Testament. Moreover, it was also a message that was implicit in the teaching of evangelical preachers such as George Whitefield; by 1774 and 1775, it was a message of deliverance that, much to the alarm of slaveholders, was being trumpeted openly and loudly in the lowcountry by black as well as by white preachers. In Charleston, for example, David Margate, the English-based black preacher dispatched to the southern mainland by the Countess of Huntingdon's Connection, declared himself to be the black Moses who would lead his people to freedom. It was only the timely intervention of James Habersham of Georgia that prevented David's lynching by irate white Charlestonians.[16] For his part, John Burnet, a Scottish minister, was said to have "often appointed Nocturnal Meetings of the Slaves under the Sanction of Religion," and "repeatedly inculcated such doctrines" that "were principally instrumental" in fomenting Jerry's rebellion.[17]

Such was the mood, the enormity of the panic, and the dread felt by the Charleston authorities that by the summer of 1775 they had turned the city into what amounted to a heavily fortified garrison. As a correspondent wrote from Charleston in June, "In our situation we cannot be too watchful, and we may require much strength, for our negroes have all high notions of their liberty."[18] Writing to his father a month later, Gabriel Manigault was rather more sanguine. He noted, "We have been alarmed by idle reports that the Negroes intended to rise, which on examination proved to be of less consequence than was expected." But, even so, Manigault concluded, "a Strick [sic] watch has been Kept for fear of the worst."[19]

Everywhere in the lowcountry, white anxieties had been exacerbated by a rumor that had clearly influenced Jerry and his followers. By late 1774 and early 1775, word was spreading like wildfire throughout the southern mainland that — reminiscent of the law that had been enacted, but never implemented, in Georgia twenty years earlier[20] — the British intended to arm enslaved people, now not against an external continental European enemy but in an attempt to impose their will on the Patriots. As Georgia Governor James Wright wrote to the Earl of Dartmouth in the spring of 1775, "A report has been propagated that [the] administration have it in view to send over troops to Carolina and at the same time to attempt to liberate the slaves and encourage them to attack their masters." This "report," which Wright discounted as "absurd and improbable," had "thrown the people in Carolina and this province into a ferment."[21] In November 1775, the "absurd and improbable" was transformed into reality when John Murray, Lord Dunmore, Virginia's royal governor, issued a proclamation offering freedom to slaves belonging to Patriot owners who were willing to take up arms on behalf of the British.[22]

As John Adams famously, and correctly, remarked in September, 1775, "The Negroes have a wonderfull [sic] Art of communicating Intelligence among themselves. It will run," he continued, "severall [sic] hundreds of Miles in a Week or Fortnight."[23] So it was that within a month, news of Dunmore's proclamation had reached the lowcountry, and its effect was electrifying.[24] Far from being deterred by the recent fate of Jerry, enslaved people did not stop to wonder whether Dunmore's offer applied to them. Instead, they made their way in the "hundreds" from the surrounding countryside to the port towns of Charleston and Savannah in the hope, and maybe also the expectation, that they would be taken aboard the British warships anchored there, and many of them were.[25] Patriot politicians such as Henry Laurens imagined that their worst nightmare — a wide black rebellion aided and abetted by the British — was about to be unleashed on the lowcountry. Some favored simply shooting the enslaved men, women, and children who had taken refuge on Tybee and Sullivan's islands as a deterrent to other would-be runaways.[26] This barbaric policy was never implemented, but every would-be runaway, female as well as male, young as well as old, knew full well that if they were apprehended, they were liable to be whipped, executed, or deported to what most believed were the even harsher plantation regimes of the Caribbean.

Between late 1775 and 1778, when the British had effectively abandoned the lowcountry and were so heavily engaged militarily further north in the American mainland, with one notable exception the working lives of enslaved people in the lowcountry returned to something approaching their familiar routines. In the countryside, the majority of women, as well as men, continued to work as field hands, with a few of each sex being employed as domestic servants. On larger plantations, the petty but highly influential managerial position of driver was reserved for enslaved men although, as we shall see, this did not mean that enslaved women field hands were totally devoid of influence.[27] With the exception of spinning and weaving, enslaved men also dominated most other artisanal and craft occupations, particularly those such as blacksmithing that required an apprenticeship.

Both on land and at sea, men filled virtually all the jobs that were associated with the transportation of goods: they worked as sailors, riverboat men, and pilots, and in towns such as Savannah and Charleston as porters and draymen. It should be noted, however, that sailors, riverboat men, and draymen carried rather more than commodities from place to place: throughout the war, they remained, as they had long been, vitally important conveyors of information.[28] Significantly, planters such as Henry Laurens were far more concerned by the illicit trading in commodities carried out by boatmen such as Adam and Abraham than they were by their potentially damaging two-way trade in hard news and hearsay.[29]

In Savannah and Charleston, as well as in such smaller towns as Georgetown and Beaufort, most enslaved men worked around the docks, loading and unloading goods, or as artisans, while most enslaved women were employed either as domestic servants, washerwomen, or market women. Depending upon their age, these women, like some women field hands, might also be employed temporarily in a secondary and, often by virtue of being hired out, an income-generating capacity as wet nurses. By definition, this was the one occupation that was confined to women. Much the same was also true of midwifery, although by the time of the American Revolution, a handful of white men, usually described as apothecaries or doctors, were beginning to practice this occupation.[30]

Whether they worked in the public market or in white households, either in their owners' employ or in that of those who hired their services, urban women played a comparable role to sailors and riverboat men in the gathering and spreading of news. For example, house servants such as Betty, in Charleston, were very well-placed either to overhear or be sufficiently trusted to be privy to the conversations that took place between the members of the white families on whom they waited. These women seem to have been no means reluctant to pass on what they had heard, or thought that they had heard, to their own family members and friends.

Precisely the same was true of the enslaved women who, by the 1760s, dominated the public markets of Savannah and Charleston.[31] Significantly, not only did these women constitute another crucial link between town and countryside, but it seems that many of their daily business dealings and conversations were with other women of color. Enslaved women, as well as enslaved men, brought their own, as well as their owners', goods in from the countryside to sell in urban markets, but most of those sent to these markets on a fairly regular basis by their owners to buy in various foodstuffs, but especially fresh foodstuffs, were female domestic servants such as Betty.

In addition to their markets, and despite their urban watches, the low-country towns offered enslaved people innumerable other opportunities to meet and socialize, sometimes in gender-specific and at other times in non-gender-specific groups of varying sizes. Churches, which in the case of evangelical congregations became increasingly dominated by women, offered regular opportunities for the exchange of news. In the urban world outside the churches, taverns were almost exclusively male preserves, as were cockfights. Horse racing in Charleston, on the other hand, tended to be a gender-mixed affair, with women often attending races with a view to vending their wares.[32]

FIELD HANDS like Hannah and Dinah Lining may well have lived at some distance from Charleston, and of course precisely the same was true of hundreds of other enslaved women in the lowcountry, but thanks in no small part to riverboat men and women market traders, they were by no means ignorant of either the unfolding imperial crisis or of the vagaries of the war that followed — and what women like the Linings learned was quickly spread through the surrounding countryside. Hiring out and fam-ily visits, as well as trade with enslaved people on neighboring plantations and visits, often after dark, to country stores all involved the gathering and the transmission of news and rumor.[33]

Precisely the same was true when it came to both the licit and the illicit gatherings of enslaved people for traditional marriage and burial ceremo-nies. Some indication of the numbers involved in these services may be gathered from James Barclay's description of the nighttime weddings that took place on lowcountry plantations on the eve of the War of Independence. If the couple to be married were "well acquainted in the place," he wrote, "multitudes of men, women and children, to the amount of several hundreds, would flock together from the neighbouring plantations" to participate in the festivities.[34] Christian ceremonies being conducted by the likes of David and Phillis George at Silver Bluff, and in Charleston by the "Negro Preachers" invited by Patrick Hinds to "deliver Doctrines to large Numbers of Negroes . . . in his House and on his Grounds," also provided regular opportunities for the gathering and spreading of news.[35]

On a more secular note, what appear to have been both widespread and regular gatherings of enslaved people for dances — again usually at night, sometimes in the countryside and sometimes in the towns — served a virtually identical function to religious ceremonials when it came to the gathering and dissemination of information. In the early 1770s, for example, a visitor to the lowcountry reported that he "had once an opportunity of seeing a Country-Dance, Rout, or Cabal of Negroes, within 5 miles distance of [Charleston] on a Saturday night." Although as many as two hundred enslaved people at a time were said to attend "such assemblies," this particular gathering had "consisted of about 60 people, ⅚th from Town." Essentially similar events, the visitor continued, consisting of "seldom fewer than 20 or 30 people . . . are frequent in Town." There they were held "either at the houses of free negroes, [or] apartments hired to slaves." It may be safely assumed that women domestics such as Betty were instrumental both in facilitating and organizing those social events that took place in "the kitchens of such Gentlemen as frequently retire, with their families, into the country for a few days,"[36] as well as those, like Betty's employer James Laurens, who during the war years left their homes for months, if not years, at a time.

With only one important exception, the worlds of women's and men's work did not change dramatically with the onset of war. What did alter, though, beginning with the Patriots late in 1775, and ironically given their fear of black insurrection, was the conscription of enslaved people, women as well as men, to help bolster the defenses of Savannah and Charleston. Significantly, but unsurprisingly perhaps, at different times different demands were made of women and men. In November 1775, for example, without specifying their sex, South Carolina's Provincial Council ordered that "a sufficient number of negroes" be hired to complete the defenses of Dorchester and James Island.[37] In Georgia, too, in mid-1776, the Council of Safety issued a non-gender-specific order that "a number of negroes" be hired "to finish . . . the intrenchments [*sic*] at Sunbury." A few months later, one hundred enslaved people were conscripted "to enclose the public magazine."[38] It seems highly likely that throughout the lowcountry, as the war got under way, enslaved women found themselves being forced to undertake grueling, backbreaking work alongside men on behalf of the Patriots.

Exactly the same would be true toward the end of the war, in 1778 and 1779, as the long-anticipated British attempt to reoccupy the lowcountry began. In August 1779, for instance, the South Carolina Assembly issued a call for "2,000 Negroes between the ages of 18 and 40 years . . . to throw up lines and necessary works of defence."[39] Significantly, no mention was made of gender.

Unsurprisingly, certain kinds of war work were limited to enslaved men. Thus, early in 1776, the South Carolina Provincial Council agreed that enslaved men should be "employed, without arms, for the defence of the several batteries in Charles-Town, Fort Johnson and other batteries."[40] Presumably their work would involve fetching and carrying the arms and ammunition, together with any other supplies required by the white defenders of these batteries. At this stage in the war, and given the events in Charleston only a few months earlier, there was no possibility whatsoever of South Carolina's and Georgia's Patriots putting guns into the hands of slaves, regardless of the possible cost to themselves. This pattern of gendered war work continued. In 1777, for example, when the Commissioners of the Navy advertised in the *South Carolina Gazette and American General Advertiser* for "a Number of Negro Ship Carpenters or Caulkers," they had no need to mention gender because everyone, black and white, knew that these skills were restricted to enslaved men.[41]

Once the British launched their long-awaited assault on the lowcountry, conscripted enslaved workers in places such as Charleston, and smaller settlements like Hampstead, often found themselves in terrifying life-threatening situations. As the Patriot John Lewis Gervais commented, during the British bombardment of Hampstead, "The Negroes were a little frightened at first, but they continued their work." What Gervais singularly failed to add was that any enslaved person deserting his or her post was likely to be summarily executed by officers such as Thomas Horry, who were "attending the negroes on the public works."[42] The fact of the matter was, whether or not they wished to do so, scores, if not hundreds of enslaved women and men found themselves being forced to assist the Patriots' war effort.

As the British forces advanced across the lowcountry, and not for the first time, enslaved people found themselves facing what were often extraordinarily difficult choices. Enslaved women and men were no more unified, no more homogenous, in their decision making than were their owners and other whites. Despite the temptation to cast them in a uniformly heroic role, by no means were all enslaved women selfless heroines; neither, of course, were they all hapless victims.

In 1778, and certainly by 1779, the prospect of liberation by the British must have seemed an entirely realistic prospect, principally because in 1779 General Henry Clinton issued his Phillipsburg Proclamation, which was similar in its essentials to that so dramatically announced by Lord Dunmore four years earlier.[43] Given the large number of enslaved women in the Upper South who, with or without their menfolk, had made their way to Dunmore's lines and endured the many hardships of life in what became known as his Ethiopian Regiment, Clinton could scarcely have been surprised when enslaved women, as well as enslaved men, made their way to his headquarters. These women not only accompanied the Black Brigade but also contributed enormously important services to the Black Brigade that served on the British side for the remainder of the war.

It has to be said, though, that however much they might have welcomed the British advance, enslaved women, as well as enslaved men, made often starkly different choices. On the one hand, there were enslaved women who voluntarily guided British troops across what to them was the lowcountry's totally unfamiliar terrain; on the other hand, there were enslaved women who, perhaps out of fear of these soldiers or because of affection and loyalty, warned their owners of the impending arrival of these troops.[44] Given the uncompromising attitude of the Patriots, and understandably so, many women, and indeed many men, may well have been deterred from traveling even comparatively short distances in the hope of encountering British or Hessian troops.

As Sylvia Frey has rightly pointed out, in town and countryside alike, the majority of enslaved women and men made a carefully considered decision to avoid unnecessary risk, to stay where they were, at least for the time being, to see how events unfolded.[45] This did not necessarily reflect apathy on their part, let alone an internalized and uncritical fondness for their masters and mistresses. It is quite clear that, as had been the case before the war, and would be again after it, enslaved women would not take flight if this meant abandoning their young children or putting those children at unnecessary risk. There is not a single example in the scores of wartime advertisements placed in the lowcountry's newspapers of a woman run-away who was said by her owner or overseer to have abandoned her baby or infant. Whether or not it was their intention to reach the British, those women who did run away usually did so either alone or in the company of a husband or a male relative. It would be erroneous to infer from this that enslaved women who ran away with men would not have done so alone. Enslaved women did not necessarily feel totally dependent upon the pro-tection likely to be offered by their male companion, although it seems reasonable to suggest that it was something they appreciated. What this pattern of running away does point to is the sheer strength and depth of the affection that bound together enslaved couples and their children.

In some cases, the sudden appearance of British troops in the vicinity made up women's minds that it was now safe for them to take flight. This was true, for example, of the thirty-four-year-old, half-blind Hannah Lin-ing and her sixty-two-year-old mother Dinah, as indeed it was of numerous other enslaved women. We do not know for how long mother and daugh-ter might have been considering running away, or why they did so together rather than in the company of a man, or men.[46] What we do know is that when, in 1780, some British soldiers passed close to the Lining Plantation upon which they worked, the slaves judged that now the time was right, that perhaps they would never have a better opportunity, to make a bid for freedom. Hannah and Dinah traveled with the British forces until, on October 31, 1783, they were evacuated from the port of New York on board the brig *Elijah* and taken to begin a completely new life in Port Mouton, Nova Scotia.[47]

We will never know the exact number of enslaved women from the lowcountry who, with or without men, managed to join up with the Brit-ish and Hessian forces as they advanced upon Savannah and Charleston, although toward the end of the war "well over four thousand Negroes of both sexes and all ages" were said to have accompanied General Cornwal-lis on his march north.[48] Some of these women spent only a few days, or weeks, with the troops. For example, the *South Carolina Gazette* reported that "a negro wench named Kate" had been captured on Edisto Island. All that we know about Kate is her name, that "her master's name is William Pendarvis," and that she had been "following the English army."[49] Unfortunately there is not one shred of evidence as to how, why, or when she decided to join up with the British troops or the circumstances surrounding her separation from them. Much the same is true of the Sally who as a young girl had been forcibly taken from Guinea to Savannah. All that we know of her is that she took advantage of the British advance on Savannah to take flight. Like Hannah and Dinah Lining, she also managed to reach New York City — how and when we do not know — and, at age twenty-three, was taken on board the *Hesperus*, which set sail for St. John, New Brunswick, on July 29, 1783.[50]

However long they spent with British and Hessian regiments or with the Black Brigade and the Black Pioneers, enslaved women faced a life of deprivation, danger, and, it seems, varying degrees of discrimination. For example, like their menfolk, those women of color who accompanied General Leslie on his southern campaigns were required to carry tickets upon which were written their names, those of their owners, and that of the army corps with which they were traveling.[51] Generally speaking, women like Peg Boden, who traveled together with her carpenter husband Cato in an artillery regiment, performed essentially the same, mainly domestic chores, as did those lower-rank white women who had for so long accompanied British regiments in both Europe and the Americas. For her part, Peg spent an unknown part of her time "employed as a servant to Major Traill."[52] All that can be said with any certainty is that, regardless of their color and legal — but not their social — status, women camp followers like Peg cooked and washed, they made and repaired soldiers' clothing, and they tended the wounded and dying both on and off the battlefield.[53]

In at least one Hessian regiment, and probably as far as all of the British and allied forces were concerned, the social rank and ethnicity of women camp followers was both recognized and reinforced. Thus, in this particular German regiment, according to his rank, each officer was allocated at least "one Negro," while in another, "Every officer had . . . three or four Negroes, as well as one or two Negresses for cook and maid." A hint at the way in which the Hessian officer class conceptualized the intersection between race, rank, and gender is suggested by the fact that "Every soldier's woman . . . also had a Negro and Negress . . . for her servants."[54] Similarly, there is some evidence that in other, British, regiments operating in the Lower South, women of color, rather than lower-rank white women, were assigned such particularly unpleasant tasks as burying offal.[55]

Unfortunately, the lack of their voices makes it impossible to say how this imposed hierarchical relationship actually affected relationships be-tween the black and white women concerned. However, what is clear is that far from being irrelevant or insignificant, the many contributions of black women were absolutely vital in ensuring the health and hygiene of all the fighting men, and not simply that of their male companions, in the regi-ments they accompanied.

It is impossible to ascertain exactly how many slave husbands, male relatives, and friends, as well as enslaved women, died fighting or from dis-ease as they traveled with British and Hessian regiments, or with the Black Brigade and the Black Pioneers. Similarly, as an unknown number of re-lationships were irretrievably broken by war, others were being formed by enslaved women and men who met and fell in love while on the road. For example, although we do not know exactly when or where it happened, Phillis Clarke, who at the beginning of the war had run away from her owner Joseph Lagree's plantation on the Santee River, appears to have met her partner Pompey, originally from Boston, Massachusetts, while both were working for the general hospital department. At the end of November 1783, the couple left New York on board the *Danger* for Port Mouton, Nova Scotia.[56]

Other enslaved women — married, single, and widowed — gave birth during the time they were traveling with their regiments.[57] Only in those cases where the woman's husband is mentioned can we be reasonably cer-tain of paternity. Equally problematic is the issue of miscegenation, be it between women of color and the officer class or with soldiers of the line. Regimental records remain largely silent on this issue, as do the postwar memoirs of British and Hessian officers. We can reasonably infer that some interracial sexual relationships of varying durations were formed, but no evidence survives that they were on a significantly large scale.

As the British and Hessian forces made their way through the low-country, enslaved people, including many women, were not the only ones who took flight. Some Patriot planters, fearful of being taken or killed by the British, left their estates for what they hoped would be safer climes. Sometimes with, and sometimes without, their human property, several made their way to what, by 1780, was the relative security of the Upper South. Thus it was that sixty-nine of James Habersham's enslaved people found themselves being transported to Virginia, as did eighteen enslaved men, eight enslaved women, and seven enslaved children belonging to Jo-seph Clay.[58] Sometimes, as was the case with George Hancock of South

Carolina, these enslaved evacuees were sold off in order to support owners and their families who found the inflated cost of living in the Upper
South way beyond their means. In August 1781, Hancock, who had taken
sixty-three people from South Carolina to Virginia, sold five men and one
woman. Eight months later, he sold another six men and three women.[59]
For these and for other enslaved people in a similar situation, their enforced
removal from the lowcountry, together with their subsequent sale, might
well entail separation if not from family members then almost certainly
from friends and other associates.

For those, the majority of enslaved women in the countryside, who
opted to stay where they were, or who were not removed by their anxious
owners ahead of the British advance, much depended upon whether or not
their owners or overseers remained in situ. Clearly, although the absence of
white supervisors raised the very real possibility of an easier escape, by no
means did all enslaved workers opt for this course of action. As with Hannah and Dinah Lining, the appearance of British, Hessian, or black troops
in the vicinity could make an enormous difference. By no means exception-
ally, this seems to have been the case on Mepkin, one of Henry Laurens's
plantations. Early in 1780, some British troops arrived at Mepkin and, when
they left, they were accompanied by "Simon mary old Cuffey's daughter ou-
gene Stine and his wife fullow prince and Binah tom Savage and antelope."
Stepney, one of those who absconded, had second thoughts — why he did
so is unrecorded — and subsequently returned to Mepkin.[60]

As Henry Laurens for one was to learn, wartime dislocations, the lack
of overseers, and the unspoken specter of both individual and organized
resistance greatly strengthened the bargaining power of those plantation
slaves who chose to employ it, not to secure their liberation but to improve
their living conditions. The only historical footprint left by an enslaved
woman named Ruth, probably a field hand, strongly suggests the influence
that she, and no doubt other women, chose to exert — not only within
their families but also over other enslaved women and men. As the war
was drawing to a close, a South Carolina planter named William Snow
wrote to his overseer, warning him to be careful in his dealings with Ruth
because, "If you say the least about [her] she will run off, for she is an arch
bitch."[61]

The evidence is sparse, but it does seem that, possibly because of the
prestige associated with both age and the possession of sacred skills, some
women assumed leadership roles in the organization of what, on some

plantations, were tantamount to embryonic trade unions. Henry Laurens was one who was made to feel the full force of the bargaining power being exerted by organized groups of slaves, rather than by individual women and men. In 1780, a group of his plantation slaves ran away and were emboldened to inform Laurens, through his agent, James Custer, that they were willing to return to work, "to go home," provided that their overseer, a man named Campbell, was fired. Custer managed to cut a deal with the enslaved strikers, who almost certainly included women field hands, promising them that if they came back they could choose for themselves which plantation they worked on. As Custer reported to Laurens, he had been "obliged to make this offer as they openly declared to me that they would never stay with Campbell again."[62]

In late 1775 and early 1776, enslaved women and men from the countryside had flooded into Charleston and Savannah in the hope of being freed by the British; exactly the same thing appears to have happened once the British reoccupied these two towns. Some indication of their willingness to serve the British in the interim, and of the British to recruit if not necessarily to free them, is evident from the lists published in the *Royal Gazette* in March 1781. At this stage in the war, 515 men, 141 women, and 15 children worked for the British in various military departments.[63] Yet their and other enslaved peoples' aspirations for freedom, at least in the short term, were quickly dashed as the British recognized the property rights being claimed by Loyalist owners. In Charleston, for example, scores of enslaved people who were roaming the streets found themselves being picked up and incarcerated in the town's Sugar House. If they could be identified, and enslaved prisoners had absolutely no reason to reveal this information, their owners were "requested" by the British authorities "to take them away to prevent further expense and injury to their health from long and close confinement."[64]

Yet there were some ways, albeit falling far short of immediate liberation, in which the British occupation of Savannah and Charleston proved beneficial to many women of color. The scores of soldiers and sailors now crowded there had to be fed, and they created a demand that produced something of a boom time for market women as well as for their rural suppliers. Before the war, Colonial officials had found it virtually impossible to totally control these women's activities, and particularly their growing monopoly of a wide range of fresh foodstuffs, for which they could charge whatever they liked, whatever the market was willing to bear. The British authorities were equally vexed by the initiative displayed by these women. The stream of threatening advertisements they placed in local newspapers, together with beefed-up patrols seeking to contain women's marketing activities, proved completely ineffectual.[65]

Through no particular fault of their own, other women of color — especially newcomers like Phillis George, who lacked longstanding local ties of family and friendship — found it hard to find work, and they did whatever they could to try to scrape together a living for themselves and their families. The only job that Phillis could find in Savannah was that of working as a laundress for General Clinton. As her husband David subsequently commented, "Out of the little she got, she maintained us."[66]

In many ways, as they had always done and would continue to do in the postwar years, women of color displayed a considerable amount of initiative during the British occupation of Savannah and Charleston. For those like Phillis George, initiative was displayed in the gendered world of work. For others, like Betty in Charleston, it seems to have been a case of stretching the boundaries of what was, and what was not, acceptable behavior in the eyes of their owners. This was by no means a new mode of female behavior, but it took on an entirely new, and for owners both a frustrating and an alarming, dimension during the years of British occupation. For example, according to Henry Laurens, his brother's enslaved woman Betty was a source of constant irritation to him. On one occasion, early on in the war, she took what to Laurens was the liberty of presenting him "with a list of grievances," and either refused to work or to pay him anything from whatever she was supposed to be earning as a result of being hired out.[67] An exasperated Laurens hoped that Betty's good behavior might best be secured by threatening to send her to "the Country," presumably to work as a field hand. There is no evidence that he actually carried out his threat, and in fact, just a month after making it, he noted that Betty "does not behave so well as she ought to."[68] Two years later Betty was still in Charleston, still misbehaving, and Laurens was once again threatening "to Send her in the Country." As in 1775, there is no evidence that he did so. Betty may have succeeded in what was clearly her objective of staying in Charleston, partly because Laurens continued to hold out some hope, however faint, that at some point in the future she would mend her ways and generate an income for him. Betty's periodic bouts of ill health, and more especially Laurens's reaction to them, also served to ensure not only that she would remain where she wanted to be, at least in the short term, but also continue to avoid being made to work. Sometime late in 1774 or early 1775, Betty conceived and, during the latter stages of her pregnancy, before she gave birth to a baby girl in August 1775, Laurens allowed her to stay with her mother for about six weeks. He was also receptive to her request, or demand, for "some Sugar & some half a dozen other articles."[69]

In Charleston and Savannah, as well as in the smaller towns of the lowcountry, enslaved women's initiatives — their stretching of the boundaries in ways that fell short of absconding — were by no means limited to the world of work. Early in 1782, for instance, a group of women reworked what were clearly already well-established social events in and around Charleston in a way that, albeit for very different reasons, white and black Charlestonians alike must have found truly astounding. Four years earlier, in 1778, Ebenezer Hazard, a visitor to the lowcountry, remarked that South Carolina "has one peculiarity which I did not hear of in any other state . . . the black dances as they are called." These, he continued, "are balls given by Negro and Mulatto women, to which they invite the white gentlemen." In a way reminiscent of the Quadroon balls that had already become a feature of New Orleans' racially gendered social life, "These women . . . dress elegantly, and have no small acquaintance with polite behavior." Hazard concluded his remarks with the intriguing comment that elite white women had no objections to their menfolk "attending at these black dances . . . they have been said to be even more fond of them on that account."[70]

On January 1, 1782, as General Nathanael Greene's forces were advancing on Charleston, three women of color — Hagar Rousell, Isabella Pinckney, and Mary Fraser — "assuming their mistresses' names" organized "an Ethiopian Ball," similar to those described by Hazard, but now with a crucial difference: their guest list. On cards just like those used by their mistresses, they limited their invitations to "Officers of the [British] Army (and our female slaves only)." If nothing else, the three women as well as their enslaved invitees were openly parodying, and thereby mocking, both their masters and their mistresses. The enslaved women who attended the ball "dress'd in taste, with the richest silks, and false rolls on their heads, powder'd up in the most pompous manner." But this was not all. The British officers collected their dance partners from their homes and "drove through the streets in pomp alongside of them, many of these wretches were taken out of their houses before their mistresses faces." Once at the ball, which was held at a private house, 99 Meeting Street, they and their hosts enjoyed a lavish dinner and "danc'd ... until four o'clock in the morning."[71]

Even though they must have known of similar dances, such as those described by Ebenezer Hazard and the anonymous correspondent to the *South Carolina Gazette*, it seems safe to say that never before had Charlestonians, black and white, witnessed anything like this brazenly public, racially and gendered, assault on such symbols of elite dominance. Previously, such assaults — such lampooning of elite behavior and fashions — had taken place in private, at the all-black dances held both in the countryside and in Charleston. These dances usually "opened, by the men copying (or taking off) the manners of their masters, and the women those of their mistresses."[72]

For the three women who organized this ball, as well as for the unknown number of enslaved women who attended it, this was a relatively safe form of defiance — at least in the short term. But why did British officers lend it their support? Unfortunately we do not have their explanations, but two possibilities suggest themselves. First, they might well have been intrigued, and fascinated, by this opportunity to attend what for them would in all probability have been a unique, and an exotic, social occasion. Maybe they too were only too happy to employ mimicry to thumb their noses at the behavior, the ungentlemanly behavior, of the lowcountry's self-styled gentlemen. At the same time, of course, their acceptance of this invitation, their choice of dance partners, involved an equal, if not an even greater, insult to Charleston's "ladies."

Even as they were dancing the night away with enslaved women, British officers were already becoming preoccupied with the defense of Charleston. As they had done in the Upper South since 1775 and in the lowcountry since 1778, the British conscripted enslaved people — women as well as men — to help them buttress the town's defenses. Simultaneously, Greene and his officer corps were doing exactly the same thing: putting large numbers of slaves — women as well as men — to the often heavy work involved in clearing trails and moving their military equipment. Toward the end of 1780, for example, they were forced "to mend the Causeway in the South of Nelsons Ferry" and, a few months later, to demolish "the Works upon Savannah River."[73]

Once the American assault began in earnest, enslaved women were no more immune from danger and deprivation than anyone else. They worked alongside enslaved men, sometimes taking their children with them, on what became a rapidly shrinking front line. Early in 1782, for example, it was reported to General Nathanael Greene that on John's Island the British had "every Negro Woman as well as Men on that Island out with them throwing up the works."[74] We simply do not know how many of these women, or those who were required to do exactly the same kind of work as Greene advanced upon Charleston, were killed or maimed, and how many of them returned to their Patriot owners once the British had surrendered.

The British evacuation of Savannah, Charleston, and New York City in 1783 offered what many enslaved women and men gathered in and around those port towns must have thought was their very last chance of securing their liberation from bondage, at least for the foreseeable future. Even as those who had managed to persuade British and American officials of their eligibility for freedom were boarding the vessels that would take them away from the newly independent United States, the British and Americans were already squabbling over the exact numbers involved.[75] As Cassandra Pybus has pointed out, their deep disagreements continue to permeate recent scholarship on the subject.[76] The one thing that most scholars agree upon is that we can never know for certain the exact number of black evacuees. This is simply because, unlike those who sailed from New York, Charleston, and Savannah — those who, by hook or by crook, managed to find a place on smaller vessels, or who traveled overland to Florida and the backcountry — did not leave a paper trail.

What we do know is that 5,327 black people are known to have been evacuated from Charleston and an estimated 3,500 from Savannah, but unfortunately we do not have a gender breakdown for them.[77] Moreover, it appears that these particular evacuations did not result in freedom for most of those concerned. Around 60 percent of the women and men who left Charleston were taken, often by their Loyalist owners, to the even harsher plantation regimes of the British Caribbean.[78]

In the case of New York, 208 women and girls age fourteen or over from the lowcountry were among the 3,000 or so evacuees from that port.[79] One hundred and thirteen of them were in their twenties, which meant that they had left their owners in their late teens or very early twenties; 48 of them were in their thirties; and only 21 of them were age forty or over. The oldest, at the age of sixty-two, was Dinah Lining.

Only 20 of these women, or just fewer than 10 percent of them, were said to have a husband, while another 26 of them traveled with, and in the *Book of Negroes* were listed in close proximity to, a man who shared the same surname. The men in question may have been husbands or male relatives, or have had the same owner, and adopted the same surname, as the women with whom they were traveling. There is simply no way of knowing which of these possibilities was actually the case. At least 80 women had spent varying amounts of time accompanying British, Loyalist, and Hessian regiments, or the Black Pioneers, and the Black Brigade.

In keeping with the destinations of most of the evacuees from New York, 184, or 88 percent, of women from the lowcountry found themselves being taken to one or other of the Maritime Provinces.[80] Once there, they often found themselves in the harshest of physical conditions — a marked contrast to those of the lowcountry — and experiencing an all-too-familiar racism. By the mid-1790s, several saw no future for themselves in this bleak part of the world, and enthusiastically embraced the Sierra Leone project.[81]

Significantly, the evacuees from the three major port towns included women as well as men from the lowcountry who had either been born legally free or granted their freedom by their owners. The 208 women of color who departed from the port of New York included 13 free women. Further south, Phillis and David George also chose to leave with the British. Almost certainly, they and the free women who left from New York believed that their continuing legal right to freedom was infinitely safer in the hands of the British than it was in those of the new Georgia and South Carolina governments, which were so firmly committed both to domestic slavery and the continuance of the transatlantic slave trade.

There is abundant evidence that, whether legally free or enslaved, male or female, by no means all of those who wished to do so were able to leave with the British. Some seem to have equivocated as to whether or not they wished to abandon familiar surroundings, and probably also friends if not family members, and eventually decided to stay where they were, even if this meant continuing enslavement. Some — and probably a minuscule proportion of — departing owners actually gave their enslaved people a choice as to whether they wished to stay or go. For example, when Josiah Smith and his family decided to leave Charleston for what was still the slaveholding city of Philadelphia, they took with them "four Servants, Peggy, Tenah, Hannah, & Girl Lidia." Smith's wife "chose to leave behind" their "Washer Woman, Nelly, with her Aged Mother Peggy," while "Frank, his Wife (my

Cook) Dolly, and her Son Cesar, all refusing to come hither were left in Charlestown." Somewhat optimistically, perhaps, Smith was confident that they would be both able and willing to send him "some Wages."[82]

Understandably, some women simply got caught up in the chaotic conditions surrounding the evacuations of Savannah and Charleston and, quite literally, missed the boat. Some of them, together with other women who had been abandoned by their Loyalist owners, found themselves being given as payment by the cash-strapped governments of Georgia and South Carolina to their returning officers and soldiers of the line. For many, this could mean enforced separation from loved ones and friends as they and their new owners moved to the backcountry.[83] Other women, who may or may not have hoped to leave with the British, tried to blend in with the black urban crowds of Charleston and Savannah, surviving the best they could, and perhaps awaiting another opportunity to make a bid for freedom. Perhaps simply because of bad luck, being in the wrong place at the wrong time, the immediate postwar years saw several of these women being picked up and returned to slavery.[84] Precisely the same would be true of the unknown number of women who joined forces with the enslaved men who hoped to continue the armed struggle for freedom from a camp they established in the swamps just north of Savannah.

In what would be one of the greatest ironies in the Revolutionary history of the lowcountry, in the summer of 1787, just as the founding fathers were in the process of fixing chattel slavery upon the new nation for the foreseeable future, the combined forces of the Georgia and South Carolina militias finally managed to dislodge this maroon community. Lewis, the community's second-in-command, was captured and taken to Savannah for what everyone involved knew would be a sham trial. Three of the women, Betty, Peggy, and Juliet, who had been taken with Lewis, were called as witnesses, and the evidence suggests that even though well aware of what the outcome would be, they did what they could to try to save him. These women were returned to slavery; Lewis was taken to be hanged and, once dead, "his head [is] to be cut off and stuck upon a pole . . . on the Island of Marsh . . . in Savannah River."[85] If only in a symbolic fashion, the judicial murder of Lewis marked the end of the armed revolutionary struggle for black freedom. But what it did not do, and could not do, was to dispel those "notions of liberty" that had been so powerfully expressed by enslaved women, as well as by enslaved men, in the preceding twenty years.

NOTES

1. Benjamin Quarles, *The Negro in the American Revolution* (Chapel Hill: University of North Carolina Press for the Institute of Early American History and Culture, 1961); Sylvia R. Frey, *Water from the Rock: Black Resistance in a Revolutionary Age* (Princeton, N.J.: Princeton University Press, 1991); Philip D. Morgan, *Slave Counterpoint: Black Culture in the Eighteenth-Century Chesapeake and Lowcountry* (Chapel Hill: University of North Carolina Press for the Omohundro Institute of Early American History and Culture, 1998); and Robert A. Olwell, *Masters, Slaves, and Subjects: The Culture of Power in the South Carolina Low Country, 1740–1790* (Ithaca, N.Y.: Cornell University Press, 1998).

2. For a pioneering essay that deals with the Revolutionary South as a whole, see Jacqueline Jones, "Race, Sex, and Self-Evident Truths: The Status of Slave Women during the Era of the American Revolution," in *Women in the Age of the American Revolution*, ed. Ronald Hoffman and Peter J. Albert (Charlottesville: University Press of Virginia for the United States Capitol History Society, 1989). For the lowcountry, see Ingeborg Irene Dornan, "Women Slaveholders in the Georgia and South Carolina Low Country, 1750–1775," (PhD diss., University of Cambridge, 2001); Carla Anzilotti, *In the Affairs of the World: Women, Patriarchy, and Power in Colonial South Carolina* (Westport, Conn.: Greenwood, 2002); Betty Wood, "Some Aspects of Female Resistance to Chattel Slavery in Low Country Georgia, 1763–1815," *Historical Journal* 30, no. 3 (September 1987), 603–22; and idem, *Gender, Race and Rank in a Revolutionary Age: The Georgia Lowcountry, 1750–1820* (Athens: University of Georgia Press, 2000).

3. Kenneth Coleman, *The American Revolution in Georgia, 1763–1789* (Athens: University of Georgia Press, 1958), 10–24.

4. For the opening of the transatlantic slave trade to Georgia, and its scope and significance before 1775, see Betty Wood, *Slavery in Colonial Georgia, 1730–1775* (Athens: University of Georgia Press, 1984), 98–104.

5. For Sally's evacuation from the port of New York in 1783, see the Inspection Roll of Negroes, Book 1, 47, Nova Scotia Museum, Black Cultural Database.

6. The most renowned member of the Lining family was Dr. John Lining (1708–1760). Born in Scotland, he moved to Charleston in 1730, where he became renowned for his meteorological observations. For his scientific career and its significance, see Everett Mendelson, "John Lining and His Contribution to Early American Science," *Isis* 51, no. 3 (September 1960): 278–92. For a brief biography of Hannah and her mother, see Remembering Black Loyalists. Black Communities in Nova Scotia, at http://museum/gov.ns.ca/blackloyalists/17751800/people1775/dinahandhannah.htm.

7. James Laurens (1728–1784), the older brother of Henry Laurens (1724–1792). By the eve of the American Revolution, Henry Laurens, who lived mainly in Charleston, was one of lowcountry South Carolina's wealthiest merchant-planters. James Laurens moved to England for reasons of health in 1775. During his absence, Henry Laurens took charge of his planting and other interests. Philip M. Hamer,

ed.; George C. Rogers Jr., asst. ed.; and Maude E. Lyles, ed. asst., *The Papers of Henry Laurens*, 20 vols. (Columbia: University of South Carolina Press for the South Carolina Historical Society, 1968–2003), 1:xiv–xxii, 139n5. Note that vols. 5–10 were edited by George C. Rogers Jr. and David R. Chesnutt, and vols. 11–16 by David R. Chesnutt and C. James Taylor. There is no full-length biography of James Laurens. For Henry Laurens, see David Duncan Wallace, *The Life of Henry Laurens. With a sketch of the life of Lieutenant-Colonel John Laurens* (New York: G. P. Putnam's Sons, 1915) and rather more recently, Daniel J. McDonough, *Christopher Gadsden and Henry Laurens: The Parallel Lives of Two American Patriots* (London: Associated University Press, 2000).

8. For Phillis George, see her husband David's autobiography, AN ACCOUNT OF [THE] LIFE OF Mr. David George from S.L.A. given by himself (unpaginated) at http://collections.ic.gc.ca/blackloyalists/documents/diaries/george-a-life.htm.

9. For discussions of the Stono Rebellion, see Peter H. Wood, *Black Majority: Negroes in Colonial South Carolina from 1670 through the Stono Rebellion* (New York: W. W. Norton, 1974), esp. 308–26; Morgan, *Slave Counterpoint*,.386, 455–56, 582; John K. Thornton, "African Dimensions of the Stono Rebellion," *American Historical Review* 96 (October 1991): 1101–113; Mark M. Smith, "Remembering Mary, Shaping Revolt: Remembering the Stono Rebellion," *Journal of Southern History* 67, no. 3 (August 2001), 513–34, and idem, *Stono: Documenting and Interpreting a Southern Slave Revolt* (Columbia: University of South Carolina Press, 2005).

10. For a discussion of the prohibition of slavery in 1735 and its introduction to Georgia in 1750, see Wood, *Slavery in Colonial Georgia*, 1–86.

11. See, for example, *Virginia Gazette* (Purdie and Dixon, publishers), August 27, 1772. In all probability, news of these cases was also brought to the southern mainland by sailors, including black sailors, who were involved in transatlantic trade. Morgan, *Slave Counterpoint*, 238–39.

12. For a discussion of the abortive Virginia rebellion, see Sylvia R. Frey and Betty Wood, *Come Shouting to Zion: African American Protestantism in the American South and British Caribbean to 1830* (Chapel Hill: University of North Carolina Press, 1998), 69–70.

13. Thomas Hutchinson to the Council of Safety, Chehaw, July 5, 1775, ed. Chesnutt et al., *Papers of Henry Laurens*, 10:208.

14. For Jerry's trial and execution see ibid., 184, 206–08 and 320–22.

15. For the origins and evolution of black millenarianism in the Southern mainland see Frey and Wood, *Come Shouting to Zion*, 69, 93, 101, 103.

16. For a discussion of David Margate's preaching, see ibid., 112–13.

17. Thomas Hutchinson to the Council of Safety, Chewhaw, July 5, 1775, in Chesnutt et al., *Papers of Henry Laurens*, 10:206–7.

18. Extract of a Letter from Charlestown, South Carolina, June 19, 1775, in *Virginia Gazette* (Purdie), August 4, 1775. For a more detailed discussion of the panic that seized white Charlestonians following Jerry's rebellion, see Robert A. Olwell, "'Domestick Enemies': Slavery and Political Independence in South Carolina, May 1775–March 1776," *Journal of Southern History* 55, no. 1 (February 1989): 21–48.

19. Gabriel Manigault Jr. to Gabriel Manigault Sr., Charleston, July 8, 1775, in Maurice A. Crouse, ed., "Papers of Gabriel Manigault, 1771–1784," *South Carolina Historical Magazine* 64, no. 1 (January 1973): 1.

20. For a discussion of this legislation, see Wood, *Slavery in Colonial Georgia*, 117–20.

21. Governor James Wright to the Earl of Dartmouth, Savannah, May 25, 1775, in K. G. Davies, ed., *Documents of the American Revolution, 1770–1783*, 21 vols. (Shannon, Eire: Irish University Press, 1972–81), 9:144.

22. For the full text of Dunmore's proclamation see *Virginia Gazette* (Purdie), November 24, 1775.

23. L. H. Butterfield, ed., *Diary and Autobiography of John Adams*, 4 vols. (Cambridge, Mass.: Belknap Press of Harvard University Press, 1971), 2:183.

24. On December 19, 1775, Henry Laurens, then the president of the South Carolina Council of Safety, reported that, "Lord Dunmore had . . . received and armed all Negroes who would come to him." Letter written by Henry Laurens, Charles-Town, December 19, 1775, in Minutes of the South Carolina Council of Safety. In the Council of Safety [Charlestown] December 20, 1775, in William Bell Clark, ed., *Naval Documents of the American Revolution* (Washington, D.C.: U.S. Government Printing Office, 1914–1968), 3:191. For news of Dunmore's proclamation reaching Georgia, see *Georgia Gazette*, January 3, 1776.

25. Henry Laurens to John Laurens, Charles Town, August 14, 1776, in *Papers of Henry Laurens*, ed. Chesnutt and Taylor, 11:224. In many ways this rush to reach Charleston and Savannah marked the beginnings of what Nadelhaft has described as the "disorders of war" in the lowcountry; Jerome J. Nadelhaft, *The Disorders of War: The Revolution in South Carolina* (Orono: University of Maine at Orono Press, 1981).

26. See, for example, Colonel Stephen Bull to Colonel Henry Laurens, president of the Council of Safety in Charles Town, Head Quarters, Savannah, March 14, 1776, in *Documentary History of the American Revolution*, 3 vols., ed. R. W. Gibbes (New York: New York Times, 1971), 1:267.

27. Morgan has suggested that the wives of drivers were often given such preferential jobs as cooks and seamstresses (Morgan, *Slave Counterpoint*, 222). These jobs did not necessarily give the women concerned as much prestige in the slave quarters as, for example, the possession of sacred specialties that involved a particular knowledge of both the benign and the malign applications of the lowcountry's flora. For a brief discussion of these skills, especially during the prewar years, see Frey and Wood, *Come Shouting to Zion*, 57–62.

28. For enslaved men as boatmen and sailors, see Morgan, *Slave Counterpoint*, 55–57, 338–42.

29. Henry Laurens to Timothy Creamer, Charles Town, June 26, 1764; to Abraham Schad, Charles Town, April 30, 1765; to John Smith, Charles Town, June 4, 1765; 1 October 1765, in *Papers of Henry Laurens*, ed. Hamer, Rogers, and Chesnutt, 4:319, 633.

30. There is as yet no comprehensive study of either midwifery or wet nursing

in the eighteenth-century Lower South. For a brief discussion, see Morgan, *Slave Counterpoint*, 324–25, 626–29. For the antebellum South, see Sally G. McMillen, "Mothers' Sacred Duty: Breast-feeding Patterns among Middle- and Upper-Class Women in the Antebellum South," *Journal of Southern History* 51, no. 3 (August 1985): 333–56; idem, *Motherhood in the Old South: Pregnancy, Childbirth, and Infant Rearing* (Baton Rouge: Louisiana State University Press, 1990). One of the first signs of men's entrée into midwifery came in an advertisement placed in the *South Carolina Gazette* on December 1, 1768, when an English migrant named T. Lowther declared that in addition to his experience in Bristol as an apothecary, he had also been employed "for some years" as a midwife. Lowther went on to declare that "he offers his attendance *Gratis* to every person in Charles-Town, whose circumstances or situation demands it. The Poor," he concluded, "may also be assisted with advice in all cases."

31. For the domination of Savannah and Charleston's public markets by women of color, see Philip D. Morgan, "Black Life in Eighteenth-Century Charleston," *Perspectives in American History*, New Series, 1 (1984): 187–232; idem, "Black Society in the Lowcountry, 1700–1810," in *Slavery and Freedom in the Age of the American Revolution*, ed. Ira Berlin and Ronald Hoffman (Charlottesville: University Press of Virginia, 1983), 83–141; idem, *Slave Counterpoint*, 250–52; Betty Wood, *Women's Work, Men's Work: The Informal Slave Economies of Lowcountry Georgia* (Athens: University of Georgia Press, 1995), esp. 80–100; and Robert A. Olwell, "'Loose, Idle and Disorderly': Slave Women in the Eighteenth-Century Marketplace," in *More Than Chattel: Black Women and Slavery in the Americas*, ed. David Barry Gaspar and Darlene Clark Hind (Bloomington: Indiana University Press, 1996), 97–110.

32. For cockfights and horse racing, see Morgan, *Slave Counterpoint*, 416–18. For a more recent discussion, see William Hunt Boulware, "The Evolution of Sport and Recreation in Early South Carolina and Georgia" (PhD diss., University of Cambridge, Faculty of History, 2007).

33. For the comparative ease with which enslaved people were able to leave their plantations after nightfall, see Charles Ball, *Fifty Years in Chains* (1837; repr., New York: Dayton and Asher, 1969), 191. For the exchange of information in the slave quarters after the day's work, see Morgan, *Slave Counterpoint*, 122.

34. James Barclay, *The Voyages and Travels of James Barclay, Containing Many Surprising Adventures, and Interesting Narratives* (London: Printed for the Author, 1777), 32.

35. For David George's preaching, see Frey and Wood, *Come Shouting to Zion*, 116–17; for Patrick Hinds, see Grand Jury Presentments, District of Charles-Town, February Sessions, 1775, in the *South Carolina Gazette*, March 14, 1775.

36. Letter, the *South Carolina Gazette*, September 17, 1772. For the illicit renting of houses by enslaved people in late colonial and Revolutionary Savannah, see Wood, *Women's Work, Men's Work*, 129–30.

37. William Edwin Hemphill, ed., Wylma Anne Wates, asst. ed., *The State Record of South Carolina. Extracts from the Journals of the Provincial Congress of South Carolina, 1775–1776* (Columbia: South Carolina Archives Department, 1960), 109, 115, 151.

38. Allen D. Candler, ed., *The Revolutionary Records of the State of Georgia*, 3 vols. (Atlanta: Franklin-Turner Company, 1908), 1:136, 199.

39. William Edwin Hemphill, Wylma Anne Wates, and R. Nicholas Olsberg, eds., *The State Records of South Carolina. Journals of the General Assembly and House of Representatives, 1776–1780* (Columbia: Published for the South Carolina Department of Archives and History by the University of South Carolina Press, 1970), 114, 179, 180, 242, 254.

40. The incentive for these enslaved men was vague. Those who "behave well in time of action" were promised "suitable rewards," but there is no suggestion that the latter would ever include freedom from bondage. Minutes of the South Carolina Council of Safety. In the Council of Safety [Charleston] Monday, January 22, 1776, in Clark, *Naval Documents*, 3:929.

41. *South Carolina and American General Gazette*, May 15, 1777. For more on the employment of enslaved men by the naval forces of South Carolina during the early stages of the war, see A. S. Salley Jr., ed., *Journal of the Commissioners of the Navy of South Carolina, October 9, 1776–March 1, 1779* (Columbia: Printed for the Historical Commission of South Carolina by the State Company, 1912), passim.

42. Anon, ed., "The Siege of Charleston," *Southern Quarterly Review* 38 (October 1848): 289.

43. For the full text of the Phillipsburg Proclamation see Morris J. McGregor and Bernard C. Nalty, eds., *Blacks in the United States Armed Forces: Basic Documents*, 13 vols. (Wilmington, Del.: Scholarly Resources, 1977), 1:29. For a discussion of the Proclamation, see Frey, *Water from the Rock*, 108, 113–14, 118–19, 121, 141, 175, 192. For more on the Black Brigade, the Black Pioneers, and other black units that fought on the British side, see Americanrevolution.org, "The Loyalist Pages: Black Loyalists," http://www.americanrevolution.org/black loyalists.html.

44. Caroline Gilman, ed., *Letters of Eliza Wilkinson: during the invasion and possession of Charlestown, S.C., by the British in the Revolutionary War*, (New York: S. Colman, 1839), letter 3.

45. Frey, *Water from the Rock*, 168–69.

46. It appears that Hannah, but not her mother had run away in 1761 but had either been recaptured — when, where, and by whom is unknown — or voluntarily returned to the Lining Plantation (*South Carolina Gazette*, June 6–13, 1761).

47. Inspection Roll of Negroes, Book 2, 17, 18, Nova Scotia Museum, Black Cultural Database. In 1784, a year after a disastrous fire in Port Mouton, Hannah and Dinah moved to Guysborough. Hannah married twice, the first time to James Lennox and, after his death, for the second time to either Samuel Aitkens or Samuel Hawkins. Dinah lived to the age of eighty-nine and Hannah to eighty. Mother and daughter are buried side by side in the cemetery of Christ Church, Guysborough (Remembering the Black Loyalists, http://museum.gov.ns.ca/BlackLoyalists/17751800/people1775/dinahandhannah.htm).

48. Joseph P. Tustin, trans. and ed., *Diary of the American War. A Hessian Journal. Captain Johann Ewald — Field Jager Corps* (New Haven, Conn.: Yale University Press, 1979), 305.

49. *South Carolina Gazette*, December 10, 1779.

50. Inspection Roll of Negroes, Book 1, 47, Nova Scotia Museum, Black Cultural Database.

51. A. R. Newsome, ed., "A British Orderly Book, 1780–1781," *North Carolina Historical Review* 9 (October 1932): 171, 286, 280.

52. Peg, who in 1783 was twenty-three years old, and Cato, who was twenty-eight, when they were evacuated from New York in 1783, claimed that they had been born free. Before joining the British forces, Cato had lived on St. John's Island, South Carolina. There is no record of Peg's birthplace (Inspection Roll of Negroes, Book 1, 13, Nova Scotia Museum, Black Cultural Database).

53. Sylvia R. Frey, *The British Soldier in America: A Social History of Military Life in the Revolutionary Period* (Austin: University of Texas Press, 1981), 17, 20, 57, 59–62, 64, 76–77. See also "On the Strength: Wives and Children of the British Army," http://www.royalengineeers.ca.femkid.html. For a comparable study of the lower-rank women who accompanied the Patriot armies, see Holly A. Mayer, *Belonging to the Army: Camp Followers and Community in the American Revolution* (Columbia: University of South Carolina Press, 1999).

54. Tustin, *Diary of the American War*, 305. For more on the people of color, but especially the men and boys, who accompanied Hessian regiments, see George Fenwick Jones, "The Black Hessians: Negroes Recruited by the Hessians in South Carolina and Georgia," *South Carolina Historical Magazine* 83, no. 4 (October 1982): 287–307.

55. Newsome, "British Orderly Book," 371.

56. At the time of their evacuation, Phillis was ages thirty and Pompey, who had been enslaved to a Doctor William Clarke of Massachusetts, was thirty-three (Inspection Roll of Negroes, Book 3, 3, Nova Scotia Museum, Black Cultural Database).

57. Unfortunately, there is no record of infant mortality.

58. August 28, 1780, Charlotte County, Virginia; February 5, 1781, At a Court held for Amherst County &c, in William P. Palmer, ed., *Calendar of Virginia State Papers and other Manuscripts Preserved in the Capitol at Richmond*, 11 vols. (1875–1993; repr., New York: Kraus Reprint., 1968), 1:371.

59. Memorial of George Hancock Late of South Carolina to the Executive of Virginia, August 1, 1781, Powhatan County, ibid., 2:281; May 17, 1782, in H. R. McIlwaine, ed., *Journals of the Council of the State of Virginia* (Richmond, Va.: Division of Purchasing and Printing, 1931–), 91–92.

60. Samuel Massey to Henry Laurens, Charles Town, June 12, 1780, in *Papers of Henry Laurens*, Chesnutt and Taylor, 15, 305.

61. William Snow to Mr. Rhodes, September 9, 1781, cited in Quarles, *Negro in the American Revolution*, 126.

62. James Custer to Henry Laurens, Charles Town, June 1780, in *Papers of Henry Laurens*, Chesnutt and Taylor, 15:303–4.

63. These women and men were distributed between the different departments as follows: "NEGROES IN THE ENGINEERS DEPARTMENT. That joined the Army since the Landing of Sir HENRY CLINTON, in 1780, "The Engineers Department: 123 men; 89 women; and 4 children (*Royal Gazette*, March 7–10, 1781); "NEGROES IN

ENGINEER DEPARTMENT that joined the ARMY in GEORGIA, IN THE YEAR 1779," 68 men, 29 women, and 11 children; "LIST OF NEGROES in the COMMISSARY GEN-ERAL'S DEPARTMENT IN Charlestown, February 11, 1781," 17 men, 3 women; "LIST OF NEGROES in the QUARTER-MASTER GENERAL'S DEPARTMENT, 121 men; no women; "LIST OF NEGROES employed in the BARRACK MASTER'S DEPARTMENT", 82 men, no women; "LIST OF NEGROES employed in the COMMISSARY OF PRISON-ERS DEPARTMENT," 2 men, no women; "RETURN OF NEGROES EMPLOYED in the ROYAL ARTILLERY DEPARTMENT," March 2, 1781, 93 men, no women; "RETURN OF NEGROES employed in the service of his Majesty's GENERAL HOSPITAL, Charle-stown," 11 men, 20 women; *Royal Gazette*, March 10–14, 1781. Only in the case of the general hospital, where the women were described as "nurses" and the men as "labourers," was any reference made to specific occupations.

64. *South Carolina and American General Gazette*, September 6, 1780. Between May 1 and October 6, 132 men and 50 women were recorded as being held in the Sugar House. The numbers of those taken in at the Sugar House was almost certainly higher than this: the women and men named in the records were those who could not or would not identify their owners, or whose owners (be they Patriot or Loyalist) had for one reason or another abandoned Charleston, either permanently or temporarily. For the names of those incarcerated, see *Royal Gazette* (all dates 1781): May 2–5, May 30, June 30–July 4, July 28–August 1, September 1–5, and October 3–6.

65. See, for example, South Carolina, Charlestown District, October 15, 1779, Presentments of the Grand Jury, in *South Carolina and American General Advertiser*, December 2, 1779; see also the notices placed in the *Georgia Gazette*, June 21, 1775; the *Gazette of the State of South Carolina*, May 5 and 9, 1777; and the *South Carolina Gazette and American General Gazette*, December 3, 1779, February 7, 1781.

66. AN ACCOUNT OF [THE] LIFE OF Mr. David George from S.L.A. given by himself (unpaginated) at http://collections.ic.gc.ca/blackloyalists/documents/dia-ries/george-a-life.htm.

67. Henry Laurens to James Laurens, Charles Town, September 22, 1775; March 1, 1776, in Chesnutt and Taylor, *Papers of Henry Laurens*, 10:414, 11:135.

68. Henry Laurens to James Laurens, Charles Town, October 20, 1775, ibid,, 10:482. Henry Laurens to John Lewis Gervais, Philadelphia, September 5, 1777, ibid., 11:486.

69. Henry Laurens to James Laurens, Charles Town, July 2, 1775; August 20, 1775, in *Papers of Henry Laurens*, ed. Chesnutt and Taylor, 10:203, 317, 318.

70. H. Roy Merrens, "A View of Coastal South Carolina in 1778: The Journal of Ebenezer Hazard," *South Carolina Historical Magazine* 73, no. 4 (October 1972): 190.

71. Daniel Stevens to John Wendell, Gen'l Greene's Head Quarters near Cha'ston, So. Carolina, February 20, 1782, in *Proceedings of the Massachusetts Historical Society* 48 (October 1914–June 1915): 342–43.

72. Letter, *South Carolina Gazette*, September 17, 1772.

73. From Colonel Francis Marion, Black River [SC], December 22, 1780, to Joseph Clay, Camp before Ninety-Six (SC), June 9, 1781, in *The Papers of General Nathanael Greene*, 13 vols., ed. Richard K. Showman (Chapel Hill: University of

North Carolina Press for the Rhode Island Historical Society, 1976–2005), May 11, 1779–October 31, 1779, 4:605; 7:361.

74. From Thomas Farr, Ashley River, S.C., January 10, 1782, in *The Papers of General Nathanael Greene*, ed. Dennis M. Conrad, December 3, 1781–April 6, 1782, 10:177.

75. For the standard work on the number of black evacuees from the port of New York, see Graham Russell Hodges, *The Black Loyalists Directory: African Americans in Exile after the American Revolution* (New York: Garland in association with the New England Historic Genealogical Society, 1996).

76. Cassandra Pybus, "Jefferson's Faulty Math: The Question of Slave Defections in the American Revolution," *William and Mary Quarterly* 62, no. 2 (April 2005): 243–64.

77. Coleman, *American Revolution in Georgia,* 145.

78. Almost half the evacuees from Charleston were taken to Jamaica, and just under 10 percent to St. Lucia. Of the remainder, just over a third were shipped to Florida, while the rest were taken either to the Maritime Provinces or to England.

79. This analysis is based on the names recorded in the *Book of Negroes.*

80. The destinations of the remainder included England, Germany, Belgium, and the West Indies. For black émigrés in Britain, see Mary Beth Norton, "The Fate of Some Black Loyalists of the American Revolution," *Journal of Negro History* 58 (October 1973): 402–26; Norma Myers, *Reconstructing the Black Past: Blacks in Britain, 1780–1830* (London: Frank Cass, 1996). As Pybus has pointed out, a handful of evacuees, not necessarily originating from the lowcountry, traveled even farther afield and were instrumental in the creation of Australia's first black community. See Cassandra Pybus, *Epic Journeys of Freedom: Runaway Slaves of the American Revolution and Their Global Quest for Liberty* (Boston: Beacon Press, 2006).

81. For studies of the formation and early history of the black communities of the Maritime Provinces, and the subsequent movement of many of the original settlers to Sierra Leone, see John N. Grant, "Black Immigrants into Nova Scotia, 1776–1815," *Journal of Negro History* 58, no. 3 (July 1973): 253–70; Harvey Amani Whitfield, "Black Loyalists and Black Slaves in Maritime Canada," *History Compass* 5, no. 6 (2007): 1478–542; and Frey, *Water from the Rock,* 194–98.

82. "Josiah Smith's Journal," *South Carolina Historical Magazine* 24, no. 2 (April 1933): 67.

83. For further discussion, see Frey, *Water from the Rock,* 213–15.

84. See, for example, the advertisements placed in the *South Carolina Gazette and General Advertiser,* November 25–December 2, 1783; February 7–19, 1784; and July 24–27, 1784.

85. The community's leader Cudjoe, or "Captain Cudjoe" as he styled himself, was killed in the skirmish. For Lewis's trial, see Betty Wood, "'Until He Shall Be Dead, Dead, Dead': The Judicial Treatment of Slaves in Eighteenth-Century Georgia," *Georgia Historical Quarterly* 71 (Fall 1987): 390–92. For further discussion, see Timothy J. Lockley, *Maroons in the Swamps of South Carolina* (Columbia: University of South Carolina Press, 2008).

Vincent Carretta

"I began to feel the happiness of liberty, of which I knew nothing before"

Eighteenth-Century Black Accounts of the Lowcountry

EXCLUDING criminal narratives, accounts of the lives of only seven English-speaking authors of sub-Saharan African descent, all male, were published before 1800.[1] The term "author" here subsumes both the subject and primary source of the published account. The author may or may not also have been the writer. When the subject and writer differed, the writer was a white amanuensis, who transcribed and edited the author's oral account. Of the seven authors, only Olaudah Equiano is widely known. But five of them had significant lowcountry affiliations and associations, including Equiano, who spent far more time than he would have liked in the lowcountry, especially Georgia. South Carolina played an important role in the lives of all five. It was Boston King's birthplace, and may have been Equiano's as well.[2]

Evangelical Christianity and the American Revolution affected all five men.[3] And the accounts of their lives all originally appeared in London between 1785 and 1798. One of the greatest challenges in dealing with these writings as historical or literary documents is trying to identify the "black message in a white envelope," to use John Sekora's inspired metaphor to describe so-called as-told-to slave narratives.[4] The three earliest narratives, by John Marrant, George Liele, and David George, are problematic as-told-to tales. King speaks more directly to us through a white publisher. Of the five, the self-published Equiano tells us his story most directly.

The five individual lives are statistically insignificant representations of the approximately five hundred thousand people of African descent living throughout British North America at the beginning of the American Revolution. These narratives nonetheless demonstrate that although the lowcountry was economically, geographically, socially, and politically at the edge of the British Empire, it was a fully integrated part of that empire, and consequently of the larger transatlantic and circum-Atlantic world as well. Just over 50 percent of the tens of thousands of enslaved Africans forced on the Middle Passage across the Atlantic from Africa to North America arrived through the port of Charlestown, South Carolina, renamed Charleston after the American Revolution.[5] But the lowcountry was also the source of thousands of people of African descent who voluntarily crossed the Atlantic in the opposite direction following the Revolution. The five cases discussed here represent the range of opportunities for refashioning political and religious identities embraced publicly by some of the black sons of the lowcountry during the last quarter of the eighteenth century.

Approaching Marrant, Liele, George, King, and Equiano from the perspective of their lowcountry connections enables us to appreciate the complexity of such terms as "diaspora," "freedom," "oppression," and "identity" during and following the Revolution. Liele, George, Marrant, and King, and perhaps Equiano as well, each participated in a diaspora from an original homeland in North America, not Africa, seeking freedom under British protection from the oppression they had every reason to associate with the colonists' side in the war. Each man served, or at least felt the need to claim to have served, with the British Army or Navy, fashioning himself as a black Loyalist. How does one classify authors of African descent like David George and Boston King, who were born in what would become the United States, immigrated to Canada, and moved from there to settle in Africa? Or John Marrant and Olaudah Equiano, who ultimately chose to live and die in England? Or George Liele, who fled from the lowcountry to Jamaica? Neither "African British" nor "African American" is a category capacious enough to cover the five diasporan authors.

Recognizing the similarities and differences among the publication venues, means of dissemination, forms, contents, and omissions of the accounts by and about these five lowcountry authors demonstrates the value and limitations these accounts have as historical documents. First published in London, the narratives targeted mainly British and overwhelmingly white readers, most of whom had little personal experience with blacks or threats of slave revolts. The publisher of the edited accounts by Liele and George also distributed them in Savannah and Charleston, returning their subjects in print to the lowcountry they had no desire to ever see again in person, and to post-Revolutionary white American readers who presumably needed to be reassured that the evangelical agenda promoted in these texts would not subvert the lowcountry regime that enabled whites to control the enslaved people surrounding them. Whether as-told-to accounts or not, all five narratives are generically spiritual autobiographies, whose primary agendas are religious. Their subjects are intended to serve their readers as models of Christian converts. But the religious agendas and consequently the implications for slavery of these tales of the lowcountry varied: Liele's and George's "Accounts" were published as Baptist texts; Marrant's *Narrative* as a Huntingdonian Methodist work; King's "Memoirs" as a Wesleyan Methodist autobiography; and Equiano's *Interesting Narrative* as a multigeneric story of someone who professes Calvinist Methodism but acts more like an Arminian Methodist, and whose subscribers included both the Countess of Huntingdon and John Wesley.

Eighteenth-century Methodism was not a unified movement within the Church of England. George Whitefield preached the doctrine of the sixteenth-century Protestant theologian John Calvin. Calvinism held that very few Christians were among the elect — that is, those predestined, or elected, by the grace of God to be saved. Everyone else was a reprobate, doomed to eternal damnation, despite faith or acts of charity. Whitefield benefited from the organizational skills of his authoritarian patron, Selina Hastings, the Countess of Huntingdon, who established the "Huntingdonian Connexion" of Calvinist Methodist chapels throughout Britain.[6] She was compelled to begin registering Huntingdonian chapels as dissenting meetinghouses in 1779, when a British court ruled that the Anglican Church had not authorized her ministers to preach. Huntingdonian Methodists increasingly felt obligated to choose between the Connexion and the church. John Wesley embraced a more liberal, or Arminian, interpretation of the requirements for salvation, teaching that all who believed and repented of their sins might be saved. Like Whitefield, Wesley published his own sermons, but he also published the works of others, both indirectly through plagiarism, and openly in abridged versions of classic religious texts. In 1778, he began the *Arminian Magazine*, renamed the *Methodist Magazine* after his death in 1791.

Their much stronger emphasis on faith rather than works inclined Calvinist Methodists to a relatively quietist attitude toward slavery as an unfortunate condition to be endured in this world. Because Whitefield and Huntingdon were ameliorationists, who sought to improve the conditions of slavery, not to eradicate it, they saw no contradiction between their understanding of Christianity and their ownership of slaves. At Whitefield's death in 1770, Huntingdon inherited the orphanage that Whitefield had established at Bethesda, twelve miles from Savannah, Georgia. With the orphanage, Huntingdon also inherited slaves. Wesley, on the other hand, was an emancipationist who actively opposed slavery as being unchristian. Whitefield's ameliorationist and Wesley's emancipationist positions are expressed respectively in *A Letter to the Inhabitants of Maryland, Virginia, North and South-Carolina, Concerning their Negroes* (Savannah, 1740) and *Thoughts upon Slavery* (London, 1774).

Whether Calvinist Methodist, Arminian Methodist, or Baptist (which also included both Calvinist and Arminian branches), evangelical Protestantism appealed to blacks for a number of reasons. Baptists and Methodists actively proselytized in the lowcountry, making little distinction between blacks and whites as potential converts, and preaching the spiritual equality of all believers. Both denominations were also relatively egalitarian in their assignment of leadership roles, which, unlike Presbyterians and non-Methodist Anglicans, did not require advanced levels of literacy and education. Like all Protestant sects, however, Methodists and Baptists stressed the need for direct access to the Bible, thus authorizing and promoting the spread of literacy among believers, including slaves. Both evangelical denominations approved of the emotional appeal and expression of faith, and the immediacy of the born-again experience. And both were perceived as critical of, if not hostile to, slavery.

Of the five published lives of eighteenth-century people of African descent, only the ones written by their authors are overtly eighteenth-century abolitionist texts, supporting the abolition of the transatlantic slave trade. King mentions the trade once in passing; Equiano announces in his dedication to the members of Parliament that "the chief design" of his book is the exposure of "the horrors of that trade" (7).[7] Moreover, only Equiano and King anticipate nineteenth-century abolitionists in calling for the abolition of slavery. King explicitly condemns slavery in his final paragraph, while Equiano constructs his argument so as to compel his readers to conclude that slavery must be ended. But even Equiano emphasizes his *Interesting Narrative*'s primary status as a spiritual autobiography by initially introducing himself to his readers with a frontispiece showing him extending an open Bible to them. The as-told-to narratives of Marrant, Liele, and George are ameliorationist rather than emancipationist texts. For evidence of more radical positions taken by these five authors, especially of those whose voices come to us explicitly edited by white amanuenses, we must often look at their actions or words outside their texts. Attending to the similarities and differences among these five works demonstrates the challenges they present to anyone trying to approach them as abolitionist, emancipationist, or African American texts.

Once hostilities in the American Revolution broke out, both sides recognized that the institution of slavery was the weakest link in the rebels' ideological and military positions. In November 1775, and again in June 1779, British proclamations offered freedom to any slave who deserted a rebel master and sought refuge behind British lines. The British did not offer the same opportunity to the slaves of Loyalists. British motives were pragmatic rather than ideological. They faced severe military and labor shortages. Moreover, recruiting enemy-owned slaves with promises of freedom caused great economic and social problems for the rebels, especially in the slave-based societies of the lowcountry. Many of the black refugees served the British military as soldiers, sailors, and auxiliaries. In response to the British success in luring their slaves away, and to meet their own manpower shortages, eventually, and often begrudgingly, all but two of the rebellious colonies agreed to take black slaves and freemen into military service, with the promise of freedom for the former. The two colonies that did not were Georgia and South Carolina. In 1775, South Carolina's population included approximately seventy thousand whites and one hundred thousand blacks. Nearly seventy-three thousand blacks lived in the lowcountry districts of Beaufort, Charleston, and Georgetown, the vast majority as slaves. Of Georgia's total population of approximately thirty-three thousand in 1775, about fifteen thousand, overwhelmingly slaves in the lowcountry, were black.

Not surprisingly then, most of the eighteenth-century blacks whose voices we can recover chose a British rather than an American identity when given the opportunity, taking advantage of the British promises of emancipation for refugee slaves of the Colonial rebels. Of the half-million blacks in the thirteen colonies, the overwhelming majority of whom were slaves, approximately five thousand served the rebels' cause while tens of thousands emancipated themselves by taking advantage of British offers of freedom. Such self-emancipation carried substantial risk, however. Facing the prospect of a British invasion, South Carolina in 1776 made it a capital crime for any slave who escaped from a rebel owner to serve in the British Army or Navy, and any slaves who fled to the British were gambling with their lives on Britain's willingness and ability to honor its promise of free-dom should it fail to conquer the rebels. Free as well as enslaved blacks saw allegiance to Britain rather than to rebellious Americans as a safer bet for their future.

John Marrant (1755–91) was born in New York on June 15, 1755, to free black parents. When his father died four years later, his mother moved with him to St. Augustine, then in Spanish Florida, where he began his school-ing. After Spain joined France at the beginning of 1761 against Britain during the Seven Years' War (1756–63), Marrant's mother fled with him to Georgia. When he was eleven years old, they moved to Charleston, South Carolina. There he was apprenticed to a carpenter and learned to play the French horn and violin. Thirteen-year-old Marrant experienced spiritual rebirth after hearing George Whitefield preach in Charleston, probably in early December 1768, at the beginning of what would be the last of White-field's seven North American preaching tours. Marrant responded so pow-erfully to the preacher he had been told was "a crazy man" that he "was struck to the ground" when he heard him (113).[8]

Because his family opposed his conversion, Marrant sought solace in the wilderness, trusting God to sustain him. He was sentenced to a hor-rible death when an Indian hunter brought him to a Cherokee town. The miraculous conversion of the executioner, however, gained him a reprieve. Marrant lived with the Indians for two years before returning to his family, who at first did not recognize him. At the end of the American Revolution, Marrant went to London, where he worked for a clothing merchant. On May 15, 1785, in Bath, England, Marrant was ordained as a minister in the Huntingdonian Connexion. Naval records do not support Marrant's claim that he was pressed into the British Royal Navy as a musician during the American Revolution. Nor do they support his claims to have been at the siege of Charleston in 1780 and the fight with Dutch forces off the Dogger Bank in the North Sea in 1781. If Marrant invented a British naval career for himself, he may have done so to reinforce the African British identity he projects in his autobiography.

Shortly after Marrant's ordination, in 1785 his as-told-to *A Narrative of the Lord's Wonderful Dealings with John Marrant, a Black . . .* was published in London. Its "black message" was delivered in the "white envelope" formed by the "Preface" of Marrant's amanuensis/editor, Rev. William Aldridge, and a concluding affidavit from Marrant's landlord attesting to his character and Christianity, at least in the fourth edition (1785). Only the fourth edition claims to have been "PRINTED FOR THE AUTHOR." Absent the phrase "a Black" in the title in all editions, and a reference only in the fourth edition to Marrant as "the free Carpenter," nothing in Aldridge's "Preface" or the *Narrative* itself indicates that Marrant was of African descent. The lack of such references reflects the rhetorical constraints exerted by the *Narrative*'s generic form. As a spiritual autobiography, particularly one mediated by a white clergyman, its primary subject is an individual's conversion to universal Christianity available to anyone. From Aldridge's perspective at least, Marrant's ethnicity is irrelevant to his conversion narrative, and significant rhetorically solely because it demonstrates that the gospel is designed for everyone, regardless of complexion or status.

Marrant's ethnicity is explicitly referred to within the *Narrative* only in the edition he claims to have published himself. The fourth edition is also the only one that says Marrant interacted with slaves, teaching them religion, despite the objections of their owners, one of whom became the prototype of the excessively cruel white female slave owner who frequently reappears in subsequent slave narratives. Mediated by an amanuensis and patronized by a slave owner, even the fourth edition of Marrant's *Narrative* carefully avoids making an emancipationist attack on the institution of slavery. Indeed, the ameliorationist message of the two paragraphs added to the fourth edition argues that Christianity will render slaves more docile and obedient.

Employed as a carpenter on "a plantation belonging to Mr. Jenkins, of Cumbee [Combahee], about seventy miles from Charles-Town," Marrant unexpectedly became a lay preacher to Jenkins's slaves, initially by "reading God's Word, singing Watts's hymns and in Prayer" with "the little negro children" (123). Jenkins was probably a member of the numerous Jenkins clan in Colleton County, between Charleston and Beaufort.[9] Marrant soon began teaching the Lord's Prayer and the catechism to the children and their parents. When Mrs. Jenkins heard of what Marrant had been doing, she incited her husband, who had tolerated Marrant's proselytizing, to oversee the flogging of their slaves. She was disappointed that she might not also have Marrant flogged, who, as her husband reminded her, was a free man who "would take the law of him" (124). Marrant's *Narrative* is far more sanguine about the legal status of free blacks in the lowcountry than Equiano's experiences justify. Mr. Jenkins admitted to Marrant that rather than being the revolutionary egalitarian ideology his wife feared, Christianity had rendered their slaves better workers: "they did their tasks sooner than the others who were not instructed." Consequently, shortly after "it pleased God to lay his hand upon their Mistress, and she was seized with a very violent fever," which killed her "in a very dreadful manner, . . . her husband gave them liberty to meet together as before, and used sometimes to attend with them." The liberty that Jenkins granted his slaves was not emancipation, but merely permission to worship together. Jenkins later told Marrant that "it was made very useful to him" (124).

Marrant's actions and writings express a more hostile attitude toward slavery, and a more active resistance toward oppressive whites, only after he left the lowcountry, and only when his words were published unmediated by a white amanuensis. Sponsored by Huntingdon, Marrant left England a few months after the appearance of his *Narrative* to preach in Nova Scotia to the native Micmac Indians and doctrinally more moderate black and white Wesleyan Methodists. He alienated several white ministers when his preaching lured their parishioners to his all-black chapels. Despite his success in Canada as a preacher, Marrant never received financial aid promised by the countess, forcing him to move in 1787 to Boston. There he served as chaplain to the first lodge of African Masons, founded by Prince Hall three years earlier. Marrant married Elizabeth Herries, a Black Loyalist, on August 15, 1788. He published *A Sermon* in Boston in 1789, before returning to London in 1790, where he continued his ministry. His last publication was *A Journal . . . To Which are Added Two Sermons* (London, 1791).[10] Marrant died in Islington, then a London suburb, on April 15, 1791.

George Liele (ca. 1751–1825), known by his friends as Brother Liele, was "called also George *Sharp* because his owner's name was [Henry] *Sharp* (325)."[11] Liele was born in Virginia, the son of slaves Liele and Nancy. Sharp soon moved Liele's family to Georgia, where Sharp was a deacon in Burke County, located between Augusta and Savannah. Blacks and whites there considered Liele's father to be "the only black person who knew the Lord in a spiritual way in that country" (326). Liele "had a natural fear of God from [his] youth" (326), but a sermon by the Baptist minister Matthew Moore on the necessity of grace disabused him of his belief that good works earned salvation. After a few months of despair, Liele felt the call of divine grace, was baptized by Moore, and became a member of Moore's Buckhead Creek Baptist Church in Burke County. Liele's owner was a deacon in the same church. Liele became the first person of African descent licensed and ordained to serve as a Baptist preacher-missionary in North America. Liele was soon preaching to both black and white audiences near Savannah, where he remained until the British evacuated the city in June 1782. Sometime before that, Liele was freed by his owner, Sharp, an officer in the Loyalist militia who was killed during the American Revolution. Some unidentified people refused to acknowledge his manumission and had him thrown in jail, but with the help of his friend Colonel Moses Kirkland, and the proper papers, he was released.

The British evacuated Liele, his wife, and their four children to Jamaica in 1783. To pay off his debts, Liele indentured himself to Kirkland as a servant. With Kirkland's recommendation, Liele spent two years in the employ of the governor of Jamaica, enabling him to settle his debts and regain his freedom. Liele established the first Baptist church in Jamaica when he began preaching in Kingston around September 1784. He initially had a congregation of four. He quickly gained a following among the poor, especially the slaves. Readers are assured though that "We receive none into the church without a few lines from their owners of their good behaviour towards them and religion" (327). Persecuted at meetings and baptisms, Liele applied for and received legal sanction for his itinerant ministry, which soon numbered 350 congregants throughout Jamaica. Although he reportedly received nothing for his services, he also established a school for both white and black children. Liele's as-told-to tale was published in London 1793 in *The Baptist Annual Register, for 1790, 1791, 1792, and Part of 1793*, whose colophon tells us that it "May Be Had of the Baptist Ministers in New York, Philadelphia, Boston, Richmond, Savannah, and Charleston, in America." Liele was jailed, tried, and acquitted on a charge of sedition in 1794. He was able to support his Jamaican ministry with the help of the charity of British Baptists, though financial problems at least once caused him to be imprisoned for debt (1797–1801).

Information not included in the *Baptist Annual Register* suggests that Liele may not have been as accommodating to whites as his as-told-to narrative claims:

During the early part of his ministry, Mr. Liele suffered much opposition, and was often treated with contumely and insult. On one occasion, when the church was about to celebrate the Lord's Supper, a gentleman (so called) rode into the chapel, and, urging his horse through the midst of the people to the very front of the pulpit, exclaimed in terms of insolence and profanity, "Come, old Liele, give my horse the Sacrament!" Mr. Liele coolly replied, "No, sir, you are not fit yourself to receive it." After maintaining his position for some time the intruder rode out. On another ordinary Sabbath, three young gentlemen walked into the chapel during service, and, going up to the table where the bread and wine had been placed, one of them took the bread, and, breaking it, gave it to his companion, who, with a horrid oath, swore that it was good ship-bread, and presented it to the third, who refused to take it. It must not be withheld that the two former were in a few days removed into the presence of that God with whose Institution they had so profanely trifled. One died in a state of awful madness from brain-fever; the other went out of the harbour in a boat, which was upset, and he was never seen again.[12]

David George (1743?–1810) was born to enslaved Africans, John and Judith, in Sussex County, Virginia.[13] George escaped from his abusive owner in 1762, when he was about nineteen years old. Relentlessly pursued by his owner's son, George fled farther and farther south, seeking sanctuary with various Indian peoples. The Natchez Indians eventually sold him to a white trader, George Galphin, in Silver Bluff, South Carolina, fourteen miles northwest of Savannah. David George married Phillis, another slave, around 1770. A fellow black introduced him to Christianity, and George began attending Baptist services conducted by his friend George Liele, as well as by Wait Palmer, a white itinerant Baptist evangelist from Connecticut. George assures his readers that Liele and Palmer preached to the slaves only by permission of their owners. Sometime in the early 1770s, George became a founder of the Silver Bluff Baptist Church, probably the first exclusively African American church. Having been taught by white children to read, George became an occasional preacher in the church. In 1778, George seized the chance to enlist with advancing British troops, helping them fortify Savannah when rebel forces unsuccessfully besieged it in 1779. Working there as a butcher, he preached to fellow blacks behind the British lines. In 1783, George and his family were among the thousands of former slaves evacuated by the British from Charleston, Savannah, and New York City, and resettled in Nova Scotia, Canada.

Despite resistance from black and white Anglican and Methodist denominations, George preached the Baptist word throughout Nova Scotia and New Brunswick to both black and white audiences. George helped John Clarkson recruit black Loyalists and their families for the Sierra Leone Company's project to establish a colony of free blacks in Africa at Freetown, Sierra Leone. George, his wife, and their four children were among the twelve hundred settlers in 1792. George established the first Baptist church in Africa. As one of the settlement's three superintendents, he went to England in 1792 with Clarkson to meet fellow Baptists and to raise money for his African mission. He returned to Africa in 1793, where he died in 1810. Like the story of Liele's life, George's as-told-to narrative appeared in *The Baptist Annual Register, for 1790, 1791, 1792, and Part of 1793*. As with Liele, evidence external to George's "Account" indicates that he had even more of a mind of his own than his "Account" suggests. Writing from Sierra Leone on June 3, 1797, to Rev. John Newton in England, Zachary Macaulay, the governor of Sierra Leone, reports that he has denied George's request to be sent from Africa to Jamaica to aid Liele in his mission there because of

> the striking declension in point of piety which seemed to have taken place not only in [George's] people, but in himself, and the prevalence among them of irregularities, wholly inconsistent with the simplicity of the Gospel. . . . I saw enough in his absolute unfitness for the business to lead me to continue, as I did, to hold out all the discouragements I could to his quitting the Colony . . . even to the prevention of those irregularities to [which] I allude above, and which serve not only to injure the Baptist interest, but what ought to be dearer to us all, the interests of Christ.[14]

Unfortunately, Macaulay does not identify the "irregularities."

Unlike the narratives of Marrant, Liele, and George, each of the autobiographies of Boston King and Olaudah Equiano is written *in propria persona*. The Methodist preacher Boston King (1760?–1802) was born a slave around 1760, on a plantation owned by Richard Waring III close to Slann's Bridge on the Ashley River, about twenty-eight miles from Charleston.[15] Boston's African-born father, a slave-driver and later mill-cutter, and his mother, a seamstress and practitioner of folk medicine, were both favored by their owner. Boston's father was also a lay preacher to his fellow slaves. When Boston was sixteen years old, his owner apprenticed him to a brutal carpenter, who severely punished Boston for the misdeeds of other workers. To escape further punishment, he sought refuge and freedom with the

British forces occupying Charleston since 1780. Once behind British lines, Boston "began to feel the happiness of liberty, of which [he] knew nothing before" (353).[16] He probably assumed the surname King about the same time, perhaps as an expression of his Loyalist allegiance to the British monarch. When he contracted smallpox he was quarantined and left behind with the Loyalist militia as the British regular forces withdrew from their position. Recovered with the aid of a militiaman, King rejoined the regular forces as the servant to the commander, and as a carrier of dispatches through enemy lines. Around 1781, he sailed aboard a British warship from Charleston to New York City, also under British control. There he married a former slave named Violet, twelve years his senior. He was captured by an American whaler while he was working at sea, and taken to New Jersey, but he soon escaped, returning to New York City.

At the end of the war in 1783, the Kings were among the more than three thousand former slaves evacuated by the British from the former thirteen colonies and resettled in Birchtown, Nova Scotia, Canada. There, first Violet and then Boston King had their Christian conversion experiences, and King began preaching in 1785. Faced with general famine and the resentment of competing white workers, their life was extremely difficult until King found regular employment as a carpenter. Conditions improved even further in 1791, when King was appointed the Wesleyan Methodist preacher to the black settlement at Preston, near Halifax.

Despite his comfortable situation in Canada, King felt the call to participate in the Sierra Leone Company's project to establish a colony of free blacks in Africa at Freetown, Sierra Leone, in part because of the company's intention, "as far as possible in their power, to put a stop to the abominable slave-trade" (363). Boston and Violet sailed with David George and his family to Sierra Leone in 1792. Like many of the new settlers, Violet soon died of fever. King remarried by 1793. His very limited success as a schoolteacher and missionary to the native Africans prompted the company to send him to England in 1794 for several years of education at the Methodist Kingswood School, near Bristol. His reception in England and his experience there as a preacher enabled him finally to overcome the prejudices against whites that his experiences in the lowcountry had given him:

> In the former part of my life I had suffered greatly from the cruelty and injustice of the Whites, which induced me to look upon them, in general, as our enemies: And even after the Lord had manifested his forgiving mercy to me, I still felt at times an uneasy distrust and shyness towards them; but

on that day the Lord removed all my prejudices; for which I bless his holy Name. . . . I have great cause to be thankful that I came to England, for I am now fully convinced, that many of the White People, instead of being enemies and oppressors of us poor Blacks, are our friends, and deliverers from slavery, as far as their ability and circumstances will admit." (366)

King returned to Freetown in 1796 and became a somewhat more successful teacher. King's narrative, "Written by Himself," was first published in the *Methodist Magazine* in London in March 1798. Soon after King returned to Freetown, he left to continue his ministry one hundred miles to the south, among the Sherbro people, where he died in 1802. The 1802 Sierra Leone census records that he was survived by a daughter and two sons.

In *The Interesting Narrative of the Life of Olaudah Equiano, or Gustavus Vassa, the African. Written by Himself*, published in London in March 1789, Equiano (1745?–97) claims that he was born in what is now southeastern Nigeria. He says that he was kidnapped into slavery around the age of eleven and taken to the West Indies for a few days before being brought to Virginia and sold to a local planter. Michael Henry Pascal, an officer in the British Royal Navy on leave, soon bought him from the planter, renamed him Gustavus Vassa, and brought him to London. Documentary evidence, however, disputes Equiano's account of his early life. His baptismal and naval records say that he was a son of the lowcountry, born in South Carolina rather than Africa. Shipping records prove that he first reached England in December 1754. Equiano served under Pascal during the Seven Years' War, but rather than granting Equiano the freedom he expected, at the end of 1762 Pascal sent him to the West Indies to be sold.

Soon after Equiano arrived at Montserrat in early 1763 he was bought by the Quaker merchant Robert King, about whom we know very little beyond Equiano's account. From his bases in Philadelphia and Montserrat, King participated in the eighteenth-century globalization of trade. The lowcountry was at the geographical center of King's commercial empire, in which he transshipped enslaved Africans and agricultural products from the Caribbean to North America in exchange for goods from Philadelphia. Because the training and education Equiano had received during his time with the Royal Navy rendered him too valuable a slave to be doomed to plantation labor, King quickly made him an agent in his intercolonial trade empire, enabling Equiano to conduct private intercolonial and international business transactions while working for King. Equiano's participation through King in the global market allowed him to purchase his freedom in 1766.

Equiano remained in King's employ for a year as a free man, making several more trading trips to Georgia, South Carolina, and Pennsylvania.[17] First as King's slave, and later as his employee, Equiano visited the low-country, particularly Savannah, at least five times between February 1765 and April 1767. He was certainly there even more often, but external evidence of additional trips is lacking because the *Georgia Gazette* suspended publication between December 1765 and June 1766 in response to the passage of the Stamp Act. Equiano tells us that he was in Charleston when news of the repeal of the act was celebrated there in May 1766. Whether as a slave or free man, Equiano found the lowcountry an inhospitable place. Equiano's experiences in the lowcountry provide us with by far the fullest account we have of the dangers faced by a person of African descent, enslaved or free, even one who had Equiano's extraordinary advantages, opportunities, and mobility.

On his first voyage beyond the Caribbean as King's slave, Equiano sailed to Savannah, then a town of fewer than three thousand people. He arrived on February 7, 1765, aboard King's sloop, *Prudence*, commanded by Thomas Farmer. The cargo was "a load of new slaves" (123). On the following Sunday, Equiano heard the celebrated George Whitefield preach there. Perhaps subconsciously unwilling or unable to associate any positive experience with the lowcountry, in a very rare lapse of memory Equiano records in his *Interesting Narrative* that he heard Whitefield preach in Philadelphia in 1766. Whitefield, however, was in Great Britain between July 7, 1765, and September 16, 1768. The *Georgia Gazette* and shipping records document that Equiano and Whitefield were both in Savannah during the second week of February 1765. The accessibility and emotional appeal of Methodist preaching remarked by Equiano help account for its attractiveness to poor whites as well as slaves and free blacks like Marrant, who were generally ignored by more conservative Anglican divines. Equiano tellingly notes an affinity between Whitefield and enslaved people, and thus, perhaps unwittingly, between the economy and society of South Carolina and the West Indian model on which they were based:

> I came to a church crowded with people; the church-yard was full likewise, and a number of people were even mounted on ladders, looking in at the windows. I thought this a strange sight, as I had never seen churches, either

in England or the West Indies, crowded in this manner before. I therefore made bold to ask some people the meaning of all this, and they told me the Rev. George Whitefield was preaching. I had often heard of this gentleman, and had wished to see and hear him; but I had never before had an opportunity. I now therefore resolved to gratify myself with the sight, and pressed in amidst the multitude. When I got into the church I saw this pious man exhorting the people with the greatest fervour and earnestness, and sweating as much as ever I did while in slavery on Montserrat beach. I was very much struck and impressed with this; I thought it strange I had never seen divines exert themselves in this manner before, and was no longer at a loss to account for the thin congregations they preached to. (132)

Equiano had ample reason to recall the lowcountry in negative terms. When King at one point threatened to sell Equiano, he told him that he would do so to "a severe master . . . in Carolina" (124). Before Equiano first reached the lowcountry, he "always much wished to lose sight of the West Indies" (123), but he discovered Georgia and South Carolina to be little better than cultural extensions of the Caribbean; "particularly in Charles Town, [he] met with buyers, white men, who imposed on [him] as in other places" (124). The last time Equiano was in Charleston, in 1766, he barely escaped alive because as a slave he had no legal recourse when a white man cheated him in trade and threatened to bind and flog him.

Equiano was not so lucky during his second trip to Savannah, sometime between the arrival of the *Prudence* after the beginning of March and when it left on April 20, 1765 (*GG*, May 9, 1765; November 4, 1765). "Worse fate than ever" attended Equiano when Doctor John Perkins, "a very severe and cruel man, came in drunk" on a Sunday night to find Equiano socializing with his slaves. "Not liking to see any strange negroes in his yard," Perkins and a white employee beat Equiano bloody and senseless, and the next morning dragged him off to jail (129). Perkins was a significant figure in Savannah, soon to be appointed quartermaster and surgeon of the first troop of Georgia Rangers on May 9, 1765 (*GG*, May 9, 1765). Fortunately for Equiano, Captain Farmer was able to find him. Acting out of what Equiano assumed was friendship, Farmer rescued him from jail and forced Perkins to back down by challenging him to a duel. All the lawyers consulted by Farmer, however, "told him they could do nothing for [Equiano] as [he] was a negro" (130). The beating caused Equiano to meet one of the very few good white men he encountered in the lowcountry.

After being told by "the best doctors in the place" that [Equiano] could not recover," Farmer brought him to "Dr. Brady," a "worthy man [who] nursed and watched [him] all the hours of the night and [Equiano] was, through [Farmer's] attention, and that of the doctor, able to get out of bed in about sixteen or eighteen days" (130). Equiano's "Dr. Brady" was almost certainly Doctor David Brydie, well known for ministering to slaves (*GG*, May 16, 1765; October 11, 1769).[18]

Equiano gained his long-awaited manumission on July 11, 1766, from his begrudging owner, King, who had promised him when he bought him that he would allow Equiano to purchase his freedom for the price King had paid for him. But before agreeing to honor his word, King coerced Equiano into agreeing to continue working for him as a paid employee supervised by Farmer for another year. Equiano was reasonably optimistic. King had purchased a larger vessel, the *Nancy*, for Farmer to command, thus giving Equiano space to carry more goods to sell privately. Once free, however, Equiano soon learned that in the lowcountry "there was little or no law for a free negro," rendering the life of a free person of African descent no less precarious and dangerous than that of a slave. Indeed, it was often more so because neither a slave nor a free black could testify in court against a white. Moreover, as legal pieces of property, slaves were often protected by their owners from injury or theft by other whites because they were considered investments (139).

Equiano received his first lesson about the fragility of freedom in Savannah at the hands of James Read near the end of his October 7–November 8, 1766, visit. Read was one of the most successful, upstanding, respected, and philanthropic residents in the whole lowcountry. Read and his partner, James Mossman, were significant merchants conducting intercolonial, international, and transatlantic trade in goods and people from their wharf in Savannah. For example, they advertised in the *Georgia Gazette* on September 23, 1767, the sale at their wharf of "European and East-India Goods. Also, Jamaica Rum and Sugar," and on July 4, 1765, they invited customers to buy "Between FIFTY and SIXTY very likely Healthy NEW NEGROES, just arrived from the Gold Coast." More locally, Read and Mossman dealt in land as well as goods. Read also owned a plantation and some fifty slaves, several of whom were ungrateful enough to run away from him during the 1760s, and from his heirs following his death in 1778 (*GG*, December 30, 1767; August 23, 1781).[19]

A man of formidable legal and political clout, Read was presumably considered by his fellow whites to have been something of an ethical and moral paragon. He was appointed a justice of the peace on May 10, 1764, sworn in as a member of the governing council on February 5, 1765, and chosen as Speaker of the Upper House of Assembly in Georgia on May 26, 1764.[20] In 1767 alone, he was one of the magistrates of the province of Georgia who publicly endorsed "An act for the more effectual suppressing prophane Cursing and Swearing," as well as "An act for preventing and punishing Vice, Profaneness, and immorality, and for keeping holy the Lord's Day, commonly called Sunday," and "An Act for the better ordering and governing Negroes and other Slaves in this province" (*GG*, January 21, 1767). Read was chosen a vestryman of the parish of Christ Church in April (*GG*, April 22, 1767), and in May he became one of the commissioners charged with soliciting proposals for the construction of a *lazaretto*, a hospital for treating contagious diseases (*GG*, May 27, 1767). In November 1767, Read and Mossman were appointed commissioners in charge of repairing Christ Church. The following year, Read was seeking subscriptions for a school (*GG*, June 1, 1768), and appointed a trustee for regulating the market in Savannah.[21]

Equiano faced a formidable enemy in Read, an eminent and influential figure in Georgia. Equiano discovered that Read also deserved his reputation as "a very spiteful man" (140). Equiano soon experienced the harsh realities a free black man faced in the slave societies of the West Indies and the lowcountry. The month after being manumitted he sailed aboard the *Nancy* in a "state of serenity" over "smooth seas" with "pleasant weather" to the Dutch West-Indian colony of St. Eustatia for cargo, and then on to Savannah (138). Fending off frightening alligators in Georgia as he brought agricultural products downriver to the *Nancy* was the least of the dangers he experienced there. One evening, at or near Read's wharf, one of Read's slaves verbally abused Equiano without provocation. Knowing that "there was little or no law for a free negro," Equiano patiently tried to diffuse the situation, but the slave only grew more intemperate. He became so overwrought that he hit Equiano, who then "lost all temper, and fell on him and beat him soundly." Fearing the possible repercussions, the next morning Equiano told Captain Farmer of the incident, and asked him to go with him to talk to Read. Farmer thought he was exaggerating the significance of the fight, assuring him that he would mollify Read if necessary. Later that morning Equiano discovered he had reason for concern. Read came to the wharf where the *Nancy* was docked and demanded that Equiano come ashore to be "flogged all round the town, for beating his negro slave." Ignoring Equiano's claim that he acted only in self-defense, Read told Farmer to turn him over. Farmer's response astounded his crewmember: "he said he knew nothing of the matter, I was a free man." "Astonished and frightened" by Farmer's statement, Equiano realized that in some ways black freemen were virtually slaves without masters, more vulnerable to abuse than chattel slaves protected by owners guarding their property. Farmer's response reminded Equiano that with neither law to protect him, nor apparently anyone in power with a vested interest in his well-being, "might too often overcomes right" in slave societies.

Recognizing that his was a case where discretion was the better part of valor, he refused to go ashore to be flogged "without judge or jury." Seething with anger, Read swore he would return with all the town's constables to remove Equiano from the vessel. Equiano had seen enough instances of the abuse of black freemen not to doubt Read's word. For example, he knew a carpenter who was thrown into jail merely for requesting the money he had earned from a white man, who later had him removed from Georgia, falsely accused of having planned "to set the gentleman's house on fire," and to have "run away with his slaves" (139).

Equiano was less upset about the possibility of physical injury than by the threat Read posed to his sense of honor as a free man. Faced with Farmer's feckless behavior, Equiano at first briefly let his hard-won freedom go to his head: "I dreaded, of all things, the thoughts of being stripped, as I never in my life had the marks of any violence of that kind. At that instant a rage seized my soul, and for a while I determined to resist the first man that should attempt to lay violent hands on me, or basely use me without a trial; for I would sooner die like a free man, than suffer myself to be scourged by the hands of ruffians, and my blood drawn like a slave." The captain and others eventually convinced him, however, that Read was such a spiteful man that resistance would be futile. Equiano agreed to take refuge in a house their landlord owned outside of town. Just after he left town, Read returned with his constables, swearing to take him "dead or alive." Five days passed before Farmer took any action on Equiano's behalf, and only then in response to the threats some of Equiano's friends made to put him on another vessel. Farmer begged Read to forgive Equiano, a man of good character, flawless reputation, and an essential crewmember. Read begrudgingly gave in, saying Equiano "might go to hell" for all he cared. Thinking he had succeeded in his mission, Farmer had to be reminded that he needed to retrieve the warrant from the constables before the affair was legally ended, and Equiano was safe from his "hunters" (140). At last, he could safely return to the *Nancy*, though he was stuck with paying all the legal expenses.

Captain Farmer died on the voyage back to Montserrat in mid-November 1766. Equiano may never have been told that his first antagonist in the lowcountry, Dr. Perkins, died around the same time (*GG*, November 19, 1766). Equiano made his next and last trip to the lowcountry under the command of Farmer's incompetent successor, William Phillips. Returning to Georgia brought Equiano back to the harsh realities of slavery and the limitations it placed on his freedom. He spent his first evening in Savannah at the home of his enslaved friend Mosa, talking past nine. The light in the house drew the attention of the watchmen, who decided to investigate it. Invited in by Mosa, and offered punch, they asked Equiano for some of his limes, which he readily gave them. After accepting Mosa's hospitality, they suddenly announced that Equiano must go to the watch-house with them because "all negroes, who had a light in their houses after nine o'clock were to be taken into custody, and either pay some dollars or be flogged. Some of these people knew that I was a free man; but, as the man of the house was not free, and had his master to protect him, they did not take the same liberty with him they did with me" (158). Ignoring Equiano's protests that he was a free man, newly arrived from the Bahamas, and well known in Savannah, they forced him to come with them. He could not help but think he was about to experience the same sort of robbery he had suffered elsewhere. But the watchmen had something worse in mind. The next morning they "flogged a negro man and woman that they had in the watch-house, and then they told me that I must be flogged too." Equiano's challenge to their right to do so "only exasperated them the more, and they instantly swore they would serve [him] as Doctor Perkins had done . . ." Fortunately for Equiano, one of them had second thoughts about the legality of such abuse, giving him the chance to call once again on Dr. Brydie, who gained his release.

Equiano sometimes actively resisted abuse. Just outside of Savannah he "was beset by two white men, who meant to play their usual tricks with me in the way of kidnapping." When one of them, claiming Equiano as his runaway slave, was about to lay his hands on him, Equiano "told them to be still and keep off, for I had seen those tricks played upon other free blacks, and they must not think to serve me so." One of the whites initially responded to Equiano's threats much as others had to his earlier claims to legal rights, but this time the now-free man was ready to act as well as speak to defend his rights: "they paused a little, and one said to the other — it will not do; and the other answered that I talked too good English. I replied, I believed I did; and I had also with me a revengeful stick equal to the occasion; and my mind was likewise good. Happily, however, it was not used; and, after we had talked together a little in this manner, the rogues left me" (159). Significantly, Equiano's responses to threats during his times in the lowcountry brought him to the brink of violence, implying that the next incident might get him to cross the line: he submitted to Dr. Perkins in 1765, resisted Read by flight in 1766, and was prepared to defend himself physically in 1767 during his last visit.

Equiano's final act in Georgia was to become, after John Marrant, the second person of African descent to record his role as a "parson" in the lowcountry, albeit also unintentionally and in a lay capacity:

> Before I left Georgia, a black woman who had a child lying dead, being very tenacious of the church burial service, and not able to get any white person to perform it, applied to me for that purpose. I told her I was no parson; and, besides, that the service over the dead did not affect the soul. This however did not satisfy her; she still urged me very hard; I therefore complied with her entreaties, and at last consented to act the parson for the first time in my life. As she was much respected, there was a great company both of white and black people at the grave. I then accordingly assumed my new vocation, and performed the funeral ceremony to the satisfaction of all present; after which I bade adieu to Georgia. . . . I thus took a final leave of Georgia; for the treatment I had received in it disgusted me very much against the place; and when I left it . . . I determined never more to revisit it. (160)

He never went back to the lowcountry.

In 1767, Equiano returned to London, and for the next six years he worked on commercial vessels sailing to the Mediterranean and the West Indies, commenting on all the versions of slavery he observed. After joining an expedition to the Arctic seeking a Northeast Passage in 1773, he returned to London, where he embraced Methodism. Soon again growing restless, in 1775–76 he briefly helped his friend and former employer, Dr. Charles Irving, in a short-lived attempt to establish a plantation in Central America, with Equiano acting as buyer and driver (overseer) of the black slaves. Returning to London in 1777, he pursued a variety of careers, including merchant seaman. He became increasingly involved in efforts to help his fellow blacks, with the project to resettle the black poor in Sierra Leone, and with the drive to abolish the African slave trade. In 1792, Equiano married an Englishwoman, Susanna Cullen, a fact he mentions in later editions of his autobiography.

What Equiano chooses not to mention in his abolitionist *Interesting Narrative* are the emancipationist positions he took in the hostile newspaper reviews of proslavery books, and the argument in favor of interracial marriage he published in newspapers during 1788. Nor does he mention his ties to radicals, such as his landlord Thomas Hardy, founder of the London Corresponding Society, for which Equiano recruited members during his 1789–94 book tours throughout England, Ireland, and Scotland. At various times in his *Interesting Narrative*, Equiano comes very close to crossing the line between amelioration and emancipation. For example, as he closes his account of his life as a slave in the lowcountry and the West Indies, he likens himself to Moses, and quotes Beelzebub from John Milton's *Paradise Lost* positively, apparently to lead his readers to conclude that slave rebellions are unavoidable and justified, only to step back rhetorically to promote an ameliorationist solution: "By changing your conduct, and treating your slaves as men, every cause of fear would be banished. They would be faithful, honest, intelligent and vigorous; and peace, prosperity, and happiness would attend you" (112).[22]

We can only speculate about why the lowcountry plays such a disproportionate role in the development of early black autobiography, especially in the four texts that depended on the mediation of whites for their transmission and distribution. The question is probably ultimately unanswerable: the total number of texts is very small, and the disproportion may simply be fortuitous. From a demographic perspective, however, one would expect the far more numerous enslaved people of African descent living in the Chesapeake and Upper South regions before 1800 to have produced more accounts of the lives of individual slaves than exist from the lowcountry. (Virginia, for example, had over twice as many slaves during the last quarter of the eighteenth century than South Carolina.) One would expect the relatively better-educated blacks in the North, with comparatively greater access to print and a longer history of exposure to Christianity, to have authored more spiritual autobiographies than people in the region with the highest level of black illiteracy in North America, and who have often been thought to have been most resistant to evangelical Christianity.

The answer, if there is one, may reflect rhetorical considerations rather than demography. Paradoxically, the great odds against the predominance of lowcountry autobiographies may help account for their relative frequency. The authors, editors, and publishers of these five texts may have appreciated that the more obstacles their subjects overcame, the more effectively their religious agendas would be served. Moreover, emphasizing the conversion and emancipation of enslaved people may also have been intended, at least in part, to enable a British audience to salvage a moral victory from the loss of the thirteen colonies.[23] If so, the more brutal the regime of slavery from which the blacks were saved, the better the British looked. A contemporaneous work of fiction, also published in London, suggests that the lowcountry provided the model of such a regime for anyone who wanted to stress the positive role Britain played in the lives of the black Loyalists liberated from its colonies lost in North America, while ignoring its dominant role in the transatlantic slave trade and the harsh conditions of slavery in its West Indian colonies.[24] When J. Hector St. John de Crèvecoeur (1735–1813) turns to the issue of slavery in his *Letters from an American Farmer* (London, 1782), he sets the scene of the barbaric punishment of a slave not in New York, where he had been a member of a society with slaves, nor in Virginia, where he had observed a slave society. Instead, he chooses South Carolina, where he may never have been, to epitomize the horrors of North American slavery. At least one modern historian validates Crèvecoeur's choice of the lowcountry.[25]

The contemporaneous black clergyman and author Richard Allen (1760–1831) recognized the dangers that the lowcountry posed for any person of African descent, enslaved or free. In *The Life, Experience, and Gospel Labours of the Rt. Rev. Richard Allen* (Philadelphia, 1833), Allen recounts that when asked in 1785 to go to the South as a missionary he declined:

> Rev. Bishop Asberry sent for me to meet him at Henry Gaff's. I did so.
> He told me he wished me to travel with him. He told me that in the slave
> countries, Carolina and other places, I must not intermix with the slaves,
> and I would frequently have to sleep in his carriage, and he would allow me
> my victuals and clothes. I told him I would not travel with him on these
> conditions. He asked me my reason. I told him if I was taken sick, who
> was to support me? and that I thought people ought to lay up something

while they were able, to support themselves in time of sickness or old age. He said that was as much as he got, his victuals and clothes. I told him he would be taken care of, let his afflictions be as they were, or let him be taken sick where he would, he would be taken care of; but I doubted whether it would be the case with myself. He smiled, and told me he would give me from then until he returned from the eastward to make up my mind, which would be about three months. But I made up my mind that I would not accept of his proposals. (11)

George Liele, David George, John Marrant, Boston King, and (perhaps) Olaudah Equiano might all be called sons of the lowcountry, but each took the opportunity to put himself up for adoption. With the possible exception of Equiano, for them the eighteenth-century African diaspora did not mean the forced expulsion from Africa to the Americas. Their voluntary diasporas moved from the new world to the old, from west to east, north to south, and back and forth in many directions as they redefined themselves several times over. For some, the Middle Passage led back to Africa. If David George had had his way, he would have voluntarily undertaken a Middle Passage from Africa to Jamaica. Fortunately for Liele, George, Marrant, and King, despite intense American pressure, the British felt honor-bound to evacuate from Savannah, Charleston, and New York City those to whom they had promised freedom. After the war, most present and former slaves in the British Empire saw Britain and not the new United States as the promised land of freedom. All of these authors stress that they chose to be subjects of the British monarch, and demonstrated their loyalty by serving in his military forces. Equiano refers to "England, where my heart had always been" (147), and writing from the Sierra Leone settlement in Africa, David George calls England his "home" (343).

Although the post–American Revolution diaspora was a relatively very small part of the larger eighteenth-century African diaspora, and although the diasporan authors from Georgia and South Carolina were few in number, the eighteenth-century black diaspora from the lowcountry played a pivotal role in the development of transatlantic black literature. By the 1780s, conditions in the lowcountry allowed a British public to congratulate themselves on having offered freedom and new identities to the enslaved who had fled their rebel owners to join the British cause. Perhaps Marrant, Liele, and George, or their amanuenses, as well as King and Equiano, all felt that simply describing those horrible conditions in ostensibly ameliorationist texts rendered the stories of their lives implicitly emancipationist as well. The lowcountry of Georgia and South Carolina has a strong claim to be recognized as the site where the African American slave narrative originated, even though the words and actions of all the founders of that genre show that they "determined never more to revisit it."[26]

NOTES

I am very grateful to Queen Mary, University of London, for a Distinguished Visiting Fellowship, which enabled me to complete the research and writing of this essay. I am greatly indebted to the staffs and collections of the British Library, the British National Archives, the Charleston County Public Library, the Georgia Historical Society, the Houghton and Widener Libraries at Harvard University, the Library of Congress, and McKeldin Library, University of Maryland. I thank Philip D. Morgan and the two anonymous readers for the University of Georgia Press for their comments on earlier versions of this essay. I am particularly grateful for the aid and support of Dr. Nicholas Butler and Henry Louis Gates Jr.

1. All seven accounts that cover the period from the author's birth to the time of narration are reproduced in Vincent Carretta, ed., *Unchained Voices: An Anthology of Black Authors in the English-Speaking World of the Eighteenth Century*, rev. ed. (Lexington: University Press of Kentucky, 2004. Two of the accounts have no lowcountry associations: *A Narrative of the Most Remarkable Particulars In the Life of James Albert Ukawsaw Gronniosaw, an African Prince, As Related by Himself* (Bath, England, 1772), and *A Narrative of the Life and Adventures of Venture, a Native of Africa: But Resident above Sixty Years in the United States of America. Related by Himself* (New London, Connecticut, 1798).

2. The documents reporting that Equiano was born in South Carolina are reproduced and discussed in Vincent Carretta, *Equiano, the African: Biography of a Self-Made Man* (2005; repr., New York: Penguin, 2007). The most recent argument that Equiano was born an Ibo in Africa is made by Paul Lovejoy, "Autobiography and Memory: Gustavus Vassa, alias Olaudah Equiano, the African," *Slavery and Abolition* 28 (2006): 317–47. For what I see as significant flaws in Lovejoy's argument and methodology, and Lovejoy's reaction, see my "Response" and his "Rejoinder," *Slavery and Abolition* 28 (2007): 115–25. A fuller and more balanced treatment than Lovejoy's of the question of Equiano's birthplace is in Alexander Byrd, "Eboe, Country, Nation and Gustavus Vassa's *Interesting Narrative*," *William and Mary Quarterly* 63 (2006): 123–48.

3. Historians disagree about the degree to which people of African descent in the Upper South and lowcountry embraced Christianity before 1800. Those arguing that the conversion rate was very low include Albert J. Raboteau, *Slave Religion: The "Invisible Institution" in the Antebellum South* (New York: Oxford University Press, 1978); Marvin L. Kay and Michael and Lorin Lee Cary, *Slavery in North Carolina, 1748–1775* (Chapel Hill: University of North Carolina Press, 1995). Those arguing that the rate was significantly higher include Mechal Sobel, *Trabelin' On: The Slave*

Journey to an Afro-Baptist Faith (Westport, Conn.: Greenwood Press, 1979); Nathan O. Hatch, *Democratization of American Christianity* (New Haven, Conn.: Yale University Press, 1989); Sylvia R. Frey and Betty Wood, *Come Shouting to Zion: African American Protestantism in the American South and British Caribbean to 1830* (Chapel Hill: University of North Carolina Press, 1998); Philip D. Morgan, *Slave Counterpoint: Black Culture in the Eighteenth-Century Chesapeake and Lowcountry* (Chapel Hill: University of North Carolina Press, 1998); Dickson D. Bruce Jr., *The Origins of African American Literature, 1680–1865* (Charlottesville: University Press of Virginia, 2001); Thomas S. Kidd, *The Great Awakening: The Roots of Evangelical Christianity in Colonial America* (New Haven, Conn.: Yale University Press, 2007).

For the importance of the American Revolution in the lives of former slaves, see Simon Schama, *Rough Crossings: Britain, the Slaves and the American Revolution* (New York: HarperCollins, 2006); Cassandra Pybus, *Epic Journeys of Freedom: Runaway Slaves of the American Revolution and Their Global Quest for Freedom* (Boston: Beacon Press, 2006).

4. John Sekora, "Black Message/White Envelope: Genre, Authenticity, and Authority in the Antebellum Slave Narrative," *Callaloo* 32 (Summer 1987): 482–515.

5. I thank Philip D. Morgan for bringing this statistic to my attention.

6. On Huntingdon, see Edwin Welch, *Spiritual Pilgrim: A Reassessment of the Life of the Countess of Huntingdon* (Cardiff: University of Wales Press, 1995); Boyd Stanley Schlenther, "'To Convert the Poor People in America': The Bethesda Orphanage and the Thwarted Zeal of the Countess of Huntingdon," *Georgia Historical Quarterly* 77 (Summer 1994): 225–56; Boyd Stanley Schlenther, *Queen of the Methodists: The Countess of Huntingdon and the Eighteenth-Century Crisis of Faith and Society* (Durham, U.K.: Durham Academic Press, 1997).

7. All quotations from Equiano's writings, cited parenthetically, are taken from *The Interesting Narrative and Other Writings*, rev. ed., ed. Vincent Carretta (New York: Penguin, 2003).

8. All quotations from *Marrant's Narrative*, cited parenthetically, are taken from Carretta, *Unchained Voices*.

9. I am indebted for this information to Dr. Nicholas Butler, Special Collections manager, Charleston County Public Library.

10. Marrant's *Journal* and other writings are included in Joanna Brooks and John Saillant, eds., *"Face Zion Forward": First Writers of the Black Atlantic, 1785–1798* (Boston: Northeastern University Press, 2002).

11. All quotations from Liele's "Account," cited parenthetically, are taken from Carretta, ed., *Unchained Voices*.

12. John Clark, Walter Dendy, and James M. Phillippo, *The Voice of Jubilee: A Narrative of the Baptist Mission, Jamaica, from its Commencement* (London, 1865), 31–32.

13. See Grant Gordon, *The Life of David George* (Hantsport, Nova Scotia: Lancelot Press, 1992).

14. Lambeth Palace Library, London, Newton Papers MS 2935, ff. 270r–272v: Macaulay to Newton, June 3, 1797.

15. See *The Life of Boston King: Black Loyalist, Minister and Master Carpenter*, ed. Ruth Holmes Whitehead and Carmelita A. M. Robertson (Halifax: Nimbus Publishing Limited and the Nova Scotia Museum, 2003), 3.

16. All quotations from King's "Memoirs," cited parenthetically, are taken from Carretta, ed., *Unchained Voices*.

17. Equiano's account of his times spent in the lowcountry can be verified, corrected, and supplemented by archival sources, as well as by the *Georgia Gazette*, hereafter cited parenthetically in the text as *GG*.

18. William Gibbons Jr. Papers, 1765–68 file, 1769 file, William R. Perkins Library, Duke University; Telfair Papers, 1775, Georgia Historical Society, Savannah, in Betty Wood, *Slavery in Colonial Georgia, 1730–1775* (Athens: University of Georgia Press, 1984), 152, 153. Woods does not mention Equiano, but cites several examples of Dr. Brydie's giving medical treatment to slaves between 1765 and 1775. I have found no references to a "Dr. Brady" in the relevant archives or the *Georgia Gazette*.

19. In a June 3, 1766, petition for a grant of additional land adjoining the property of James Mossman, Read says that he needs it to sustain his "Wife, five Children, and fifty Negroes" (*The Colonial Records of the State of Georgia*, Vol. 9: *Proceedings of the Minutes of the Governor and Council, January 4, 1763, to December 2, 1766* [Atlanta: Franklin-Turner, 1907], 513).

20. *The Colonial Records of the State of Georgia*, Vol. 9: *Proceedings of the Minutes of the Governor and Council, January 4, 1763, to December 2, 1766* (Atlanta: Franklin-Turner, 1907), 179, 302.

21. *The Colonial Records of the State of Georgia*, Vol. 10: *Proceedings of the Minutes of the Governor and Council, January 6, 1767, to December 5, 1769* (Atlanta: Franklin-Turner, 1907), 647, 648.

22. On Equiano's allusions to Moses, see Eileen Razzari Elrod, "Moses and the Egyptian: Religious Authority in Olaudah Equiano's *Interesting Narrative*," *African American Review* 35 (Fall 2001): 409–25; George Boulukos, *The Grateful Slave: The Emergence of Race in Eighteenth-Century British and American Culture* (Cambridge: Cambridge University Press, 2008). On Equiano's allusions to Moses and John Milton's *Paradise Lost*, see Vincent Carretta, "Equiano's Paradise Lost," in *Imagining Transatlantic Slavery*, ed. J. R. Oldfield and Cora Kaplan (London: Palgrave, forthcoming).

23. On the effects in Britain of its defeat in the American Revolution, see Linda Colley, *Britons: Forging the Nation, 1707–1837* (New Haven, Conn.: Yale University Press, 1992); Carretta, *Equiano, the African*; Christopher Leslie Brown, *Moral Capital: Foundations of British Abolitionism* (Chapel Hill: University of North Carolina Press, 2006).

24. Of the five lowcountry authors, only Equiano — the least constrained by the mediation of whites, the most concerned with the ongoing transatlantic slave trade, and the only one who claims not to have born in North America — treats West Indian slavery at length.

25. Morgan, *Slave Counterpoint*, 267.

26. Equiano, *Interesting Narrative*, 160.

Michael A. Gomez

Africans, Culture, and Islam
in the Lowcountry

THE HISTORY and experience of African Muslims and their descendants is critical to understanding the lowcountry. Long viewed as the source and reservoir of Gullah culture, it is now clear that coastal islands such as Sapelo, St. Simons, St. Helena, and their environs were also the collective site of the largest gathering of African Muslims in early North America, establishing a legacy that continues to the present day.

We learn a great deal about these Muslims through advertisements for enslaved runaways, as they contain unique and substantial information on individual ethnic and cultural traits. These advertisements are important in part because they occasionally provide names that are clearly Muslim but rarely identified as such.[1] Names such as Bullaly (Bilali), Mustapha, Sambo, Bocarrey (Bukhari, or possibly Bubacar from Abu Bakr), and Mamado (Mamadu) are regularly observed in the advertisements for runaway slaves. Unless slaveholders clearly understood the origin of these names, they would not necessarily associate them with Islam.[2] A good example of this concerns the name Sambo or Samba, which can mean "second son" in the language of the Hausa and Fulbe.[3] The January 9–12, 1782, publication of Charleston's *Royal Gazette* sought the return of Sambo, or Sam, described as having a "yellowish complexion . . . and his hair is pretty long, being of the Fulla country."[4] The connections between Sambo, Islam, and the Fulbe become even more apparent when the preceding advertisement is juxtaposed with another notice in which a decidedly Muslim name is identified with the same ethnicity: the June 17, 1766, edition of Charleston's *South-Carolina Gazette and Country Journal* features an ad in which Robert Darrington sought the return of one "Moosa, a yellow Fellow . . . is of the Fullah Country."⁵ A final example comes from the May 24, 1775, edition of Savannah's *Georgia Gazette*, in which appeared a notice for three missing men, including twenty-two-year-old Sambo, reportedly "of the Moorish country."⁶ This association with the Moorish country may be more a reference to Sambo's Muslim identity than to his actually having hailed from North Africa, but it should be borne in mind that Moors, or Arabo-Berbers from Mauritania and elsewhere in North Africa, were in fact also imported into North America.⁷

The appearance of incontestably Muslim names in the runaway slave notices is relatively infrequent. More commonly, slaveholders seeking the return of runaways associated them with particular regions of origin (for example, Gambia or Senegal) or provided an ethnic identity (such as Mandingo or Fula). The *Charleston Courier*, for example, advertised the finding of a "new Negro BOY, of the Fullah nation, says his name is Adam."⁸ In the case of supposed region of origin or ethnic derivation, one cannot conclusively argue that the individual in question is Muslim, but given both the African background and the tendency among American planters to conflate Muslims, ethnicity, and region of origin, the probability is high that many of these persons were Muslims.

In addition to runaway slave advertisements, Muslim identity and naming patterns come together in an intriguing fashion in the slave registers of the John Stapleton plantation at Frogmore on St. Helena Island, South Carolina.⁹ In May 1816, a list of the 135 enslaved persons on the Frogmore estate was drawn up, on which the following individuals appear: Sambo, eighty-five years old and African-born; Dido, a fifty-six-year-old "Moroccan"; Mamoodie and his wife Eleanor, both African-born and age twenty-eight and twenty-nine, respectively; and the family of Nelson, Venus, and child Harriett. Sambo and Dido were probably Muslim. Mamoodie and Eleanor had a child named Fatima in 1814 (who died in infancy), so they were very likely Muslim also. The more interesting individuals are Nelson and Venus, who were twenty-nine and twenty-seven, respectively, and both African-born. In a subsequent enslaved list drawn up in 1818, their child Hammett appears. Hammett (Hamid or Ahmad) is a Muslim name, which would suggest that one or both of the parents were Muslim. Again, the remaining names on the 1816 list are not African, but twenty-eight people are listed as African-born. It is therefore possible that others were Muslim, as Nelson or Venus may have been, but the absence of a corroborating Hammett prevents any such identification.

That many examples of Muslim runaways come from South Carolina and Georgia, especially along the coast, is due to the role of Charleston (and Savannah) as a preeminent slave port, surrounded by major slaveholding areas devoted to rice and indigo cultivation.[10] Senegambians and Sierra Leonians, possibly in great demand for their agricultural skills, tended to come from areas in which there was a Muslim presence. Given their alleged preference for enslaved persons from these areas and distaste for Africans from the Bight of Biafra, South Carolina and Georgia planters paid close attention to ethnicity. In contrast, Virginia planters may not have been as discriminating, and their alleged indifference to ethnicity, as opposed to any actual disproportion, may explain the relative absence of references to Muslims from Senegambia and Sierra Leone.[11]

Consistent with the preponderance of runaway notices featuring Muslims in South Carolina and Georgia newspapers is the quantitatively greater amount of information available on Muslims and their descendants living along the Georgia coast, both on the various sea islands and on the mainland near Savannah. The data provide a rare glimpse into the lives of African-born Muslims, their progeny, and the associated community of believers. What emerges is an incomplete but substantive picture of individuals who pursued their religion with diligence and purpose, and this in an atmosphere charged with Christian catechism and the allure of competing African religions. There is even evidence of non-Muslim Africans converting to Islam. And the manner in which the grandchildren and subsequent progeny of these African-born Muslims relate their stories betrays considerable pride and admiration, suggesting a strong and clear identification with an Islamic heritage, if not an actual embrace of the religion.

To begin, it would appear that the number of enslaved Muslims in this area was significant indeed. In May 1802, for example, two Muslim men named Alik and Abdalli escaped from Sapelo Island; both men were likely African-born, as one spoke "bad English" and the other's facility in the idiom was only slightly better.[12] Toney, Jacob, and eighteen-year-old Musa also escaped from Sapelo Island in March 1807, contesting the proprietary claims of one Alexander Johnston.[13] Conceivably, all three men were Muslim.

Reference to Sapelo Island underscores the fact that Sapelo, along with

St. Simons Island, was the conjoined site for the most important Muslim community in Georgia–South Carolina and, arguably, the whole of antebellum North America. The famous Hopeton plantation on St. Simons was one of a number (both on the island and along the Altamaha River) owned by John Couper (1759–1850) and his son James Hamilton Couper (1794–1866). In an 1827 document detailing the sale of Hopeton by John Couper to James Hamilton (a close friend) and his son James, 381 names of the enslaved are listed.[14] Of these names, Fatima is repeated six times, Mahomet twice, and there is one Maryam, all probably Muslims. However, the principal Muslim on the plantation was Salih Bilali, who is listed as "Tom" in the document. How many more Muslims were at Hopeton cannot be discerned from the available data, but there probably were others whose Islamic identities are hidden behind such anglicized monikers. Indeed, James Hamilton Couper himself wrote that "there are about a dozen negroes on this plantation, who speak and understand the Foulah language; but with one exception, they appear not to have been native born Foulahs, and to have acquired the language, by having been for sometime in servitude among that nation."[15] Hamilton's conjecture that many speaking Pulaar had been first enslaved in West Africa, while speculative, is quite possible.

Salih Bilali remained a devout Muslim his entire life. Born around 1765, he grew up in Maasina, along the upper Niger valley.[16] Initially captured around 1790, Salih Bilali was eventually taken south and sold at Anomabu, along the Gold Coast. That he exited West Africa from Anomabu rather than the Senegambian coast, the anticipated site of embarkation for captives from the upper Niger, suggests the variety of options available to those trafficking in such captives.[17] Arriving in the Bahamas, he was repurchased around 1800 and brought to Hopeton plantation on St. Simons, where by 1816 (at the age of fifty-one) he was the head driver at Cannon's Point Plantation. His acclaim arose from his considerable managerial skills; such were his abilities and his reliability that the plantation owner left Salih Bilali in charge of the entire plantation for months at a time, absent any other supervision. The date of Salih Bilali's death is uncertain, but it may have been in the late 1850s.

Ben Sullivan was eighty-eight and living on St. Simons when interviewed by the Works Progress Administration (WPA) in the 1930s.[18] He was the grandson of Salih Bilali, and his father's name was "Belali," an indication of the grandfather's desire to pass on his Islamic identity. In addition to his father and grandfather, Ben Sullivan (Bilal ibn Sulayman?) remembered two other Muslims in the community, "Ole Israel" and Daphne. Concerning the former, Ben reported: "Ole Israel he pray a lot wid a book he hab wut he hide, and he take a lill mat an he say prayuhs on it. He pray wen duh sun go up and wen duh sun go down. . . . He alluz tie he head up in a wite clawt an seem he keep a lot uh clawt on hand." The book to which Sullivan refers may well have been the Qur'ān. Daphne also prayed regularly, bowing "two aw tree times in duh middle uh duh prayuh," a clear reference to prescribed Muslim prayer in which *rak'a* and *sujūd* (bowing and prostration) are performed. Daphne, described as having a visage that was "shahp-feechuh . . . an light uh complexion," also wore a veil.

On nearby Sapelo Island was the large plantation of Thomas Spalding (1774–1851), the driver of which was Salih Bilali's coreligionist and contemporary Bilali (d. 1859, pronounced "Blali" in the Sapelo community), also referred to as "the Old Man."[19] Otherwise known as known as "Ben Ali," Bilali originated somewhere in "Guinea" and, like Salih Bilali, may have spent time in the Bahamas before he was brought to Sapelo (perhaps the two met in the Bahamas, if not before).[20] Also like Salih Bilali, Bilali was a dependable driver who was called upon to manage the Sapelo plantation of four or five hundred enslaved persons.[21] He is perhaps most noted for an extant collection of excerpts from an Islamic, Maliki legal text known as the *Risāla* of Ibn Abī Zayd.[22] Bilali also served as the model for Joel Chandler Harris's caricature "Ben Ali."[23]

As one observer stated in 1901, based upon her memories of the late 1850s, Bilali's large family of twelve sons and seven daughters all "worshiped Mahomet."[24] Some details of their religious practices are provided by Katie Brown, who at the time of the WPA interviews was "one of the oldest inhabitants" of Sapelo Island.[25] She was also the great-granddaughter of Bilali, or "Belali Mahomet." She enumerated Bilali's seven daughters as "Margret, Bentoo, Chaalut, Medina, Yaruba, Fatima, and Hestuh," most identifiably Muslim names. Margaret was the grandmother of Katie Brown, who went on to say:

> Magret an uh daughter Cotto use tuh say dat Bilali an he wife Phoebe pray on duh bead. Dey wuz bery puhticluh bout duh time dey pray and dey bery regluh bout duh hour. Wen duh sun come up, wen it straight obuh head an wen it set, das duh time dey pray. Dey bow tuh duh sun an hab lill mat tuh kneel on. Duh beads is on a long string. Belali he pull bead an he say, "Belambi, Hakabara, Mahamadu." Phoebe she say, "Ameen, Ameen."[26]

Margaret also wore a head covering that extended to her shoulders, a practice emulated by Katie (whose head covering, however, was not as elaborate). In addition to such observances, it would seem that Bilali adhered to Islamic prescriptions concerning marriage, as Brown remarked, "Magret she say Phoebe he wife, but maybe he hab mone one wife. I spects das bery possible."[27]

It would also appear that there was some attempt to adhere to Islamic dietary proscriptions. Information is rather meager on this question, but Cornelia Bailey offers a glimpse with her observation that Bilali's children would not eat "wild" animals or "fresh" meat, and that seafood such as crab was avoided, as were certain kinds of fish.[28]

Taken together, the testimonies of Ben Sullivan, Cornelia Bailey, and Katie Brown provide the essential contours of Muslim life in early Georgia — prayer mats, prayer beads, veiling, Qur'āns, dietary regulations, and daily, ritualized prayer. The composite picture is consistent with a serious pursuit of Islam.

Nothing is known about Bilali's twelve sons, which suggests either a breakup of the family in the Bahamas (assuming they were there), or an idealization resulting from iconographic forces that helped shape his memory. However, his daughters are verifiable persons who were possibly African-born and forced into captivity along with their parents, and were just as religious.[29] Shad Hall of Sapelo, another descendant of Bilali through his grandmother Hestuh (Esther?), describes the daughters as follows: "Hestuh an all ub um sho pray on duh bead. Dey weah duh string uh beads on duh wais. Sometime duh string on duh neck. Dey pray at sun-up and face duh sun on duh knees an bow tuh it tree times, kneelin' on a lill mat."[30]

A sense of a closely knit community emerges from these interviews. Katie Brown refers to Salih Bilali of St. Simons as "cousin Belali Sullivan." Shad Hall states that his grandmother Hestuh bore a son called "Belali Smith," who in turn was Phoebe Gilbert's grandfather, also a Sapelo resident.[31] Phoebe Gilbert's other set of grandparents were Calina and Hannah, both of whom were Ibo. Sapelo inhabitant Nero Jones was also related to "Uncle Calina and An Hannah" and says that they were "mighty puhticuluh bout prayin. Dey pray on duh bead. Duh ole man he say 'Ameela' and An Hannah she say 'Hakabara.'"[32] The last quote is fascinating, for it strongly suggests that Calina and Hannah converted to Islam in America, as the Ibo of southeastern Nigeria were not Muslim.[33] Furthermore, the Ibo population in early America was substantial but never identified with Islam.

Sapelo also provides evidence of cultural practices primarily associated with Muslim women that were derivative of West African Islamic societies. The evidence centers around the production and significance of "saraka" cakes which, according to Diouf, are often distributed during Ramadan in fulfillment of the requirement to pay alms or *zakāt*. Diouf further argues

> there is little doubt that these words [*sakara/saraka*] are slight corruptions of the Arabic word *sadakha*. *Sadakha* are voluntary alms that the believer offers to acquire merit with Allah. . . . The Sea Islands *saraka* and the Brazilian *saka* are the exact transportation to America of an African Muslim custom. The rice ball is the traditional charity given by West African women on Fridays. . . . The cake is still made in West Africa in the same way that Bilali's daughter made hers. . . . The confection of the rice cakes represents the only recorded example of Islamic behavior specifically expressed by slave women. As slaves, as women, as Africans, and as Muslims, Muslim women did not receive much attention during and after slavery.[34]

Such tradition appears to relate to customs recorded in Trinidad and Brazil, where (at least in Trinidad) a portion of the prepared foods included rice sweetened with sugar.[35] At least two of Bilali's daughters, Margaret and Hestuh, participated in his hemispheric-wide custom. According to granddaughter Katie Brown, Margaret

> make funny flat cake she call "saraka." She make um same day ebry yeah, an it big day. Wen dey finish, she call us in, all duh chillun, an put in hans lill flat cake an we eats it. Yes'm, I membuh how she make it. She wash rice, an po off all duh watuh. She let rice sit all night, an in mawnin rice is all swell. She tak dat rice an put it in wooden mawtuh, an beat it tuh paste wid wooden pestle. She add honey, sometime shuguh, an make it in flat cake wid uh hans. "Saraka" she call um.[36]

Shad Hall's "Gran Hestuh" also made a "strange cake, fus ub ebry munt. She call it 'saraka.' She make it out uh meal an honey. . . . Sometime she make it out uh rice." Those times during which *saraka* was prepared were clearly special occasions, the Islamic nature of which was underscored by Hestuh's invocation of "Ameen, Ameen, Ameen" prior to the cake's consumption.[37]

Islam along coastal Georgia was by no means confined to the descendants of Bilali and Salih Bilali. The WPA interviews of Ed Thorpe of Harris Neck, Rachel and Alec Anderson and Rosa Grant of Possum Point, and Lawrence Baker of Darien reveal that their ancestors were also Muslim.[38]

Like the Bilali families, these early Muslims prayed three times daily, ending their prayers with "Ameen, Ameen, Ameen." In fact, Rosa Grant says of her grandmother Ryna that "Friday wuz duh day she call huh prayuh day." This is not a reference to daily prayer, for Grant had already stated that her grandmother's prayers began "ebry mawnin." Rather, this is a reference to the Muslim observance of Friday prayer, at which time Muslims congregate in the early afternoon. Whether Grant and others actually gathered for the prayer is not known, but she at least attempted to keep alive the significance of the day.

Despite the vitality of the Islamic tradition and the strength of their bonds, Muslims in early Georgia–South Carolina faced certain distinct challenges to the preservation of their faith. For although they may have gathered in small numbers and clandestine places to pray, they could not openly maintain Qur'ānic schools or *madrasas*, nor did they have access to Islamic texts. It was inevitable that their collective memory would eventually falter. As an example, Bilali, author of the "Ben-Ali Diary," put together passages from Ibn Abī Zayd's *Risāla* in such a haphazard way that Nigerian clerics, upon reviewing the document, declared it to be the work of *jinn* (spirits).[39] Likewise, Salih Bilali, although claiming to possess a Qur'ān, apparently could not write Arabic coherently.[40] Allowing for exceptional cases such as Bilali's, the gradual loss of Islamic knowledge, combined with the parochial application of Arabic to religious discourse, constituted a blow to the continuation of Islam in the early American South.

Additional challenges to Islam include the fact that it was in competition with other African religions, especially prior to the nineteenth century. In the American South, most Africans adhered to non-Islamic beliefs. The host society, although at times amused by religious variations, became increasingly concerned with controlling the religion of its captive population as the nineteenth century progressed. The gradual increase in the number of Christian converts among African Americans resulted from both their own desire to embrace an Africanized version of Christianity, together with a campaign within the post-1830 militant South to use religion as a means of social control. As Africanized Christianity slowly became a force, Islam suffered.

The process by which Christianity began to compete with and eventually overtake Islam can be viewed in the Sapelo community. The progeny of African-born Muslims (who tended to restrict their social interactions with non-Muslims) eventually began attending the Tuesday, Thursday, and

Sunday night "prayer houses" held by each community on the island, while continuing with their own Muslim gatherings. With the establishment of the First African Baptist Church in May 1866, however, the open and collective pursuit of Islam became increasingly rare, although it is difficult to say when, exactly, it ended on the island.[41]

In addition to the impact of Christianity, it should be noted that ethnocentricity, combined with other cultural differences, probably restricted efforts at proselytization among non-Muslims. Continuity of the Islamic tradition was heavily dependent upon a cultural transfer within existing Muslim families and over generations. This was a formidable task, especially as the importation of non-Muslims into North America greatly exceeded that of Muslims in the late eighteenth and early nineteenth centuries; many Muslims had little choice except to marry non-Muslims. Further, African-born Muslims may have been unable to effectively communicate with their children and grandchildren and would have been frustrated in their attempts to convey the tenets of Islam adequately.[42] Enslavement itself introduced structural impediments to such matters as a formal education, circumcision, the formation of brotherhoods, the maintenance of moral proscriptions, and the observance of basic dietary rules. The children of African Muslims would have been socialized within the context of the larger, non-Muslim slave culture and deeply influenced by this process. In short, Muslims would have had great difficulty in preserving Islam within their families, assuming a stable enslaved family. With Louisiana as a possible exception, such an assumption is most unwarranted.[43]

It is therefore with the children and grandchildren of African-born Muslims that questions concerning the resilience of Islam take on significance. While it cannot be established with certainty that the progeny were Muslim, the Islamic heritage was certainly there; individuals bore Muslim names and retained a keen memory of the religious practices of their ancestors. However, their reluctance to be unequivocal on the question of their own adherence to Islam can be observed in the responses of Georgian coastal blacks to queries posed by WPA interviewers. Indeed, a careful review of these interviews reveals considerable anxiety among the informants, understandable given the politics of the time. If they were practicing Muslims, they were certainly not going to tell whites in the rural South of the 1930s.[44]

One account given by the interviewers underscores the ambiguity of religious affinities and supports the contention that the informants did not reveal all. It concerns one Preacher Little, who was encountered on Sapelo Island and whose physical appearance, demeanor, and dress were initially described as "Mohammedan looking."[45] Although the interviewers were subsequently assured that the minister was Christian (and they went on to witness the minister preside over a religious service), their first impressions are instructive, especially as this encounter took place after the interviews with the descendants of Salih Bilali and Bilali. Preacher Little may have been a Muslim who dissembled in the interviewers' presence, but he could have also been the embodiment of a certain Islamic-Christian synthesis. Indeed, this possibility is enhanced by the reflections of Charles Jones in 1842, who wrote that African-born Muslims related Yahweh to Allah and Jesus to Muhammad.[46] His observation contains a number of potential meanings, including the possibility that Africans, while ostensibly practicing Christianity, were in reality reinterpreting Christian dogma in light of Islamic precepts. If Jones was correct, such correlations were probably more Muslim than Christian in their worldview, since Islam had already shaped their perspective. It is therefore conceivable that their descendants may have continued this kind of syncretism (or dissimulation).

A further example again comes from Sapelo and the descendants of Bilali.[47] Cornelia Bailey's grandmother would tell the former about the life of Harriet Hall Grovner, Bailey's great-grandmother and the granddaughter of Bentoo, Bilali's daughter. Harriet was a practicing Muslim until the First African Baptist Church was organized in 1866, at which time she joined. Although she became very active in the Sunday school, it is possible that, because she frequently retreated into the woods to pray, she was also practicing Islam, since she would have had no reason to continue her clandestine activities unless she was praying something other than Christian prayers. The fact that Harriet died in 1922 and may have still been practicing Islam at such a late date and as a direct legacy of an African Islamic tradition is highly significant, for as such she would have been an organic link to an African Muslim past while at the same time contemporaneous with the dawn of Islamically informed movements among African Americans in the early twentieth century.

Evidence for the Muslim presence in the American South is also supported by reference to the African background. Senegambia was the major source of Muslims for the American South, supplying as much as 23.6 percent of the entire trade volume to North America, nearly the same as that of West Central Africa (with 23.7 percent).[48] Of the estimated 210,477 enslaved persons imported into the Carolinas and Georgia, some 44,682, or 21 percent of the total, hailed from Senegambia, an immense region where coastal populations began converting to Islam en masse late in the eighteenth century, though smaller Muslim communities had been there for many centuries.[49] Sierra Leone and the Windward Coast were also sources of the enslaved, supplying 17.1 percent of the total number imported, followed by the Gold Coast (present-day Ghana), supplying some 14.5 percent of the total trade to North America.[50] Finally, the Bight of Benin contributed some 2.3 percent to North America's total volume.[51] Stretching from the Volta to the Benin River, the area witnessed struggles in the 1780s and 1790s that, along with *jihadic* activity in (what is now) northern and southwestern Nigeria in the first third of the nineteenth century, produced numerous captives. Mississippi slaveholders spoke of preferences for Africans "of the Bornon, Houssa, Zanfara, Zegzeg, Kapina, and Tombootoo tribes."[52]

These five regions constitute the zones from which the overwhelming majority of Muslims came to the American South, and supplied approximately 57.6 percent of all those imported to North America. Thus, of the estimated 388,747 Africans imported into British North America during the slave trade, nearly 224,182 came from areas influenced by Islam. It is therefore reasonable to conclude that Muslims arrived in North America by the thousands, if not tens of thousands.[53]

It would be a mistake, however, to solely focus on the Muslim population, as Islam's influence in West Africa was not confined to the converted, practicing community. Many non-Muslims were acquainted with a number of its tenets through the activities of Muslim traders and clerics. The Muslim trading networks, through which the Juula, Yarse, and Hausa merchants supplied disparate West African communities with goods from as far away as the Mediterranean, also linked the savannah with the forest area, from Senegambia to Lake Chad. Their apolitical, nonproselytizing code of conduct also helps to explain the receptivity of many Muslim and non-Muslim communities to their commercial endeavors. At the same time, Muslim clerics performed religious and diplomatic services for royal courts and commoners alike, providing amulets for both Muslims and non-Muslim. Mosques and *madrasas* (Qur'ānic schools) were invariably established in the Muslim part of town or in the nearby Muslim village, and as a result, many non-Muslims were exposed to Muslim dress, dietary laws, and overall conduct.[54]

To be sure, it was not unusual for those who had converted to Islam to retain aspects of their previous beliefs; Islam in West Africa underwent a number of reforms in an effort to achieve orthodoxy.[55] However, to the degree that these non-Islamic tendencies were not in conflict with the fundamental tenets of the faith (one God, Muhammad as God's messenger, daily prayer, fasting during Ramadan, and so on), the integrity of these practitioners and the veracity of their confession is not open to challenge.

One of the more interesting aspects of the Muslim experience in the early American South was the impact of this religious community upon the process of stratification within African and African American society. Given that it was largely a society of the enslaved, such stratification began with the perception of the slaveholders. Vis-à-vis other Africans, Muslims were generally viewed by slaveholders as "more intelligent, more reasonable, more physically attractive, more dignified people."[56] Phillips has written that planters found the Senegalese to be the most intelligent, as they "had a strong Arabic strain in their ancestry."[57] William Dunbar, a prominent Natchez planter, specifically preferred Muslims from what would become northern Nigeria over Senegambians, but the former were Muslims nonetheless.[58] The belief in the superiority of the "Mohammedans" was a consistently held view throughout the Colonial and antebellum periods. As an example, Salih Bilali is described as "a man of superior intelligence and higher cast of feature."[59] To a great extent, this view of the Muslim was informed by the physical appearance of the Fulbe and certain Mande speakers, who were believed to be phenotypically closer to Europeans than other Africans.[60] European travelers invariably commented upon Fulbe features: Gray and Dochard described them as "much resembling the European," as did Callié, whereas Jobson stated that the Fulbe were "a Tawny people, and have a resemblance right unto those we call Egyptians."[61]

As a result of their experience and perceived advantage, as well as for reasons to be explored shortly, many Muslims in the early American South were given more supervisory responsibilities and privileges than other slaves. Alford writes that Muslim slaves were used as "drivers, overseers, and confidential servants with a frequency their numbers did not justify."[62] Prime examples of Muslim privilege include the careers of Bilali and Salih Bilali, who were both placed in positions of high authority and used that authority to jointly quell a slave insurrection. Zephaniah Kingsley Jr., a slaveholder who advocated the "benign" treatment of the enslaved, recorded that along the Georgia coast during the War of 1812, there were "two instances, to the southward, where gangs of negroes were prevented from deserting to the enemy [England] by drivers, or influential negroes, whose integrity to their masters and influence over the slaves prevented it; and what is still more remarkable, in both instances the influential negroes were Africans; and professors of the Mahomedan religion," an apparent reference to Bilali and Salih Bilali.[63] Not only did they crush the revolt but, as previously mentioned, Bilali defended Sapelo Island in 1813 with eighty armed slaves, preventing access to the English. It is likely that the great majority of these eighty persons were Muslim, given the extensive nature of Islam in the Georgia–South Carolina coastal corridor, combined with Bilali's statement that he could depend only upon fellow Muslims, as opposed to the general enslaved population whom he characterized as "Christian dogs."[64]

Bilali and Salih Bilali appear to have served as models for a character named "Old King" in an otherwise crude apologist literature published in 1853.[65] Old King had come to a North American coastal island as an enslaved adult and as a "Mahomedan," and was subjected to both the company of "pagan negroes" and the authority of "Christian dogs," a phrase resonating with preceding testimony. He soon became a "lord of the Isle," who in "retirement" carried himself with the "dignity of a retired field-marshal, and the authority of a patriarch," having served as a driver during his productive years. Such was his prestige and elevated status that even the slaveholder treated him with respect, demonstrated by an imagined conversion in which the slaveholder deferentially asks him to show an overseer how to prepare a field (appropriately named King-field). In the conversation, Old King addresses the holder by his first name, and initially replies, "I'll think about it Jacob, and let you know in the morning." The slaveholder is greeted the next day by King's deliberation: "I am sorry to disappoint you, Jacob, but I have concluded not to go to King-field this morning," to which the holder eventually responded, "Really, King, I thought certainly you would be more obliging." The holder's disappointment turns to cheer when King elects to compromise. Such an embellishment of the Bilali–Salih Bilali legacy, whereby it assumed mythlike proportions, was premised upon the very real phenomenon of Muslim privilege, and for that reason enjoyed more than a sliver of plausibility.

As the careers of Bilali and Salih Bilali suggest, there were certain tensions between Muslim and non-Muslim slaves, whether the latter were African-born or not. In the first place, there is evidence that some American-born slaves condescended to newly arrived Africans.[66] To the extent that African Muslims encountered such a reception, they would have experienced pressures to modify or discontinue their Muslim/African practices in order to conform to what was acceptable in the new setting, or they would have found the resolve to remain faithful to their convictions. The evidence shows that, despite pressure from Christianity and African indigenous traditions, the majority resisted coercion to abandon their faith.[67] Stories of Muslim piety and determination include that of Salih Bilali, described by his owner as "the most religious man that he had ever known"; another depicted him as a "strict Mahometan" who refused alcohol, holding "in great contempt, the African belief in fetishes and evil spirits."[68]

With the foregoing in mind, it is not surprising to read of Bilali's characterization of his fellow (or actually subordinate) slaves as Christian dogs, a characterization that comports perfectly with statements by Abd ar-Rahman, a fellow Fulbe who was enslaved in Mississippi. Cyrus Griffin records Abd ar-Rahman's comments, in which "he states explicitly, and with an air of pride, that not a single drop of negro blood runs in his veins."[69] This attitude was confirmed by the children of Bilali, all of whom were Muslims, and who were described as "holding themselves aloof from the others as if they were conscious of their own superiority."[70] Bailey essentially verifies this, stating that not only did Bilali "keep his distance" from others because he "did not like mixing" with them, but that Muslims and non-Muslims as a whole tended to "keep to themselves," although they generally "got along" and could work together for specific purposes or special occasions.[71]

The attitude of Muslim superiority must first be explained within the context of the West African background. The fact that these people themselves had been slaveholders in the Old World influenced their view of the enslaved. The African experience was shaped along the lines of highly stratified societies in which the servile population was seen as inferior. The ethnic factor is relevant here as well, in that there are considerable data on the ethnocentricity of the Fulbe.[72] Originating long ago in present-day southern Mauritania, many of the Fulbe claim descent from the Arab general 'Uqba b. Nāfi', who in 667 led Muslim armies as far south as Kawar in the Fezzan.[73] This clear fiction reflects the larger truth of their mixed ancestry, resulting, in some instances, in the view of the non-Fulbe as inferior. Park remarked upon this attitude, stating that "the Foulahs of Bondou . . . evidently consider all the Negro natives as their inferiors, and when talking of different nations, always rank themselves among the white people."[74]

A second factor in explaining Muslim attitudes of superiority concerns Islam itself. To live as a Muslim in eighteenth- and nineteenth-century West Africa was to live in an increasingly intolerant society. This was the period of *jihād*, of the establishment of Muslim theocracies, of self-purification and separation from practices and beliefs seen as antithetical to Islam. Abu Bakr al-Siddiq of Jamaica summarized the perspective of the Muslim when he wrote:

> The faith of our families is the faith of Islam. They circumcise the foreskin; say the five prayers; fast every year in the month of Ramadan; give alms as ordained in the law; marry four free women — a fifth is forbidden to them except she be their slave; they fight for the faith of God; perform the pilgrimage to Mecca, i.e. such as are able to do so; eat the flesh of no beast but what they have slain for themselves; drink no wine, for whatever intoxicates is forbidden to them; they do not keep company with those whose faith is contrary to theirs, such as worshippers of idols.[75]

It is clear, then, that fundamental differences between Islam and other religions could have further militated against a uniform experience of enslavement, along with such considerations as regional differences, urban versus rural conditions, and so on.

But a third factor in Muslim attitudes of superiority is as important as the first two — namely, a number of these enslaved Muslims were from prominent backgrounds in West Africa. In fact, it was more common than not that West African Muslims were recipients of an Islamic education and were therefore literate, and the various documents that concern notable Muslims invariably comment on the fact that they could write in Arabic (or in Arabic script). From the observer's vantage point, this was quite incredible. However, it should be appreciated that literacy within the West African Muslim community was widespread; most Muslim villages and towns maintained Qur'ānic schools, to which boys and girls from ages seven to fourteen went for instruction.[76] Reducing such an educated elite to the status of slaves — a status shared with those of humble birth — was particularly demeaning.

Reflecting the pastoral background of many Africans and referring to considerations of differentiation within the servile condition, it is important to note that some of the enslaved Muslims were completely unaccustomed to agricultural labor. Dr. Collins remarked that the Muslims of Senegambia "are excellent for the care of cattle and horses, and for domestic service, though little qualified for the ruder labours of the field, to which they never ought to be applied."[77] The doctor's observations accord remarkably well with the 1903 report of a French official in Guinea, who wrote that "the Fula is poorly endowed by nature for physical labor, puny and sickly . . . with no resource other than cultivation by his slaves."[78] The aristocratic or pastoral background of some West Africans, combined with the aforementioned agricultural expertise of others, meant that Muslims were, in the eyes of the host society, better suited for domestic and/or supervisory roles, a determination that widened the schism between Muslim and non-Muslim. The early twentieth century provides evidence that Fulbe slaveholders viewed agricultural work as servile and beneath them; it may be that this attitude was present as early as the eighteenth century, so that decisions by North American planters to place the Fulbe and other Muslims in nonagricultural positions may have also been influenced by such sensibility.[79]

Finally, it is probable that some Muslims were deeply affected by racist views of whites toward other Africans, views that included a vision of the Fulbe as fundamentally different from and superior to others similarly enslaved, views consistent with "Lord" Lugard's 1903 assessment of domestic slavery in what would become northern Nigeria, where the enslaved populations in "the towns of Kano and Sokoto are ruled by *an alien race* who buy and sell the people of the country in large public slave markets."[80] In 1844, Hodgson wrote unequivocally that

> The Foulahs are *not* negroes. They differ essentially from the negro race, in all the characteristics which are marked by physical anthropology. They may be said to occupy the intermediate space betwixt the Arab and the Negro. All travelers concur in representing them as a distinct race, in moral as in physical traits. To their color, the various terms of *bronze, copper, reddish*, and sometimes *white* has been applied. They concur also in the report, that the Foulahs of every region represent themselves to be *white* men, and proudly assert their superiority to the black tribes, among whom they live.[81]

While acknowledging that the Fulbe's nappy hair placed them among the "oulotric" ("wooly haired") populations of the world, Hodgson insisted that this was an inconsequential feature.[82] In view of such sentiments, the Fulbe and other Muslims would have been encouraged to distance themselves from the average African and descendant of Africans, even to the point of denying any kindred relationship to them. If Abd ar-Rahman did not initiate the idea that he had no "negro blood," he certainly did not dispute the claim that he was a Moor; on the contrary, he placed "the negro in a scale of being infinitely below the Moor."[83] Mark Twain's view of Abd ar-Rahman, however, underscores the dilemma of those seeking an accommodation with such racism: the inescapability of blackness, and the unattainability of whiteness. Learning of Abd ar-Rahman's return to West Africa, the irascible Twain offered the following good wishes:

> I, for one, sincerely hope that after all his trials he is now peacefully enjoy-
> ing the evening of his life and eating and relishing unsaleable niggers from
> neighboring tribes who fall into his hands, and making a good thing out of
> other niggers from neighboring tribes that are saleable.[84]

The matter of claiming Moorish or Berber ancestry was not unique to Abd ar-Rahman and was not entirely without foundation. Given the validity of some claims, incredulity over the 1937 statement of centenarian Silva King of Marlin, Texas, issues into uncertainty: "I know I was borned in Morocco, in Africa, and was married and had three children befo' I was stoled from my husband. I don't know who it was stole me, but dey took me to France, to a place called Bordeaux, but drugs me with some coffee, and when I knows anything 'bout it, I's in de bottom of a boat with a whole lot of other niggers."[85]

Although there is evidence of strained relations between Muslims and non-Muslims, there are also instances of cooperation. Charles Ball mentions his acquaintance and friendship with a number of Muslims.[86] Abd ar-Rahman himself, in an ironic twist, married a Baptist woman in 1794 (perhaps a concession to necessity), had several children by her, returned to Liberia with her in 1829, and expired in her arms a few months later. But it was Muhammad 'Ali b. Said, or Nicholas Said, who perhaps best exempli-fies the Muslim who made common cause with others. Born around 1833 in the Islamic state of Bornu near Lake Chad (bordering Hausaland), he was taken captive around 1849, whereupon he began a most circuitous voyage to the United States, after initially crossing the Sahara, where he was sold in Tripoli to owners in Mecca, then Turkey, then Russia, after which he traveled to various European destinations before his tour of the Americas as a free man between 1860 and 1862. By 1863, he had become a teacher in Detroit, Michigan, as he was fluent in French and Italian, and probably English. He then joined the Fifty-fifth Regiment of Massachusetts Col-ored Volunteers and served until his exit from the Union Army in South Carolina in 1865. Marrying, he subsequently died in Brownsville, Tennes-see, in 1882.[87]

It remains to examine both the viability and impact of Islam on the lowcountry. To begin, it is not always easy to know the extent to which Muslims had opportunities to engage in corporate expressions of faith. At first glance, such opportunities would seem highly improbable, but evidence suggests that they were in fact afforded. The record from the Georgia–South Carolina coast is replete with references to individuals praying regularly, such as "Ole Israel," Daphne, and the Ibo couple Calina and Hannah; presumably there were times when they prayed together. Salih Bilali of St. Simons was a devout Muslim who fasted during Ramadan; Bilali of Sapelo wore a fez and kaftan, prayed daily (facing the east), and also observed the Muslim feast days, practices observed by his wife and daughters as well as others among the faithful along the Georgia–South Carolina coast.[88] It would appear that Abd ar-Rahman continued to practice Islam, and that after either a flirtation with Christianity or a conscious strategy of dissimulation (to gain support for his repatriation), he immediately reaffirmed his Muslim beliefs upon returning to Africa.[89] Charles Ball, enslaved in Maryland, South Carolina, and Georgia for forty years, also witnessed certain Muslim observances among the fellow enslaved, for he wrote, "I knew several who must have been, from what I have since learned, Mohammedans; though at that time, I had never heard of the religion of Mohammed."[90] Ball took particular interest in one Muslim in South Carolina who prayed "five times every day, always turning his face to the east," and records his account of life in the West African *sāhil*, where he was captured as a lad by Tuareg (Arabo-Berber inhabitants of the desert) and served for two years as *bella* (slave) before his ultimate transfer to the Atlantic trade. Ball, like other observers, took note of Muslim behavior but did not know enough to recognize what he saw.

Individual examples of adherence to Islam suggest that many practiced the religion, perhaps clandestinely, or perhaps in full view of unsuspecting eyes such as Ball's. In any event, that Muslims congregated for prayer is informed by a second factor; the general tendency among the enslaved to steal away into secluded areas for religious and social purposes. It has generally been assumed that stealing away involved the enslaved's pursuit of their particular brand of Christianity, or indigenous African religions, but there is absolutely no reason to preclude Muslims from similar activity. Thus, we have the example of Harriet Hall Grovner of Sapelo Island, who found it necessary to regularly seek refuge to pray as late as 1922. The probability that Muslims gathered in groups to pray is increased when the question of contact between Muslims is considered. Bilali and Salih Bilali, residing on plantations on neighboring sea islands, were considered the best of friends and were in contact with others who were Muslim, many apparently Fulbe. Religion and religious observances must have constituted an important, if not central, component of Muslims' bond. Abd ar-Rahman and Samba, his fellow Pullo (singular of Fulbe) enslaved on the same farm, were able to associate closely with each other, and the two communicated with at least one other Muslim, a Mandinka in this instance, from Natchez.[91] As coreligionists, they surely sought opportunities to re-create sacred space in corporate prayer.

It would also appear that Muslims struggled not only to maintain their bonds with each other, but that they also attempted to preserve Islamic education, particularly the knowledge of Arabic and the Qur'ān. One Dr. Collins, who wrote a manual on the medical treatment of the enslaved, stated that many individuals from Senegal "converse in the Arabic language, and some are sufficiently instructed even to write it."[92] LeConte recalled "an old native African named Philip," a Muslim who during the antebellum period demonstrated the outward expressions of the religion "by going through all the prayers and prostrations of his native country."[93] Abd ar-Rahman would write the *Fātiha* (opening *sūra*, or chapter, of the Qur'ān) for whites who believed they were receiving the "Lord's Prayer" in an exotic hand.[94] There are many other examples of Arabic literacy among the enslaved in North America.[95]

Muslims struggled not only to preserve their traditions but also to pass them on to their progeny. Thus, Bilali bestowed Muslim names upon most, if not all, of his daughters, and apparently taught all but the youngest Pulaar (language of the Fulbe) and possibly Arabic, as they regularly communicated with one another in a "foreign tongue."[96] Samba, the companion of Abd ar-Rahman, had at least three sons, and gave them all Muslim names.[97] In 1786, Sambo and Fatima escaped Edward Fenwicke of Johns Island; Sambo was "of the Guinea country" and probably Muslim, but Fatima was described as country-born, so she may have either converted to Islam or had at least one Muslim parent.[98] The recurrence of Muslim names among the American-born enslaved is corroborative evidence of the desire among many to keep their religion and culture alive.[99]

Islam's legacy in the lowcountry continued well into the twentieth century, and a major source of substantial corroboration for the presence of a sizeable Muslim community in coastal Georgia–South Carolina continues to be the underused, pathbreaking work of Lorenzo Turner. Three-fourths of the personal names he collected during his fifteen-year study, which began in 1932, were collected in coastal Georgia, principally in St. Simons, Sapelo, Harris Neck, and the vicinity of Darien, while the remainder were gathered in coastal South Carolina, including the islands of Edisto, St. Helena, Hilton Head, Johns, James, and Wadmalaw. Of the hundreds of names in the study, some 274 have a possible Muslim connection.[100] While not all are incontestably Muslim names, such are to be found in the Turner collection, including Adamu, Ali, Amina, Aminata, Ayisata, Bakari, Baraka, Bilali, Binta, Bintu, Birahima, Birama, Fatimata, Fatima, Fatuma, Gibril, Haruna, Hasana, Mamadi, Mamadu, Male, Mare, Mori, Moriba, Musa, and Safiyata. The linguistic evidence also suggests that Muslim amulets were widely distributed; for example, the Hausa female name Makari bears a relationship to amulets (literally "an antidote" or "protection"), and is consistent with other terms found by Turner such as *juju*, used throughout Senegambia for amulets of various sorts (including non-Muslim varieties), and *kafa*, possibly derived from Hausa as the name for a "charm" of some kind.[101]

The Muslim presence in coastal Georgia–South Carolina (and possibly elsewhere along the Atlantic) was therefore active, vibrant, and compelling, and may well have informed the subsequent rise of such organizations as the Moorish Science Temple, founded by Nobel Drew Ali, and the Nation of Islam. An admittedly speculative tie concerns one Sambo Swift (1811–84). Enslaved in Darien, Georgia, right in the epicenter of the Muslim world in coastal Georgia, he managed to reach Mecca, Indiana, a region from which were later attracted a number of adherents to the Moorish Science Temple in the early twentieth century. Indeed, Nobel Drew Ali relocated his headquarters from Newark, New Jersey, to Chicago because of the Midwest's allegedly greater affinity for Islam. The matter is complicated and poorly understood, but it could be that Sambo Swift, who hailed from the lowcountry, was part of a spiritual foundation for the emergence of a variant of Islam in the twentieth century, the reverberations of which remain to this day.[102]

NOTES

1. For examples of names that probably have African origins, see Charles Lyell, *A Second Visit to the United States of America*, 2 vols. (New York: Harper and Brothers, 1849), 1:263. For discussions of names as ethnic markers, see John C. Inscoe, "Carolina Slave Names: An Index to Acculturation," *Journal of Southern History* 49 (1983): 527–34; Cheryll Ann Cody, "There Was No 'Absalom' on the Ball Plan-

tations: Slave-Naming Practices in the South Carolina Low Country, 1720–1865," *American Historical Review* 92 (1987): 563–96.

2. Lathan Windley, comp., *Runaway Slave Advertisements: A Documentary History from the 1730s to 1790*, 4 vols. (Westport, Conn.: Greenwood Press, 1983); Inscoe, "Carolina Slave Names," 533–35.

3. In Mende and Vai, however, the name Sambo implies disgrace. See Lorenzo Dow Turner, *Africanisms in the Gullah Dialect* (1949: repr., New York: Arno Press and the New York Times, 1969); Keith E. Baird and Mary A. Twining, "Names and Naming in the Sea Islands," in *The Crucible of Carolina: Essays in the Development of Gullah Language and Culture*, ed. Michael Montgomery (Athens: University of Georgia Press, 1994).

4. Windley, *Runaway Slave Advertisements*, 3:593.

5. Ibid., 3:605.

6. Ibid., 4:64.

7. For example, some of the evidence for Moors in America comes from Midlo Hall's research, in which the appellation "Nar," a Wolof term for Moor, is used to characterize a number of enslaved persons in Louisiana. See Gwendolyn Midlo Hall, *Slavery and African Ethnicities in the Americas: Restoring the Links* (Chapel Hill: University of North Carolina Press, 2005). Also see Paul B. Barringer, *The Natural Bent: The Memoirs of Dr. Paul B. Barringer* (Chapel Hill: University of North Carolina Press, 1949), 3–13; and James W. Hagy, "Muslim Slaves, Abducted Moors, African Jews, Misnamed Turks, and an Asiatic Greek Lady: Some Examples of Non-European Religious and Ethnic Diversity in South Carolina prior to 1861," *Carologue: A Publication of the South Carolina Historical Society* 9 (1993): 12–13, 25–27. This information is derived from the South Carolina Council Journal, vol. 21, pt. 1, 298–99, March 3, 1753, South Carolina Department of Archives and History.

8. *Charleston Courier*, May 1, 1809.

9. John Stapleton Papers (South Caroliniana Library, University of South Carolina, Columbia), microfilmed on reels 6 and 7, series A, pt. 2, *Records of Ante-Bellum Southern Plantations from the Revolution through the Civil War*, gen. ed. Kenneth M. Stampp.

10. See Michael A. Gomez, *Exchanging Our Country Marks: The Transformation of African Identities in the Colonial and Antebellum South* (Chapel Hill: University of North Carolina Press, 1998), 1–113. The author has only partially reviewed early Mississippi and Louisiana newspapers, so the assessment is subject to revision. Also see Charles Joyner, *Down by the Riverside: A South Carolina Slave Community* (Urbana: University of Illinois Press, 1984), 14–15; Peter H. Wood, *Black Majority: Negroes in Colonial South Carolina* (New York: Knopf, 1974), 58–62; Daniel C. Littlefield, *Rice and Slaves: Ethnicity and the Slave Trade in Colonial South Carolina* (Baton Rouge: Louisiana State University, 1981), 76–98.

11. See Philip D. Curtin, *The Atlantic Slave Trade: A Census* (Madison: University of Wisconsin, 1969), 156–58; James A. Rawley, *The Transatlantic Slave Trade: A History* (New York: Norton, 1981), 334–35. Littlefield (*Rice and Slaves*, 31–32) disagrees with the view that Virginia planters were unconcerned about ethnic origins.

To the contrary, Littlefield maintains not only that Virginians were concerned but also that they preferred the Ibo and others from the Niger delta (Littlefield's position is predicated upon Darold D. Wax, "Preferences for Slaves in Colonial America," *Journal of Negro History* 58 (1973): 374–75. Rawley, in turn, states that Virginians preferred those from the Gold Coast and Windward Coast, accepted the Ibo in large number, disliked those from Angola. See also Judith Ann Carney, *Black Rice: The African Origins of Rice Cultivation in the Americas* (Cambridge: Harvard University Press, 2001). That either African agricultural skills or planter preferences for specific African ethnicities practicing such skills were in any meaningful way influential on the patterns of slave importation into the lowcountry has been vigorously contested. See David Eltis, Philip Morgan, and David Richardson, "Agency and Diaspora in Atlantic History: Reassessing the African Contribution to Rice Cultivation in the Americas," *American Historical Review* 112 (December 2007): 1329–58.

12. *Columbia Museum and Savannah Advertiser*, May 11, 1802.

13. Ibid., March 27, 1807.

14. State of Georgia Archives, GRG2–009 and GRG2–029 (Georgia Department of Archives and History, Atlanta).

15. Letter from James Hamilton Couper, in William Brown Hodgson, *Notes on Northern Africa, the Sahara, and Soudan* (New York: Wiley and Putnam, 1844), 68–74.

16. See Ivor Wilks, "Salih Bilali of Massina," in *Africa Remembered: Narratives of West Africans from the Era of the Slave Trade*, ed. Philip D. Curtin (Madison: University of Wisconsin, 1967); Allan D. Austin, *African Muslims in Antebellum America: Transatlantic Stories and Spiritual Struggles* (New York: Routledge, 1997), 309–16.

17. Philip D. Curtin, *Economic Change in Precolonial Africa* (Madison: University of Wisconsin Press, 1975), 159–68.

18. Georgia Writers' Project, *Drums and Shadows: Survival Studies among the Georgia Coastal Negroes* (Athens: University of Georgia Press, 1940), 178–83.

19. Cornelia Bailey interview, July 1992. Cornelia Walker Bailey was born in Bell Marsh on June 12, 1945. Bilali is her great-great-great-grandfather through his daughter Bentoo (Arabic "Binta"). Bailey presently lives in Hog Hammock Community on Sapelo with her husband and family. The interview was taped, and notes were taken during the interview. Both tapes and notes are in the author's possession. For more on Sapelo Island, see William S. McFeely, *Sapelo's People: A Memory of Slavery, an Appointment with Freedom* (New York: W. W. Norton, 1994).

20. Austin, *African Muslims*, 6. Katie Brown maintained that Bilali's wife Phoebe "come by Bahamas. She speak funny words we didn know." Whether or not Phoebe was African-born is therefore unclear, but Brown maintains that by the time Bilali and Phoebe and their daughters arrived in Sapelo, the "whole fambly wuz mos grown up." This conflicts with the testimony of Shad Hall, who claims that "Belali an all he fambly come on same boat frum Africa." See Georgia Writers' Project, *Drums and Shadows*, 161–62, 166.

21. Lydia Parrish, *Slave Songs of the Georgia Sea Islands* (New York: Creative Age

Press, 1942), 27–28; Allan D. Austin, *African Muslims in Antebellum America: A Sourcebook* (New York: Garland Publishing, Inc., 1984), 265–68.

22. The manuscript is entitled "The Ben-Ali Diary," and was held by the Georgia State Law Library until 1997, when it was transferred to the University of Georgia Library in Athens. See also Joseph H. Greenberg, "The Decipherment of the 'Ben-Ali Diary,' a Preliminary Statement," *Journal of Negro History* 25 (1940): 372–75; B. G. Martin, "Sapelo Island's Arabic Document: The 'Blali Diary' in Context," *Georgia Historical Quarterly* 78 (1994): 589–601.

23. Joel Chandler Harris, *The Story of Aaron (so named), the Son of Ben Ali* (Boston: Houghton, Mifflin, 1896).

24. Parrish, *Slave Songs*, 28n22.

25. Georgia Writers' Project, *Drums and Shadows*, 158–60.

26. Ibid., 161.

27. Ibid.

28. Cornelia Bailey interview, July 1992.

29. Although Bilali was African-born, his wife and children may not have been. According to Bailey, his wife Phoebe was "from the islands" (the Caribbean), meaning that she was either West Indian–born or "seasoned" there. Because Bilali came to Sapelo with his entire family (except for his alleged twelve sons), the family may have developed in the Caribbean rather than Africa (Cornelia Bailey interview, July 1992).

30. Georgia Writers' Project, *Drums and Shadows*, 165–68.

31. Ibid., 164.

32. Ibid.

33. In response to a direct question about this, Bailey responded that Calina and Hannah were indeed Muslims, and that they came to Sapelo via the Caribbean. Thus, they could have converted to Islam while in the Caribbean (Cornelia Bailey interview, July 1992).

34. Sylviane A. Diouf, *Servants of Allah: African Muslims Enslaved in the Americas* (New York: New York University Press, 1998), 64–66.

35. Maureen Warner-Lewis, *Guinea's Other Suns: The African Dynamic in Trinidad Culture* (Dover, Mass.: Majority Press, 1991), 5–6, 115–16.

36. Georgia Writers' Project, *Drums and Shadows*, 162.

37. Ibid., 166–67.

38. Ibid., 120–21, 144–45, 154–56.

39. Greenberg, "Ben-Ali Diary." But see Ronald A. T. Judy, *(Dis)forming the American Canon: African-Arabic Slave Narratives and the Vernacular* (Minneapolis: University of Minnesota Press, 1993), for an alternative analysis.

40. Austin, *African Muslims, A Sourcebook*, , 321.

41. Cornelia Bailey interview, July 1992.

42. Indeed, in the Georgia coastal area, none of the descendants of African-born Muslims claim to be Muslim themselves in the WPA interviews.

43. Following Midlo Hall, colonial Louisiana pursued a slave policy that provided for some sense of familial security. See Gwendolyn Midlo Hall, *Africans in Colo-*

nial Louisiana: The Development of Afro-Creole Culture in the Eighteenth Century (Baton Rouge: Louisiana State University Press, 1992), 168.

44. For example, Rosanna Williams of Tatemville, Georgia, became so alarmed at the questions of the interviewers that she asked, "Wut yuh doin? Is yuh gonuh sen me back tuh Liberia?" (Georgia Writers' Project, *Drums and Shadows*, 71).

45. Ibid., 169–70.

46. Charles C. Jones, *The Religious Instruction of the Negroes* (Savannah, Ga.: Thomas Purse, 1842), 125.

47. Cornelia Bailey interview, July 1922.

48. See David Eltis and Martin Halbert, The Trans-Atlantic Slave Trade Database, http://www.slavevoyages.org/tast/assessment/estimates.faces?yearFrom=1501&yearTo=1866&disembarkation=205.203.201.202.204;http://www.slavevoyages.org/tast/assessment/estimates.faces?yearFrom=1501&yearTo=1866&embarkation=1&disembarkation=205.203.201.202.204.

49. Ibid., http://www.slavevoyages.org/tast/assessment/estimates.faces?yearFrom=1501&yearTo=1866&disembarkation=203;http://www.slavevoyages.org/tast/assessment/estimates.faces?yearFrom=1501&yearTo=1866&embarkation=1&disembarkation=203. See Jean Suret-Canale and Boubacar Barry, "The Western Atlantic Coast to 1800," in *History of West Africa*, 2nd ed., 2 vols., ed. J. F. Ade Ajayi and Michael Crowder (New York: Columbia University Press, 1976), 1:466; Jean Boulègue and Jean Suret-Canale, "The Western Atlantic Coast," in *History of West Africa*, 3d ed., ed. J. F. Ade Ajayi and Michael Crowder (New York: Longman, 1985), 519; Paul Lovejoy, *Transformations in Slavery: A History of Slavery in Africa* (Cambridge: Cambridge University Press, 1983), 58. Regarding written accounts, Mollien observed that "Mahometanism is making daily progress, and will soon become the only religion of the country of Cayor," while Jobson's early-seventeenth-century description of "Marybuckes" (*marabouts*, or Muslim clerics) and Islam along the Gambia is echoed by Smith and Moore's early- and Park's late-eighteenth-century observations, demonstrating Islam's growing influence. See G. Mollien, *Travels in the Interior of Africa to the Sources of the Senegal and Gambia* (London: H. Colburn, 1820), 61; Richard Jobson, *The Golden Trade, or a Discovery of the River Gambra, and the Trade of the Aethiopians* (1623; repr., London: Dawsons of Pall Mall, 1968), 78–99; Frances Moore, *Travels into the Inland Parts of Africa* (London: E. Cave, 1738), 12–26; Mungo Park, *Travels in the Interior Districts of Africa* (London: W. Bulmer and Co., 1799), 15–35; William Smith, *A New Voyage to Guinea* (1744; repr., London: Cass, 1967), 26–27. Eyewitness written accounts include Saugnier's report in 1784 that the Serrakole's religion was "nearly allied to Mahometanism, and still more to natural religion"; by 1821, Gray and Dochard essentially said the same: "From a state of Paganism these people are progressively embracing the Mahometan faith." See M. Saugnier and M. Brisson, *Voyages to the Coast of Africa* (1792; repr., New York: Negro Universities Press, 1969), 220; Major William Gray and Surgeon Dochard, *Travels in Western Africa, in the Years 1818, 19, 20, and 21* (London: J. Murray, 1825), 266. David Robinson, "The Islamic Revolution in Futa Toro," *International Journal of African Historical Studies* 8 (1975): 185–221; Michael A. Gomez, *Pragmatism*

in the Age of Jihad: The Precolonial State of Bundu (Cambridge: Cambridge University Press, 1992); Abdoulaye Bathily, "La traite atlantique des esclaves et ses effets économiques et sociaux en Afrique: La cas du Galam, royaume de l'hinterland sénégambien au dix-huitième siècle," *Journal of African History* 27 (1986): 269–93; compare with Curtin, *Economic Change*.

Regarding earlier events, evidence from a clerically led revolt along the coast in the 1670s, known as the *tubenan* movement, supports this contention. The term *tubenan* is from the Arabic *tawba*, or "to repent"; the Wolof word *tub* essentially carries the same meaning. For more on *tubenan*, or "la guerre des marabouts," see Philip D. Curtin, "Jihad in West Africa: Early Phases and Inter-Relations in Mauritania and Senegal," *Journal of African History* 12 (1971): 11–24; Boubacar Barry, "La guerre des marabouts dans la region du fleuve Sénégal de 1673 à 1677," *Bulletin de l'Institut Fondamental* (formerly *Français*) *d'Afrique Noire* 33 (1971): 564–89; Suret-Canale and Barry, "Western Atlantic Coast," 1:470; P. Cultru, *Premier voyage du Sieur de la Courbe fait à la Coste d'Afrique en 1685* (Paris: É. Champion, 1913), 30. Anne Raffenel, *Voyage dans l'Afrique occidentale . . . executé, en 1843 et 1844* (Paris: A. Bertrand, 1846), 299.

50. Eltis and Halbert, Database, http://www.slavevoyages.org/tast/assessment/estimates.faces?yearFrom=1501&yearTo=1866&embarkation=2.3&disembarkation=205.203.201.202.204;http://www.slavevoyages.org/tast/assessment/estimates.faces?yearFrom=1501&yearTo=1866&embarkation=4&disembarkation=205.203.201.202.204. See, for example, John Matthews, *A Voyage to the River Sierra-Leone* (1788; repr., London: Cass, 1966), 17–18; compare with Joseph Corry, *Observations upon the Windward Coast of Africa* (1807; repr., London: Cass, 1968), 41–44; Walter Rodney, *A History of the Upper Guinea Coast* (Oxford: Oxford University Press, 1970), 95–113, 244–55. Gray and Dochard's emphasis on Futa Jallon's strict observance of Islam is echoed by Callié's depiction of its people as "extremely fanatical," underscoring the seriousness of the *jihād*. See Gray and Dochard, *Travels in Western Africa*, 39–40; René Callié, *Travels through Central Africa to Timbuctoo* (London: H. Colburn and R. Bentley, 1830), 222. One consequence of Asante expansion in the mid-eighteenth century (in the interior of the Gold Coast) was the defeat of Gonja, a Muslim territory vitally connected to the middle Niger valley. See Lovejoy, *Transformations in Slavery*, 56; Ivor Wilks, *Asante in the Nineteenth Century: The Structure and Evolution of a Political Order* (Cambridge: Cambridge University Press, 1975); Wilks, in *Asante in the Nineteenth Century*; Peter B. Clarke, *West Africa and Islam* (London: Edward Arnold, 1982), 50–60; Melville Herskovits, *The Myth of the Negro Past* (New York: Harper and Brothers, 1941); and idem, *The New World Negro* (Bloomington: Indiana University Press, 1966), 90–93.

51. Eltis and Halbert, Database, http://www.slavevoyages.org/tast/assessment/estimates.faces?yearFrom=1501&yearTo=1866&embarkation=5&disembarkation=205.203.201.202.204.

52. Charles Sackett Sydnor, *Slavery in Mississippi* (New York: D. Appleton-Century, 1933), 141.

53. Eltis and Halbert, Database, http://www.slavevoyages.org/tast/assessment/

estimates.faces?yearFrom=1501&yearTo=1866&embarkation=2.4.1.3.5&disembark
ation=205.203.201.202.204. Also see Gomez, *Exchanging Our Country Marks*, 65–
67; Curtin, *Atlantic Slave Trade*, 83–89; Paul Lovejoy, "The Impact of the Atlantic
Slave Trade on Africa: A Review of the Literature," *Journal of African History* 30
(1989): 365–94; Rawley, *Transatlantic Slave Trade*, 428.

54. For more on the Juula, see Timothy F. Garrard, *Akan Weights and the Gold
Trade* (London: Longman, 1980); Ivor Wilks, "Wangara, Akan and Portuguese in
the Fifteenth and Sixteenth Centuries," *Journal of African History* 23 (1982): 333–49
(pt. 1); 463–72 (pt. 2). Regarding the role of clerics and amulets, see Jack Goody, ed.,
Literacy in Traditional Societies (Cambridge: Cambridge University Press, 1968), and
Mervyn Hiskett, *The Development of Islam in West Africa* (New York: Longman,
1984).

55. For an introduction to this discussion, see I. M. Lewis, ed., *Islam in Tropical
Africa*, 2nd ed. (Bloomington: International African Institute in association with In-
diana University Press, 1980), or Nehemiah Levtzion, ed., *Conversion to Islam* (New
York: Holmes and Meier, 1979).

56. Newbell N. Puckett, *Folk Beliefs of the Southern Negro* (Chapel Hill: University of North Carolina Press, 1926), 528–29; Lyell, *Second Visit*, 1:266.

57. U. B. Phillips, *American Negro Slavery: A Survey of the Supply, Employment
and Control of Negro Labor as Determined by the Plantation Regime* (New York:
D. Appleton, 1918), 42.

58. Sydnor, *Slavery in Mississippi*, 141.

59. Puckett, *Folk Beliefs*, 528–29; Lyell, *Second Visit*, 1:266.

60. Dr. Collins, *Practical Rules for the Management and Medical Treatment of
Negro Slaves* (1811), 37; Austin, *African Muslims, A Sourcebook,*, 81.

61. Gray and Dochard, *Travels in Western Africa*, 40; Callié, *Travels through Central Africa*, 222; Jobson, *Golden Trade*, 42.

62. Terry Alford, *Prince among Slaves* (New York: Oxford University Press, 1977),
56.

63. Zephaniah Kingsley, *Treatise on the Patriarchal or Co-operative System of Society as it Exists in some Governments, and Colonies in America and in the United States
under the Name of Slavery, with Its Necessity and Advantages* (n.p.: 1829), 13–14. See
also Parrish, *Slave Songs*, 25; Austin, *African Muslims, A Sourcebook*, 268.

64. Ella May Thorton, "Bilali — His Book," *Law Library Journal* 48 (1955):
228–29. Cornelia Bailey disagrees with the idea that the Muslims of Sapelo enjoyed
advantages over non-Muslim slaves and maintains that slaveholders treated both
groups the same (Cornelia Bailey interview, July 1992).

65. See David Brown, *The Planter: Or, Thirteen Years in the South, by a Northern
Man* (1853: repr., New York: Negro Universities Press, 1970), 120–28. Reference to
Old King was first made by Austin, *African Muslims: Transatlantic Stories*, 37.

66. For example, see Puckett, *Folk Beliefs*, 58–29.

67. See John W. Blassingame, *The Slave Community: Plantation Life in the Antebellum South* (New York: Oxford University Press, 1979), 73.

68. Austin, *African Muslims, A Sourcebook*, 316, 321.

69. Cyrus Griffin, "The Unfortunate Moor," *African Repository* (February 1828): 365–67. See Austin, *African Muslims: Transatlantic Stories*, 65–80. Austin argues that Cyrus Griffin played a prominent role in transforming Abd ar-Rahman into a Moor.

70. Georgia Bryan Conrad, *Reminiscences of a Southern Woman* (Hampton, Va.: Hampton Institute Press, n.d.), 13.

71. Cornelia Bailey interview, July 1992.

72. For the Fulbe in West Africa, see Paul Riesman, *Freedom in Fulani Social Life* (Chicago: University of Chicago Press, 1977); Victor Azarya, *Aristocrats Facing Change: The Fulbe in Guinea, Nigeria, and Cameroon* (Chicago: University of Chicago Press, 1978); Marguerite Dupire, *Organisation sociale des Peuls* (Paris: Plon, 1970); idem, *Peuls nomades: étude descriptive des WoDaaBe du Sahel Nigérien* (Paris: Institut d'ethnologie, 1962); Paul Marty, *L'Islam en Guinée: Foûta-Diallon* (Paris: E. Leroux, 1921); G. Vieillard, *Notes sur les coutumes des Peuls au Foûta Djallon* (Paris: Larose, 1939); Claude Rivière, *Mutations sociales en Guinée* (Paris: M. Rivière et Cie, 1971); M. Z. Njeuma, *Fulani Hegemony in Yola (Adamawa), 1809–1902* (Yaoundé, Cameroon: Pub. and Production Centre for Teaching and Research, 1978).

73. Paul Irwin, *Liptako Speaks: History from Oral Tradition in Africa* (Princeton, N.J.: Princeton University Press, 1971), 46–77.

74. Park, *Travels in the Interior District*, 59.

75. Wilks, "Abu Bakr al-Siddiq of Timbuktu," in *Africa Remembered: Narratives by West Africans from the Era of the Slave Trade*, ed. Philip O. Curtin (Madison: University of Wisconsin Press, 1967), 162–63.

76. Marty, *L'Islam en Guinée*, 108–47; Jean Suret-Canale, "Touba in Guinea: Holy Place of Islam," in *African Perspectives*, ed. Christopher Allen and R. W. Johnson (Cambridge: Cambridge University Press, 1970); and Gomez, *Pragmatism in the Age of Jihad*, 26–28.

77. Collins, *Practical Rules*, quoted in Douglas Grant, *The Fortunate Slave: An Illustration of African Slavery in the Early Eighteenth Century* (London: Oxford University Press, 1968), 81.

78. Quote from Paul Guebhard, found in Martin Klein, *Slavery and Colonial Rule in French West Africa* (Cambridge: Cambridge University Press, 1998), 141.

79. Ibid., 182–83, 217.

80. In Paul E. Lovejoy and Jan S. Hogendorn, *Slow Death for Slavery: The Course of Abolition in Northern Nigeria, 1897–1936* (Cambridge: Cambridge University Press, 1993), 27.

81. William Brown Hodgson, *Notes on Northern Africa*, 49–50.

82. Hodgson (50) maintained that the Fulbe were the descendants of Arab fathers and "Taurodo" mothers, the latter an apparent reference to sub-Saharan communities living in the *sāhil* and in contact with the Arabo-Berber populations of Mauritania. Hodgson's remarks relate to the Fulbe claim of descent from the Arab general 'Uqba b. Nāfi' discussed in the text. The *Torodbe* (singular *Torodo*) of Futa Toro were in fact a clerical community that rose from humble origins to provide leadership for various theocratic states in Senegambia.

83. Griffin, "Unfortunate Moor," 365–67.

84. Mark Twain, "American Travel Letters, Series 2," *Alta California*, August 1, 1869, final letter.

85. George P. Rawick, *The American Slave: A Composite Autobiography* (Westport, Conn.: Greenwood Publishing Company), 4:290.

86. Austin, *African Muslims, A Sourcebook*, 127–31; Ball, *Slavery in the United States*, 164–65, 167, 186; also see Charles Ball, *Fifty Years in Chains, or the Life of an American Slave* (New York: H. Dayton, 1858).

87. See "A Native of Bornoo," *Atlantic Monthly* (October 1867): 485–95; Austin, *African Muslims: Transatlantic Stories*, 173–85.

88. Austin, *African Muslims, A Sourcebook*, 265, 321.

89. Alford, *Prince among Slaves*, 57–58; Austin, *African Muslims, A Sourcebook*, 6–7.

90. Charles Ball, *Slavery in the United States* (1837; repr., New York: Negro Universities Press, 1969), 164–65, 167–86.

91. Alford, *Prince among Slaves*, 43–44, 77.

92. Collins, *Practical Rules*, quoted in Grant, *Fortunate Slave*, 81.

93. William Dallam Armes, ed., *The Autobiography of Joseph LeConte* (New York: D. Appleton, 1903), 29–30.

94. Austin, *African Muslims, A Sourcebook*, 129; see n. 64.

95. See Michael A. Gomez, *Black Crescent: The Experience and Legacy of African Muslims in the Americas* (New York: Cambridge University Press, 2005).

96. Ibid., 265, 272–75. Cornelia Bailey maintains that Arabic was not taught but that "some African" was spoken.

97. Alford, *Prince among Slaves*, 77–78. Two of the sons were named "Sulimina" (but called "Solomon" and "Samba"").

98. *State Gazette of South Carolina*, July 31, 1786, in Windley, *Runaway Slave Advertisements*, 3:400.

99. Windley, *Runaway Slave Advertisements*, passim.

100. Turner, *Africanisms in the Gullah Dialect*, 41–190.

101. Ibid., 190–208.

102. See Gomez, *Black Crescent*, 185–275; Amir Nashid Ali Muhammad, *Muslims in America: Seven Centuries of History, 1312–2000: Collections and Stories of American Muslims* (1998: repr., Beltsville, Md., 2001), 46–48. According to Muhammad, Sambo had three children: Abrahim (?), Mollie, and Alonzo.

Erskine Clarke

"They shun the scrutiny of white men"

Reports on Religion from the Georgia Lowcountry and West Africa, 1834–1850

IN THE EARLY 1830s, an escaped slave made his way into the deep swamps of the Medway River in Liberty County, Georgia, not far from the little town of Sunbury. Eluding white authorities who sought to capture him, he began to make contact with the surrounding slave settlements. Word soon spread that he was a powerful conjurer, and the people from the settlements began to risk dangerous nighttime journeys to see him in his hiding places and to receive from him some of the power of his conjuring. Some apparently sought protection from threatening spirits or angry neighbors; others may have sought help in attracting a lover or in punishing an enemy with a hidden charm, while still others may have turned to him for revenge against a master's brutal discipline. Whatever their reasons, all sought help from the conjurer's knowledge of secret powers and from his skill in reading signs and explaining events that could not be understood or controlled. To whites he was seen as "that ridiculous Conjurer" who turned "the ignorant people crazy; cheating them out of their time and money, creating quarrels and confusion among them, and leading them into trouble."[1]

One of those who slipped away from a nearby slave settlement was Sam, the driver, the "chief man," at Laurel View, a twenty-five-hundred-acre rice and Sea Island cotton plantation owned by the estate of U.S. Senator John Elliott. Sam's grandfather Ned had been the driver at the nearby Novarre Plantation in the early years of the century as had his uncle for the next generation of those who lived in the Novarre settlement. Sam's mother had been a longtime member of the Sunbury Baptist Church, and by the time Sam visited the conjurer in the swamps, he himself was a leader in this important Baptist congregation. So Sam came from one of the most influential families of the Gullah-speaking slave community of Liberty County, and he was married to a woman who worked in the home of the white Baptist preacher at Sunbury. Sam was remarkably prosperous, too, for a lowcountry slave, owning at the time of his death "twelve or sixteen head of cattle, sixty head of hogs, a saddle horse, and poultry of all kinds, with at least forty dollars." Clearly Sam was a man with deep roots in the Gullah community, a man of means and of influence, and a leader in the Baptist church.[2]

When Sam first slipped away to the conjurer, people in the settlements thought he was in cahoots with him. But Sam thought the conjurer was a charlatan and fraud and laid a plan to have him captured. The conjurer was taken and shipped out of the county. His inability to protect himself or to see through Sam's pretense undercut his authority, and a white observer believed that "the foolish and ignorant people that trusted in him were brought to shame."[3]

In this way, two men out of the Georgia lowcountry Gullah community confronted one another. One man stood in a tradition of conjuring that reached back to West and West Central Africa.[4] The other man stood in a tradition of Baptist piety and practice that reached back to English and Continental Protestants. Both traditions were thus part of an Atlantic world, and both traditions were also part of African American life and culture in the Georgia lowcountry of the antebellum period.[5] As traditions of an Atlantic world, they had not remained static in the Georgia lowcountry, frozen in time, but had been dynamic religious forces evolving in complex ways as they interacted not only with one another but also with the social and cultural realities of the region, especially the brutal conditions of chattel slavery.[6] By the 1830s, both traditions had been a part of the lowcountry Gullah community for several generations. Clearly the evolving tradition of Baptist piety in which the driver Sam stood was a part of a rapidly developing African American Christianity among the Gullah people. This tradition, deeply influenced by the radical wing of Puritanism, emphasized personal faith in Jesus, an experience of conversion, adult baptism, and a disciplined Christian life.[7] But the traditions of the conjurer, even though he had been captured and shipped, would also continue for generations to be a powerful part of a lowcountry African American world.[8] The traditions of the conjurer pointed toward a sacred cosmos, an interior landscape of the mind and imagination that for many Gullah people encompassed and was in turn shaped by the marshes and fields, the settlements and secrets of the lowcountry.

This essay seeks to explore the competing and overlapping worlds of the conjurer who hid in the Medway swamps, of Sam the Baptist leader, and of a fetish priest in West Africa whom we shall introduce shortly. In what ways were their worlds, each with its own sacred cosmos, part of a transatlantic world?[9] I want to explore these competing and overlapping worlds in a limited and modest manner as a historian and not an anthropologist by looking at two revealing encounters: one between Sam and the conjurer in the Georgia lowcountry in the 1830s; and the other between a white lowcountry missionary and a West African fetish priest in the 1830s. And I want to explore these worlds, again in a limited and modest manner, by looking through a particular set of lenses, the extensive reports from two contemporary lowcountry observers — one who visited regularly among the slave settlements of Liberty County during the 1830s and 1840s, and one who lived and traveled extensively in Western Africa for seventeen years during the same period and encountered the fetish priest. Both were missionaries; both were white southerners with deep roots in the lowcountry; both were keen observers and famous in their day for their work; and both were bearers of similar worldviews, assumptions, and prejudices. The lens through which they looked and made their careful observations was obviously ground and shaped by their whiteness, by their nineteenth-century lowcountry backgrounds, and by their religious commitments as Protestant missionaries. In other words, their reports are from within a particular European American world with its own sacred cosmos. But their extensive and careful reports are nevertheless among the most important primary sources available to the historian seeking to understand these overlapping worlds, and within their limitations the reports invite our serious attention.

Before exploring these worlds and their relationship to each other, however, we must acknowledge at least briefly some daunting historical and methodological issues. The first of these issues swirls around what is often called the Frazier-Herskovits debate, named after the African American historian E. Franklin Frazier and the white anthropologist Melville Herskovits. Simply put, the Frazier side of the debate has emphasized the brutal character of the transatlantic slave trade and the conclusion of Frazier's that "probably never before in history has a people been so nearly completely stripped of its social heritage as were the Negroes who were brought to America." In addition, Frazier argued that an African past was primarily a matter of "Forgotten Memories."[10] So, from this perspective, the world of the Medway conjurer was largely a new world, created de novo on this side of the Atlantic. Herskovits and his followers, on the other hand, have emphasized continuities between African traditions and social structures and those of the African American diaspora in the Western hemisphere, including the lowcountry Gullah people. On the Herskovits side of the debate, it has been argued that African Americans were essentially Africans "whose commitments to their ancestral past made them culturally different from other Americans." Their world was largely a transplanted African world. On the Frazier side, African Americans, including the Gullah people, were "merely Americans who had not been able to acculturate fully because of their oppression."[11]

Even to mention the Frazier-Herskovits debate has long seemed to some historians like beating a dead horse since the debate has been so intense and of such extended duration.[12] Yet this particular dead horse, however hard it has been beaten in the past, has the uncanny ability to struggle to its feet and to give indications of being alive if not well. One reason the debate lingers are the ideological commitments and assumptions that swirl beneath the competing interpretations and political implications of the debate. How do we understand the African American experience, and consequently how do we understand the American experience itself? In particular, are the Gullah people a largely marginal group in American society and consequently an attraction for tourists seeking an exotic and fading culture in modern America? Or is the Gullah experience, rather than being marginal, a part of a broad American experience and a window into the very character of American history? To know central themes of American history with its oppressive racism, goes this side of the debate, we must look at the experience of African Americans, including Gullah people.[13]

Closely connected to the Frazier-Herskovits debate is the question of the African origins of the Gullah people. Were the Gullah predominantly from one cultural group? Some histories, for example, have emphasized

Gullah connections with Sierra Leone or the Windward Coast.[14] Others have emphasized that the Gullah people came from widely disparate ethnic and cultural groups — from Gambia in the north to Angola in the south.[15] With such a diverse cultural background, how is it possible, it has been asked, to speak of continuities with something called "West African cultural traditions"? Some scholars, on the other hand, have suggested there was a generalized Western African cultural heritage, shared by different ethnic groups, that was brought to the lowcountry and which provided the deep assumptions of Gullah culture.[16] But to claim such a generalized African cultural heritage has been attacked by some scholars of Western African history as naïve and uninformed in regard to the deep differences between Western African cultures.[17]

A third issue has to do with the idea of tradition itself and with traditional religious belief in particular. Once again, for more than a decade, scholars of African history have been asserting that what is called "traditional African religion" is a contemporary construct, an illusion that covers over the dynamic and diverse character of religious life in Africa. The concept of African traditional religion, it is argued, tries to find an essence of African religious life that is frozen in time rather than seeing a diverse African religious life that is dynamic and evolving.[18]

Finally, there is the question of missionary reports. Missionaries in western Africa were not only among the first and most important observers of western African cultures from outside the region, they were also people who went into those cultures with the intent to change them. That intent, together with the inevitable worldviews and assumptions brought by the missionaries, helped shape what they observed and how they reported on what they observed. The same was true in the Georgia lowcountry. The intent of missionaries among the Gullah people was to change and convert them, and that intent shaped what the missionaries observed and how they interpreted and reported on what they saw.[19]

With these warnings, I want to see how these historical and methodological issues unfold as we explore, from a historian's perspective, the competing and overlapping worlds of the Liberty County conjurer, of Sam, and of a West African fetish priest.

CHARLES COLCOCK JONES was a wealthy Liberty County planter and Presbyterian minister who, after studying in the North, became convinced both that slavery was a great evil and also that the path of duty led him back to Liberty County to be a missionary among the Gullah people and an advocate for their welfare within the system of slavery. Beginning in 1831, the slave preacher Sharper became Jones's mentor, taking him under his wing and carefully and no doubt selectively introducing him to the beliefs and practices of the slave settlements. Sharper stood in a line of black preachers who went back several generations and was by the early 1830s the most respected man in the settlements.[20] "He has been preaching the Gospel to his colored brethren," Jones wrote in 1833, "for almost twenty years, with fidelity." Not only had Sharper been preaching, he had also been visiting in the slave settlements of the county for years. In the evenings around nighttime fires after worship services, the black preacher had had opportunities to talk with those who had been born in Africa and to see the ways that African beliefs and practices were a part of life in the settlements. "He gives me," said Jones, "more insight into the nature of my work amongst the Negroes in one conversation, than I gain in the observation of weeks. The ground is all familiar to him, and I esteem it a privilege and a blessing, that we labor together in the same field."[21]

Jones also knew Sam and his family. Jones had spent the summers of his youth in the little village of Sunbury, and his family was an integral part of the tightly knit white families of Liberty County — including the family of Senator Elliott. As an adult, Jones often visited the settlement at Laurel View where Sam was the driver, and when Sam died his family asked Jones to conduct his funeral service. This Jones did and by the content of his eulogy indicated a long and respectful association with Sam even as it reflected the assumptions of a paternalistic white.[22]

In these ways and through his own pastoral visitation and work during the 1830s and 1840s, Jones caught a glimpse of the world of the conjurer and the world of Sam. What did he see?

First, Jones saw Africans among the Gullah people as he visited in the slave settlements of Liberty County. At Seabrook Plantation, not far from where Sam lived, Jones met Dublin, who had been born in Africa and who would teach his neighbors a long-remembered African dance song.[23] Jones also knew that Fanny who lived at his own Montevideo Plantation had grown up in Africa. She had been bought as a young woman by Jones's father at a Savannah slave sale together with her two African-born children, Elvira and Marcus. Fanny would struggle all her life with English and would as an old woman speak at best a kind of broken pidgin English. But her children would grow up in Liberty County and would speak the Creole dialect of the Gullah people.[24] Jones thought that the acculturated Gullah like Elvira and Marcus were "more intelligent, neater in their persons, more respectable in their dress, and [spoke] better English than the *native Africans*." By the 1830s, however, he was noting that "Native Africans are rapidly decreasing" in the Georgia lowcountry.[25] Nevertheless, he saw continuing African influences in the Gullah settlements. "They believe," he wrote, "in second-sight, in apparitions, charms, witchcraft, and in a kind of irresistible Satanic influence. The superstitions," he said, "brought from Africa have not been wholly laid aside."[26] What Jones the missionary derisively called "the superstitions brought from Africa" constituted fundamental elements of the conjurer's world and provide for us primary links across the Atlantic to the complex religious life of West Africa.

Perhaps most visible were the "charms." Jones knew they were widely used in the Liberty County settlements, and he discovered that they could be employed for a variety of reasons. Some charms, he said, "will enable the possessor to make free use of any part of his owner's property without detection, and others . . . will remove sickness or the mediated revenge of enemies, or in the midst of dangers, preserve the person invulnerable." He found "the *composition* of these charms" to be "singular": "A bunch of Negro or animal hair, or wool, crooked sticks, glass of bottles, rusty nails, roots, etc. prepared in size and quality, and with various incantations, suitable to persons and circumstances."[27] Sometimes the charms would be placed in a little bag to be worn around the neck or buried under a door or planted along a path to keep at bay malignant forces. At other times the charms might be composed of secret roots to heal a sore or of black cat ashes and graveyard dirt, a piece of fingernail and a strand of hair to be stirred into some powerful potion. Jones thought that all of these charms reflected the extreme superstition of the people that was rooted in ignorance and in the neglect of whites in caring for the welfare of the slave population. But he also believed that the charms were the tools of what he called "designing men" within the African American community, in particular those who might rise in resistance to the oppression of slavery. He named Denmark Vesey in Charleston and Nat Turner in Virginia as dangerous examples of those "who wish to gain an ascendancy" over the people by availing "themselves of their ignorance and superstition."[28] For Jones the danger with all conjurers was in their "pretensions to courage, to divine protection, to the exercise of peculiar power in consummating their own plans . . . They avail themselves of the passions and prejudices of the poor people and thus fit them for their own purposes. They proceed to predict events, or to see visions and dream dreams, or to give out *charms* of various kinds and for various purposes."[29]

Distinct from the conjurer's charms but a part of the conjurer's world were the witches who were said to roam the lowcountry nights. They could slip into different shapes, creep into cabins at night and onto a sleeper's chest so that their victims awoke feeling not only terrified but as if they were smothering. A neighbor or an old woman who lived alone might be a witch who would wait for a moonless night to travel dark paths through swamp and marsh, to hide in dark corners of the settlements and bring sickness and trouble.[30]

Jones lumped witches, sorcerers, and conjurers together as deceivers living among the settlements. He told a crowded congregation of Gullah people at the North Newport Baptist Church that these deceivers "pretend only to do wonders, and tell fortunes and give charms . . . And we may defy all of them in the world to tell our fortunes, what is coming to pass, to make us well or to bewitch us, by their old roots and rusty nails and hair and wool and old bags and sticks and marks and mutterings. They lie and do not [tell] the truth." What they are after, Jones warned his Gullah congregation, is your money.[31]

In spite of such warnings, Jones became increasingly aware of how difficult it was to challenge these deep-seated beliefs. He came to believe that a "religious teacher *cannot always meet and put down a superstition. He must depend upon a gradual increase of knowledge.* When light enters the mind, darkness will vanish."[32] But even light and knowledge were not sufficient when a person had come under the influence of a conjurer. The conjurer's "power is dreaded," wrote Jones, and a threat from the conjurer was "sufficient to produce trembling and obedience." He believed that there was "no way in the world to break this power, to deliver the people from this delusion, but by breaking the [conjurer] himself."[33]

Jones was clearly intent on converting the people from the world of the conjurer to the world of Sam and the Christian convictions he represented. Such an intention shaped what Jones saw when he peered into the conjurer's dangerous world.[34] It was dangerous in part, Jones believed, because the conjurer was a threat to the established ways of a lowcountry plantation society, and his charms were weapons in an arsenal of strategies that could be turned against whites.

Yet Jones was also aware of the secret character of the conjurer's world; indeed, that was part of its threat to the authority of white masters. After years of visiting in the slaves' settlements among the sick and troubled, he wrote, "Persons live and die in the midst of Negroes and know comparatively little of their real character. . . . The Negroes are a distinct class in a community, and keep themselves very much *to themselves*. They are one thing before the whites, and another before their own color."[35] Consequently, as Jones sought to peer into the conjurer's world, his sight was not only limited by his missionary intentions and the assumptions of a white plantation owner but also by the hidden character of the conjurer and the deliberate strategy of the Gullah people to keep much of their common life hidden from the eyes of whites.

WHILE JONES WAS trying to make his way among the slave settlements of Liberty County, John Leighton and Jane Bayard Wilson were working among the Grebo people of Liberia and then the Mpongwe of Gabon. The Wilsons were lowcountry people — he from South Carolina, she from Georgia. Her family was one of the most distinguished of Georgia families; her grandfather was General Lachlan McIntosh, after whom McIntosh County was named, and her father Nicholas Bayard was an eminent Savannah physician and a founder of the Georgia Medical Society. In the 1830s, Jane and Leighton Wilson freed their slaves, including thirty lowcountry Gullah people who at their own request and at the Wilson's expense sailed from Savannah and became a part of the young colony at Cape Palmas in Liberia, West Africa. There the Wilsons helped them to become established among the other colonists.[36]

During the coming years — while Jane Wilson taught school and nursed sick and dying missionaries — Leighton Wilson traveled thousands of miles not only along the coast but also into the interior of West and West Central Africa. This Presbyterian minister, who was serving under the interdenominational American Board of Commissioners for Foreign Mission, was a keen observer of the land, its flora and fauna, and was deeply interested in the social and cultural history of the many peoples he encountered. A vigorous opponent of the international slave trade, he worked hard for the strengthening of the British fleet's efforts to stop the trade and took the side of the Mpongwe people against the imperialist incursions of the French into Gabon. He wrote an encyclopedic *Western Africa, Its History, Conditions, and Prospects* (1856) in which he described in great detail the kingdoms and tribes of the region. This history, which was the culmination of his research and observations on the societies of western Africa, is still used by historians and anthropologists as an early resource on precolonial Africa.[37] A recent French historian has called Wilson "a remarkable man" and has said that in comparison to other American and European travelers and commentators in nineteenth-century Gabon, one "admires his work, his activism, his moderation, and the generosity and justice of his judgments."[38]

Wilson traveled and observed an African world that was dynamic and evolving, especially as it adapted to the increasing intrusions by Europeans and European Americans. By the 1830s and 1840s, several generations had passed since most lowcountry slaves had been taken and brutally transported to America, yet the African world that Wilson observed was not isolated from that earlier African world but rather stood in deep continuity with it.

Not long after he arrived in Liberia, Wilson encountered a conjurer or, as he called him, "a *fetish priest.*" The man had come into the little settlement in Monrovia, and Wilson was immediately struck by what he called the "singular and ludicrous" character of his dress. An animal skin decorated with seashells sat upon his head and tumbled over his forehead and down onto his shoulders. Around his neck were long strings of beads, and around his wrists and ankles were rings of iron and ivory. A long tail reached toward the ground with a bell on its end that "made a loud dinging at each step," and around his waist he wore a narrow strip of cloth. Wilson immediately perceived that the man carried himself erect with great dignity and with a sense of self-confidence. In a remarkable encounter, Wilson approached the man and began to examine minutely what Wilson called "his articles of ornament." This examination, said Wilson, gave the conjurer great offense. "He resented my curiosity by taking hold of the sleeve of my coat and twisting it with an air of contempt." In this way the missionary and the fetish priest examined one another and confronted one another with contempt across the great cultural divide that separated their worlds. Wilson, far from his lowcountry context, quickly learned to be more circumspect and prudent as he sought to explore the world of the West African conjurer.[39]

"The interior life of the people," Wilson would write some twenty years later, "their moral, social, civil, and religious condition, as well as their peculiar notions and customs, have always been a sealed book to the rest of the world."[40] While Wilson thought his own investigations over many years were a "faithful and unpretending record" of the societies of Western Africa, he remained aware of how difficult it was to comprehend

In Liberia, Leighton Wilson, a Presbyterian minister, met a conjurer or "fetish priest." When he approached the man and fingered his clothing of seashells and animal skins, the conjurer, offended by Wilson's presumptuous act, boldly took hold of Wilson's sleeve and examined him. Thus the two men encountered one another across a great cultural divide. In the late eighteenth and early nineteenth century the four continents of the Atlantic basin saw a massive exchange of people, a situation that occasioned frequent encounters between cultures that had previously remained alien. From Robert Hamill Nassau, *Fetichism in West Africa* (New York: Charles Scribner's Sons, 1904), frontispiece.

"the interior life" of other peoples. "It is not an easy task," he would write in the 1850s, "to give a full and satisfactory exposition of the religious creed of the pagan tribes of Africa. Those who have lived longest in the country, and have had the best opportunities to make themselves acquainted with the subject, have not always been able to satisfy their own minds in relation to what they really believe and hold as their religious creed." He had discovered through his years of investigation and travel that West and West Central Africa were composed of a mosaic of richly diverse cultures, religions, and languages. And he had also discovered that the people everywhere were reluctant to make known their religious beliefs to whites. "They naturally shun," he wrote, "the scrutiny of white men."[41]

In spite of the cultural and religious diversity that Wilson found in West and West Central Africa, and in spite of the difficulties of penetrating and grasping the complexities of religious belief over this vast region, Wilson did believe that he had identified certain common beliefs that provided coherence to the religious life of the region. These included belief in "one Supreme Being," belief in a "Future Existence," belief in "Witchcraft," and a belief in "Demons." Most prominent, however, was a belief in charms or fetishes.[42]

Perhaps remembering his early confrontation with the conjurer, Wilson wrote in the 1850s that when a stranger first plants "his feet upon the shores of Africa," his eyes immediately encounter fetishes.

> He steps forth from the boat under a canopy of fetishes, not only as a security for his own safety, but as a guaranty that he does not carry the elements of mischief among the people; he finds them suspended along every path he walks; at every junction of two or more roads; at the crossing-place of every stream; at the base of every large rock or overgrown forest tree; at the gate of every village; over the door of every house, and around the neck of every human being whom he meets.[43]

These fetishes, he wrote, are "little else than a charm." They may be "made of a piece of wood, the horn of a goat, the hoof of an antelope, a piece of metal or ivory," and they may include the hair of someone's head or a fingernail clipping. Once prepared, the fetish "needs only to pass through the consecrating hands of a native priest to receive all that the supernatural powers which it is supposed to possess."[44]

While Wilson found that fetishes were used for reasons "almost without number," he believed their chief purpose was as a "defense against witchcraft." He acknowledged that a belief in witchcraft had "prevailed to a greater or less extent among most of the nations of the earth," but he was convinced that a belief in witches could be regarded "as one of the heaviest curses" that rested upon much of western Africa. A person possessed of the "mysterious art" of the witch was said to have almost omnipotent power. Wilson found that "there is nothing too hard for the machinations of witchcraft. Sickness, poverty, insanity, and almost every evil incident to human life, are ascribed to its agency. Death, no matter by what means, or under what circumstances it takes place, is spontaneously and almost universally ascribed to this cause."[45]

AS A REMEDY to witchcraft, Wilson found almost everywhere that he traveled some form of what was called the "red-water ordeal." A person, he wrote, accused of being a witch, of causing a death or some illness or misfortune, was forced to drink a red-water concoction. Those who vomited it up were innocent, but those who fell down and lost their self-control were guilty and were immediately set upon and killed by the people.[46] Warnings against witches and other dangers often came through dreams believed to have been sent by the spirits of the dead. The people, Wilson wrote, "are eager to receive communications from the spirits of their deceased friends, especially as they are supposed to have emerged from the uncertainties and darkness of this to the clearer light of another world."[47]

Wilson as a Christian missionary and Presbyterian wanted to bring some theological coherence to these diverse beliefs — a quest that was itself apparently an act of imposing Western cultural assumptions. Yet as a careful observer, Wilson knew the complexity and diversity of religious life in West and West Central Africa. So as he wrote and made his reports, he tried to hold in tension the diversity with what he found to be certain common beliefs and practices.

WHAT THEN of the conjurer in the Medway swamp and of Sam? What glimpses into their worlds open before us through a careful reading of the extensive reports of a lowcountry missionary in West and West Central Africa?

Most obviously the conjurer's world contained certain material retentions from an increasingly distant African homeland. The physical character of charms in the lowcountry — with their roots, strands of hair, and bits of fingernail — reflected remembered ways of constructing fetishes.

Yet even the physical character of the charms showed that they were constructed in the lowcountry and not West or West Central Africa. The bottles and rusty nails used in the lowcountry charms were rare in the lands through which Wilson traveled, while antelope hooves and other distinctive African animals and plants were not available for lowcountry charms. Cultural accommodations to the basic physical realities of the lowcountry had been shaping the conjurer's world.[48]

At the same time, the conjurer in the Medway swamp had to take into account the social realities of the lowcountry. Unlike the fetish priest who boldly confronted Wilson, the lowcountry conjurer hid in the Medway swamp. He clearly knew the harsh realities of a slave society. Wilson in his reports on West African fetishes noted that they continued to be used by slaves in the American South, but, he said in a telling comment, "in a less open form."[49] The conjurer hiding in Liberty County could not walk confidently out of the Medway swamp wearing the regalia of a fetish priest and confront the driver Sam or Charles Colcock Jones. Powerful social, cultural, and religious forces kept him hiding in the swamp and made the lowcountry practice of conjuring fundamentally different from that practice in western Africa, where the fetish priest was surrounded by social, cultural, and religious systems that supported his practice of conjuring. The Medway conjurer stood in a tradition of conjuring that had been adapting over several generations to both the physical and social realities of the lowcountry. By the 1830s, this tradition had become an African American — and not simply an African — tradition of conjuring. Conjuring, a cultural practice transmitted from one social context to new social circumstances, did not hang suspended above the Georgia lowcountry in some essential, unchanging form, but was transformed by historical figures such as the Medway conjurer into an African American practice of conjuring.

Similar observations can be made of lowcountry witchcraft so closely associated with the world of the conjurer. While witchcraft has been practiced in many cultures, including the white South, the widespread belief among Gullah people in witches suggests strong continuities with West and West Central African beliefs. Yet in the lowcountry, the belief in witches was "in a less open form." Witchcraft was always on the margins of lowcountry life, largely hidden and out of sight, slipping in and out of view like a phantom of some social reality. Unlike its African origins, lowcountry witchcraft was not supported by dominant social, cultural, and religious systems and had to adapt to its marginality. Certainly there was no parallel in the lowcountry to the public red-water ordeal so fundamental to much of the world of West and West Central Africa. Witchcraft in the lowcountry was an African American and not simply an African phenomenon.[50]

What then about the role of dreams in the religious life of West and West Central African people? Can that role provide another glimpse into the world of the Medway conjurer and into that of Sam's? Wilson emphasized that throughout his travels he found dreams understood to be communications from the spirits of the dead, and Jones found in Liberty County that dreams played an important role in the religious life of the Gullah people. People sought out the conjurer because he had visions and dreamed dreams and claimed to predict events. But the people also had their own dreams, and those dreams were Liberty County dreams, arising out of the places they laid their heads at night and the life they lived in the lowcountry settlements. These dreams became a part of the Baptist tradition of Sam. A man came to Jones "professing to be under some convictions of sin" and said, "Last night I dreamt that two white ladies, all dressed in white, with smiling faces, said to me, will you come with us and serve the Lord? I answered — I am not ready. Said they, you must get ready and come, and with that they vanished out of sight." Another man, who had been excommunicated, wished to be readmitted to the church. He went to a watchman, an African American church leader, and told him a dream he had had: "He fell into a hole, and that was full of fire. A white man appeared and took him out, and told him to go and tell T. the watchman."[51] These and other dreams reported later in slave narratives point toward the dynamic and evolving character of the conjurer's world and of Sam's world. Within the Gullah community, an African dream tradition had been interacting with a Protestant theological tradition represented by Sam the driver and leader at the Sunbury Baptist Church. One result of this interaction was an African dream tradition appropriated and adapted into a lowcountry African American Christianity.[52]

BENEATH THESE beliefs and practices we can discern at least some of the complex ways the Gullah people of the Georgia lowcountry in the 1830s and 1840s were part of an Atlantic world. Charms, witchcraft, and dreams linked them to a West and West Central Africa world where sickness, death, and troubles of many sorts were *caused* by social conflicts, by the animosity of a neighbor or the harmful intent of a witch.[53] In such a world, the causes of a misfortune could be discovered through divination, a dream, or a vision. These "deep assumptions" about causality and divination had not been lost in the traumas of the Middle Passage. But such deep assumptions had to function on a different side of the Atlantic in a world of American slavery, in the midst of an evolving European American culture, and in dynamic relationship with an emerging African American Protestant tradition that also had strong ties with European Protestantism. Both the Medway conjurer and Sam were thus part of competing and overlapping worlds — European and African, European American and African American.

And what then of the fetish priest in Liberia? He too was part of an Atlantic world as he encountered not only a white lowcountry missionary but also Gullah people who brought with them to Liberia their own African American traditions that been forged under the harsh conditions of the Georgia lowcountry. Indeed, the history of Liberia for generations to come would be largely marked by the encounter between Americo-Liberians and indigenous people.[54]

By the 1830s and 1840s, the broad Atlantic had thus served as a highway across which people had moved in both directions. To be sure, most of the movement had been in one direction, and it was the brutal, involuntary movement of chattel slaves. Yet the movement had gone in both directions, and traveling with those who moved or were moved were remembered ways and dreams, religious commitments, and deep assumptions. Among those who were a part of this Atlantic world were Gullah people. By the 1830s, they had established their own distinct religious life that was not a simple replication of some West African religious traditions or of European Protestant piety. Nor was their religious life a new thing under the sun that had emerged from the landscape of the lowcountry unadorned and without a history. Rather it was a part of a developing African American religious tradition, rooted in West and West Central Africa and also in a transatlantic Protestant tradition. A dynamic and evolving Gullah community had been seeking to adapt to the physical and social landscape of the Georgia lowcountry even as it helped to shape those landscapes.

NOTES

1. "Samuel Elliotts Funeral Sermon," *Charleston Observer*, October 13, 1838.
2. Ibid.
3. Ibid. I have been unable to identify any more specific details about the conjurer — the plantation he came from or the persons who captured him, who were most likely whites.
4. For links between lowcountry conjuring and West and West Central Africa,

see Philip D. Morgan, *Slave Counterpoint: Black Culture in the Eighteenth-Century Chesapeake and Lowcountry* (Chapel Hill: University of North Carolina Press, 1998), 614–18; Margaret Creel, *"A Peculiar People": Slave Religion and Community-Culture among the Gullah,* (New York: New York University Press, 1988); and Theophus Smith, *Conjuring Culture: Biblical Formations of Black America* (New York: Oxford University Press, 1994), 3–15.

5. The concept of an "Atlantic world" with an "Atlantic history" has become a rapidly developing field of historical study. See Bernard Bailyn, *Atlantic History: Concept and Contours* (Cambridge, Mass.: Harvard University Press, 2005).

6. For the brutality of slavery, see, for example, Orlando Patterson, *Slavery and Social Death: A Comparative Study* (Cambridge, Mass.: Harvard University Press, 1982).

7. A convenient place for a comprehensive review of Baptist piety and belief can be found in Sydney E. Ahlstrom, *A Religious History of the American People* (New Haven, Conn.: Yale University Press, 1972).

8. For the continuing role of lowcountry conjurers into the twentieth century, see Georgia Savannah Unit, Georgia Writers' Project, Works Projects Administration, *Drums and Shadows: Survival Studies among the Georgia Coastal Negroes*, with an introduction by Charles Joyner (1940; repr., Athens: University of Georgia, 1986).

9. For an important introduction to this question, see Thornton, *African Religions and Christianity in the Atlantic World*, 235–71.

10. E. Franklin Frazier, *The Negro Family in the United States* (Chicago: University of Chicago Press, 1939), 21, and chap. 1.

11. Melville J. Herskovits, "The Negro in the New World," *American Anthropologist* 32 (1930): 145–55. See also, for example, Melville J. Herskovits, *Life in a Haitian Valley* (1937; repr., New York: Doubleday Anchor, 1971), 260; and Mintz and Price, *Birth of African-American Culture*, 61–66.

12. Richard Waterman, "On Flogging a Dead Horse: Lessons Learned from the Africanisms Controversy," *Ethnomusicology* 7 (1963): 83–87.

13. Stephan Palmié, review of *Africanisms in American Culture*, ed. Joseph E. Holloway, in *Africa* 63, no. 2 (1993): 273–76.

14. See, for example, Margaret Washington Creel, "Gullah Attitudes toward Life and Death," in *Africanisms in American Culture*, ed. Joseph E. Holloway (Bloomington: Indiana University Press, 1990), 69–70; and Creel, *"Peculiar People,"* passim.

15. Morgan, *Slave Counterpoint*, 58–76, shows in great detail the "growing heterogeneity" of the Gullah. See also Darold D. Wax, "'New Negroes Are Always in Demand': The Slave Trade in Eighteenth-Century Georgia," *Georgia Historical Quarterly* LXVIII (1984): 193–220.

16. Mintz and Price, *Birth of African-American Culture*, 7–12, 44–45.

17. Cf. Palmié, review of *Africanisms in American Culture*, 274–75.

18. For the "invention of tradition," see Eric Hobsbawn and Terence Ranger, eds., *The Invention of Tradition* (Cambridge: Cambridge University Press, 1983). For the problematic character of "traditional African religion," see J. D. Y. Peel, "Historicity and Pluralism in Some Recent Studies of Yoruba Religion," *Africa* 64, no. 1 (1994): 150–66; Sean Hawkins, "Disguising Chiefs and God as History: Questions on the

Acephalousness of Lodagaa Politics and Religion," *Africa* 66, no. 2 (1996): 202–47; and Rosalind Shaw, "The Invention of 'African Traditional Religion,'" in *Religion* 20 (1990): 339–53. Cf. V. Y. Mudimbe, *The Invention of Africa: Gnosis, Philosophy, and the Order of Knowledge* (Bloomington: Indiana University Press, 1988).

19. For some of the problems and advantages in the use of missionary reports, see J. D. Y. Peel, "For Who Hath Despised the Day of Small Things? Missionary Narratives and Historical Anthropology," *Comparative Studies in Society and History* 37, no. 3 (1995): 581–607; Femi J. Kolapo, "The 1858–1859 Gbebe Journal of CMS Missionary James Thomas," *History in Africa* 27 (2000): 159–92; and Paul S. Landau, "Hegemony and History in Jean and John L. Comaroff's *Of Revelation and Revolution*," *Africa* 70, no. 3 (2000): 501–19.

20. Erskine Clarke, *Dwelling Place: A Plantation Epic* (New Haven, Conn.: Yale University Press, 2006). See esp. 152–66.

21. Charles Colcock Jones, "Journal of a Missionary to the Negroes in the State of Georgia,'" *Charleston Observer*, August 31, 1833; February 21, 1835.

22. "Samuel Elliotts Funeral Sermon," *Charleston Observer*, October 13, 1838.

23. Lydia Parrish, *Slave Songs of the Georgia Sea Islands* (1942; repr., Athens: University of Georgia Press, 1992), 45–47; Clarke, *Dwelling Place*, 152.

24. Clarke, *Dwelling Place*, 470.

25. "Journal of a Missionary to the Negroes in the State of Georgia," *Charleston Observer*, September 7, 1833.

26. Charles C. Jones, *The Religious Instruction of the Negroes, In the United States* (Savannah, 1842), 127–28. For the character and volume of the slave trade into Savannah and Charleston during the closing years of the eighteenth century and the early years of the nineteenth, see James A. McMillin, *The Final Victims: Foreign Slave Trade to North America, 1783–1810* (Columbia: University of South Carolina Press, 2004).

27. "Journal of a Missionary to the Negroes in the State of Georgia," *Charleston Observer*, September 21, 1833.

28. Ibid.

29. "Samuel Elliotts Funeral Sermon."

30. For lowcountry witches, see Georgia Writers' Project, Works Projects Administration, *Drums and Shadows: Survival Studies among the Georgia Coastal Negroes* (Athens: University of Georgia Press, 1940), 112–32; Michael Mullin, *Africa in America: Slave Acculturation and Resistance in the American South and the British Caribbean, 1736–1831* (Urbana: University of Illinois Press, 1992), 68–72; Morgan, *Slave Counterpoint*, 615–25; Albert J. Raboteau, *Slave Religion: "The Invisible Institution" in the Antebellum South* (New York: Oxford University Press, 1978), 80–86, 275–88; Smith, *Conjuring Culture*, 140–58. A massive anthropological literature seeks to understand or explain witchcraft, conjurers, and magic. Good entry points into the literature are Brian Morris, *Anthropological Studies of Religion: An Introductory Text* (Cambridge: Cambridge University Press, 1987), and idem, *Religion and Anthropology: A Critical Introduction* (Cambridge: Cambridge University Press, 2006).

31. Charles C. Jones, "Simon the Sorcerer," Charles Colcock Jones Papers, "Sermon File," Howard-Tilton Memorial Library, Tulane University.

32. "Journal of a Missionary to the Negroes in the State of Georgia," *Charleston Observer*, January 25, 1834.

33. "Journal of a Missionary to the Negroes in the State of Georgia," *Charleston Observer*, September 21, 1833.

34. The dynamics of conversion and its intentions have received prominent attention by historians and anthropologists. See, for example, Robert W. Hefner, ed., *Conversion to Christianity: Historical and Anthropological Perspectives on a Great Transformation* (Berkeley: University of California Press, 1993), esp. 3–44; and Andrew Buckser and Stephen D. Glazier, eds., *The Anthropology of Religious Conversion* (Lanham, Md.: Rowman and Littlefield Publishers, 2003).

35. Clarke, *Dwelling Place*, 229.

36. For biographical information on the Wilsons, see Hampden C. DuBose, *Memoirs of Rev. John Leighton Wilson, D.D.* (Richmond, 1895); Henry H. Bucher Jr., "John Leighton Wilson and the Mpongwe: The 'Spirit of 1776' in Mid-Nineteenth Century Africa," *Journal of Presbyterian History* 54, no. 3 (Fall 1976): 291–316.

37. See, for example, K. David Patterson, *The Northern Gabon Coast to 1875* (Oxford: Clarendon Press, 1975), passim; Hubert Deschamps, *Quinze Ans de Gabon: Les Débuts de L' établissement Français 1839–1853* (Paris: Société Française D'Histoire D'Outre-Mer, 1965); and K. David Patterson, "The Vanishing Mpongwe: European Contact and Demographic Change in the Gabon River," *Journal of African History* 16, no. 2 (1975): 217–38.

38. Deschamps, *Quinze Ans de Gabon*, 101; also 331.

39. John Leighton Wilson, "Journal of J. Leighton Wilson on a Missionary Tour to Western Africa in the Year of 1834," February 1, 1834, Archive, American Board of Commissioners for Foreign Missions, Houghton Library, Harvard University (microfilm, Columbia Theological Seminary Library).

40. John Leighton Wilson, *Western Africa: Its History, Condition, and Prospects* (New York, 1856), iii.

41. Ibid., 208.

42. Ibid., 209–11.

43. Ibid., 214. Wilson spelled "fetish" as "fetich." I have changed his spelling to the modern spelling.

44. Ibid., 211–15.

45. Ibid., 216, 222.

46. Ibid., 221–28. Accounts of "witchcraft executions" in Gabon are given in Robert Hamill Nassau, *Fetichism in West Africa: Forty Years' Observation of Native Custom and Superstitions* (New York: Charles Scribner's Sons, 1904), 128–38. For more recent accounts of this ordeal, see Misty L. Bastian, "'The Daughter She Will Eat Agousie in the World of the Spirits' Witchcraft Confessions in Missionised Onitsha, Nigeria," *Africa* 72, no. 1 (2002): 85–110; Thornton, *Africans and the Making of the Atlantic World*, 241; Christopher J. Gray, *Colonial Rule and Crisis in Equatorial Africa: Southern Gabon, Ca. 1850–1940* (Rochester, N.Y.: University of Rochester

Press, 2002). Gray points toward the increase in "witchcraft accusations, poison or-deals, and the poisoning of rivals" in the midst of colonial dislocations of the late nineteenth century. See esp. 49–50.

47. Wilson, *Western Africa*, 211.

48. Mintz and Price, *Birth of African-American Culture*, 52–60; Robert Hall, "African Religious Retentions in Florida," in Holloway, *Africanisms in American Culture*, 98–118. Pointing to "distinctive cultural patterns" of African origins among the Gullah in nineteenth-century Florida, Hall insists these "Africanisms had be-come Americanisms" (106).

49. Wilson, *Western Africa*, 215.

50. Cf. Charles Joyner, *Down by the Riverside: A South Carolina Slave Commu-nity* (Chicago: University of Illinois Press, 1984), 141–43.

51. "Journal of a Missionary to the Negroes in the State of Georgia," *Charleston Observer*, September 17, 1833.

52. Other examples of an African American dream tradition can be found in Clifton H. Johnson, ed., *God Struck Me Dead: Religious Conversion Experiences and Autobiographies of Ex-Slaves* (Philadelphia: Pilgrim Press, 1969), especially "behold I am a doctor," 150–52; and "more than conqueror," 169–72. See also Mechal Sobel, *Trabelin' On: Slave Journey to an Afro-Baptist Faith* (Princeton, N.J.: Princeton Uni-versity Press, 1988).

53. E. E. Evans-Pritchard made the connection between witchcraft and a theory of causation in *Witchcraft, Oracles and Magic among the Azande* (Oxford: Oxford University Press, 1937), and argued that witchcraft is an intellectual coherent system. Cf. Mintz and Price, *Birth of African-American Culture*, 9–10, and J. Omosade Awo-lalu, *Yoruba Beliefs and Sacrificial Rites* (Essex, UK: Althelia Henrietta PR, 1979), 81–84.

54. For the religious life of the settlers at Cape Palmas, Liberia, and their stormy relationship with the indigenous people, see Richard L. Hall, *On Afric's Shore: A History of Maryland in Liberia, 1834–1857* (Baltimore: Maryland Historical Soci-ety, 2003). For the late-twentieth-century civil war in Liberia, see Stephen Ellis, *The Mask of Anarchy: The Destruction of Liberia and the Religious Dimension of an Afri-can Civil War*, updated ed. (New York: New York University Press, 2006).

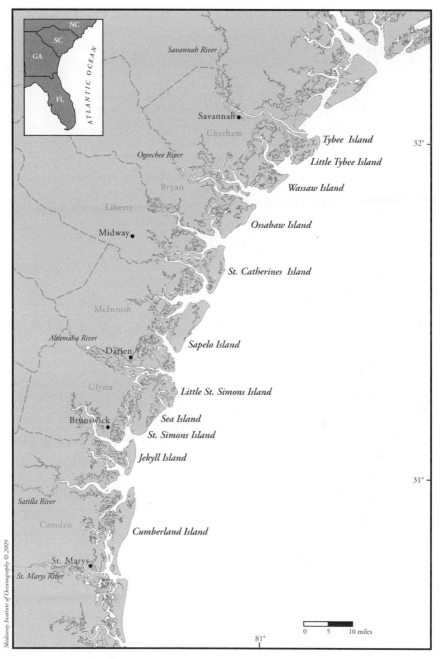

Map of coastal Georgia

Coastal Georgia from the Savannah River to the St. Marys River. The network of tidal rivers and creeks defines the principal rice-growing areas of the coast. Courtesy of the Graphics Department at Skidaway Institute of Oceanography.

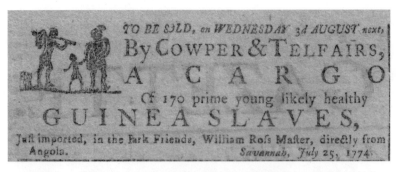

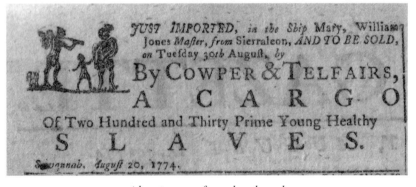

Advertisements for enslaved people

The firm Cowper and Telfairs imported five hundred Africans — from Angola, the Gold Coast, and Sierra Leone — during a six-week period in 1774. Information on the slave trade in Georgia over the previous decade indicates that about 41 percent of the enslaved were embarked from Senegambia, 22 percent from Sierra Leone and the Windward Coast, 8 percent from Angola, and 7 percent from the Gold Coast. Cowper and Telfairs, a firm of Scotsmen, was the largest importer of enslaved Africans in Georgia. From the *Georgia Gazette*, July 27, August 3, and August 24, 1774. Courtesy of the Georgia Historical Society.

Sunbury, 20th June, 1766.

RUN AWAY from my plantation at Sunbury, about seven weeks ago, FOUR NEGROES, viz. three men and one woman: BRIDGEE, a stout fellow about 40, five feet ten inches, with a high nose; he was first purchased by the Portuguese, and sold to the Spaniards (by which he speaks both languages) taken last war, bought by Capt. James Dunbar, who sold him to me: CELIA, his wife, a likely wench about 26: PRINCE, a tall handsome young fellow about 23: ABOO, a thick short fellow about 25, with a cut in his face, to the best of my remembrance on his right temple. The men are all prime sawyers. When they first went off, having some connections with Mr. Martin's and other negroes upon South-Newport, they were supposed to have gone there; but after having committed several outrages, particularly upon Mr. Ross at the Ferry, and a chained canoe being cut away some nights after from a wharf at Sunbury, and no people missing, they are suspected to be the villains, and are gone to the Northward. Whoever will apprehend all or any of the aforesaid negroes, and deliver them to the goal-keeper in Savannah, to Mr. Thomas Carr in Sunbury, or to me at Frederica, shall receive for each upon delivery the sum of 20s. sterling, with all reasonable charges. MARK CARR.

Advertisement for runaway slaves

The majority of runaway slaves in colonial Georgia were from Africa or the West Indies. Mark Carr, a retired Scottish officer, advertised for Bridgee — who had been purchased by the Portuguese, sold to the Spanish, and could speak both languages — Bridgee's wife, Celia, and two other men, Prince and Aboo. The three escaped men were "prime sawyers" — much-valued cutters who turned timber into lumber. Canoes, rafts, and flatboats were prized means of escape. Given their background, these runaway slaves may have been headed to Savannah to attempt to embark on a ship. From the *Georgia Gazette*, July 2, 1766. Courtesy of the Georgia Historical Society.

Map of western Africa
Map of western Africa, including the six principal slave-trading areas: Senegambia, Sierra Leone, the Gold Coast, the Bight of Benin, the Bight of Biafra, and Angola. From J. Leighton Wilson, *Western Africa: Its History, Condition, and Prospects* (New York: Harper and Brothers, 1856), 100.

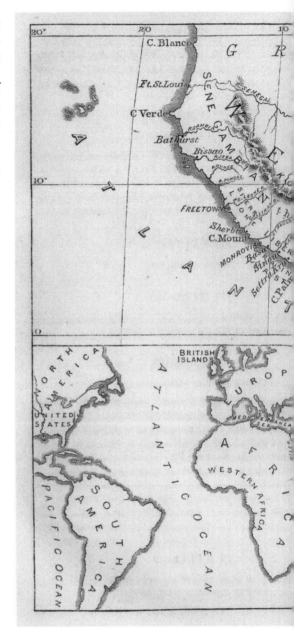

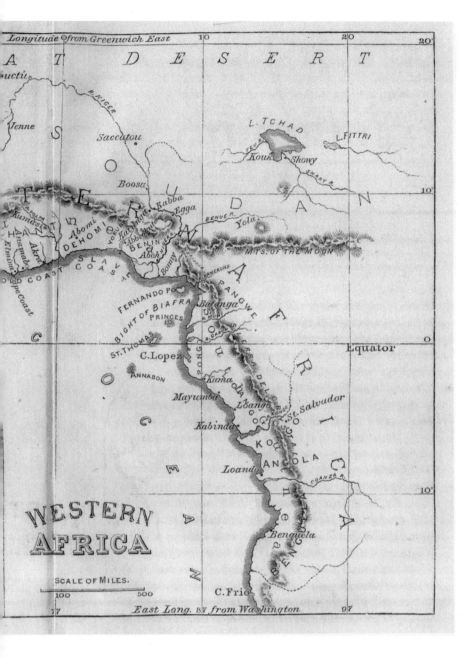

AT   D E S E R T

uctu

S
Jenne   Saccatou   L. TCHAD   L. FITTRI

R. NIGER   O   Kouk   Showy

Boosa   U   D   A   N   10

T E R   Rabba   SHARY R.

Abomi   Egga

Kumasi   DEHOMI   BENUE R.   Yola

Abo   YORUBA   BENIN   Aboh   MTS. OF THE MOON

Elmina   SLA   VE   Bonny

GOLD COAST   COAST   CAMEROONS   A

ope Coast   FERNANDO PO   PANGWE   F

C   BIGHT OF BIAFRA   Batanga

FERNANDO PO   PRINCES   R. CAMA   R   Equator   0

ST. THOMAS   R. GABOON

C. Lopez

ANNABON   PONGO   SERRA DEL   I

Kama

Mayumba   L'Bango   St. Salvador   C

O   Kabinda   KONGO

E   KO   A

Loando   ANGOLA

A   COANZA R.   10

WESTERN
AFRICA

N   Benguela

SCALE OF MILES.

100   500   C. Frio

Olaudah Equiano

Author of a literary masterpiece that captures his life as an enslaved person and later as an abolitionist, Olaudah Equiano wrote of his several voyages to Savannah in vessels owned by Robert King, a Quaker who ran a trading operation between the island of Montserrat and Philadelphia. In at least six trips during the mid-1760s, Equiano found Georgia to be little better than a cultural extension of the Caribbean. He was nearly beaten to death in one instance, was taken to the guardhouse to be whipped in another, drew the ire of a leading merchant who put local constables on his trail on still another occasion, and in a final instance escaped being kidnapped by the slimmest of margins. Frontispiece from the first edition of volume 1 of Olaudah Equiano's *Interesting Narrative* (London, 1789). The John Carter Brown Library at Brown University.

George Liele

Growing up on a farm between Savannah and Augusta during the 1760s, George Liele experienced a profound religious awakening and joined the Buckhead Creek Baptist Church, where his owner was a deacon. Baptized, Liele became the first person of African descent licensed and ordained to serve as a Baptist preacher and missionary in North America. His sermons delivered at Silver Bluff Plantation before the Revolution stirred a call to ministry in David George, an enslaved person who in turn founded the Silver Bluff Baptist Church, probably the first exclusively African American church on the continent. Both men came to Savannah during the Revolution and preached to fellow blacks behind British lines. In 1782, Liele accompanied the British to Jamaica, where he founded the first African American Baptist church on that island. From Edgar G. Thomas, *The First African Baptist Church of North America* (Savannah, Ga., 1925). Courtesy of the Georgia Historical Society.

Andrew Bryan

In his work in Loyalist Savannah, George Liele baptized Andrew Bryan, an enslaved person born in Goose Creek, South Carolina. When Liele departed in 1782, Bryan assumed leadership of the nascent Savannah fellowship and, despite severe beatings and imprisonment, gained a following. Six years later, a white minister, accompanied by a black colleague, came to town and ordained Bryan while baptizing forty of the faithful. The newly ordained minister founded First African Baptist Church, arguably the first independent African American Baptist church in the United States. He later purchased his own and his family members' freedom, bought property for church construction in 1794, and began a hauling enterprise that made him a relatively wealthy small slaveholder. From Emmanuel King Love, *History of the First African Baptist Church, from Its Organization, January 20th, 1788, to July 1st, 1888* (Savannah, Ga.: The Morning News Print, 1888). Courtesy of the Georgia Historical Society.

First African Baptist Church

Organized in 1788, First African Baptist Church (called First Colored during its early years) is one of the oldest black congregations in North America. Under Andrew Bryan and his successors, the church developed a unique spiritual and cultural identity by blending African folkways and Christianity. By the 1820s, it numbered several thousand people, including offshoot congregations in rural communities. In 1802, church elders organized a second congregation to relieve overcrowding, the Second African Baptist Church. As a result of a controversy in the early 1830s, the original congregation split, with First African locating on Franklin Square and the remainder forming Third African Baptist Church, later renamed First Bryan Baptist Church. From Thomas, *The First African Baptist Church of North America*. Courtesy of the Georgia Historical Society.

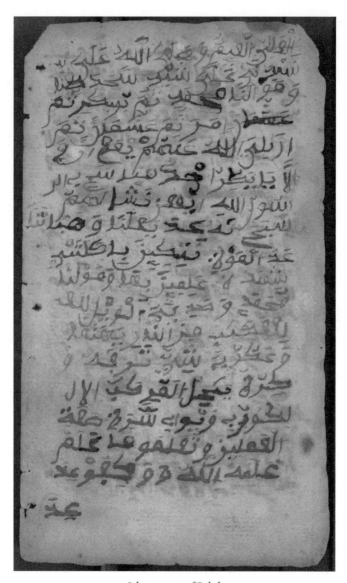

Islamic text of Bilali

The Georgia sea islands, especially St. Simons and Sapelo, were a center of Muslim life in the early American South. Muslims on these islands made genuine and persistent efforts to observe their religion. A central figure was Bilali, otherwise known as "Ben Ali," head driver for over four hundred enslaved people on the Thomas Spalding plantation on Sapelo Island. He originated somewhere in "Guinea" and may have spent time in the Bahamas before he was brought to the island. He is most noted for an extant collection of excerpts from an Islamic legal text known as the Risāla of Ibn Abī Zayd. Bilali also served as the model for Joel Chandler Harris's caricature "Ben Ali." One observer later stated that his large family of twelve sons and seven daughters all "worshiped Mahomet." Courtesy of Hargrett Rare Book and Manuscript Library, University of Georgia Libraries.

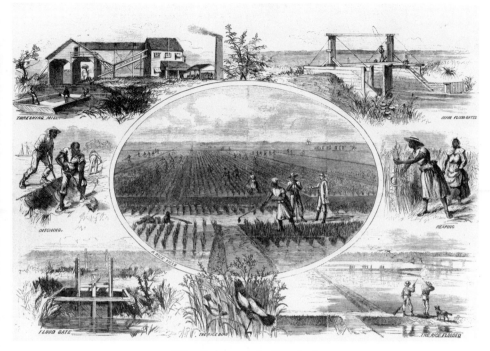

"Rice Culture on the Ogeechee"

"Rice Culture on the Ogeechee, Near Savannah, Georgia," an image by A. R. Waud that appeared in *Harper's Weekly* on December 12, 1867, depicts enslaved Africans working in the rice fields. The vignettes illustrate the various stages in rice cultivation, including ditching, flooding, reaping, and threshing. Recent scholars have demonstrated that Africans and African Americans contributed much more than brute labor to the development of the rice industry along coastal Georgia and South Carolina. Many believe that various technologies involved in rice cultivation in the lowcountry originated in rice-producing regions in West Africa and were transferred across the Atlantic by slaves. Whatever the origins of the technology, blacks succeeded in negotiating a degree of autonomy through the task system, an agreement that a worker would accomplish a certain task each day and be free to use the remaining time for his or her own purposes. Courtesy of V & J Duncan Antiques, Prints & Books, Savannah, Ga.

Hoeing a rice field

A woman hoeing a rice field alongside three men in coastal Georgia. Women's roles in rice culture developed in West Africa where women worked in the fields at the specialized tasks of hoeing, sowing, weeding, and transplanting rice seedlings. Courtesy of V & J Duncan Antique Maps, Prints & Books, Savannah, Ga.

Winnowing rice

(*Facing page*) As late as the early twentieth century, African Americans winnowed rice using techniques brought from West Africa. This woman is shaking and rotating rice grain in a traditional flat basket so that the empty husks and chaff move to the edge, where they are jettisoned. Courtesy of Georgia Archives, Vanishing Georgia Collection, sapo94.

Plowing a rice field

Two enslaved people plowing a rice field near Savannah, ca. 1855. Rice growing involved flooding fields periodically to cause the seeds to germinate, control weeds, and support the stalks of rice in their final stage. This photograph illustrates how the soft soil of the lowcountry discouraged the use of horses, mules, or oxen to pull plows. It speaks to the harsh labor and the vulnerability of enslaved people to the deadly respiratory and waterborne illnesses that proliferated in the swampy land. Item 1, Georgia Historical Society collection of stereographs, MS 1361-SG, Georgia Historical Society, Savannah, Ga. Courtesy of the Georgia Historical Society.

Hulling rice

(*Facing page*) Women on Sapelo Island hulling rice using mortar and pestle. Until the advent of milling machinery in South Carolina at the end of the eighteenth century, use of the African mortar and pestle proved an effective processing method because it removed the hull while minimizing grain breakage. Rice planters relied on enslaved women as much as on the labor of enslaved men. Courtesy of Georgia Archives, Vanishing Georgia Collection, sap093.

Sorting sea island cotton

Sea island cotton, a luxury staple characterized by long, thin fibers, was the predominant crop on barrier islands. Its cultivation began in the first decade after the American Revolution and declined precipitously after the Civil War. Planting involved both men and women. The preparation of sea island cotton for the market each fall was a communal affair. Women worked in the gin house to "sort" or remove dead leaves, stems, and yellowed cotton before ginning took place. Younger children were left in the quarters under the care of an older person. Sketch by James E. Taylor, *Harper's Weekly*, August 17, 1869. Courtesy of Library of Congress, Prints and Photographs Division, reproduction number LC-USZ62-116578.

Plantation quarters, St. Catherines Island
Women and children in front of the plantation quarters on St. Catherines Island. The
structures were made of tabby, a combination of oyster shells, sand, water, and lime
produced from mixing burnt oyster shells with wooden ash. The cabins contained two
rooms on either side of a brick chimney, each room inhabited by a family. Much of life
was lived outside plantation cabins. Families cooked, talked, visited, and repaired clothing and equipment out-of-doors. They typically supplemented the meager food rations
provided by plantation owners with a small garden behind the house that grew vegetables
native to Africa — groundnuts, benne (sesame), melons, and gourds. Image no. 211, William E. Wilson photographs, photograph album, and gelatin dry plate negatives, MS 1375,
Georgia Historical Society, Savannah, Ga. Courtesy of the Georgia Historical Society.

Man riding in an ox-drawn cart, Sapelo Island

This timeless photograph could just as easily have been taken in 1815 as in 1915. The barrier islands formed the heart of Africa-America, the Gullah-Geechee culture of the South Carolina and Georgia sea island region. Gullah usually refers to West African traditions in South Carolina, Geechee to those traditions in Georgia. Saltwater Geechee referred to those who lived on islands like Sapelo; freshwater Geechee to those who lived along tidal rivers and creeks. Living in an environment of few whites, blacks of both the islands and the coast showed greater continuity with African work patterns and folk culture than African Americans in other regions. Courtesy of Georgia Archives, Vanishing Georgia Collection, sap074.

Man with a homemade fiddle

Musical instruments from Africa represent an array of devices: the one-stringed fiddle, known especially in Islamic Africa; the drum; flutes of bamboo; and a lute with a gourd bowl, probably the forerunner of the banjo. At Christmas and New Year's Day, black men and women celebrated in a fashion that recalled West African customs, strumming stringed instruments made out of horsehair and animal bladders while beating out rhythms on drums of raccoon hide stretched over hollow logs. Photograph by O. Pierre Havens. Courtesy of Georgia Archives, Vanishing Georgia Collection, ctm352-92.

The Hermitage Plantation

African American men in front of the former slave cabins on the Hermitage Plantation. Built in 1850, fifty-two cabins housed two hundred enslaved men and women who
worked on the nearly four-hundred-acre plantation on the Savannah River. The forebears of these workers, shown circa 1900, produced Savannah gray brick at the kilns of
the plantation, center for brick production in southeast Georgia. Courtesy of Library of
Congress, Prints and Photographs Division, reproduction number LC-USZ62-110813.

Daguerreotype portrait

Daguerreotype portrait of a white child being held by an African American woman attired in traditional African headdress, ca. 1853. This house servant lived with her master, cared for his children, and participated in most of the household routine. Nevertheless, more than one lowcountry person remarked that black people did not easily reveal themselves to the white race, succeeding in maintaining an outward veneer that hid another, deeper life. Daguerreotype by J. W. Miller. Courtesy of Georgia Archives, Vanishing Georgia Collection, ctm347-87.

Firefighter, Savannah

Urban life offered rich possibilities. This unidentified firefighter, whose dress and countenance reflect great pride in his work, was most probably a free black. In the mid-1850s, several hundred slaves and 140 free men of color made up the Savannah Fire Department. The annual "Colored Fire Companies Parade" featured seven engine companies, two hose companies, and one hook and ladder company. The largely wooden city depended on its African American population for its protection. Photograph of an African American fireman in Savannah, Ga., ca. 1856, Manuscript, Archives, and Rare Book Library, Emory University.

Drayman, Savannah

A drayman stands next to his wooden cart with bales of cotton along the waterfront of Savannah. On this street fronting the river, draymen, sailors, laborers, ship carpenters, food suppliers, merchants, and retailers mingled as upland cotton was loaded for the textile mills of New England, Great Britain, and France. The four-story buildings behind the cart doubled as counting houses and warehouses. Courtesy of V & J Duncan Antique Maps, Prints & Books, Savannah, Ga.

First African Baptist Church

The First African Baptist Church on Franklin Square, where construction began in the late 1850s. The Baptist faith provided both a training ground and a forum for black leaders, male and female. The congregation of First African raised the money and provided the skills to construct this striking edifice with its grand tower. With four thousand members, this self-governing institution provided a degree of cultural autonomy that challenged the slaveholders' ideology of black dependence and inferiority. The many-storied tower collapsed at a later time. Today, the tower retains the first two stages and a smaller steeple. From Love, *History of the First African Baptist Church*. Courtesy of the Georgia Historical Society.

Andrew Marshall

The Reverend Andrew Marshall, pastor of First African Baptist Church from the early nineteenth century until his death in 1856. Marshall was the nephew by marriage of Andrew Bryan, founder of the church. Born a slave in South Carolina, he had purchased his freedom, built a successful drayage business in Savannah, and owned considerable property, including for a brief while several slaves. His congregation included many in small rural congregations throughout the lowcountry. Marshall walked a fine line in his sermons but encoded in them an emotional message of hope for the dawn of freedom and a day of reckoning. When he died at age one hundred, a throng of blacks and whites accompanied his hearse to Laurel Grove Cemetery. From Love, *History of the First African Baptist Church*. Courtesy of the Georgia Historical Society.

Ad for largest slave sale in Georgia

The largest sale of enslaved people in the state of Georgia took place in March 1859 at the Ten Broeck Race Course outside Savannah. To satisfy his creditors, Pierce M. Butler, resident of Philadelphia, sold 436 men, women, and children from his Butler Island and Hampton plantations near Darien. The breakup of families and the loss of home became part of the African American heritage remembered as the "weeping time." The event was reported extensively in the northern press and reaction to the sale deepened the nation's growing sectional divide immediately preceding the Civil War. From the *Savannah Republican*, February 22, 1859.

Contrabands, 1865

As Sherman marched his troops towards Savannah, thousands of black men, women, and children joined the advancing columns, eager to secure their freedom. The refugees tried to make themselves useful, offering to cook and wash, revealing hidden supplies and livestock, and providing military intelligence. The northern soldiers viewed the contrabands with mixed feelings but increasingly came to see them as a liability. After an incident at Ebenezer Creek near Savannah where dozens of blacks drowned attempting to cross the water, Sherman found himself under pressure from Washington to address their situation. From *Frank Leslie's Illustrated Newspaper*, March, 18, 1865. Courtesy of Library of Congress, Prints and Photographs Division, reproduction number LC-USZ62-112169.

Green-Meldrim House

On January 12, 1865, three weeks after entering Savannah, General Sherman met with twenty black leaders, mostly Baptist and Methodist ministers, on the second floor of the elegant house of Charles Green, an English cotton factor, to discuss the future of newly emancipated African Americans. In the wake of that meeting, Sherman issued Special Field Order No. 15, confiscating plantations on barrier islands and along tidal rivers and calling for the settlement of black families on the land. Sherman's revolutionary order was to provide land to many thousands of African Americans until Congress overturned the measure. Photograph by Branan Sanders, Historic American Buildings Survey, 1934. Courtesy of Library of Congress, Prints and Photographs Division, HABS, reproduction number HABS GA, 26-SAV, 22-1.

Freedmen's Bureau

At the end of the Civil War, Congress created the Freedmen's Bureau (Bureau of Refugees, Freedmen, and Abandoned Lands) to oversee the transition of newly emancipated blacks from slavery to freedom. Many white agents of the Bureau worked diligently to ensure fair treatment of African Americans in labor contracts as well as to protect them from random violence. This illustration from the July 23, 1868, edition of *Harper's Weekly* represents an idealized version of their role. The reality was more complex. On Ossabaw Island, the white agent attempted to use his position to create a sea island cotton plantation with labor working directly for him. Courtesy of Library of Congress, Prints and Photographs Division, reproduction number LC-USZ62-10555.

Map of Middle Place Plantation, Ossabaw Island

On its eleven thousand acres of upland, Ossabaw Island held four plantations before the Civil War. With Sherman's Special Field Order No. 15, demobilized federal troops from South Carolina received warrants for land at Middle Place Plantation. Visible in the map are former slave cabins, the fields for growing sea island cotton, and, on either side of the fields, salt marsh. The superintendent of the Freedmen's Bureau created a firm to grow cotton using black sharecroppers and, in the process, worked to undermine the recipients of outright land grants. Matters deteriorated to the point that federal troops intervened to prevent a conflict between white authorities, black recipients of grants, and former slaves who resented having been excluded from the grants. Courtesy of the Ossabaw Island Foundation.

HARTWELL

Tunis Campbell

Before the Civil War, Tunis Campbell was a successful preacher who doubled as a caterer and hotel steward in New York City. With the help of Secretary of War Stanton, Campbell was appointed to supervise land claims and resettlement on five Georgia sea islands. Campbell arrived at St. Catherines Island with his own blueprint for government. He established a militia of over one hundred blacks. Harassed by whites, unable to feed the colony, and beset by internal dissension, Campbell left the island to found a new colony in McIntosh County. He became justice of the peace in Darien, vice president of the Republican Party in Georgia, and state senator. After Democrats regained power in 1871, Campbell was arrested for "malfeasance" and sentenced to a convict labor camp. Courtesy of Howard University.

Family working in a cotton field

After the Civil War, both sea island cotton, with its long, thin fibers, and upland cotton, with its short, coarse fibers, were grown. The work was demanding and the hours long. Although posed, this photograph indicates the importance of the family unit in the field and the extended ties that bound kin together. The presence of babies and children in the field was not untypical. Image no. 105, William E. Wilson photographs, photograph album, and gelatin dry plate negatives, MS 1375, Georgia Historical Society, Savannah, Ga. Courtesy of the Georgia Historical Society.

Stacking bales of cotton, Savannah

Laborers stacked bales of cotton on the bottom floor of a four-story building on the waterfront that served as a counting house and warehouse. The fourth floor looked over Bay Street atop Savannah's forty-foot bluff. Blacks formed a critical part of the maritime community: laborers on the docks, coopers and ship carpenters, draymen carrying bales of cotton, sailors, and boatmen carrying produce from coastal farms and plantations. From *Frank Leslie's Illustrated Newspaper*, October 14, 1871. Courtesy of Library of Congress, Prints and Photographs Division, reproduction number LC-USZ62-37837.

Loading cotton on a Savannah dock

African Americans and whites loading a bale of cotton on board a vessel. Stevedores on the Savannah waterfront divided into two labor unions, the white Workingmen's Benevolent Association, organized by Irish immigrants, and the black Workingmen's Union Association, founded by freedmen. By the 1880s, the WUA achieved the same pay for the same work for its members, something that did not occur in other cities. A decade later, it suffered a devastating defeat in a strike, saw its most skilled longshoremen leave for other ports, and folded. Photograph by O. Pierre Havens. Courtesy of Georgia Archives, Vanishing Georgia Collection, ctm345-86.

Sugarcane production

Because growing conditions for sugarcane were generally favorable throughout the coastal plain, many farmers grew the crop for household and local use. The cane could be processed with a pressing machine operated by horse or oxen, a simple mill, and vats. Production remained on a small scale because processing the sugar for commercial purposes required a formidable investment for clarifying the juice into crystals, drying the sugar, and draining out the molasses. African Americans participated as workers and small farmers, and sorghum formed a notable part of the diet for many families. Image no. 115, William E. Wilson photographs, photograph album, and gelatin dry plate negatives, MS 1375, Georgia Historical Society, Savannah, Ga. Courtesy of the Georgia Historical Society.

Carrying food to market near Savannah

African Americans carrying food to market in baskets and by ox-drawn cart. The women walk with the produce on their heads in African fashion. From slavery to the early twentieth century, black people supplied the markets of coastal towns with the produce of their garden plots, including African foods like okra, yams, benne seed, black-eyed peas, and watermelon. E. A. Abbey, "Going to market — a scene near Savannah, Georgia," *Harper's Weekly*, May 29, 1875. Courtesy of Library of Congress, Prints and Photographs Division, reproduction number LC-USZ62-102153.

City Market, Savannah

Once in Savannah, African Americans sold produce at the City Market. In this structure opened in the 1870s, black women dominated the marketing of vegetables and other produce, setting the prices and serving as part of the informal economy that existed outside the system controlled by whites. The City Market became the focal point for the sale of meat, vegetables, and other produce and, as such, brought white and blacks together in intimate ways. Box 7, folder 8, item 1265, Georgia Historical Society collection of photographs, MS 1361-PH, Georgia Historical Society, Savannah, Ga. Courtesy of the Georgia Historical Society.

Huckster

(*Facing page*) Black men and women peddled fresh vegetables, baked goods, and handicraft items on the streets of towns and between farms and plantations. "Hucksters" walked through neighborhoods with distinctive voices, calling out their wares in a Gullah-Geechee dialect. In the late nineteenth and early twentieth centuries, they were a vital part of the distribution of foodstuffs in the lowcountry. Box 22, folder 22, item 4441, Georgia Historical Society collection of photographs, MS 1361-PH, Georgia Historical Society, Savannah, Ga. Courtesy of the Georgia Historical Society.

Oxcart and driver in Savannah, 1880s

The ox provided basic transportation for African Americans, whether they lived on barrier islands or in towns. Photograph by William O. Wilson. Courtesy of Georgia Archives, Vanishing Georgia Collection, ctm340-84.

African American family

An African American family engaged in home chores in a rural setting. In the wake of Reconstruction, even those blacks who managed to acquire a few acres of land had little hope of accumulating more that a few household items: bed linens and bedsteads, a spinning wheel for cotton, cooking utensils, clothing, a Bible and perhaps a few school-books, a horse or ox and a wagon, a cow and a calf, and two or three hogs. The sons and the father might seek jobs in Savannah, Darien, or Brunswick during the winter when work was slack on the farm but busy on the docks of the ports. Photograph by O. Pierre Havens. Courtesy of Georgia Archives, Vanishing Georgia Collection, ctm351-92.

Baptism at Pin Point

A baptism at Pin Point, a small African American neighborhood outside Savannah. The settlement took shape in the 1890s when tenant farmers on Ossabaw and other islands came to the mainland in search of land and built a community around crabbing, shrimping, and oyster harvesting. Described in *Drums and Shadows* (1940; repr., University of Georgia Press, 1986), the village existed in isolation until well after World War II. Today it represents one of the few traditional communities remaining on the coast of Georgia. The tidal creek that fronted Pin Point served as the place for baptisms. Box 15, folder 1, item 3105, Georgia Historical Society collection of photographs, MS 1361-PH, Georgia Historical Society, Savannah, Ga. Courtesy of the Georgia Historical Society.

Ring shout
"Shouting" often took place after a prayer meeting or worship service. Men and women circled in a counterclockwise direction while shuffling their feet and clapping their hands and often singing or praying aloud. In earlier times, the shout took place in a praise house, a small wooden structure in an out-of-the-way place where blacks could express their deepest feelings and celebrate their religion. The ring shout demonstrated how African culture redefined itself in the New World, a proud assertion of the human spirit. Courtesy National Park Service, Fort Frederica National Monument, Georgia Historical Society, The Margaret Davis Cate Collection, MS 997, photograph box 6, folder 40.

Sylvia Bond Anderson

Sylvia Bond Anderson was the granddaughter of David Bond, an enslaved person at Middle Place Plantation on Ossabaw Island. Her father, Benjamin Bond, was a leading figure in the Hinder Me Not Baptist Church on Ossabaw and led many of the residents off of the island to found a new community at Pin Point. Much of the culture and values of Ossabaw were recreated in this isolated village devoted principally to oystering and crabbing. Living in isolation, the residents displayed a fierce sense of independence, a quiet dignity, and close-knit family ties. The child in this photograph is a relative. Photograph by Muriel and Malcolm Bell Jr., 1939. Courtesy of Malcolm Bell III.

Lewis McIver

Lewis McIver was the prime netmaker at Pin Point. Injured on the water, he gave up the life of a fisherman to devote himself to providing nets for the several dozen men who took small bateaus into Ossabaw Sound to catch crabs, oysters, and shrimp. The construction of the last bateau by residents took place in the 1970s. Photograph by Muriel and Malcolm Bell Jr., 1939. Courtesy of Malcolm Bell III.

Katie Brown

Katie Brown of Sapelo Island was the great-granddaughter of Bilali or "Bilali Mahomet," the head driver of Thomas Spalding's plantation, with its more than four hundred enslaved persons. Bilali's numerous children practiced Islam well into the nineteenth century. Brown and her relatives recalled the essential contours of Muslim life in early Georgia — prayer mats, prayer beads, veiling, the Qur'ān, dietary restrictions, and daily ritualized prayer. At the time of the Works Progress Administration interviews, she was one of the oldest inhabitants of the island. Photograph by Muriel and Malcolm Bell Jr., 1939. Courtesy of Malcolm Bell III.

Graveyard sculptures, Sunbury

Graveyard sculptures by Cyrus Bowen, ca. 1920, Sunbury, Georgia. Mourners often placed broken bottles and other ornaments on gravesites as an expression of religion and magic. To call them decorations is missing the point. The broken bottles as well as the sculptures by Bowen are an integral part of the belief system of the interred. The carvings are original creations yet suggest an African influence. Photograph by Muriel and Malcolm Bell Jr., 1939. Courtesy of Library of Congress, Prints and Photographs Division, reproduction number LC-USZ62-137160.

Emory S. Campbell
Emory Campbell, descendent of five generations on Hilton Head Island, helped lead the movement to preserve Gullah culture and make Gullah people living in rural areas more aware of their uniquely rich African heritage. He served for twenty-two years as executive director of the Penn Center on St. Helena Island and participated in the translation of the New Testament into the Gullah language. Courtesy of the family of Emory S. Campbell.

Perry and Rosa Williams
Perry and Rosa Williams, maternal grandparents of Emory Campbell. As a boy, Campbell recalls growing up speaking two languages, that of his maternal grandmother, who spoke only in the Gullah-Geechee language, and that of his paternal grandmother, who spoke the King's English with deliberation. Tying those worlds together was a strong sense of family, a spirituality rooted in a belief in one God, and a taste for rice dishes, okra, and tomatoes. Courtesy of the family of Emory S. Campbell.

Solomon Campbell

Solomon Campbell, paternal grandfather of Emory Campbell. The grandson of an enslaved African who came to Hilton Head Island in the 1820s, Solomon Campbell and
his wife were teachers shortly after Reconstruction. They were avid readers and called
everyone by their legal rather than "basket" names (nicknames given at birth). Courtesy
of the family of Emory S. Campbell.

Theresa A. Singleton

Reclaiming the Gullah-Geechee Past

Archaeology of Slavery in Coastal Georgia

LOWCOUNTRY Georgia was the birthplace for the archaeological study of African American life that has now blossomed into the research field known as archaeology of the African diaspora. Although it was not the site of the earliest archaeological study of people of African descent, the research conducted by Charles Fairbanks, an archaeologist, and Robert Ascher, a cultural anthropologist, at Rayfield Plantation on Cumberland Island in 1969 set the stage for the study of slavery and plantation life as the interdisciplinary pursuit practiced today.[1] Their precedent-setting study combined descriptive accounts obtained from a variety of written sources — slave narratives, travelers' accounts, and public records — with archaeological findings to piece together slave life within the quarters. While some of their assumptions and interpretations may be considered naïve compared to our present-day understanding of slavery, Ascher and Fairbanks demonstrated the potential of archaeology to provide a new and different perspective on slavery and African American life. They chose to examine slavery during the well-documented antebellum period (1830–60) of American history as they rejected the idea that writing was superior to other sources in providing information on past human activities. Because most enslaved men and women were unable to write about their lives, Ascher and Fairbanks reasoned that archaeology could shed some light on aspects of slave life that written records authored by whites could not.[2] This argument, elaborated on by later generations of archaeologists, became the chief rationale for future archaeological investigations of slavery.

In this essay, archaeological research of slavery on the Georgia coast is examined from a perspective on archaeology of the African diaspora in the wider Atlantic world. Slavery is the focus of the vast majority of African American sites investigated to date on the Georgia coast and elsewhere in the Americas. This archaeological research is directly linked to Gullah-Geechee communities in keeping with Ray Crook's recent declaration that "African-American archaeology in this tidewater region [from southern North Carolina to northeastern Florida] is Gullah-Geechee archaeology."[3] To be sure, the people who once occupied these sites were the forebears of the present-day Gullah-Geechee communities. Making an explicit connection between the archaeology and Gullah-Geechee carries a responsibility for archaeologists to enable the Gullah-Geechee to reclaim this aspect of their heritage, should these communities choose to do so. It is anticipated that future archaeological studies of African American life in the area will provide opportunities for Gullah-Geechee to actively participate in these efforts.

This essay is organized around the following themes: First, to provide background to the subject, the circumstances that made the Georgia coast an attractive testing ground for archaeological study of slavery are briefly summarized. Second, discussion of the substantive archaeological findings from the Georgia coast and how these compare to the archaeology of slavery generally constitute the bulk of this essay. Third, as a conclusion, ways in which archaeologists can better achieve the goal of linking Gullah-Geechee communities with their archaeological heritage are considered.

WHY THE GEORGIA COAST?

A number of factors, both academic and practical, coalesced into making the Georgia coast the initial site for the archaeological study of slavery. Charles Fairbanks had been a specialist in the archaeologies of Georgia and Florida focusing on Native American heritage for at least two decades before undertaking research on African Americans. His knowledge of the area along with the close proximity of the University of Florida — where he and his students were based — facilitated the development of a long-term field research program in which several plantations as well as many other

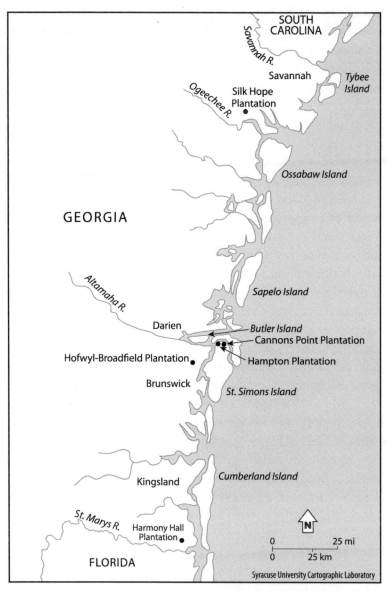

Map of coastal Georgia showing many of the locations discussed in this essay.
Courtesy of Syracuse University Cartographic Department.

archaeological sites were investigated between 1968 and 1982. This research program produced graduate students who wrote the first doctoral dissertations and masters' theses on the archaeology of slavery and plantations.[4]

The cultural distinctiveness of Gullah-Geechee communities played a role in the selection of the Georgia sea islands as a site for the archaeological study of slavery. Anthropological interest in the African American communities of the South Carolina–Georgia coasts dates back to the early twentieth century. Indeed, Melville Herskovits, in his classic book *The Myth of the Negro Past* (New York: Harper & Row, 1941), frequently referenced the language and cultural practices of Gullah-Geechee people as evidence that they and other African American communities retained and reinterpreted many aspects of African cultural heritage in the making of African American culture. Since Herskovits's work, scholars of numerous disciplines have sought out the sea islands of Georgia and South Carolina to make cultural connections between the Gullah-Geechee and peoples of West and West Central Africa, specifically areas in present-day Senegal, Gambia, Sierra Leone, Liberia, and Congo-Angola. Archaeologists have also attempted to search for artifacts of African practices in their exploratory studies of slavery, but when these studies failed to produce such finds, many archaeologists began to address other kinds of questions, such as everyday slave life, plantation social structure, master-slave relationships, and slave consumption. A significant amount of archaeological research of the African diaspora, however, continues to be directed toward understanding how African ways of knowing were transformed in the Americas.[5]

Extant ruins are usually good indicators that deposits of archaeological materials buried around them are well-preserved. Ruins of plantation buildings constructed of tabby — a masonry product made from oyster shell, lime, and sand that could be poured like cement, molded into bricks, or used as mortar — made the Georgia coast attractive for plantation studies. Long before archaeological studies of slavery, archaeology was utilized to dispel a now-forgotten myth regarding the origin of the tabby ruins extending south from Beaufort, South Carolina, to northern Florida. The ruins had captured the imagination of both lay and professional historians who claimed that these remains were vestiges of the short-lived, seventeenth-century Spanish missions. This myth emerged in the early 1900s at the same time a revival of interest in the Spanish missions of California inspired an architectural and furniture style known as mission. For a quarter of a century, the Spanish mission myth dominated the interpretation of tabby ruins until both archaeological and historical research in the 1930s pointed to their nineteenth-century plantation origins.[6] Spaniards may have initially introduced tabby to the southeastern United States through their permanent settlement at St. Augustine, Florida, but it was reintroduced to Georgia during the 1800s because it was seen as an inexpensive, durable material that could possibly withstand hurricanes.[7] Although the archaeology of tabby ruins was not concerned with slavery, it established that plantation sites associated with these ruins were well-preserved for future archaeological investigation.

Preservation of slave sites on the Georgia coast was greatly enhanced by the absence of sustained postemancipation occupation at former slave settlements. Following emancipation, many coastal slave settlements were abandoned, never reoccupied nor built upon at a later time.[8] These conditions produce undisturbed deposits for archaeological study. In contrast to the Georgia coast, abandoned slave settlements in many inland areas of the plantation South were plowed over and farmed intensely to produce cotton and other crops; therefore, very few archaeological traces of slave life would be preserved at such locations. Excellent site preservation combined with previous archaeological and anthropological study of the area came together during the burgeoning development of African American studies in academia to make the Georgia coast a viable place to begin initial studies of slavery using archaeology.

AN ATLANTIC PERSPECTIVE ON ARCHAEOLOGY
OF SLAVERY IN COASTAL GEORGIA

In the more than forty years since initial investigations of plantations began in Georgia, archaeological study of slavery has been conducted throughout the Americas. In the United States, plantations have been investigated in every former slave state of the South as well as in several places in the Northeast. The Caribbean is second to the United States in numbers of plantations investigated, and has become a leader in innovative approaches to the archaeological study of plantation landscapes, Afro-Caribbean pottery, maroon communities, and informal slave economies. Increased research is also taking place in mainland Latin America, primarily in Brazil. Preliminary work has begun on haciendas of Mexico, Peru, and Argentina, but these operations did not exclusively use enslaved African labor.

Given the tremendous volume of plantation research, it makes sense to evaluate archaeological findings of the Georgia coast from a perspective engaging the broad literature on the archaeology of slavery. Through such a lens, it is possible to examine the ways in which the archaeology from the Georgia coast is similar to, yet different from, archaeology in other plantation settings. Lowcountry Georgia is compared herein primarily with the former British West Indies with which it has had historical relationships; for example, there were close familial and business ties between Bahamian planters and Georgia coast planters. Familial and cultural linkages may well have existed between the slave communities in the two places. The trajectory of Bilali of Sapelo Island, Georgia, demonstrates that linkages between enslaved people of the Bahamas and coastal Georgia can be established. Bilali (also spelled Belali, Bu Allah, Ben-Ali, et al.), born in Africa, appears to have been first enslaved in the Bahamas and then later sold to Thomas Spalding, a planter on Sapelo Island, Georgia. Bilali became a patriarch of the slave community on Sapelo and a legendary figure for the Gullah-Geechee people of the Georgia coast.[9]

Comparison are also made, on a smaller scale, between Georgia and South Carolina and, when possible, with different districts along the Carolina-Georgia coast. Archaeological research is very site-specific, which provides the opportunity to examine how specific plantations operated and ways in which particular districts of the Carolina-Georgia coast were perhaps distinct from each other. In this way, archaeology contributes to building micro-histories of particular Gullah-Geechee communities, while at the same time promoting a general understanding of Gullah-Geechee culture as a whole. The discussion below focuses on four areas of material culture that have been important to slavery studies: pottery production and consumption, housing and plantation space, foodways, and religious beliefs and practices.

Archaeological findings from the excavations of slave quarters during the period of approximately 1968–84 focused on plantations established after the American Revolutionary War (1775–83), and therefore have yielded information on slavery during the period from 1790 to 1860. More recent archaeological studies undertaken in the 2000s uncovered evidence of earlier eighteenth-century housing and artifacts, but for the most part archaeological investigation from the Georgia coast contributes to understanding slavery in the nineteenth century. This contrasts with the archaeological findings in South Carolina, which have emphasized eighteenth-century sites, although numerous nineteenth-century sites have been investigated in South Carolina as well. Archaeologists have at various times attempted to compare and contrast the archaeologies of slavery in South Carolina and Georgia, with varying degree of success; while there are similarities, there are also distinct differences in recovered artifacts.[10] The most striking difference is in the presence of an undecorated earthenware (pottery) that archaeologists refer to colonoware. This pottery is abundant in South Carolina, but virtually absent in Georgia.

Pottery Production and Consumption

"Colonoware" is a term used to designate numerous varieties of earthenware pottery produced in colonial situations in eastern North America. It is a hand-built (potters using their hands to form the shape of the vessel rather than a potter's wheel) earthenware fired in open pits rather than in kilns used to fire bricks and other kinds of ceramics. Colonoware was originally termed colonial-Indian because the varieties recovered from British, French, and Spanish colonial sites resemble local Native American pottery, sometimes made into European-shaped vessels such as pitchers, plates, or pans.[11] In Virginia, where the pottery was first identified, both documentary records and ethnographic accounts indicate Native American communities such as the Pamunkey made pottery and traded it to both blacks and whites well into the early twentieth century.[12] The recovery of colonoware vessels fired on the plantations in South Carolina strongly supported the proposition that enslaved people produced some of this pottery. This slave-made pottery, however, is found predominately in the South Carolina lowcountry. Colonoware is also found on slave sites in the Chesapeake, but in smaller quantities, and there is some debate as to whether or not African Americans produced these wares, as direct evidence of plantation-produced pottery has not been forthcoming from Virginia sites.[13] Occasionally, colonoware has been found on sites associated with African Americans in upland areas of the South, and a few fragments have even turned up in New England, but most of these finds are in very small quantities.[14]

Colonoware and similar hand-built earthenwares found on plantations throughout the Caribbean and in Brazil have been important in archaeological studies of slavery as pottery is one of the few handcrafted items associated with enslaved people. In general, there are few, if any, written references to enslaved people making pottery or even using pottery; therefore, the recovery of slave-made pottery has been a finding on slave life that has been discovered entirely from archaeological research. Before iron pots and pans were introduced to West Africa through European trade, Africans, like most preindustrial peoples, prepared their food in clay pots and on griddles. Slave production and use of pottery is significant because it suggests that some traditional African ways of preparing, serving, and consuming foods, beverages, or medicines were practiced on plantations where the pottery is found. At some sites, both iron and clay pots have been found, suggesting that clay pots continued to be used, perhaps for preparing and consuming special dishes or medicines. Ann Yentsch, for example, found in her research of African American foodways in the Chesapeake that earthenware pots, unlike those made of iron, prevented vegetables like okra from turning black.[15] In a similar vain, William Gilmore Simms, a nineteenth-century author and native of Charleston, South Carolina, commented that "okra soup was always inferior if cooked in anything, but an Indian pot."[16] The reference to "Indian pot" is insightful because it describes a kind of pottery — low-fired earthenware — characteristic of all Native American pottery in the eastern United States as well as all colonoware whether it was made by Native Americans or African Americans.

In the past three decades since archaeologists first suggested that people of African descent had a role in making this pottery, there have been efforts to identify pottery made by Africans and their descendants and those made by Native Americans. Some archaeologists distinguish between the Native American–made pottery and the slave-made pottery based upon construction techniques used to shape the vessel and, to a lesser extent, surface finishes and vessel forms. From analyses of various colonoware collections, Native Americans are thought to have used the coil method, wherein coils or rolls of clay are built up to establish the circumference and height of the vessel, and the finish surface of the vessel is highly polished. On the other hand, enslaved Africans and African Americans formed the vessel through pinching and squeezing one piece of clay, and surface finishes were crudely smooth or polished.[17] Other archaeologists, however, see colonoware as a Creole product combining the pottery traditions of Africans, Native Americans, and Europeans that developed from interactions between Africans and Native Americans possibly when they were both enslaved on early-eighteenth-century plantations in South Carolina.[18] When viewed as a product originating from multiple sources due to colonial interactions, it is difficult to ascribe an ethnic designation to particular pots. We can say, however, with a high degree of certainty that South Carolina colonoware was produced by Africans and their descendants as well as Native Americans.

Little is known about the production sites of colonoware. Even vessels recovered in urban contexts are presumed to have been produced in rural settings at nearby plantations.[19] According to Carl Steen, colonoware is a very localized craft in which the core area of production is restricted to Charleston, Berkeley, and Georgetown counties or the area extending northward from Charleston to south of Myrtle Beach, and inland about thirty miles. Colonoware is found south of Charleston and other areas of South Carolina but in smaller quantities than the core area.

Two forms of colonoware are most commonly found in excavations of plantations: (1) small, open bowls with or without foot rings (a circular foot at the base of the bowl); (2) larger, rounded bottom jars often with evidence of soot suggesting that they were used for cooking.[20] Colonoware is most prevalent on eighteenth-century sites, and it significantly decreases in the nineteenth century but it continues to be used to the time of emancipation. Additionally, fewer of the larger jars are found on nineteenth-century sites, which suggests that the use of pottery for cooking had declined, but the pottery was still being used for other purposes. Christopher Espenshade observed that bowls with markings believed to be of religious significance began to appear on colonoware in the late eighteenth century and continued to the mid-nineteenth century. From this observation, he suggests that colonoware changed from being an everyday, utilitarian object in the eighteenth century to an object used for ritual and healing purposes in the nineteenth century.[21]

In lowcountry Georgia, colonoware is a rare find, with one recent exception, that being the Silk Hope Plantation — an eighteenth-century site on the northern neck of the Ogeechee River in Bryan County about twelve miles south of Savannah. At Silk Hope, 2,556 colonoware fragments have been recovered from excavations, approximately 42 percent of the total amount of ceramics found at the site (the other ceramics being of imported, European manufacture). The archaeologists estimate that the total fragments of colonoware represent about fifty-three whole vessels consisting of thirty-six bowls, nine jars, and eight unidentified forms used during the occupation of the site between 1759 and 1791. The vessels were made using at least three different hand-building methods, involving pinching, squeezing, and coiling. Approximately 55 percent of the vessels have evidence of soot — nineteen bowls, five jars, and five of the identi-

Fragments of colonoware, a type of pottery used for cooking and serving food
primarily found on eighteenth-century plantations in lowcountry South Carolina.
These fragments are from excavations of tabby cabins on Ossabaw Island, Georgia.
Courtesy of Dan Elliot, LAMAR Institute.

fied forms — indicating that both bowls and jars were directly placed on
fire and used for cooking.[22] The use of both bowls and jars for cooking is
unlike many South Carolina assemblages of colonoware, where only jars
display evidence of soot. The absence of religious markings along with the
large number of vessels with soot strongly suggests that the colonoware at
Silk Hope was used primarily for cooking and consuming food.[23]

Silk Hope is the earliest slave site investigated to date on the Georgia
coast, which may explain its large collection of colonoware compared to
other sites. Considerably smaller quantities of colonoware were recovered
from Cherry Hill (2 fragments) and Richmond (111 fragments) plantations,
two sites located near Silk Hope that were investigated as part of the same
research project as Silk Hope Plantation.[24] These plantations were established in the eighteenth century but were occupied well into the nineteenth
century. Only 60 colonoware fragments were recovered in test excavations
of the North End Tabbies on Ossabaw, a barrier island off the coast of
Savannah.[25]

The small percentages of colonoware on the Georgia coast is at least
partially explained by the fact that most of the sites are nineteenth century,

with many of them dating to the antebellum period, 1830–60. By that late date, iron pots were in widespread use worldwide. The only Georgian site with a sizeable quantity of colonoware is Silk Hope, an eighteenth-century site. Colonowares were evidently used there, and preliminary analyses of a few pottery fragments suggest that the vessels tested were made from clays similar to clays available in the vicinity of Silk Hope. Therefore, it is highly possible that some of the colonoware recovered from Silk Hope was both produced and used by occupants of Silk Hope.

Differences in production and usage of colonowares between Georgia and South Carolina coasts had similar parallels in the Caribbean. The making of hand-built, open-fired, Afro-Caribbean earthenwares varied from island to island. Many of the sugar islands produced wares used for sugar processing, but these are distinguished from Afro-Caribbean wares.[26] Some islands have a long tradition of Afro-Caribbean pottery making dating as far back as the late seventeenth century.[27] Potters from several islands of the former British West Indies — including Nevis, Antigua, Jamaica, and St. Lucia — have continued to produce pottery of this tradition until the present. On other islands, pottery making ended during the process of emancipation in the 1830s.[28] Still other islands — for example, the Bahamas and Barbados — never developed an Afro-Caribbean pottery tradition. The absence of good clays in the Bahamas appears to have been a major contributing factor for the absence of pottery making.[29] Barbados, on the other hand, has rich clay deposits in the Scotland district on the east coast that were extracted and used to produce ceramics for at least two hundred years initially for sugar wares and architectural products such as roof and floor tiles, and later, for wheel-thrown utilitarian, European forms. But, a Barbadian hand-built, Afro-Caribbean pottery tradition never materialized.[30]

Islandwide differences in the production and consumption of Afro-Caribbean wares are comparable to regional differences in the production and consumption of colonoware in the southeastern United States. In addition to the temporal differences between the sites investigated in Georgia and South Carolina, a variety of factors were operative that might explain these differences: the early replacement of earthenware with iron pots or other utensils for cooking, the absence of potters in certain districts to produce pottery, or the lack of time or access to clay resources needed to make pottery. The Barbados example illustrates that, even with the availability of appropriate clay sources, African-influenced potting traditions did not necessarily emerge. Diversity in pottery production and consumption offers an example of how particular plantation districts along the coast may have differed from each other.

Colonoware found in Georgia thus far is concentrated around Savannah (the northern neck of the Ogeechee River and Ossabaw Island). Only negligible amounts of colonoware have been reported south of the Ogeechee River. This distribution suggests that pottery was not produced or traded south of outlying areas near Savannah. Unfortunately, few excavations have been undertaken in Savannah; therefore, virtually nothing is known about the production or consumption of colonowares in Savannah. Based upon studies undertaken in Charleston, however, colonowares were commonplace; diverse residents of the city used them during the Colonial period, but this usage declines in the late eighteenth century, after which urban slaves become the primary consumers of colonoware.[31] This consumption pattern is similar to what archaeologists have outlined for South Carolina lowcountry plantations. At this point, however, data for colonowares in Georgia are too fragmentary to offer general interpretations on consumption or production of them beyond the Silk Hope site. Given the finds at Silk Hope, the core area for colonoware production designated by Steen may need to be extended further south to include the Ogeechee River.

Slave Housing and Plantation Space

Of all the material culture associated with slavery, slave housing has received the greatest attention from scholars in architecture, archaeology, folklore, geography, and history. Studies of visual sources including paintings, prints, maps, and photographs combined with verbal descriptions of slave quarters have produced an impressive literature on construction materials, approximate size, layout, and overall physical appearance of slave quarters. Archaeological studies of slave houses complement this scholarship by supplying details on construction techniques, building modifications, and maintenance of particular structures as well as insights into how enslaved people lived in their quarters. Despite the insights gained from archaeological research on slave housing, however, such studies rarely yield direct evidence on construction materials made from organic substances such as thatched roofs or wooden shingles, floors, or walls. Thatch is made from highly perishable plant fabrics that leave no traces in the archaeological record. Wood products are more durable than thatch, but once a

wooden building was abandoned, construction materials were probably recycled for building or repairing other buildings, or used for firewood. Consequently, archaeologists focus their studies of slave housing on remains of
standing ruins and materials preserved buried below ground.

Throughout the Americas, slave housing ranged from small dwellings made from weaving together twigs, poles, and palm leaves that are
difficult to identify from archaeological investigations to substantial masonry buildings for which extant ruins often exist. Construction materials
were not only diverse, but material selection and construction techniques
changed through time. What kind of slave housing enslaved people lived
in depended upon the resources slaveholders were willing to invest in quar-
tering enslaved laborers. Early slave houses tended to be made from readily
accessible, natural products: clay or mud, thatch, and roughly hewn wood.
By far the most common type of slave housing found in the Caribbean
and tropical areas of mainland Latin America was of wattle-and-daub construction (wattle refers to a wooden lattice or frame and daub to a plaster-
like substance made from clay, mud, or lime-based mixtures used to fill in
the frame forming the walls of the structure both inside and out). Whereas
in the United States, earthfast construction — consisting of posts set in
the ground without sills or footings, roughly split clapboards, and earthen
floors — was the dominant type of slave quarter until log and timber frame
structures began supplanting it in the mid-eighteenth century.[32]

Clay-walled slave houses resembling wattle-and-daub houses found
elsewhere in the Americas have been excavated at eighteenth-century plantations in South Carolina.[33] Several references to clay-walled slave houses
in eighteenth-century documents suggest such houses were not unusual
in Colonial South Carolina, and may have even been commonplace.[34] A
slave house similar to those recovered in South Carolina was excavated at
the previously mentioned Silk Hope Plantation in Bryan County, Georgia. The Silk Hope house was apparently occupied shortly after the plantation was established in 1759, making this structure one of the earliest
slave houses identified on the Georgia coast thus far. The lack of postholes
— holes dug to support timber posts — used in the Silk Hope case to raise
the floor off the ground suggest that the house apparently had a dirt floor
and possibly a gable roof made from thatch.[35] Construction of mud-walled
slave houses was primarily an eighteenth-century practice in lowcountry
South Carolina and Georgia, but oral tradition suggest that a few enslaved
people on the Georgia coast built variations of wattle-and-daub housing

well into the nineteenth century. Recent archaeological evidence of wattle-and-daub housing from nineteenth-century slave settlements on Sapelo Island supports the oral tradition.

Perhaps the most well-known reference to a slave-built, mud-walled house is that of Okra, an African enslaved on Altama Plantation on the Altamaha River. Ben Sullivan of St. Simons Island described Okra's house to interviewers in 1930s as a hut measuring approximately twelve by fourteen feet of basket weave with clay plaster on it. The house lacked windows, and the roof was flat and made from palmetto bushes. According to Sullivan, Okra built the house because he wanted a house like the one he had in Africa. Okra's owner, James Couper, however, ordered that the house be torn down because he did not want an African house on his plantation.[36] The story of Okra may be apocryphal, but the description of the house is very similar, if not identical, to other plastered-wattle houses described elsewhere in the Americas and used widely for slave housing. Sullivan also heard rumors of another enslaved African building a house of cane or corn stalks, mud, and straw filling.[37] On Sapelo Island, according to oral tradition, some enslaved people were permitted to build African-style houses at Thomas Spalding's plantation.[38] Through excavations at Behavior and New Barn Creek — two slave settlements at Thomas Spalding Plantation — fragments of tabby mortar with impressions of wooden wattles were recovered from slave houses suggesting that the walls of these buildings were constructed with a daub or plaster made of tabby mortar.[39] The usage of tabby mortar for daub or plaster in wattle-and-daub construction may be a variation on the use of lime-based daubs for building on Caribbean plantations of the former British and Danish West Indies (U.S. Virgin Islands).[40] Most Caribbean plantations produced and used lime for a building material and for whitewashing buildings.[41] Whether these excavated slave houses on Sapelo were the ones the oral tradition referred to as African-styled is unknown. The wattle framework may have been considered African, but the tabby daub possibly was not.

Wattle-and-daub slave housing is often assumed in the examples above and elsewhere to be of African derivation. Numerous preindustrial societies in Africa, Europe, and in the Americas, however, utilized some form of wattle-and-daub or plaster-wattle construction. As the use of engineered materials (clapboards, shingles, masonry) became widely available, this traditional method of house construction was abandoned. Scattered references to the presence of wattle-and-daub construction in nineteenth-century plantation settings is usually associated with African-born peoples, because by that time most European Americans in the United States had abandoned it. Eighteenth-century wattle-and-daub slave houses, on the other hand, may not have been entirely an African tradition, as is often assumed, because at that time both European and Native American wattle-and-daub traditions were still being practiced. Carl Steen, for example, notes that all of the clay-wall houses excavated in South Carolina were located on plantations owned by French immigrants who would have been familiar with the French tradition of clay-wall construction common on French colonial sites.[42] Thus, the excavated mud-wall structures at Silk Hope and at South Carolina sites may have been an amalgamation of African, European, and Native American architectural traditions.

From the exterior, timber or log slave houses were often indistinguishable from the houses of white laborers. Enslaved people attempted, however, to modify interior spaces to suit their needs whenever they could. The digging of subfloor pits is an example of such a modification that was prolific on plantations in the Upper South, particularly in eighteenth-century Virginia. The pits were dug directly through earthen floors or below wooden floor boards and were used for storage of food and personal items. A few have been interpreted as sacred shrines.[43] Several of the slave quarters have multiple subfloor pits, with one containing twenty-two in a single structure.[44] These pits are seldom found in lowcountry South Carolina and Georgia. Only one subfloor pit has been tentatively identified in lowcountry South Carolina, at Spiers Landing in Berkeley County. This is the site of an earthfast structure presumed to be a slave quarter with one irregular-shaped sub-floor pit, which Leland Ferguson interpreted as a root cellar.[45] At Silk Hope in Georgia, several storage pits were identified but were not associated with houses, and were therefore interpreted as detached root cellars.[46] Many of the subfloor pits studied in Virginia have little or no archaeological evidence of the slave houses once associated with the pits; therefore, it is possible that further analysis of the Silk Hope storage pits may indicate that they are similar to the subfloor pits in Virginia. Despite these few lowcountry examples of subfloor pits, enslaved people of the lowcountry did not regularly dig these pits like enslaved people of Virginia and other areas of the upland South. A reason for this difference may lie in how these pits were used. If the pits were used primarily for food or personal storage, enslaved people of the lowcountry may have stored these items in other kinds of containers: barrels, cupboards, or trunks. Keys and padlocks are frequently recovered from excavations of lowcountry slave quarters and may be indications that personal possessions, possibly even food, were placed in locked containers. If subfloor pits were used as sacred places such as shrines, then enslaved people of the lowcountry apparently did not practice these rituals or did not practice them within their quarters.

Most slave houses excavated on the Georgia coast were built in the nineteenth century, and artifacts recovered from these excavations help to determine when they were occupied. Some houses were in use as early as 1800, whereas others date no earlier than the antebellum period (post-1820 or later), and were abandoned before the 1850s. A few others were occupied until the eve of the Civil War. Many of the antebellum slave quarters exhibit some features typical of the so-called reform slave housing. Reform slave housing refers to quarters designed to meet recommendations slaveholders developed in response to criticisms of abolitionists and other social reformers regarding the poor quality and crowded conditions of slave quarters. Efforts to reform or improve the living conditions of both slave and nonslave workers became a worldwide phenomenon that influenced nineteenth-century slave housing throughout the Atlantic world.[47] Architectural historian Edward Chappell links the move to new and better housing to fundamental changes in the systematic management of resources — crops, animals, or people — that accompanied agrarian capitalism of the nineteenth century.[48] In the United States, recommendations published in southern agricultural journals of the day typically described an ideal dwelling for a single slave household unit as consisting of sixteen by eighteen feet, placed at least seventy-five feet from neighboring dwellings, and raised upon building piers of two to three feet. Recommendations also included the use of plank floors and large fireplaces.[49] While examples of well-built slave quarters conforming to some, if not, all of these criteria are known in extant examples, it is doubtful that most slave laborers lived in housing meeting all these criteria.

Excavations of reform-period slave housing in coastal Georgia support this interpretation and have shown that slave housing varied considerably not only from plantation to plantation but often on the same plantation, and within the same slave settlement. At the south slave settlement at Cannon's Point on St. Simons, one slave house was built on brick piers at least two feet above the ground, while the other three were built directly on the ground, presumably with earthen floors. Archaeologists often interpret a larger or better-built slave house within a slave village as belonging to a driver (a slave overseer) or some other high-status head of household. Suzanne McFarlane who wrote the excavation report for the Cannon's Point site, however, proposed an alternative interpretation. She suggested the house with the brick piers replaced a slave house that was destroyed, possibly by a hurricane. She based this interpretation on her observation that the slave house appeared to have built from salvaged materials, possibly from an earlier slave house, and that the construction pit for one of the brick piers was dug through an earlier garbage pit.[50] Though alternative interpretations are plausible for MacFarlane's observations, her argument implies that improvements to slave housing were implemented on a gradual or as-needed basis. In other words, slave houses were improved only when it was deemed necessary to build new quarters or rebuild old or damaged ones. Such a practice may explain disparities found in slave quarters at other plantations. At Hampton Plantation, also on St. Simons, the slave houses in the settlement known as Jones constructed in 1801 continued to have dirt floors throughout the antebellum period.[51] The houses constructed at St. Anne's in 1824, however, were built with raised floors.[52] By that date, slaveholders had begun to articulate the advantages of raised floors for air circulation. Another reason the floors at St. Anne's were raised may have been due to the fact that the slave settlement was located on reclaimed marsh similar to the slave houses at Butler Island, a rice plantation south of Darien. Excavations of slave houses at both St. Anne's and Butler Island revealed the primary material used to raise the floors were wooden posts, not bricks as recommended by reformers or shown in later photographs of Butler Island. The use of wood plank floors was documented by the recovery of a large portion of wood flooring from one of the excavated houses at Butler Island.[53]

The size and dimensions of slave houses were considerably smaller in some cases, while others met or exceeded reform recommendations. Measurements ranged from eleven to eighteen feet wide and sixteen to twenty-one feet long for a single unit, and thirteen to twenty feet wide and forty to forty-six feet long for a duplex, a structure that housed two slave households.[54] Small amounts of window glass suggest that a few quarters had a least one glazed window, but windows in most quarters were unglazed. Archaeological recovery of shutter latches and hardware indicate that windows were opened and closed with wooden shutters.

Archaeological investigations have also shown the extent to which the reform mandate for order, cleanliness, and good hygiene was implemented.

As with improvements in slave housing, cleanliness and good hygiene varied considerably from plantation to plantation. Some slave villages were equipped with privies and wells, slave yards were swept of debris, and trash deposited out of sight of the village possibly in a nearby ravine or river.[55] At other sites, large amounts of trash accumulated in and around slave houses, which attracted rats (the bones of which were found in these trash heaps) and other pests.[56] These trash accumulations contained large amounts of oyster shell presumably collected for the purpose of making tabby, but they made slave communities vulnerable to disease.

In addition to domestic spaces around slave houses, archaeologists, as well as other scholars, are increasingly analyzing the overall spatial organization of plantations. This scholarship demonstrates that the use of plantation space was central to understanding how plantations operated and how slavery was organized. In general, plantation layouts were designed to maximize access to fields, enhance productivity, control slave workers, reinforce the social hierarchy of the plantation, and appeal to the aesthetic sensibilities of the slaveholding class at plantations with great houses and landscaped grounds.

Archaeological studies of plantation space undertaken in the Caribbean and Chesapeake have emphasized the ways in which plantations were designed for surveillance and containment of slave activities and movement.[57] Studies in lowcountry Georgia are at a preliminary stage of research in this regard, but lowcountry slaveholders apparently did not employ the same principles of landscape design observed on many Caribbean or Chesapeake plantations. Many lowcountry planters dispersed slave villages at several locations on a plantation rather than placing all slave quarters in one central location. Dispersed slave villages mitigated against the use of panoptic devices (watchtowers or elevated structures) to observe slave activities. On most Caribbean and many southern plantations, all buildings were located in one central location, which included the residences of owners, managers, and slave laborers; outbuildings; service buildings for machines; and storage facilities. Merle Prunty, a cultural geographer, coined the term "nucleated plantation village" to refer to placing all plantation buildings together in the same location. Prunty believed this form of plantation layout was a distinctive feature of antebellum plantations as opposed to postbellum plantations.[58] The nucleated plantation form, however, is found throughout the Caribbean and Brazil (although it is not referred to by this term) on plantations of all time periods. Caribbean planters wrote essays urging the use of three or more acres for the central location of all buildings, including slave quarters.[59] Nucleated plantations are also known on many Georgia coast plantations, and Prunty used Hopeton, a cotton and rice plantation on the Altamaha River, as an example of a nucleated plantation.[60]

Dispersed slave settlements, however, were not unique to the lowcountry plantations. Tobacco culture in the Chesapeake followed a dispersed slave residential pattern in part because fertile soils for tobacco cultivation were scattered over the landscape. To take advantage of the best soils, laborers were dispersed on outlying settlements known as quarters near the major home farm or place on more distant holdings under the supervision of an overseer or family member.[61] Additionally, dispersed settlements are known in other parts of the South; for example, some Louisiana sugar plantations grouped buildings together at separate locations on the plantation property.[62] Dispersed slave settlements are found on plantations in various locations on the Georgia coast, but on four plantations of the Altamaha estuary these slave settlements have also been identified and further documented through archaeological investigation: Butler Island, south of Darien; Hampton Plantation, on Butler Point on St. Simons; Cannon's Point, also on St. Simons; and Thomas Spalding Plantation, on Sapelo.

Reasons for establishing dispersed slave settlements at the four plantations are unknown but possibly developed from numerous factors. All four plantations are located on small islands where limited space may have necessitated this arrangement. The landholdings of Butler Island, Hampton, and Spalding plantations developed over time. As these landholdings were expanded, and more areas for fields were cleared and planted, new slave settlements were established that provided easy access to fields. Butler Island and portions of Hampton consisted of marshlands that had to be reclaimed before it could be profitably used for agriculture. The four dispersed slave settlements at Butler Island were established in succession as the marsh was reclaimed, a process that took many years.[63] Similarly, St. Anne's, one of five slave settlements of Hampton Plantation and owned by the same family as Butler Island, was established in 1824 from reclaimed marsh on St. Simons.[64] At Thomas Spalding Plantation, each of the three slave settlements (Behavior, New Barn Creek, and Hanging Bull) was initially created for specific operations within the plantation complex.[65] Cannon's Point had only two slave settlements: one was part of the area that included the great house, the other was located near fields south of the great house. Both slave settlements appear to have been established around the same time.

Control of slave laborers was another consideration for developing dispersed slave settlements. Slaveholders may have seen some advantages in subdividing large slaveholdings into smaller groupings. Dispersed slave settlements eliminated a large concentration of enslaved people in close proximity to planter and manager residences, which posed a threat to small numbers of whites on the premises. Attacks directed toward white overseers or slaveholders periodically took place in the Caribbean where nucleated plantation villages prevailed. Smaller settlements promoted efficient accounting of slave productivity and the distribution of slave provisions. On the Butler estate, both at Butler Island and Hampton plantations, each slave settlement (nine in all) operated as a self-contained productive unit. Enslaved people were listed according to slave settlement with the amounts of crops planted and harvested recorded by slave village.[66] Access to large provision gardens directly attached to slave houses and to the bountiful food resources of coastal habitats were additional benefits of dispersed slave settlements that slaveholders and enslaved people could appreciate. Slaveholders could, and did, reduce the amount of plantation rations distributed to slave communities, and enslaved people could farm and procure foods to their liking, and sell any surplus.

By far the greatest advantage for enslaved people in isolated slave villages was being part of a close-knit community with which they identified and where it was possible to undertake activities — imbibing alcoholic beverages, gambling, dancing, participating in rituals, or taking short-term leaves from plantation work — away from the watchful eye of slaveholders and managers. These small slave communities nurtured the florescence of Gullah-Geechee culture, and were sites of origin for community-level cultural practices, traditions, and memories, some of which were shared with nearby slave settlements, but others unique to specific settlements.[67] Just as slaveholders identified enslaved people by settlement, enslaved people apparently identified with a slave settlement rather than the larger plantation. Even after emancipation, the tradition of identifying with a specific settlement on a sea island, and not the islandwide community, continued well into the twentieth century.[68]

Foodways

Foodways refer to all human activities associated with food — from procurement of food items through farming or hunting to preparation and consumption. Archaeological studies of the foods enslaved people procured, prepared, and consumed have greatly enhanced our understanding of slave diet. Most slave sites have yielded some food remains of items that enslaved people either raised themselves or obtained through foraging activities. Well-preserved remains of animal foods on many Georgia plantations have made it possible to conduct more detailed studies of slave subsistence than in plantation areas where bone poorly preserves.[69] Analysis of animal food bone known as zooarchaeology has shown enslaved people on the Georgia coast abundantly supplemented plantation rations with nondomestic food resources they hunted and fished. Zooarchaeologists have estimated nondomesticated animals (reptiles, wild birds, wild mammals, shellfish, and fish) may have contributed as much as 40 percent of the meat to the slave diet on lowcountry plantations in Georgia.[70] Recovered artifacts such as gun parts, animal traps, and fishing gear document the techniques they used to procure these food items. Most of the equipment and gear consisted of out-of-date muskets or, possibly, homemade firearms, fish hooks made from bending nails, and net sinkers formed from reused lead objects. The Gullah-Geechee are well-known for their handcrafted casting nets, which they still produce today, and the recovery of net sinkers implies that this craft dates to the time of slavery. The specific animal resources exploited depended upon the habitats located near the plantation as well as slave food preferences. On the barrier islands, as would be expected, enslaved people consumed a variety of marine fishes, mollusks, and sea turtles, whereas enslaved people living near freshwater marshlands consumed freshwater fishes and semiaquatic turtles. In both areas, they hunted small mammals such as rabbit, opossum, raccoon, and muskrat, as well as a variety of birds and ducks.

Analysis of food remains at St. Anne's slave settlement provides additional details regarding slave consumption of nondomestic food resources, which has implications for interpreting differential access to food resources. The occupants of one house (identified as House #4) consumed wild birds, while occupants in the other three excavated houses did not.[71] This difference suggests the residents of the first house may have had access to guns, the most expeditious way to hunt birds, and the other households did not have access to guns. House #4 also consumed considerably more turtle than all other households. Whether this difference was also a consequence of not having guns or traps to capture turtles, or the occupants had more access to the habitats where turtles are found, or simply indicates food preferences among the four households is unknown. Although

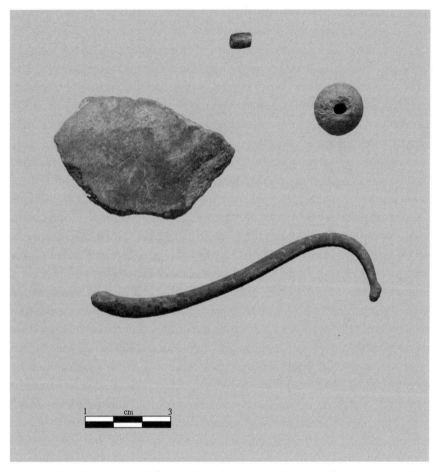

Assorted artifacts recovered from tabby cabins on Ossabaw Island. Beginning at the bottom and moving clockwise: a raccoon baculum, a fragment of colonoware, a green glass bead, and a lead fish-net sinker. Courtesy of Dan Elliot, LAMAR Institute.

one can only speculate as to the reasons for these differences, analysis of foodways from St. Anne's suggests the slave's ability to supplement their plantation rations with wild foods was perhaps more complicated than archaeologists have previously interpreted. Both written and archaeological sources have shown that some members of slave communities acquired better quality of food, clothing, and housing based upon a plantation social hierarchy. The St. Anne's faunal remains suggest that this differential access perhaps extended to the procurement and consumption of nondomestic food resources as well. In a slave settlement as remote as St. Anne's, the social structure may have been one enslaved people chose as was the case elsewhere on the Georgia coast.[72]

The St. Anne's data on foodways raises questions regarding the extent to which enslaved people prepared their food in their quarters or whether some portion of their food was prepared for them in plantation kitchens. References to plantation kitchens abound in written sources for nineteenth-century slavery in the Americas. Reform efforts combined with slaveholders' desire to control what enslaved people ate and when they ate led to the use of plantation kitchens for the preparation of at least one, possibly two, meals daily. Although few plantation kitchens have been identified from archaeological research, there may be other indications of their presence at particular plantation sites.[73] At Butler Island, for example, a small quantity of recovered food remains combined with written references to the presence of a cook's shop at each of the four slave settlements strongly suggest that there were plantation kitchens preparing some meals for the workforce.[74] The managers of Butler Island may have found preparing meals in central kitchens more efficient for such a large slaveholding (350 to 500 people), particularly during harvests and other seasons when the workday was excessively long. At other times, enslaved people may have been responsible for some or all of their own meals. Scholars often assume that enslaved people either prepared their own food or it was prepared for them in plantation kitchens. Rather than being an either-or proposition, some plantations, like Butler Island, may have operated using a combination of both plantation kitchens and slave households preparing their food within their quarters.

Archaeologists often attribute to task labor the capability of lowcountry slave communities to abundantly supplement plantation provisions with food and household goods they acquired themselves.[75] Task labor was the organizational structure for slave labor used in the production of rice and sea island cotton. Under the task system, enslaved laborers were assigned a certain amount of work by day. A task basic unit designated a set amount of land — usually one-quarter of an acre — and this basic unit formed the daily requirement for most plantation work, including clearing, draining, plowing, hoeing, weeding, and so forth. Slave workers were classified into full, three-quarter, half, and one-quarter hands according to their physical ability to perform tasks. Most tasks began at sunrise and were completed between 1:00 and 4:00 p.m. But tasks could be considerably longer, and the workday might be fifteen or sixteen hours during the peak of harvest season.[76] Task labor was unlike gang labor, wherein slave workers worked in groups or gangs under direct supervision of slave drivers from dawn to dusk. Gang labor predominated on Caribbean sugar plantations where it originated, and in the production of short-staple cotton and other crops of the Old South.

Because task labor afforded enslaved people opportunities to pursue economic activities for their own account, some archaeologists interpret the artifacts and food remains recovered from slave settlements as the residue of task labor. Ray Crook has further proposed that task labor played a major role in shaping Gullah culture, and sees the task system as "the material force underlying the construction of Gullah culture as a coherent cultural form."[77] From archaeological resources alone, however, these interpretations are problematical. The same kinds of activities are found at slave sites that did not employ task labor. While there are differences in artifacts recovered from site to site, these differences are often in the quantity and quality of artifacts, but not in the kinds of activities inferred from the artifacts. Activities typically documented at slave sites include preparing and consuming food, producing crafts, tending to gardens, procuring food, making tools and other implements from recycled materials (glass, ceramics, and metals), sewing, consumption of patent medicines and alcoholic beverages, smoking, playing games, participating in ritual, and wearing beads, jewelry, and amulets. The most striking difference in the archaeological record of slavery in lowcountry Georgia and that of slave sites located elsewhere is the abundant quantity and variety of nondomestic food resources. Is this distinctive feature a product of task labor or a product of the abundant resources available on the coast and exploited by lowcountry slave communities? Obviously, both situations contributed to slave procurement of wild foods, but enslaved people would have been able to exploit coastal food resources without task labor as they did in other plantation settings. Moreover, the animal species selected at many lowcountry sites were easy to obtain, and may be an indication of the limited amount of time they had available to procure food.[78] Task labor, perhaps, influenced the amount of *time* they spent on this pursuit, and therefore, impacted the *quantity* of food items that enslaved people were able to procure. Demonstrating this proposition from archaeological findings, however, presents a challenge to current archaeological methods. Task labor was important in the development of lowcountry slavery, but evaluating its significance from archaeological resources (artifacts and food remains) recovered from slave quarters is difficult.

Religious Beliefs and Practices

Archaeological approaches to slavery on the Georgia coast developed from an intellectual tradition that privileges economic (material) aspects of everyday life — housing, subsistence, labor, craft production, and so forth — while neglecting the influence of religious beliefs in the use of artifacts. This emphasis on materialism continues today, yet religion and spirituality were significant aspects of Gullah-Geechee life, as Cornelia Bailey has poignantly stated: "It was part of everyday life [over here on Sapelo Island] to believe in magic and signs and spirits."[79] Based on historical and ethnographic research undertaken on other sea islands, Bailey's comments can be extended to other Gullah-Geechee communities.[80] The idea that religious beliefs permeate all aspects of life is a fundamental premise of African and religions of African origins in the Americas, and one that archaeologists can no longer ignore in artifact interpretations of African diaspora peoples.

Outside of Georgia, archaeologists have begun the systematic study of African American religion, particularly during slavery at various sites in the United States. From excavations of African American sites, both slave and nonslave, archaeologists have recovered somewhat puzzling finds: pierced coins, crystals, smoothed or water-worn pebbles, shells, and worked animal bone fragments often with perforations, among other objects. Singularly, the significance of many of these objects is unclear, but when several are found together and deliberately placed in caches below floorboards, hearths, doorways, or corners of buildings, the possibility that they are of a religious nature is heightened. Such caches have been recovered at eighteenth-century slave houses in Virginia; at nineteenth- and twentieth-century urban dwellings in Annapolis, Maryland; late antebellum/post-emancipation, slave/wage laborer houses in Texas; among other places throughout the South, and a few in the Caribbean. Although there are similarities in the kinds of artifacts found in these caches, they appear to relate to different practices, and have been interpreted as such. In Virginia, the caches found in subterranean pits in slave houses have been interpreted as ancestral shrines. Those in Annapolis, Maryland, have been linked with Hoodoo, a southern term, used to refer to African American conjuring practices. Archaeologists in Texas pointed to the similarities in materials recovered from the slave/wage laborer's house and those used in Kongo rituals in the Americas.[81]

In Georgia, very few artifacts have been identified as having potential religious meanings. Archaeologists have examined collections of colonoware for ritual markings like those found on some South Carolina colonoware, but none have been reported. The strong materialist orientation in which recovered objects are classified according to obvious function obscures identification of potential symbolic usages. Cornelia Bailey, for example, recounts how her grandmother used a crystal doorknob as a "nubie" — an object suspended on a string and used for divining.[82] If recovered archaeologically, the only distinguishing characteristic of the doorknob indicating its possible use as a religious item would be the perforated hole for the string or thread. Small perforations are often the only identifiable evidence that an item had a special use other than its initial function, before it was reworked and reused for another purpose. Several small bird and mammal bones with perforations were recovered from excavations of the Tabbies at the North End Plantation on Ossabaw Island as well as numerous raccoon baculum (penis bone). Raccoon baculum have been found with perforations at other slave sites.[83] Unfortunately, the objects excavated from the Ossabaw Tabbies were not found in a cache or some other intentional deposit, like a subfloor pit; therefore, it is not possible to substantiate that these objects were used as a religious offering. Because the bones were perforated, however, they could have been strung together to form a necklace. Perforated teeth and vertebrae were recovered from excavations of a slave burial in Barbados of a presumed healer/conjurer.[84] Whether the perforated bones were nubies or worn as a necklace or anklet is also unknown. The practice of perforating bones, teeth, and other objects has been frequently reported from archaeological studies of African diaspora peoples.

Pierced coins are another example of perforated artifacts commonly found at African American sites, and have been reported from one site in lowcountry Georgia. These coins are frequently referenced in Works Progress Administration (WPA) interviews with former enslaved people. They were tied on strings and worn around ankles or necks for protection or good luck, or to prevent certain ailments like rheumatism. Two pierced coins were recovered from Harmony Hall, a small farm on a tributary of the St. Marys River in Camden County, with only six slave workers.[85] Gullah-Geechee oral tradition indicates that wearing a silver dime around the ankle for good luck was practiced in some Gullah-Geechee communities, but not in others. Additionally, when a silver dime around the ankle turned black, it was a sign that the person wearing it had been conjured.[86] The coins from Harmony Hall, however, were Spanish *reales* and not U.S. dimes. At the time the site was occupied (1793–1832) and well into the nineteenth century, Spanish currency was still legal tender in the United States. One can only speculate if the Spanish coins had the same meaning as U.S. dimes, but corroborating the archaeological finds with oral history supports an interpretation that the coins from Harmony Hall were most likely worn and used as amulets.

Beads are often significant in religions of African origin in the Americas. Archaeologists have proposed that blue-glass beads may have had special meaning to enslaved people since the inception of archaeological studies of slavery.[87] Beads are usually found on most slave sites but in varying quantities and colors; a few sites have large numbers of beads (over one hundred), while most have fewer than ten. Blue is usually, but not always, the dominant color. Oral histories, ethnographies, and travelers' accounts point to the significance of blue, particularly among Gullah-Geechee people, but no specific references to blue beads.[88] Blue beads may have been worn as amulets, kept as charms, or worn as jewelry. Any religious significance attached to beads may have been lost among later generations of enslaved people as suggested in the autobiography of Stella Martin written in 1867: "He handed me a rag of cotton cloth, tied all about with a string. I opened it, and found some blue glass beads — beads given to my mother by her mother as a keepsake when she died. I knew by that token he was a messenger from my mother. . . . I often heard her saying that nothing would make her part with these beads."[89] Martin had been enslaved in both Georgia and Alabama and apparently was unaware or (chose not to disclose) the meaning of blue beads, beyond the fact that they were an important keepsake in her maternal family line.

Interpreting artifacts as religious items always presents challenges, but greater efforts need to be directed toward this endeavor in the archaeological study of African American life in coastal Georgia than is currently the case. Functional analyses of artifacts are insufficient, because these miss other potential interpretations. Given the high frequencies of modified objects recovered at African diaspora sites, archaeologists must be open to alternative interpretations.

Reclaiming Gullah-Geechee Heritage

An important goal of archaeological studies of African diaspora today concerns developing relationships with present-day communities — referred to by archaeologists as descendant communities — whose heritage is being investigated at archaeological sites. These communities are not strictly speaking biological descendants of the people who once occupied the sites, but they have a legitimate claim to the site, and often perceive of themselves as stakeholders in the project.[90] Inclusion of descendant communities in an archaeological research project can take many forms. In some cases, archaeologists consult with descendant communities prior to beginning a project to find out what kinds of questions or issues interest them. This has led to developing partnerships or collaborations with community members who sometimes take an active role in the research. In other cases, descendant communities are considered and treated as an audience or a constituency of the research. The archaeologists, with the help of educators and other specialists, organize tours, lectures, exhibitions, and other public programs for their participation. The type of relationship developed between researchers and descendants depends on many factors, such as the scope of the project, the level of community interest, and the commitment of the archaeologists and sponsors (funding sources) of the archaeological research.

In the late 1970s and early 1980s, members of Gullah-Geechee communities were consulted primarily for interviews to aid the archaeological research. This is often the primary reason, even today, that archaeologists consult descendant communities. At that time, it was very difficult to engage the people interviewed in the research, with one notable exception. They either did not want to be reminded of a painful past associated with slavery and emancipation, or they were suffering from "interviewee fatigue" (a condition resulting from being interviewed too often by scholars, journalists, museum professionals, etc., that the interviewee develops rote responses to questions, and sometimes responses are even memorized from published sources).[91] As William Pollitzer observed, tourists see the Gullah-Geechee as "relics of a bygone era."[92] Unfortunately, these communities have often been portrayed in similar ways by scholars and other professionals, and it was the reason some members of the community near Butler Island refused to be interviewed. They were concerned that they would be depicted as quaint or odd people with strange practices or beliefs.

The most successful interview was with Rudolph Capers, who had worked for many years for the Dent family — the last owners of Hofwyl-Broadfield Plantation, just north of Brunswick in Glynn County, and now a Georgia state historic site. After the property became a state museum, Mr. Capers became a staff member of the site until his death. Mr. Capers possessed excellent skills as a storyteller and provided the researchers of the Butler Island project with information on rice planting, foodways (particularly on capturing turtles and waterfowl), and Gullah-Geechee life

Rudolph Capers, former employee of the Hofwyl-Broadfield Plantation, provided archaeologists with oral testimony of the area. Courtesy of Georgia Department of Natural Resources, Hofwyl-Broadfield Plantation State Historic Site.

during the first half of the twentieth century. He was later interviewed for a Public Broadcasting System (PBS) documentary on historical archaeology titled *Other Peoples' Garbage* (1980), and was hailed as a purveyor of local knowledge who helped fill gaps between the archaeological record and the recent past.

The researchers' experience with Mr. Capers should encourage archaeologists working today on the Georgia coast to develop dialogues and collaborations with the Gullah-Geechee communities. Archaeology of the Gullah-Geechee, unlike conducting archaeology of slavery in many other places in the Atlantic world, has the advantage of descendant communities who are cultural descendants of former occupants of archaeological sites. This is similar to archaeological studies of historic Native American and other cultural groups where there are direct links between the archaeology and the living people. These present-day communities, however, are not frozen in time, but are actively engaged in cultural production and reproduction. The ways in which Gullah-Geechee culture has changed over time should be just as important to archaeologists as the recovered evidence of their past lifeways. Archaeologists could learn a great deal from Gullah-Geechee communities that would contribute to interpretations of the archaeological record: What are their thoughts about colonoware? Do they know or had they heard of the significance of raccoon baculum? Why do they think enslaved people chose certain wild foods and not others? The Gullah-Geechee would probably be equally interested in learning of some of the archaeological findings: the resourcefulness of enslaved people to make tools and implements from materials they recycled; evidence of craft production some of which is still made today, like casting nets, while others like colonoware are no longer being produced; the use of beads, buttons, and other ornaments to make necklaces and other adornments. Although it was difficult to engage the Gullah-Geechee in archaeology of their heritage thirty years ago, it should not be as difficult to do so now with ongoing efforts to revitalize Gullah-Geechee communities in order to preserve their cultural heritage.

Archaeologists, like all students who study the past, work in the present to understand the past. Our understanding of the past is influenced by present circumstances, theories, and scholarly practices. In the archaeological study of plantations and slavery on the Georgia coast, earlier approaches and paradigms to archaeology did not encourage working with descendant communities; consequently, archaeological research has not always been perceived of as the heritage of a particular people. It is now time that we not only make this acknowledgment, but work hand-in-hand with the Gullah-Geechee so that they might learn of and reclaim their archaeological heritage.

NOTES

I would like to thank the organizers of the conference "The Atlantic World and African American Life and Culture in the Georgia Lowcountry: 18th to the 20th Century" for inviting me to participate, which gave me an opportunity to revisit and update research I undertook thirty years ago. Special thanks to Thomas Whitley and

Scott Butler of Brockington Associates Inc., Daniel Elliot of the Lamar Institute, Joe W. Josephs of New South Associates, and Ray Crook for providing me with site reports and other publications of recent work in the area. I remember fondly the time I spent doing archaeology on the Georgia coast, and I have taken the lessons I learned from working there everywhere I have worked since. I would also like to dedicate this essay to the memory of Rudolph Capers.

1. Robert Ascher and Charles H. Fairbanks. "Excavation of a Slave Cabin: Georgia, U.S." *Historical Archeology* 8 (1971): 3–7. Earlier works include: Adelaide K Bullen and Ripley Bullen, "Black Lucy's Garden," *Bulletin of the Massachusetts Archaeological Society* 6 (1945): 17–28; Ivor Noël Hume, *Excavations at Tutter's Neck in James City County Virginia, 1960–1961*, United States National Museum, Bulletin 249, *Contributions from the Museum of History and Technology, Paper 53* (Washington, D.C.: Smithsonian Institution Press, 1966); Charles Fairbanks, "The Kingsley Slave Cabins in Duval County, Florida, 1968," *Conference on Historic Site Archaeology Papers, 1971* 7 (1974): 62–93. Fairbanks's first archaeological project on slavery at Kingsley Plantation preceded the work on Cumberland Island, but was published later.

2. Ascher and Fairbanks, "Excavation of a Slave Cabin," 3.

3. Ray Crook, "Gullah-Geechee Archaeology: The Living Space of Enslaved Geechee on Sapelo Island," *African Diaspora Archaeology Network (ADAN)* (March 2008): 2, http://www.diaspora.uiuc.edu/newsletter.html.

4. Dissertations: John S. Otto, "Status Differences and the Archaeological Record: A Comparison of Planter, Overseer, and Slave Sites from Cannon's Point Plantation, 1794–1761, St. Simons Island, Georgia" (PhD diss., University of Florida, 1975); Theresa Singleton, "The Archaeology of Afro-American Slavery in Coastal Georgia: A Regional Perception of Slave Household and Community Patterns" (PhD diss., University of Florida, 1980); Sue M. Moore, "An Antebellum Barrier Island Plantation: In Search of an Archaeological Pattern" (PhD diss., University of Florida, 1981). Masters' theses: Suzanne S. McFarlane, "The Ethnoarchaeology of a Slave Community: The Couper Plantation Site" (master's thesis, University of Florida, 1975); Jennifer Hamilton, "Early History and Excavations at the LeConte-Woodmanston Plantation" (master's thesis, University of Florida, 1980).

5. Some recent studies in this vain include: Christopher C. Fennell, *Crossroads and Cosmologies: Diaspora and Ethnogenesis in the New World* (Gainesville: University of Florida Press, 2007); Patricia M. Samford, *Subfloor Pits and the Archaeology of Slavery in Colonial Virginia* (Tuscaloosa: University of Alabama Press, 2007); Akinwumi Ogundiran and Toyin Falola, eds., *Archaeology of Atlantic Africa and the African Diaspora* (Bloomington: University of Indiana Press, 2007).

6. E. Merton Coulter, ed., *Georgia's Disputed Ruins: Certain Tabby Ruins on the Georgia Coast* (Chapel Hill: University of North Carolina Press, 1937). For an archaeological study, see James A. Ford, "An Archaeological Report on Elizafield Ruins," in Coulter, *Georgia's Disputed Ruins*, 191–225.

7. John M. Vlach, *Back of the Big House: Architecture of Plantation Slavery* (Chapel Hill: University of North Carolina Press, 1993), 111.

8. John S. Otto, "Afro-American Archaeology," *Plantation Society in the Americas* 1 (1982): 4; Cornelia Walker Bailey with Christena Bledsoe, *God, Dr. Buzzard and the Bolito Man: A Saltwater Geechee Talks about Life on Sapelo Island, Georgia* (New York: Anchor Books, 2000), 49.

9. Ray Crook, "Biali — The Old Man of Sapelo: Between Africa and Georgia," *Wadabagei* 10, no. 2 (2007): 48–50.

10. Theresa Singleton, "An Archaeological Framework for Slavery and Emancipation, 1740–1880," in *The Recovery of Meaning: Historical Archaeology in the Eastern United States*, ed. Mark P. Leone and Parker B. Potter Jr. (Washington, D.C.: Smithsonian Institution Press, 1988), 345–70; J. W. Joseph, "Pattern and Process in the Plantation Archaeology of the Lowcountry of Georgia and South Carolina," *Historical Archaeology* 23, no. 1 (1989): 55–68.

11. Leland Ferguson, *Uncommon Ground: Archaeology and Early African America, 1650–1800* (Washington, D.C.: Smithsonian Institution Press, 1992), 18–32.

12. Theresa A. Singleton and Mark D. Bograd, "Breaking Typological Barriers: Looking for the Colono in Colonoware," in *Lines That Divide: Historical Archaeologies of Race, Class, and Gender*, ed. James A. Delle, Stephen A. Mrozowski, and Robert Paynter (Knoxville: University of Tennessee Press, 2000), 7.

13. Ferguson, *Uncommon Ground*, 3–7. For the debate concerning the makers of the Virginia wares, see L. Daniel Mouer et al., "Colonoware Pottery, Chesapeake Pipes, and 'Uncritical Assumptions,'" in *I, too, Am America: Archaeological Studies of African-American Life*, ed. Theresa Singleton (Charlottesville: University Press of Virginia), 47–115.

14. Colonoware has been recovered from Lethe Farm, an upland site in South Carolina that yielded 5,747 fragments. See Carl Steen, "Stirring the Ethnic Stew in South Carolina Backcountry: John de la Howe and Lethe Farm," in *Historical Archaeology, Identity Formation, and the Interpretation of Ethnicity*, ed. Maria Franklin and Garrett Fesler (Williamsburg, Va.: Colonial Williamsburg Foundation, 1999), 112. Sixty-four fragments were recovered from an urban African American site in Columbus, Georgia. See Rita F. Elliott, "A city slave is almost a Freeman . . . or not," *Early Georgia* 36, no. 1 (2008): 69. For a reference to colonoware in New England, see Stephan A. Mrozowski, *The Archaeology of Class in Urban America* (New York: Cambridge University Press, 2006), 54–55.

15. Anne E. Yentsch, *A Chesapeake Family and Their Slaves: A Study in Historical Archaeology* (New York: Cambridge University Press, 1994), 205.

16. William Gilmore Simms, "Loves of the Driver," *The Magnolia: Or Southern Monthly* 3 (1841): 122.

17. Thomas R. Wheaton and Patrick H. Garrow, "Acculturation and the Archaeological Record," in *The Archaeology of Slavery and Plantation Life*, ed. Theresa A. Singleton (Orlando, Fla.: Academic Press, 1985), 249–51; Christopher Espenshade, "The Changing Use Contexts of Slave-Made Pottery on the South Carolina Coast," Conference Proceedings, African Impact on the Material Culture of the Americas, Museum of Early Southern Decorative Arts, Winston-Salem, North Carolina, May 30–June 2, 1996.

18. Carl Steen, "Stirring the Ethnic Stew in South Carolina Backcountry," 99–103; Singleton and Bograd, "Breaking Typological Barriers," 8–9.

19. Nicole Isenberger, " 'Necessity or Commodity?' An Analysis of the Ford Plantation Colonoware, Bryan County, Georgia," *Early Georgia* 36, no. 1 (2008): 44.

20. Espenshade, "Changing Use Contexts of Slave-Made Pottery."

21. Ibid.

22. Thomas Whitley et al., The Ford Plantation Project: Archaeological Data Recovery at Silk Hope Plantation (9BN58 and 9BN176), Bryan County, Georgia, Prepared for the Ford Plantation LLC, Richmond Hill, Ga. (Atlanta: Brockington and Associates, 2003), 156–66.

23. Isenberger, " 'Necessity or Commodity?' " 47.

24. Reports on Cherry Hill and Richmond plantations are in separate volumes: Thomas Whitley et al., The Ford Plantation Project Archaeological Data Recovery at Cherry Hill Plantation (9BN49/56/67), Bryan County Ga. (Atlanta: Brockington and Associates, 2003); Scott Butler et al., The Ford Plantation Project: Archaeological Data Recovery at Dublin/Richmond Plantation (0BN44, 9BN174 & 9BM177), Bryan County, Ga. (Atlanta: Brockington and Associates, 2003).

25. Lamar Institute Inc. Archaeological Investigations at Tabbies 1 and 2 North End Plantation Ossabaw Island, Ga. *Lamar Institute Publication Series Report Number 108* (n.d.), 115.

26. Sugar wares are usually wheel-thrown and fired in kilns. The two dominant forms are sugar molds and molasses drip jars.

27. Karen Olwig, "Cultural Identity and Material Culture: Afro-Caribbean Pottery" *Folk* 32 (1990): 8.

28. Most studies of Caribbean pottery examine the history of potting on a specific island. For discussions of Afro-Caribbean occurring on several islands, see James Petersen, David Waters, and Desmond Nicholson, "Continuity and Syncretism in Afro-Caribbean Ceramics from the Northern Lesser Antilles," in *African Sites Archaeology in the Caribbean*, ed. Jay B. Haviser (Princeton, N.J.: Markus Wiener, 1999), 157–95, and Mark W. Hauser and Christopher R. DeCorse, "Low-Fired Earthenwares in the African Diaspora: Problems and Prospects," *International Journal of Historical Archaeology* 7, no. 1 (2003): 67–98.

29. Laurie A. Wilkie and Paul Farnsworth, *Sampling Many Pots: An Archaeology of Memory and Tradition at a Bahamian Plantation* (Gainesville: University Press of Florida, 2005), 252.

30. Thomas C. Loftfield, "Ceramic Evidence of Creolization in Barbados," Conference Proceedings, African Impact on the Material Culture of the Americas, Museum of Early Southern Decorative Arts, Winston-Salem, North Carolina, May 30–June 2, 1996; Dwayne Scheid, Department of Anthropology, Syracuse University, personal communication, July 2008.

31. Isenberger, " 'Necessity or Commodity?' " 42–43.

32. Samford, *Subfloor Pits*, 86.

33. Wheaton and Garrow, "Acculturation and the Archaeological Record," 243–48; Steen, "Stirring the Ethnic Stew," 98.

34. Ferguson, *Uncommon Ground*, 77.

35. Whittington et al., *Silk Hope Plantation*, 211–16.

36. Georgia Writers' Project, *Drums and Shadows: Survival Studies among the Georgia Coastal Negroes*, (1940: repr., Athens: University of Georgia Press, 1986), 179.

37. Ibid., 182.

38. John S. Otto, *Cannon's Point Plantation, 1794–1860: Living Conditions and Status Patterns in the Old South* (Orlando, Fla.: Academic Press, 1984), 43.

39. Crook, "Gullah-Geechee Archaeology," 9–10.

40. Douglas Armstrong, personal communication.

41. B. W. Higman, *Montpelier Jamaica: A Plantation Community in Slavery and Freedom, 1739–1912* (Mona, Jamaica: Press University of the West Indies, 1998), 154–55.

42. Steen, "Stirring the Ethnic Stew," 98–99.

43. Samford, *Subfloor Pits*, 118–21.

44. Ibid., 61–63.

45. Ferguson, *Uncommon Ground*, 67, 71.

46. Whitley et al., Ford Plantation Project Archaeological Data Recovery, 83–86.

47. For a discussion of specific reform efforts in slave housing outside the United States, see William Chapman, "Slave Villages in the Danish West Indies: Changes of the Late Eighteenth and Early Nineteenth Centuries," in *Perspectives in Vernacular Architecture* 4, ed. Thomas Carter and Bernard L. Herman (Columbia: University of Missouri Press, 1991), 112–15; Wilkie and Farnsworth, *Sampling Many Pots*, 150–51; Theresa Singleton, "Slavery and Spatial Dialectics on Cuban Coffee Plantations," *World Archaeology* 33, no. 1 (2001): 103–4.

48. Edward A. Chappell, "Museums and American Slavery" in *I, Too, Am America: Archaeological Studies of African-American Life*, ed. Theresa Singleton (Charlottesville: University Press of Virginia), 243.

49. Singleton, "Archaeological Framework for Slavery and Emancipation," 355.

50. McFarlane, "Ethnoarchaeology of a Slave Community," 73.

51. Moore, "Antebellum Barrier Island Plantation," 206.

52. Scott Butler, "Data Recovery Excavations at the St. Anne's Slave Settlement 99GN197), Glynn County, Georgia," *Early Georgia* 35, no. 2 (2008): 126.

53. Singleton, "Archaeological Perception of Slave Household and Community Patterns," 116, fig. 18; 126–29.

54. Singleton, "Archaeological Framework for Slavery and Emancipation," 357. I also took note of measurements given of slave quarters at Jones and St. Anne's on St. Simons, and Cherry Hill and Richmond plantations on the Ogeechee River to arrive at these ranges.

55. Whitney W. Olvey, "Where Did They Dump It? Refuse Disposal at the Ford Plantation Site," Paper presented at the Society for Historical Archaeology, Mobile, Alabama, January 8–12, 2002; Brockington and Associates, http://www.brockington.org/research.

56. Butler, "Data Recovery at St. Anne's," 130–31.

57. Some studies of plantation space include Jim Delle, *An Archaeology of Social Space: Analyzing Coffee Plantations in Jamaica's Blue Mountains* (New York: Plenum Press, 1998); Dan Hicks, *The Garden of the World: An Historical Archaeology of Sugar Landscapes in the Eastern Caribbean*, British Archaeology Reports, International Series 1632 (Oxford: Archaeopress, 2007); Mark P. Leone, James M. Harmon, and Jessica L. Neuwirth, "Perspective and Surveillance in Eighteenth-Century Maryland Gardens, Including William Paca's Garden on Wye Island," *Historical Archaeology* 39, no 4 (2005): 138–58; Terrence W. Epperson, "Panoptic Plantations: Garden Sights of Thomas Jefferson and George Mason," in *Lines That Divide: Historical Archaeologies of Race, Class, and Gender*, ed. James A. Delle, Stephan A. Mrozowski, and Robert Paynter (Knoxville: University of Tennessee Press, 2000), 58–77.

58. Merle Prunty, "The Renaissance of the Southern Plantation," *American Geographical Review* 45, no. 4 (1955): 463–66.

59. P. J. Laborie, *The Coffee Planter of Santo Domingo* (London: T. Caddell and W. Davies, 1798), 37–38.

60. Stephanie R. Joyner, "Slave Housing Patterns within the Plantation Landscape of Coastal Georgia (master's thesis, University of Florida, 2003). This thesis examines the spatial organization of fifteen plantations, of which six had dispersed slave settlements.

61. Lorena S. Walsh, "Slave Life, Slave Society, and Tobacco Production in Tidewater Chesapeake. 1620–1820," in *Cultivation and Culture: Labor and the Shaping of Slave Life in the Americas*, ed. Ira Berlin and Philip D. Morgan (Charlottesville: University Press of Virginia, 1993), 172.

62. Vlach, *Back of the Big House*, 190–91.

63. Singleton, "Archaeological Perception of Slave Household and Community Patterns," 32.

64. Butler, "Data Recovery at St. Anne's," 113–14.

65. Crook, "Gullah-Geechee Archaeology," 4.

66. Singleton, "Archaeological Perception of Slave Household and Community Patterns," 114–18.

67. Erskine Clarke, *Dwelling Place: A Plantation Epic* (New Haven, Conn.: Yale University Press, 2005), 47.

68. Bailey, *God, Dr. Buzzard*, 21, 113–15.

69. Normally acidic coastal soils do not yield good bone preservation. The prevalence of oyster shell in many of the trash deposits helps to neutralize acidic coastal soils.

70. Elizabeth Reitz et al., "Archaeological Evidence for Subsistence on Coastal Plantations," in *Archaeology of Slavery and Plantation Life*, ed. Theresa A. Singleton (Orlando, Fla.: Academic Press, 1985), 184.

71. Butler, "Archaeological Recovery at St. Anne's," 127–28.

72. Clarke, *Dwelling Place*, 47.

73. I am only aware of one plantation kitchen used to prepare slave meals that has been studied by archaeologists: at Marshall Pen, a nineteenth-century coffee plantation in Jamaica (Jim Delle, personal communication).

74. Francis Kemble, *A Journal of a Residence on a Georgian Plantation, 1838–1839*, ed. John A. Scott (1863; repr. New York: Alfred Knopf, 1961), 100.

75. William H. Adams, ed., "Historical Archaeology of Plantations at Kings Bay, Camden County, Georgia," Report Submitted to Naval Submarine Base. Report of Investigations #5, Department of Anthropology, University of Florida, Gainesville, 1987, 11–13; Ray Crook, "Gullah and the Task System," *Anthropology of Work Review* 22, no. 2 (2001): 24–28. Elizabeth Reitz, Tyson Gibbs, and Ted A. Rathbun, "Archaeological Evidence for Subsistence on Coastal Plantations," in *The Archaeology of Slavery and Plantation Life*, ed. Theresa Singleton (Orlando, Fla.: Academic Press, 1985), 183.

76. Philip D. Morgan, "Work and Culture: The Task System and the World of Lowcountry Blacks, 1700–1880," *William and Mary Quarterly* Series 3, 39 (1982): 587–91.

77. Crook, "Gullah and the Task System," 26.

78. Reitz, Gibbs, and Rathbun, *Archaeological Evidence*, 184; Lamar Institute, *Archaeological Investigations*, 140.

79. Bailey, *God, Dr. Buzzard*, 9.

80. Clarke, *Dwelling Place*, 50–51; William S. Pollitzer, *The Gullah People and Their African Heritage* (Athens: University of Georgia Press, 1999), 144–45.

81. Samford, *Subfloor Pits*, 149–73; Mark Leone, *The Archaeology of Liberty in an American Capital: Excavations in Annapolis* (Berkeley: University of California Press, 2005), 237–44; Kenneth Brown and Doreen Cooper, "Structural Continuity in an African-American Slave and Tenant Community," *Historical Archaeology* 24, no. 4 (1990): 17.

82. Bailey, *God, Dr. Buzzard*, 65.

83. Lamar Institute, *Archaeological Investigations*, 120; For a reference to another raccoon baculum, see Theresa Singleton, "The Archaeology of Slave Life," in *Before Freedom Came: African-American Life in Antebellum South*, ed. Edward D. C. Campbell Jr. with Kym S. Rice (Charlottesville: University Press of Virginia, 1991), 164.

84. Jerome S. Handler, "An African-Type Medicine Man and His Grave Goods: A Burial, from a Plantation Slave Cemetery," *International Journal of Historical Archaeology* 1, no. 2 (1997): 91–130.

85. Adams, "Historical Archaeology at Kings Bay," 123, 387: figures N and O.

86. Bailey, *God, Dr. Buzzard*, 150; Pollitzer, *Gullah People and Their African Heritage*, 145.

87. For a detailed examination of blue beads on slave and other African American sites, see Linda F. Stine et al., "Blue Beads as African-American Cultural Symbols," *Historical Archaeology* 30, no. 3 (1996): 49–75.

88. See, for example, Margaret Washington Creel, *"A Peculiar People": Slave Religion and Community-Culture among the Gullahs* (New York: New York University Press, 1988), 321.

89. John Blassingame, ed. *Slave Testimony: Two Centuries of Letters, Speeches, Interviews, and Autobiographies* (Baton Rouge: Louisiana State University, 1977), 713.

90. Theresa Singleton and Charles E. Orser Jr., "Descendant Communities: Linking People in the Present to the Past," in *Ethical Issues in Archaeology*, ed. Larry J. Zimmerman, Karen D. Vitelli, and Julie Hollowell-Zimmer (Walnut Creek, Calif.: AltaMira Press, 2003), 143.

91. I coined this term and have frequently encountered this problem when interviewing people.

92. Pollitzer, *Gullah People and Their African Heritage*, 4.

Jacqueline Jones

A Spirit of Enterprise

The African American Challenge
to the Confederate Project in
Civil War–Era Savannah

INTERVIEWED by members of the Southern Claims Commission
after the Civil War, black men and women throughout the Georgia
lowcountry testified to their remarkably resilient entrepreneurial impulses. The U.S. Congress established the commission in 1871 to compen-
sate southern Unionists whose property had been seized by federal troops
during the war. In lowcountry Georgia, most of those loyal southerners
were black men and women. When U.S. troops marched through the lowcountry in late 1864, they had confiscated livestock, food, and household
goods belonging to black people living in and around Savannah. Alexander
Steele recalled that he and other slaves on James Potter's expansive Savannah River rice plantations had "by industry and economy" stockpiled rice,
honey, and lard, and raised and marketed cows, chickens, mules, turkeys,
and hogs. Planters such as Potter allowed their enslaved laborers to work for
themselves after they finished their daily tasks in the fields, granting each
person, in Steele's words, the "liberty of trading and trafficking for himself."
Born free, Liberty County's Tony Axon accumulated livestock and the
tools of his blacksmith trade by working hard and gaining the patronage of

whites in the area. Declared Axon, "I got this property by the sweat of my brow, hard licks, Sir!" City slaves showed similar initiative. Cato Keating, an engineer in Savannah, worked for two rice mills; his master allowed him to keep a weekly allowance of four dollars. Together Keating and his wife, a washerwoman, raised hogs and sold them for a profit: "Sell and buy and sell and buy" was Keating's motto.[1]

In the mid-nineteenth century, the coastal region of Georgia and South Carolina formed a sacred landscape, home to the Gullah-Geechee culture. Linking the profane and spiritual worlds of the slaves were the waterways that laced the lowcountry, a place shaped by West African traditions of work, family, and religious faith. The Gullah-Geechee worldview contrasted mightily with that of planters and other lowcountry elites, men and women who saw the land and water primarily as components of a vast cultivation machine powered by the descendants of Africans. Where black people expressed their yearnings for freedom indirectly, metaphorically through stories and songs, wealthy whites prided themselves on speaking and acting directly and decisively. Where black people nourished a sense of community borne of their African heritage and their struggles as slaves, elites promoted individualism and money making.[2]

Nevertheless, it is possible to overstate the cultural distinctiveness of the Gullah-Geechee, and in the process to ignore the social and political values they shared with whites of all classes — in particular, ownership of land and other forms of property, full citizenship rights, and profit seeking through trade. Throughout the lowcountry, enslaved workers contributed to a regional economy based on petty commodity production; just as significantly, in concert with poor whites, they participated in a shadow economy specializing in the illicit trading of goods and services, and the labor of runaways of various kinds. True, whites took alarm from many West African cultural practices, including the beating of drums, which seemed to signal an imminent slave uprising; yet even more threatening to white hegemony was the fact that the spirit of enterprise characteristic of Savannah was not limited to elites. Indeed, trafficking between slaves and poor whites represented a political challenge to the whole system of white supremacy before and during the war. After the war, black people pressed their demands for citizenship rights, revealing in new and dramatic ways the values they shared with all white people — to send their children to school, to work for themselves, and to participate fully in the political process.[3]

Before the Civil War, white authorities realized that a rigid lowcountry social hierarchy based on ideologies of class, caste, and color existed in theory more than in fact. To maintain an enforced political separation between blacks and whites demanded novel and aggressive strategies. And so throughout the 1850s, members of the Savannah city council routinely devoted the beginning of their biweekly meetings to a curious ritual: After the council president gaveled the meeting to order, members settled back and prepared for the evening's entertainment — lawbreakers recently convicted in mayor's court were appealing their fines. Typically, the defendants, like those who appeared before the council in 1855, had surnames such as Egan, Kelly, and Gleason, and hailed from Irish counties such as Limerick, Cork, Donegal, Roscommon, Galway, and Kerry. Most operated modest businesses in the city — John McAuliffe, thirty-five, from Cork, was a grocer and barroom keeper, and Christopher Hussey, twenty-five, was a shipping master from Kerry. These men were charged with "entertaining" seamen deserters and slave runaways; with serving alcohol to blacks after curfew; fencing stolen goods received from black and white men and women alike; keeping a brothel; and making a ruckus on the Sabbath. For council members, the defendants' entrepreneurial activities bespoke a larger, troubling reality — the collusion among slaves, free blacks, and nonelite whites to profit and to provide for their families through illegal means. Yet therein lay a dilemma, for by harshly punishing white miscreants, council members risked alienating a key component of their own political constituency.[4]

The evening's real drama came in the form of the "defense" offered by each defendant's attorney. Among the lawyers representing these men were, among others, John McPherson Berrien, former judge of the eastern circuit court of Georgia, state senator, U.S. senator (1825–29, 1841–52), and attorney general under the Andrew Jackson administration; and Edward J. Harden, former judge of the city court. These distinguished attorneys predictably defended their clients by offering a spirited if spurious defense, a variation on the theme that the apprehension itself violated local or state law.[5]

Hearings like these were actually highly charged political rituals. The lawyers performed a "defense" of men and women of the white laboring and petty-proprietor classes, and urged the aldermen — their own peers, not the peers of the defendants — to drop the charges or at least reduce the fines. Many of the attorneys had political ambitions of their own and sought to appeal to members of Savannah's Democratic Party, a group that included many Irish immigrant workers and shopkeepers. Aldermen were unpredictable in passing judgment on defendants who managed to retain savvy, well-connected counsel. Yet such rituals allowed white elites to uphold the law while simultaneously currying favor among immigrants accused of petty crimes.

During the Civil War era, Savannah's merchants, bankers, cotton factors, and planters came together to initiate and sustain the Confederate project — that is, to win the allegiance of Savannah's white laboring classes in pursuit of white supremacist policies. These policies aimed to overcome the imperatives of class and fix a stark dividing line between whites and blacks. Yet Savannah's boisterous spirit of commercial enterprise remained stubbornly resistant to traditional southern hierarchies meant to reinforce caste lines between white and black, free and enslaved people. In 1860, the Confederate project mandated secession from the Union; in 1865, that project mandated resistance to Yankee military occupation, the Republican Party, and the black struggle for civil rights. Throughout this period, the Confederate project assumed a profoundly reactionary character, as whites sought to counter the aggressive efforts of black people to claim their dignity as producers, and their rights as American citizens.[6]

Savannah, in the county of Chatham, sits on a bluff forty feet above the Savannah River, eighteen miles from the Atlantic Ocean. In the late antebellum period, city leaders considered themselves proud boosters; they eagerly invested taxpayers' money in railroads, banks, and internal improvements, such as the dredging of the Savannah River. Yet several factors complicated the political agenda of the local authorities. First, substantial proportions of the white laboring classes were transient and unstable. The city's economy relied on the processing and transporting of staples, tasks that were by definition seasonal. From late fall through the spring, many Savannah laborers spent their working hours hauling raw materials from the Central of Georgia railroad depot in the western part of the city to the sawmills, cotton presses, and rice mills down by the wharf, and then loading wooden planks, tierces of rice, and bales of cotton into ships bound for Boston, New York, Havana, and Liverpool. In 1860, about one-half of all white adults in the city were foreign-born, and about 70 percent of those were Irish. Some Irish immigrants had arrived in the state in the 1840s to work on the railroads, later settling in Savannah to start families and to open grocery stores and grogshops. But many Irish workers were transients, traveling around the South in search of work, or migrating annually from New York City to labor on the docks between November and May.[7]

Unlike most other southern cities, Savannah grew rapidly in the 1850s (from fifteen thousand in 1850 to twenty-two thousand in 1860). Its substantial population of northern- and foreign-born whites, together with slaves and free people of color (six thousand to eight thousand in this period), rendered the white southern-born population a striking minority within the city overall. The foreign-born, mainly Germans and Irish, dominated the ranks of petty proprietors, and it was they who perceived city-imposed fines as routine costs of doing (illicit) business with black people in general and slaves in particular. Savannah's relatively small population of free people of color (fewer than one thousand in the 1850s), together with the city's slaves, were well integrated into the local economy; these men toiled as tradesmen (especially in the drayage business), skilled craftsmen (carpenters and bricklayers), and dockworkers and employees of cotton presses, sawmills, and rice mills. The fact that black workers contributed greatly to the city's commercial trade accounts for the latitude with which masters granted slaves the opportunity to hire themselves out and keep part of the wages they earned as mill workers, skilled craftsmen, and draymen. In all these jobs, blacks often toiled side-by-side with white men of the laboring classes.[8]

In Savannah, the geography of labor attested to elites' efforts to enforce a caste system, but also to their difficulties in doing so. The city market served as a worksite not only for white male butchers, but also for enslaved women who came in from the countryside to tend their stalls and sell seafood, eggs, and vegetables. The streets of the city were clogged with black women hawking goods, and carrying on their heads in the African style bulky loads of laundry to customers and food to market. Ironically, slaves and free people of color represented a uniquely stable presence in the regional labor market. Black men dominated the jobs of wagoner, drayman, and porter; transient Irish workers had fewer opportunities to invest in the animals and wagons necessary for this kind of business. More generally, one's legal status was not readily apparent to people at the time, or to historians since. Ulysses L. Houston, who would become pastor of the Third African (later Bryan) Baptist Church, was a butcher by trade. Hiring his own time and paying his master fifty dollars a month, Houston regularly went out into the countryside to buy cattle, selling the meat and hides from his residence in the city. Similarly, Dolly Reed (grandmother of the nurse and teacher Susie Baker King Taylor) possessed market-savvy energy and industry. Like Houston, Reed traveled between the city and its hinterland to trade, taking bacon, flour, molasses, and sugar to rural folks and returning with eggs, chickens, and cash. The city and the countryside formed a regional economy that relied on the trade conducted by slaves and free blacks.[9]

Significantly, Savannah lacked large-scale manufacturing firms, which would have yielded a more stable working class as well as white-collar positions for bookkeepers and supervisors. Elites thus had to contend with the fact that the city had no substantial middle class that might have served as intermediary between the wealthy on the one hand and the mass of white laborers on the other. In the city, charity and a strong police force, not opportunities for upward mobility, were the elite's preferred strategies in dealing with the white poor.[10]

And so how to convince white laborers that the interests of the fabulously wealthy were their own? For the most part, the city consisted of, on the one hand, a small, interlocking directorate of powerful men, and, on the other, large numbers of black and white laborers who worked together, lived in the same neighborhoods, and drank, traded, stole, swore, fought, and sometimes even struck for higher wages together. Dividing this period into three parts — antebellum, wartime, and postbellum — allows us to consider the challenges faced by Savannah's political leaders.

Before the war, Savannah's whites made a strategic error in allowing blacks, enslaved and free, any opportunity for self-direction in the form of either wage work or participation in mutual aid associations, clandestine schools, and independent churches. Authorities were less than vigilant in rooting out the several secret schools conducted by black teachers. And whites believed, wrongly, that black religious activities would serve to reinforce the power of slaveholders through biblical injunctions and calls for enslaved workers to practice humility and patience. The Georgia lowcountry boasted the first independent black Baptist church in North America, and by the 1850s, the majority of Savannah's blacks worshiped at one of three African Baptist churches in the city. Members of these congregations chose and paid the salaries of their own ministers, elected governing officers, and sponsored Sunday schools and benevolent and mutual aid associations. Church officers disciplined members for various infractions. More generally, these black churches departed from their white counterparts and developed a theology that promoted a narrative of justice and equality, a narrative that would eventually infuse partisan politics with spiritual meaning.[11]

In Savannah, the antebellum Democratic Party stood for the white laboring classes and for slavery, for "progress," profits, and states' rights. What white man could object? Indeed, so universal was the appeal of this platform that some observers were complaining in the mid-1850s that the Democrats were virtually unbeatable. Yet in order to retain their influence over the white laboring classes, party leaders often had to look the other way when dockworkers, teamsters, and seamen engaged in the kinds of petty crime that were the hallmark of any bustling port. Richard D. Arnold, a physician and mainstay of Savannah civic culture during this period, described the cardinal rule of city politics: "The Mayor and & [city] Marshall ... regulate the shopkeepers politically by *not* regulating them as to the Law." In other words, shopkeeping and laboring-class constituents expected to make money — serving black customers as well as white — without interference from authorities and other hectoring busybodies.[12]

Not all Savannah politicians reconciled themselves to this bargain; some, the reformers, retained a strong streak of righteousness in the midst of so many vice purveyors. And a small but rising political party, the Know-Nothings, resented the zeal with which Irish immigrants in particular entered the ranks of the Democratic Party and received in return jobs as public-works laborers and policemen. Of Savannah's immigrant-Democratic faithful, one observer noted, "In a twinkling, he masters the science of government and winds his way without a light through all the labyrinths of politics." And in fact, the Irish and Germans proved adept at Savannah's political game. In order to vote in municipal elections, a white man need only be twenty years old, a resident of the state of Georgia for one year, a resident of Savannah for four months. By 1854, the shillelagh had joined the bowie knife, brick, and pistol as an election-day weapon of choice among raucous and oftentimes inebriated Savannah voters.[13]

At the same time, public officeholding remained the purview of relatively few men elected at-large. During the 1850s, of the 143 slots for mayor and alderman, only 136 different men ran for office. The only substantial difference of opinion among political candidates revolved around the proper way to accommodate the restless white working classes, and particularly the growing number of Irish immigrants. Yet the Know-Nothings understood that they could never gain permanent power in Savannah politics; after all, as a matter of principle they were bent on disparaging the morals and intelligence of nearly half the electorate.[14]

Many immigrant men operated brothels, gambling operations, and all-hours grogshops because of the high demand for these services. Some enterprising boardinghouse owners made a living by "abducting" disgruntled seaman and then helping them find employment elsewhere, a practice that gave the city a bad name among ship captains up and down the East Coast. The thriving, underground economy also encouraged the hiring or "entertaining" of runaway slaves. After a hard day's work on the wharves, at the railroad depot, on in a sawmill, laborers retreated to the Yamacraw or Old Fort neighborhoods, there to slake their thirst with a pint of ale, or to risk their hard-earned wages on a game of dice. Consequently, city politics seesawed between those who appealed to immigrant voters and looked the other way when barroom owners hid runaway slaves, and those who appealed to immigrant voters and then cracked down on such behavior once they were elected.[15]

Savannah had long boasted a network of volunteer associations that knit together white dockworkers and merchants, Protestants and Catholics and Jews, and recent immigrants and long-established families. The Union Society and the Needle Woman's Society offered venues for the wealthy of all religious faiths to ameliorate some of the social ills afflicting whites and flowing naturally from an economy that relied on such a large proportion of seasonal, low-wage workers. Social groups such as the Hibernians and the Irish Union Society included men of Irish descent, regardless of class. Societies of German speakers counted among their members Jews, Catholics, and Protestants. Catholic Church parishioners included the native-born as well as German and Irish immigrants. Volunteer militias and fire companies gave expression to male bravado and a peculiarly southern martial spirit. The Democratic Party represented perhaps the most successful cross-sectional alliance of all, a testament to the mutual if wildly unequal dependence of the commercial elite on large numbers of white laborers.[16]

Like other nineteenth-century American cities, Savannah valued parades as forms of political and social expression, and indeed during any particular day the city was likely to come to a halt and watch a funeral cortege, Sunday school procession, or military drill. Among the largest and liveliest of these parades were the ones marking St. Patrick's Day on March 17 and the firemen's parade held the last Friday in May. Organized by the Hibernians, an Irish benevolent society founded in 1812, the annual St. Patrick's Day parade attracted huge numbers of spectators, not just persons claiming a heritage from the Emerald Isle, but all who wished "to drown the shamrock in mountain dew." Such parades could not help but remind the city's predominantly Protestant elite of the political clout of overlapping groups of Irish immigrants, Catholics, and the laboring classes.[17]

In fact, northern visitors observed in Savannah processions the foundation and symbol of a remarkably stable social order. The city apparently possessed no "underswell . . . [,] the motley crowd of men and boys of all nations which gather in [northern cities] on public occasions." Also conspicuous for their absence in Savannah were the "mobs . . . that fearful element in society, an irresponsible and low class"— the ugly demonstrations of unemployed workers, the pitched battles between Catholic and Protestant and between immigrant and native-born workers. In the place of civil strife, the Georgia riverport offered highly choreographed displays of overlapping systems of power and influence — the volunteer militias and fire companies, the charities, churches, fraternal orders, professional groups, and Democratic Party.[18]

The collective discipline on display in the largest city processions was but an extension of the martial spirit that played an increasingly prominent role in Savannah's public life during the 1850s. Virtually all white men belonged to some sort of military organization — native-born members of the laboring classes forming ragtag bands of volunteer home guards, the Irish sponsoring the Jasper Greens and Montgomery Guards. The wealthy joined independent companies such as the resplendently attired Republican Blues, Georgia Hussars, Chatham Artillery, or Oglethorpe Light Infantry, each complete with its own marching band of African American musicians. Together with the fire companies, the militias provided white men — and white men only — with a near-universal experience of parading and drilling.[19]

The presidential election of 1856 handed a victory to the Democrat James Buchanan; but a new party with national aspirations, the Republicans, was itself within two states of carrying the White House. Supported by northerners exclusively, the Republicans signaled the demise of a generations-old compromise between the Whigs and the Democrats on the subject of slavery. The white laboring classes of southern cities would seem to represent the Republican's best hope for extending their message into slave territory. In Savannah, some white tradesmen continued to express their long-standing resentment toward their enslaved competitors, black men hired out by their owners. White dockworkers and other manual laborers chafed under an exploitative system that paid them starvation wages

while enriching their employers and the city's financial elite more generally. Increasingly, wealthy whites interpreted working-class restlessness as
a potential threat to Democratic hegemony.[20]

Nevertheless, the urban white laboring classes showed little evidence
that they possessed either the will or the strength to act in their own economic self-interest in opposition to the town and country lords of the lash.
Some craftsmen, including typographers, master bootmen, and journey-
men tailors, did organize in the antebellum period, but these associations
more nearly resembled fraternal orders than labor unions. In the mid-1850s,
in addition to the dockworkers, white carpenters and mechanics working
for the Central of Georgia Railroad struck for higher wages. In each of
these cases, employers moved swiftly to fire the striking workers and re-
place them with blacks. Complicating the situation was the incremental
upward mobility experienced by a few albeit highly visible Irish immigrant
laborers who won jobs as foot patrolmen in the police force, and by shopkeepers who worked their way into the planter class.[21]

On a practical level, the city fathers, many of whom owned plantations in the rice kingdom or the cotton-producing sea islands, also feared
the explosive potential of a persistent, biracial waterborne traffic in alcohol
and stolen goods. Peddlers and grogshop owners were eager to exchange
alcohol — in some cases a noxious mixture of tobacco and whiskey — for
cotton, rice, produce, tools, and any kind of hardware purloined from local
plantations. To counter "the extensive and growing traffick unlawfully
carried on with slaves by white persons and chiefly by Retailers of Spiri-
tous Liquours," planters from Savannah to Augusta formed the Savannah
River Anti-Slave Traffick Association. Since this underground economy
provided a livelihood for many of the region's nonslaveholding whites, the
founders of the association had to acknowledge "it has been said that ours
was a combination to oppress the poor."[22]

During the winter and spring of 1857–58, Savannahians began to calculate the dangers of a white man's democracy. Armed conflict in Kansas
proved that slave owners could not count on sufficient votes among western settlers to preserve the institution of bondage in the territories. Might
not a pure form of democracy empower nonslaveholders? In Savannah,
this question spurred support for a renewed foreign slave trade. In 1859,
Savannah smuggler Charles Lamar had surreptitiously landed hundreds
of African slaves on Georgia's coast, and the firebrand editor of the *Savannah Morning News*, William Thompson, came out in favor of reopening

the African slave trade. (Thompson also made a point of denouncing Illinois politician Stephen Douglas and other "Recreant Northern Democrats and Southern Traitors" who wanted to let each territory decide for itself whether to become slave or free.) The editor believed that class differences between whites would recede with an infusion of more bound blacks into the South: "Every white man of capacity will own his slave. Every man of enterprise will own his labor." The "ruling race" would meet at the ballot box, and "cast their vote from the same position; as well at home as abroad they will have a common cause."[23]

Lamar himself was unapologetic in his desire to make the South less dependent on poor white men; he claimed that all manual laborers, regardless of legal status or skin color, should be disfranchised; that way they would be "more susceptible of government than the hireling labor of the Democratic [northern] states." Lamar and others thus offered a pointed critique of the current labor market in Savannah, which they believed consisted of too many workers vulnerable to the blandishments of free-soil Republicans.[24]

As early as mid-summer of 1860, the outcome of the upcoming presidential contest appeared a foregone conclusion. Such uncertain times demanded a leader of firm resolve, an energetic man of sound principles and unquestioned moral rectitude. And so on October 8, 1860, the voters of Savannah chose twenty-nine-year-old Charles C. Jones Jr. as their mayor. The son of a prominent Liberty County Presbyterian minister, Jones lost little time fulfilling his supporters' expectations; within two weeks he had ordered the arrest of several free-black sailors on the charge of "tampering with our Negroes and attempting to induce them to leave the state." The new mayor also vowed to remedy the fact that blacks in general "have forgotten their places — are responsible of gambling, smoking in the streets, drinking, and disorderly conduct generally." Behind this breakdown of order were "those offenders of foreign birth, the rum-sellers, who at the corners of our streets in their shops are demoralizing our servants and ruining them in every point of view."[25]

Within a month, the white population apparently had coalesced around the idea of southern independence. The white laboring classes became swept up in the frenzy of the moment, carried away by the speeches of fire-eaters and the fevered pitch of public meetings: to be an American now was to close ranks with other southern white men in defiance of northern abolitionists. At a mass meeting on December 12, Catholic priest Jeremiah O'Neill gave his blessing to the secessionists and exhorted his fellow Irish immigrants to join the cause; indeed, "he would be the first to *lade* them into battle, he would!" Nevertheless, later developments would suggest that a wide array of groups — rich and poor, native-born and immigrant, male and female, black and white — felt compelled to mask their true feelings in the midst of so much public posturing by a segment of influential white men.[26]

By late November, Savannah cotton factors and merchants were expressing anxiety about the "Stagnant State of business," now that political uncertainty was taking a toll on the city's businesses. A host of new questions about the future relation between Savannah and its northern creditors, and its domestic and foreign customers, was paralyzing activity in the mills, in the warehouses, and on the docks. Immigrant men had recently arrived from the North to process, haul, and load the region's cotton, rice, and timber, but now they found themselves without work, "many becoming the inmates of our poor houses and hospital," complained the city council. Banks began to curtail their operations and some stores closed their doors. Reports circulated that "the Irish draymen, rail road employees, and all depending on the transportation of cotton are out of employment."[27] Nevertheless, on Saturday, January 19, 1861, white men and women greeted the news of Georgia's secession with a celebration of fireworks and cannon salutes: "We are *a free and independent people!*"[28]

Georgia's secession delegates reconvened in Savannah on March 7 and proceeded to ratify the new Confederate constitution and revise their own. A highlight of the convention was the famous "cornerstone of the Confederacy" speech delivered by Georgia native and newly elected Confederate Vice President Alexander H. Stephens. Succinctly, Stephens went to the heart of the difference between North and South: The United States, he claimed, adhered to the idea that "all men are created equal." In contrast, "Our new government is founded upon exactly the opposite idea; . . . its cornerstone rests upon the great truth, that the negro is not equal to the white man; that slavery — subordination to the superior race — is his natural and normal condition."[29]

The revised Georgia constitution, approved by the delegates by a vote of 270-0, not only preserved slavery but also reined in the state's (white male) democratic underpinnings. The new document reduced the number of state senators, stripped the state legislature of its power to revise the constitution (in favor of a new body called for that purpose), and mandated that judges of the superior courts now be appointed by the state legislature instead of elected by the voters. Alarmed at the "anarchical spirit introduced into the community" by recent events, some prominent Savannahians felt that the new constitution did not go far enough in limiting the power of ordinary voters. Most worrisome was the fact that the document left intact the system of electing judges of inferior (local) courts; in the words of Savannah lawyer George A. Mercer, "Universal suffrage is found by sad experience to be inapplicable to the judiciary." Meanwhile, a popularly elected judge, a "notorious member of the lawless rattle-snake club," was presiding over a city court and "dispensing his own brand of justice."[30]

Keeping track of Confederate friend and Union foe in Savannah was complicated by the fact that the city was a lively hub of military and economic activity. And rather than muting distinctions between the rich and poor, the deployment of troops only highlighted them. Stationed on Tybee Island at the mouth of the Savannah River, ordinary soldiers endured "hard drilling" every afternoon, with no whiskey to erase the mind-numbing boredom. In contrast, men such as Charles C. Jones Jr. and George A. Mercer enjoyed privileges that eased the pain of isolation and physical discomfort. Many well-to-do officers went back to town often to "take a scrub," enjoy a hearty breakfast, and attend to business. In camp, they entertained visitors with meals of roasted oysters prepared by the slaves or Irish cooks they had brought from home. Most officers had slaves to wash their clothes, though Charles Jr. could count on his mother to send him clean laundry and supply him with a cornucopia of fresh food.[31]

At the same time, the whole lowcountry region was like a giant sieve, with whites as well as blacks fleeing from Confederate territory and into Union lines. In December, William Barr, who identified himself as "a native of Ireland and a citizen of Philadelphia," deserted his post at Fort Pulaski (the formidable fort downriver from Savannah) by stealing a raft; federal authorities found him to be "particularly intelligent and anxious to be useful," providing estimates of CSA troop strength at the fort and in and around Savannah. Increasingly, men like Barr, disillusioned with the southern cause for whatever reason, were hijacking flatboats, canoes, and rafts to make their escape from southern batteries and encampments. It was these men who, together with enslaved pilots and other black spies, would provide the information necessary for the Federals to capture Fort Pulaski in April 1862.[32]

That spring brought fresh woes to Savannah. From his perch on the coast, Jones could see disaster looming on the horizon: When the war started, he noted, men flocked to the cause because "the earliest and strongest tide of patriotism throb[bed] in their veins." Now fearing a long war, these same men were eager to escape a miserable existence — the "Wet tents, thin blankets, scanty rations, heavy marches, sleepless nights beneath the canopy of a dripping sky, and long hours of sickness and pain." Not to mention the specter of death and destruction at the hands of a well-armed and surprisingly disciplined enemy. Taking these factors into account, Confederate lawmakers set April 16 as the date for the first military draft in the history of North America; under its provisions all white men age eighteen to thirty-five became liable for three-year terms of service. For three hundred dollars, a drafted man could buy a substitute from a pool of men exempt from duty. However, the Confederate Congress was anxious to avoid forcible conscription wherever possible, and so it offered incentives — a fifty-dollar bounty and a sixty-day furlough — to anyone who volunteered before the law went into effect.[33]

By early March, Chatham County had sent thirty-one companies into service, but a CSA quota system mandated that they send more. Military officials called for able-bodied men to report at the parade ground on March 4. A reporter for the Charleston *Courier* recorded the scene as an estimated fifteen hundred people gathered, all in "a high state of excitement." A recruiting officer, a Georgia colonel, stepped before the crowd, declaring the very idea of conscription a disgrace to his home state. He reminded them that a cash bonus awaited men of conviction and courage, "and on the strength of these considerations, invited everybody to walk three paces in front. Nobody did it." When the exasperated officer called out for those who possessed legitimate exemptions from service, he was mobbed by the onslaught: "Did you ever see a crowd run away from a falling building at a fire, or toward a dog fight or a side-show? . . . Hats were crushed, ribs punched, corns smashed, and clothes torn." Stable hands and drygoods clerks pressed forward, clutching certificates that attested either to their infirmity or their indispensability on the job. Ten hours later, the colonel had met his quota; but only because some men "volunteered" so they could qualify for the cash bounty.[34]

By this time, Governor Joseph E. Brown feared for Savannah's security, now that more and more coastal territory was coming under control of the enemy. Still, many believed that the future of Savannah depended less upon the actual numbers of soldiers defending it and more upon the morale and discipline of those already on duty. Critics argued that, for all their expert marksmanship, backwoods recruits by nature despised authority and resisted orders. In this view, the recent recruitment plan, which allowed men to elect new company officers, only exacerbated the problem. Jones worried that would-be leaders would be forced to engage in "low, petty electioneering," and indeed he claimed that the new officers were "in very many instances mere noses of wax, to be molded and controlled at will by the men whom they should govern — have been entrusted with the command." Increasingly, rumors circulated of "mutinies" among restless troops languishing on the coast. The loyalty of Confederate soldiers was flagging.[35]

More generally, while the city had thus far escaped from playing host to Union soldiers, the war effort itself produced distressing signs of social and political disorder. On the streets, Savannahians could catch glimpses of court-martialed soldiers hobbled by balls and chains and seven-pound leg bars; these were men who had been caught rebelling against the hardships of camp life, or aiming to return to their families on the home front, or resenting the fact that they had tasted "little of the poetry and romance of war." More and more, regular troops provoked the contempt of elites, who feared that these young men were incapable of "energetic heroic action," that they were useful mainly because they "understand how to use the spade."[36]

During the first week of January 1863, the advertising pages of the local newspapers were filled with the descriptions of many men with a price on their heads. The twenty-six-year-old "quick-spoken" Frank, a slave, had absconded from work on Savannah's fortifications, probably hiding out somewhere near his former owner in the city, where the rest of the young man's family was still living. Other ads described Manly, five-feet-six-inches tall, thirty-two years old, missing one eye; and Louis, five-feet-nine-inches tall, fifty-one years old, with "a prominent nose" and a stout build (he "speaks very broken English"). However, aside from the notice for Frank, these ads for runaways all described white men, deserters from the Confederate Army. The usual reward of thirty dollars awaited the captor of Manly Hart, a carpenter, and John Makin, an Irish-born baker, both of whom had fled from the Savannah Volunteer Guards. On January 3, officers in the First Battalion of Georgia Sharpshooters took out a lengthy ad for ten deserters, men born in Georgia, Virginia, Alabama, and Germany. Indeed, by this time, ads for runaway soldiers were far outpacing ads for runaway slaves.[37]

For most working-class whites, wartime Savannah afforded little in the way of new and expanded economic opportunities, since the able-bodied at least were supposed to be in military service. In contrast, some black men and women were making a bold bid for independence in the form of wage work, trade, and other moneymaking enterprises. Behind southern lines they provided for their own families by trafficking in scarce goods and services, literally taking advantage of absent masters and distracted mistresses. Union troops rewarded men and women who sold animal pelts, moss for mattress stuffing, cotton or corn, or performed a variety of services such as cooking and clothes laundering. Enslaved men found their way through picket lines to deliver packages and letters from Savannah to soldiers stationed on batteries south of the city. Referring to blacks up and down the Georgia coast, James Henry Gooding, an African American soldier from the North, observed admiringly, "The Slaves, hereabouts, are working for the government mostly, although they can make a pretty snug little sum, peddling among the soldiers, selling fruit, &c."[38]

Free persons of color responded to cash incentives when they worked in any number of Confederate war-related industries — sawmills, brickmaking establishments, railroads, the hospital, and saltworks outside the city. Even slaves hired out by their owners made the most of the task system that included overtime pay. In 1863, Engineer Bureau slaves impressed to work on railway roadbeds dug out twelve to fifteen cubic yards by noon or so; after that, they earned a "premium" of fifteen cents per additional cubic yard excavated. Enslaved railroad hands, boatmen, and teamsters also worked on a modified task system that offered cash wages.[39]

Many slaves and free blacks found new and potentially profitable sources of income in and around the city. In Liberty County, Tony Axon continued to work as a blacksmith during the war. He decided to accept provisions in return for his services, so "I would have something which would do me more good than Confederate money." The well-to-do Anthony Odingsells went into business selling fish, oysters, meat, and other provisions to Confederate soldiers stationed in and around Wassaw Island. In the city, stable keepers, skilled construction workers, and draymen were especially in demand. The slave Rachel Bromfield hired her own time and that of her two daughters; together they kept a boardinghouse and rented out rooms. The slaves Moses Stikes and Binah Butler formed a partnership to cultivate a seven-acre garden in the city. The butcher Jackson B. Sheftall was among the most enterprising of Savannah blacks. He earned lucrative contracts from Confederate authorities. Each day, he drove cattle from the railroad to a pen, but after that work he was "allowed all the balance of the time to do my own." He received permission to keep as many of his own cows and pigs as he wished. He also retained the offal, as well as the hides, livers, and tongues of cattle, which he sold for a profit to other businesses. In early 1862 Sheftall managed to buy his wife, Elizabeth, from her owner, paying twenty-six hundred dollars for her freedom. Reviewing the butcher's record of wartime profit making (if not profiteering), one Union official noted disapprovingly that Sheftall had realized "there was a large profit in it, and went in zealously."[40]

In the midst of wartime turmoil, wealthy whites persisted in a form of consumption that was conspicuous in the extreme and increasingly resented by the poor. Now, with a population swollen by military personnel, theatre performances of all kinds offered well-heeled patrons an added touch of glamour. Lowcountry folk discovered that they could still indulge in rich foods and merrymaking, as long as they did so to honor the men in gray uniform. In Liberty County, the plantation visit of an army captain and his men called forth "a bountiful repast consisting of turkey, ham, ducks, and chickens, breads, cakes, boiled custard, syllabub, etc." And much of the Savannah social scene revolved around entertaining military officers. On February 21, 1863, at the Pulaski House hotel, Savannah women sponsored a "spirited and *recherche* entertainment" to honor General P. T. G. Beauregard and his staff. To the strains of a "fine band," the general "moved among the 'pretty faces and costly laces' with as much coolness and ease as if he were among the sterner duties of the battlefield, and seemed to partake fully of the occasion." Even some wealthy Savannahians considered these extravagant entertainments to be callous affairs, now that so many people were in mourning, and young men were daily returning home from the front, thin and shell-shocked, with all their former "gay spirits" drained out of them.[41]

Faced with widespread distress among the white laboring classes, the city council stepped up its own charitable efforts during the first half of 1863. Aldermen ordered one hundred cords of wood cut and distributed to the poor at city expense, and they appropriated emergency funds for the Board of Health, Episcopal Orphan Home, the Savannah Female Orphan Asylum, and the Widow's Society. The council also secured an interest-free loan of ten thousand dollars from the Marine Bank to open up a city store that would buy and sell basic provisions at cost. City leaders were reacting to spiraling inflation provoked not only by systematic speculators and hoarders, but also by chronic petty offenders like German-born George Ehrlich, who showed up at the city market at dawn and bought potatoes which he sold later in the day for a profit. Before long the city store had received a total of seventy-five thousand dollars in bank loans and had begun distributing large quantities of bacon, rice, flour, molasses, meal, sugar, and peas.[42]

However, by mid-April 1864, conditions in the river port had deteriorated to the point that a group of armed women conducted a "daring robbery" in the downtown area, raiding at least four different stores and seizing bacon and other items. Some shopkeepers sought to preempt the looting by handing out free supplies of rice and sugar. The Chatham County sheriff arrested three women — Mary Welsh, for robbery, and Anne McGlin and Julia McLane for disorderly conduct. All three of the women were soldiers' wives, and their plight reflected the heavy burdens borne by ordinary families.[43]

In December 1864, the city was startled to learn that a Yankee invasion would come not from the sea but from the interior of the state. General William Tecumseh Sherman and his troops swept into the city right before Christmas, and found not the elegant place of antebellum days, but a "miserable hole" full of dilapidated buildings, broken street lamps, rotting docks, and weed-choked cemeteries. Banks stood empty, bankrupt, their mortgage and bond business gone the way of Confederate money. The city's railroad lifelines with the outside world were a mass of twisted, smoldering "Sherman's hairpins."[44]

Over the next few months Sherman would establish as his highest priority the preservation of order in the city. He impressed black men into the Union Army to work as laborers, and sent black women, children, and elderly blacks to the sea islands, not to establish a landed peasantry so much as to rid himself of so many hungry mouths to feed. Union officers began to punish black men and women accused of stealing by putting them in a ball and chains and forcing them to labor under armed guard on the streets. Enraged, black leaders protested this form of public humiliation, pointing out that white thieves were fined, not set to work under slave-like conditions. In the coming months and years, the mayor and other city judges would continue the practice, which, they believed, had much to recommend it: the chain gang provided a ready, cheap source of menial labor for cleaning streets; alleviated overcrowding in the Chatham County jail;

and also reminded every pedestrian and cart driver in the city that heavily ironed freed men and women remained uniquely vulnerable within the various layers of military and civilian law that governed the city.[45]

Meanwhile, Savannah's elite made strenuous efforts to preserve what they considered to be normal operations. General Sherman complied by authorizing the city council to continue, though with diminished authority. He allowed the current mayor, the ubiquitous Richard Arnold, to establish three dozen ward committees headed by aldermen and other prominent leaders, most of them unrepentant Confederates. Yet the swiftness with which the black community organized itself alarmed whites throughout the city. Early in January an ecumenical group of preachers had formed the Savannah Education Association to provide elementary schools for black children. On the tenth of that month, white Savannahians were startled to behold a new kind of procession wending its way through the streets — hundreds of children marching from First African Church to their new school, the former Bryan slave market. Black people were claiming the streets for their own purposes. And indeed, the assertiveness with which blacks organized themselves after the occupation of the city prompted elites to devise new political strategies to maintain the neo-Confederate project.[46]

By the end of April, the state of Georgia, which had sent thirty thousand men to their deaths over the last four years, officially capitulated to Union authorities. Mayor Arnold and the aldermen were determined to reassert control over the city, and reestablish the city's traditions of order and hierarchy in the midst of various postwar crises — Yankee military occupation, the opening of local United States Freedmen's Bureau offices, and the incursion into the city of northern white men and women "adventurers" in the guise of politicians, teachers, missionaries. Yet the elites' greatest challenge was to counter the growing influence of established as well as emerging black leaders. Some, including elderly clergy, were well-known and influential before the war; many of these men continued to practice the rhetorical indirection that was the hallmark of antebellum black sermons. But other black leaders were new men on the scene: These included the former fugitive slave Aaron A. Bradley, who arrived in Savannah from Boston in late 1865, armed with a detailed knowledge of constitutional law and a defiant attitude that was the nightmare of every white Georgian; James M. Simms, throughout Reconstruction an active presence in lowcountry partisan politics and labor relations; and former rice slaves and dockhands who led militant work stoppages in their respective workplaces.

Over the next few years, the black clergy would seek to retain their influence over the Savannah black population; yet their customary circumspection, as well as their emphasis on accommodation, proved unequal to the times. An emblematic encounter took place between Bradley and an eminent preacher in December 1865. Drawn to the rich political ferment of Savannah and the lowcountry — collective stirrings on the docks, on the streets, and in the fields — Bradley had quickly set about attacking planters for seeking to return black laborers to a state of neoslavery, the mayor and military authorities for condemning black prisoners to work with ball and chain, Freedmen's Bureau officials for colluding with their former enemies in denying fundamental justice to black citizens. Armed with a bowie knife and a pistol, and dressed flamboyantly with top hat and kid gloves, the light-skinned, long-haired, freckle-faced Bradley had no difficulty drawing attention to himself. In early December he spoke at a mass meeting held in the Second African Baptist Church, and explicitly challenged the speaker who came before him — the elderly preacher Garrison Frazier, who had told his listeners, "You must not steal!" Bradley maintained that since black people were the source of all wealth, they were not stealing when they took what they had earned. He urged field hands to, in the breathless words of a *Republican* editorial, "*resist, if necessary, at the point of a bayonet, all attempts on the part of the agents of the Freedmen's Bureau to dispossess or remove*" them from the lands they currently occupied. In the coming years some of the older Savannah preachers would break publicly with their congregants who advocated a militant form of politics.[47]

In their attempt to contain black leaders' insistent claims to political and social equality, and ordinary black people's claims to autonomy from whites, Savannah elites received support from some unexpected quarters. By the fall of 1865, President Andrew Johnson had ordered Freedmen's Bureau agents to return seized coastal and island lands to their white owners. At the same time, bureau agents were trying to force rice hands back to work under labor contracts that offered black families little more than a subsistence living for a year's hard labor in the fields. Agents of the federal government and their missionary allies united in their respect for private (real) property and for contracts, now that the Confederates were vanquished.[48]

Conflicts over the land revealed once again that certain cultural val-

ues of the Gullah-Geechee people not only dovetailed with wider regional
— and American — aspirations, but also held dramatic political significance. Soon after the end of the war, James Simms wrote to U.S. government officials on behalf of the freedpeople who labored in the Ogeechee
rice district west of Savannah. Simms himself was a former slave, a skilled
carpenter who had bought his own freedom in the 1850s; now he was serving as a labor agent for the black men and women who remained rooted
to the land and determined, in his words, to honor "their Fathers and
Mothers [who] cleared these swamps and marshes, and Made them the
Fruitful Rice Fields they are." Simms condemned the southern and northern white officials who sought to limit the former slaves to landlessness
and neoslavery. In claiming the land of their forebears, Ogeechee blacks
not only expressed a cultural imperative, but also a collective impulse that
challenged the authority of federal agents and former supporters of the
Confederate States of America. Indeed, once again, the meaning inherent in black people's drive for self-sufficiency was less its cultural distinctiveness and more its universal aspects. Thus the challenge for white elites
was to renew their efforts to preserve caste relations within a lowcountry
transformed — one ravaged by war and undergoing the birth pangs of a new,
raw democracy aggressively promoted by black leaders such as Simms.[49]

On the first Wednesday in December 1865, Savannah voters went to
the polls and voted in the annual municipal election, the first since the
city's liberation. Outsiders like Carl Schurz were convinced that, in this
"hottest" of "rebel places," the "restoration of civil government is not yet
possible." Indeed, the electorate was similar to that of the antebellum and
war years. And so it was not surprising that familiar leaders once again
took the reins of power. Fifty-year-old Edward C. Anderson was elected
mayor. A former lieutenant in the U.S. Navy, Anderson had proved himself a certifiable Confederate war hero when he piloted the blockade run-
ner *Fingal* safely to Savannah, eluding federal gunboats along the way. For
the duration of the conflict, he commanded batteries along the Savannah
River. He would hold the office of mayor from 1865 to 1869. The council
too evoked antebellum days, with several members reprising earlier terms.
The city jailor, clerk of the city court, and chief of detectives, together with
the county ordinary, retained their positions in the postwar political order.
The police force, overwhelmingly composed of men with Irish surnames,
remained intact.[50]

At the same time, an intricate web of antebellum-era white fraternal, benevolent, ethnic, and religious societies slowly knit itself back together. The Savannah Benevolent Society, Odd Fellows, Masons, Georgia Medical Society, Ladies of Episcopal Orphans Home, Seamen's Benevolent Society, Hibernian Society, Irish Union Society, Hebrew Benevolent Society, and Ladies of the Hebrew Congregation were among those voluntary organizations rebounding after the war. For the most part, the white fire companies also remained intact; a new one formed in the summer of 1865, called the Metropolitan Fire Company, was composed of CSA veterans. Federal authorities outlawed the volunteer militia companies; some of them simply changed their name and called themselves "social" organizations. Hence, the Oglethorpe Light Infantry became the Oglethorpe Light Club and under that title continued to march, purchase arms, and "monitor" the polls on election day.[51]

Though divided by war and politics, Mayor Anderson and federal military officials could agree on certain fundamentals — that black people must continue to work under the supervision of whites, and that the law must deal decisively with outsiders and "troublemakers." One Union officer urged a group of mustered-out black soldiers to accommodate themselves peacefully to the new order: "The prejudices which formerly existed against you are well-nigh rooted out." This relative harmony of interests between northern and southern whites would be enshrined in the supremacy of law, variously defined. By early 1866, city police were arresting disproportionately more black men and women compared to whites for any number of offenses and on the slightest pretext. Serving as a Freedmen's Bureau court judge in early 1866, Dominick O'Byrne, a former alderman, routinely sentenced black petty-crime offenders to five or six months of hard labor "on streets and lanes with ball and chain." He also forced many to wear a "placard on back stating I am a thief, which *placard you must positively place on*."[52]

Still, developments in 1867 reminded the city's elite (if they had ever forgotten) that the black-white binary so integral to their own ideology was flawed. It is true that the majority of the city's white population — the laboring classes — believed that they gained nothing, and lost much, by black emancipation. The influx of refugees depressed wages for unskilled labor, and the bravado of victorious black troops challenged the "manhood" of vanquished Confederates regardless of status. For many of the poorest, though, the comfort of a white skin was cold indeed. A correspondent for the *New York Times* reported in the fall of 1866 that most

Savannahians lived in "miserable wooden structures — some nothing more than shanties, that offend the eye and give an unmistakable evidence of poverty." The outskirts of town were rapidly filling up with "worthless refugees and vagabonds," blacks and whites alike.[53]

Two years after the fall of the Confederacy, Congress passed two major Reconstruction acts in the spring of 1867; these mandated new southern state constitutions be drawn up by special conventions whose delegates would be chosen by black voters and a reduced electorate of white southerners. Excluded from this latter group were men who had both taken an oath of allegiance to the Union before the war and then served in an official Confederate capacity during the war. Ordinary CSA soldiers would thus be eligible to vote, along with CSA leaders who had not held a federal post before 1861. National lawmakers ordered that the new state constitutions enact universal manhood suffrage and ratify the Fourteenth Amendment. Finally, the South was divided into five districts, each under the authority of a military commander who would oversee voter registration, elections, and the process of reconstruction in general. General John Pope assumed authority of the Third Military District consisting of Georgia, Florida, and Alabama.

These revolutionary measures ignited a firestorm of political organizing and speechifying in Savannah and the lowcountry; by the spring of 1868, the whole coastal region was swept up in anticipation of the April elections, when black men would in large numbers join whites and vote on the new proposed state constitution and for candidates for state and local office. In January of that year, many lowcountry workers had refused to sign labor contracts, holding out hope that the election would lead to a widespread redistribution of land. In Savannah, Freedmen's Bureau agent Captain J. Murray Hoag spoke for many other federal officials when he suggested an inverse relation between black well-being and electioneering on the countryside. Comparing the more quiescent freedpeople in the interior to those on the coast, he claimed of the former, "Their greater prosperity I attribute to the absence of political excitement, and false teachings of ambitious adventurers."[54]

Meanwhile, the whole city of Savannah appeared to move outdoors, as blacks and whites thronged the streets and squares in an endless round of political meetings, counter-meetings, and public celebrations. The looming municipal elections, also scheduled for late April, intensified the already high level of excitement. Richard Arnold helped to form a "Conservative

Club" to appeal to both whites and blacks and to oppose "by all proper and legal means" the rule of the "Deconstructionists," which Arnold deemed "the most stupendous wrong ever attempted to be inflicted on a civilized people." He and others responded with considerable relief when Union officials announced on March 26 that they were postponing city elections out of fear that too many illegal black voters would overwhelm Savannah polling places and engulf the city in chaos. The consequences of this decision were clear: for now at least, the city government would remain largely insulated from black political influence.[55]

The election itself represented a new chapter in the long history of Savannah street theatre. On Monday, April 20, when the courthouse polls opened at 7 a.m., "the mass of the new enfranchised humanity began to surge, and . . . it was a life and death struggle as to who would get in and get squeezed." Black men turned out in large numbers not only because of the intense electioneering of the previous weeks, but also because Governor Bullock had suspended a state-sanctioned poll tax (the state legislature stipulated that such a tax was legitimate if the proceeds went to public education). The *Daily News and Herald* condemned the mass of impoverished, illiterate black voters, who, the paper claimed, flooded the city from South Carolina "to finish their hellish orgies . . . fresh from the banquet over the remains of a free constitutional government." But the *Freemen's Standard*, a new local black paper edited by James M. Simms, saw a different drama unfolding: whites came armed with sword canes, bowie knives, and revolvers in order to "intimidate and terrify the white and colored loyalists."[56]

Throughout the lowcountry, black voters spoke in a way that was hard to ignore or misunderstand: returns from Chatham County suggested the near balance between blacks and whites in Savannah, with Republican candidates just barely besting their Democratic rivals (about twenty-eight hundred votes to twenty-seven hundred for each). In the rural districts, the black majority overwhelmingly cast their ballots for the Republican candidates, ensuring the election of a number of blacks (including Simms and Bradley) and northern-born whites. However, the new state legislature had only a slight Republican majority, and it would soon become clear that party labels meant less than the overwhelming desire of all white men to control officeholding and lawmaking throughout the state. Indeed, despite the near parity between white and black voter registrants and despite gains in local offices, black Republicans were becoming increasingly discouraged; in the legislature, whites outnumbered blacks 236 to 29. Statewide, the Republican Executive Committee remained all white. White politicians of both parties hailed the election as proof that black suffrage need not translate into black political power, as long as white men dominated officeholding. And the all-white city police force continued its aggressive harassment of black men, women, and children.[57]

By late summer, with the fall elections looming, both sides positioned themselves for a bitter campaign fought not only in the streets but in the courts and the state legislature. The Republicans appeared to be on the offensive. And then in September, white lawmakers in the state legislature made a stunning move: they expelled all of the black legislators on the grounds that the state constitution did not guarantee the rights of blacks to hold office. Invoking the 1857 *Dred Scott* Supreme Court case, among other rationales, forty-six Republicans joined with thirty-seven Democrats to remove twenty-nine black senators and representatives. Soon after the expulsion, state lawmakers decided to eliminate another legal ambiguity when they voted to prohibit all Georgia blacks from serving on juries.[58]

Local machinations during the presidential election of 1868 served as a template for Savannah's effort to suppress the black vote in the coming months and years. On the morning of November 3, authorities opened the city's single polling place, in the courthouse, where approximately one thousand black men were already waiting outside. Unlike the April election, election officials now insisted that voters must present proof that they had paid a one-dollar voter registration fee before they could cast their ballots. Black leaders protested, pointing out that Governor Rufus Bullock had suspended the poll tax, but they were rebuffed by the county ordinary, who claimed he knew nothing about the suspension. By this time, Democratic challengers had crowded into the small polling place and threatened to turn away all men who could not prove with a written receipt that they had paid their taxes for the year 1867. Later estimates suggested that fully 90 percent of the black registered voters who sought to cast their ballots were prevented from doing so because of these challenges. In some cases employers had paid their workers' taxes and then deducted the money from their wages; in any case, few black men possessed written documentation.[59]

Turned out of the courthouse, angry black men regrouped on the street and sidewalk. At 8:15, about fifty employees of the Central of Georgia Railroad arrived; they "said they must vote immediately and return to work," in the words of one observer, and a contingent of police began to push aside the restless crowd of blacks, making way for the white men. Suddenly shots rang out. In all, three white policemen and three blacks died. An estimated seventeen black people were wounded. Many blacks retreated to a nearby church but eventually dispersed to their homes without voting. The melee outside the courthouse that morning was less a riot than a rout of black voters.[60]

For most Savannah whites, the policemen's deaths that day were but an unfortunate byproduct of a glorious victory for Democratic candidates. The twin strategies of intimidating black men and challenging their right to vote (claiming unpaid taxes, variously defined) proved to be a winning combination. In this, the November election, Savannah Republican candidates for office received less than one-fourth the number they had received the previous April; though the city had thirty-nine hundred registered black voters on its rolls, the Republican candidate Ulysses S. Grant received only four hundred votes.[61]

In the spring of 1869, Savannah authorities turned their attention to municipal elections. That March, the city took advantage of state law and provided for a local poll registration tax that would support the white schools. This fee would make voting a relatively expensive proposition for the majority of laborers. (There is evidence to suggest that the local Democratic Party paid the requisite fees for large numbers of white workers.) Not content to leave matters at that, the council inaugurated a new system of representation districts in the city. This system represented a break from the tradition of at-large municipal elections that diluted the power of any one constituency — in the antebellum period, Irish working-class voters especially. By the late summer of 1869, the purposes of the new system became clear. On August 30, the Conservative Party assembled in Wright Square to formulate a new way of selecting candidates for alderman and mayor. The consensus of the meeting was that the city should abandon the old free-for-all, which had allowed individuals to run on their own, with the men — or man, in the case of the mayor — receiving the highest number of votes winning the office. Now the Conservatives in each of the four districts would meet in early September and nominate three candidates for the city council, and then together a committee of twenty-eight (seven people each representing the four districts) would decide on a single candidate for mayor. Voters would cast their ballots for tickets and not for individuals. The purpose of the district system, in the words of its supporters, was to "preserve the ancient fame and good name of the Forest city from misrule — and ruin," and, they might have added, from a black electorate that constituted nearly one-half of the city's total population.[62]

On Wednesday, September 1, the *Morning News* reminded its readers of the momentous nature of the event — the first municipal election in two years: "At no period in the political history of the city of Savannah, has the election of wise, prudent and trusty men for the offices of Mayor and Aldermen required greater foresight and discretion on the part of the citizens of Savannah, than at this apparent juncture." The official Democratic ticket consisted of the forty-two-year-old railroad official and Confederate veteran John Screven for mayor and a slate of twelve new faces for the city council slots. The demographic profile of the candidates had not changed much from antebellum days, dominated as it was by "well-known gentlemen of the highest social and commercial standing"— lawyers, merchants, businessmen, and others "thoroughly identified with our people." Rounding out the ticket were two immigrants, forty-five-year-old Michael Lavin, a grocer and native of Mayo who "has transferred his warm attachment for Erin to Savannah," and a thirty-year-old Bavarian-born baker, John Schwarz, who "by his strict attention to business has won the esteem of all classes."[63]

The Democrats calculated that the voter registration fee would depress the black vote and that the disarray of the Republicans would block any semblance of a Radical (Republican) ticket of candidates. In the weeks before the election, as black men rushed to register, whites made light of the sight, claiming that recent instances of clothes pilfered from washtubs and chickens plucked from the roost provided evidence of would-be voters scrambling for a dollar to pay their registration fee. Still, the fact that "the black element takes such a lively interest in politics" remained profoundly troubling. And then at the last minute a group of dissident Conservatives threatened to put forth their own ticket, which all agreed would be disastrous for the white community. Despite this confusion, the Democratic ticket swept the October 11 election by a vote of 3:1, with all twelve of its official candidates winning city council seats.[64]

By 1870, Savannah had successfully bifurcated its political system, embracing virtually all white men and excluding virtually all black men. The Republican era of Georgia postwar politics was coming to a close. On July 15 of that year, Congress readmitted the state to the Union for the third time in five years, and approved state elections in December. That summer, the federal government closed the state's last Freedmen's Bureau office. In Savannah, black men and women confronted a grim reality — their near-total exclusion from the formal machinery of power: no black people served on the juries of any city, county, or state court; and the mayor, members of the city council, and the entire police force were all white.[65]

At the same time, complicating the project of restoring conservative rule were the sharp clashes between haves and have-nots during the late winter and spring of 1871. Black and white longshoremen on the docks and black teamsters on the streets pressed their advantage, striking for higher wages during the busiest time of the season. Trouble also came from an unexpected quarter, when the city's largely Irish police force demanded an end to the system of compensation based on the fines exacted from the men and women they arrested; but Mayor Screven broke a tie vote in the council, and the old method of compensation remained in place. In Savannah, class tensions between whites would periodically challenge, but not undermine, the white supremacist imperative.[66]

Along the coast, a lowcountry peasantry preserved the outlines of the Gullah-Geechee culture that had shaped the lives of rice and cotton slaves before the Civil War. Some household heads, like Joseph Stevens of Liberty County, owned their own modest homesteads — in Stevens's case a sixty-acre farm cut from a larger antebellum plantation. By 1872, the thirty-eight-year-old Stevens and his wife Julia, thirty-three, had little hope of accumulating more than what they already possessed: a horse and a wagon, a cow and a calf, three hogs, some bed linens and bedsteads, a spinning wheel for cotton, cooking utensils, clothing, and a Bible and a few schoolbooks. The parents of seven children ranging in age from one to twelve, Joseph and Julia pieced together a patchwork living for their family. Perhaps the sons and their father would eventually seek jobs in Savannah in the wintertime, when work was slack on the farm but busy on the docks. In the daily struggles and modest belongings of the Stevens family were revealed both the promise and the betrayal of the years following emancipation.[67]

With the machinery of law enforcement in the hands of conservative whites, and with the federal government largely indifferent to black civil rights in general, the neo-Confederate project emerged triumphant from the crucible of war and Reconstruction. Together, white men retained all positions of influence in the Savannah city government and police force, kept black men off juries, and suppressed the black vote through violent intimidation and poll taxes. In valuing social order and a revival of the region's commercial economy, northern military and bureau officials co-operated in this effort. And so the neo-Confederate project would prevail, albeit uneasily, for another century.

NOTES

1. "by industry . . . for himself": Alexander Steele, Chatham County claim no. 229, Southern Claims Commission (hereinafter SCC); "I got": Tony Axon, Liberty County claim no. 21472, SCC; "Sell and buy": Cato Keating, Liberty County claim no. 20689, SCC. See also Dylan C. Penningroth, *The Claims of Kinfolk: African American Property and Community in the Nineteenth-Century South* (Chapel Hill: University of North Carolina Press, 2003); Philip Morgan, "The Ownership of Property by Slaves in the Mid-Nineteenth-Century Low Country," *Journal of Southern History* 49 (August 1983): 399–420; John Hammond Moore, "Sherman's 'Fifth Column': A Guide to Unionist Activity in Georgia," *Georgia Historical Quarterly* 68 (Fall 1984): 382–409.

2. The literature on Gullah culture is extensive. See the other essays in this volume and, for example, William S. Pollitzer, *The Gullah People and Their African Heritage* (Athens: University of Georgia Press, 1999); Margaret Creel, *"A Peculiar People": Slave Religion and Community-Culture among the Gullahs* (New York: New York University Press, 1988); Michael A. Gomez, *Exchanging Our Country Marks: The Transformation of African Identities in the Colonial and Antebellum South* (Chapel Hill: University of North Carolina Press, 1998).

3. For an extended discussion of these themes, see Jacqueline Jones, *Saving Savannah: The City and the Civil War* (New York: A. A. Knopf, 2008).

4. Biographical information on the defendants from the 1860 U.S. manuscript census (Chatham County). See also Timothy J. Lockley, "Trading Encounters between Non-Elite Whites and African Americans in Savannah, 1790–1860," *Journal of Southern History* 1 (February 2000): 25–48.

5. See, for example, Minutes of Savannah City Council (hereinafter CC Minutes), September 6, 1855. Biographical information on the attorneys from Robert Manson Myers, ed., *The Children of Pride: A True Story of Georgia and the Civil War* (New Haven, Conn.: Yale University Press, 1972), 1464–65, 1540; and 1860 federal manuscript census (Chatham County).

6. In this sense, Savannah's story represents but a variation of Michael Johnson's discussion of secessionist Georgia in *Toward a Patriarch Republic: The Secession of Georgia* (Baton Rouge: Louisiana State University Press, 1977).

7. Herbert Weaver, "Foreigners in Ante-Bellum Savannah," *Georgia Historical Quarterly* 37 (March 1953): 1–17. See also Christopher Silver, "A New Look at Old South Urbanization: The Irish Worker in Charleston, South Carolina, 1840–1860," in *South Atlantic Urban Studies*, Vol. 3, ed. Samuel M. Hines et al. (Charleston:

University of South Carolina Press, 1979): 141–72; Monica Hunt, "Organized Labor along Savannah's Waterfront: Mutual Cooperation among Black and White Longshoremen, 1865–1894," *Georgia Historical Quarterly* 92 (Summer 2008): 177–99.

8. Ira Berlin and Herbert Gutman, "Natives and Immigrants, Free Men and Slaves: Urban Workingmen in the Antebellum American South," *American Historical Review* 88 (December 1983): 1175–1200. These comparisons are based on the studies of Frank Towers, *The Urban South and the Coming of the Civil War* (Charlottesville: University of Virginia Press, 2004), and Jonathan Daniel Wells, *The Origins of the Southern Middle Class, 1800–1861* (Chapel Hill: University of North Carolina Press, 2004). Mid-nineteenth-century Savannah, a small city without manufacturing, did not support the socioeconomic class categories discussed by either of these authors.

9. Susie King Taylor, *Reminiscences of My Life in Camp with the 33rd U.S. Colored Troops* (1902; repr., New York: Markus Wiener, 1988), 26–27; Whittington B. Johnson, *Black Savannah: 1788–1864* (Fayetteville: University of Arkansas Press, 1996); Walter J. Fraser Jr., *Savannah in the Old South* (Athens: University of Georgia Press, 2003), 287; Claudia Dale Goldin, *Urban Slavery in the American South, 1820–1860: A Quantitative History* (Chicago: University of Chicago Press, 1976), 20–24.

10. Cf. Wells, *Origins of the Southern Middle Class*, and Bruce Dorsey, *Reforming Men and Women: Gender in the Antebellum City* (Ithaca, N.Y.: Cornell University Press, 2002).

11. The literature on black churches under slavery is extensive. See, for example John Ernest, *Liberation Theology: African American Writers and the Challenge of History, 1794–1861* (Chapel Hill: University of North Carolina Press, 2004). James Sidbury discusses the historical and political significance of the African Baptist Church, founded in the vicinity of Savannah, in *Becoming African in America: Race and Nation in the Early Black Atlantic* (New York: Oxford University Press, 2007).

12. Weaver, "Foreigners in Ante-Bellum Savannah"; "The Mayor": Richard J. Shryock, ed., *Letters of Richard D. Arnold, M.D., 1808–1876* (Papers of the Trinity College Historical Society, Double Series, 18–19, 1929), 39; Richard H. Haunton, "Law and Order in Savannah, 1850–1860," *Georgia Historical Quarterly* 56 (March 1972): 1–24: Lockley, "Trading Encounters"; Anthony Gene Carey, *Parties, Slavery, and the Union in Antebellum Georgia* (Athens: University of Georgia Press, 1997); Wallace Hettle, *The Peculiar Democracy: Southern Democrats in Peace and Civil War* (Athens: University of Georgia Press, 2001).

13. "In a": quoted in Weaver, "Foreigners in Ante-Bellum Savannah," 8; Edward M. Shoemaker, "Strangers and Citizens: The Irish Immigrant Community of Savannah, 1837–1861," (PhD diss., Emory University, 1990), 291; Thomas Paul Thigpen, "Aristocracy of the Heart: Catholic Lay Leadership in Savannah, 1820–1870," (PhD diss., Emory University, 1995), 535; Richard H. Haunton, "Savannah in the 1850s," (PhD diss., Emory University, 1968), 198.

14. Haunton, "Savannah in the 1850s," 197–99, 225; Weaver, "Foreigners in Ante-Bellum Savannah," 11.

15. Fraser, *Savannah in the Old South*, 306–7. Lockley argues that during the

period under review, "Pro-shopkeeper councils" were elected in 1857 and 1858, and "Anti-shopkeeper councils" in 1859 and 1860. See Lockley, "Trading Encounters," 46n61, and CC Minutes for the following meetings: February 8, 1855; March 22, 1855; August 1, 1855.

16. On the city's charitable societies, see Timothy James Lockley, *Welfare and Charity in the Antebellum South* (Gainesville: University Press of Florida, 2007).

17. Lilla Mills Hawes, ed., "The Memoirs of Charles H. Olmstead," *Georgia Historical Quarterly* 42 (Dec. 1958); "to drown": *Savannah Morning News*, March 30, 1857; Thigpen, "Aristocracy of the Heart," 120–23; Shoemaker, "Strangers and Citizens."

18. "underswell . . . class": Nehemiah Adams, *South-Side View of Slavery* (1854; repr., New York: Negro Universities Press, 1969), 44. See also Lillian Foster, *Way-Side Glimpses, North and South* (New York: Rudd and Carleton, 1860), 52.

19. Charles C. Jones Jr., *History of Savannah, Georgia* (Syracuse, N.Y.: D. Mason, 1890), 388; Adams, *South-Side View of Slavery*, 19–20; James Silk Buckingham, *The Slave States in America* (London: Fisher, Son, 1842), 125; Shoemaker, "Strangers and Citizens," 354; John Hope Franklin, *The Militant South* (Cambridge, Mass.: Harvard University Press, 1956), 22, 75; Joseph Frederick Waring, *Cerveau's Savannah* (Savannah: Georgia Historical Society, 1973), 30–31.

20. Robert S. Starobin, *Industrial Slavery in the Old South* (New York: Oxford University Press, 1970), 17; Fred Siegel, "Artisans and Immigrants in the Politics of Late Antebellum Georgia," *Civil War History* 27 (1981): 228. See also *Savannah Morning News*, December 5, 1856.

21. Michele Gillespie, *Free Labor in an Unfree World: White Artisans in Slaveholding Georgia, 1789–1860* (Athens: University of Georgia Press, 2000), 159–61; Shoemaker, "Strangers and Citizens," 272, 293, 319; Emily Burke, *Pleasure and Pain: Reminiscences of Georgia in the 1840s* (Savannah, Ga.: Beehive Press, 1991), 81; *Savannah Morning News,* December 31, 1856; Siegel, "Artisans and Immigrants in the Politics of Late Antebellum Georgia"; Hunt, "Organized Labor Along Savannah's Waterfront."

22. "the": J. William Harris, *Plain Folk and Gentry in a Slave Society: White Liberty and Black Society in Augusta's Hinterlands* (Middletown, Conn.: Wesleyan University Press, 1985), 60; "it has": Harris, *Plain Folk*, 68; Timothy James Lockley, *Lines in the Sand: Race and Class in Lowcountry Georgia, 1750–1860* (Athens: University of Georgia Press, 2001), 57–130; Jeff Forret, *Race Relations at the Margins: Slaves and Poor Whites in the Antebellum Southern Countryside* (Baton Rouge: Louisiana State University Press, 2006).

23. All quotes from *Savannah Morning News*: "Recreant," April 2, 1858; "Every," May 26, 1858; "ruling . . . cause," May 27, 1858. See also May 29, 1858.

24. Siegel, "Artisans and Immigrants in the Politics of Late Antebellum Georgia," 229; "more": quoted in Ronald Takaki, *A Pro-Slavery Crusade: The Agitation to Reopen the African Slave Trade* (New York: Free Press, 1971), 115–16. See also Tom Henderson, *The Slave Ship Wanderer* (Athens: University of Georgia Press, 1968).

25. "tampering . . . view": Myers, *Children of Pride*, 624.

26. "he would be": Shoemaker, "Strangers and Citizens," 363–64; Myers, *Children of Pride*, 634; Mrs. G. J. Kollock in Susan M. Kollock, ed., "Letters of the Kollock and Allied Families, 1826–1884," Part 3, *Georgia Historical Quarterly* 34 (1950): 155; Mark I. Greenberg, "Creating Ethnic, Class, and Southern Identity in Nineteenth-Century America: The Jews of Savannah, Georgia, 1830–1880" (PhD thesis, University of Florida, 1997), 262–8.

27. "Stagnant . . . hospital": CC Minutes, November 21, 1860; "the Irish": George A. Mercer Diary, typescript, Georgia Historical Society, 38–39; "The Secession Movement," *New York Times*, January 17, 1861.

28. "We": Augusta J. Kollock in Kollock, "Letters," Part 4 (September 1950), 229; T. Conn Bryan, *Confederate Georgia* (Athens: University of Georgia Press, 1953), 15; Johnson, *Toward a Patriarchal Republic*, 39–41.

29. Stephens quoted in James M. McPherson, *Battle Cry of Freedom: The Civil War Era* (New York: Oxford, 1988), 244.

30. *Savannah Morning News*, March 25, 1861; Johnson, *Toward a Patriarchal Republic*, 171–73; "anarchical . . . justice": Mercer Diary, 56, 65.

31. W. H. Andrews, *Footprints of a Regiment: A Recollection of the 1st Georgia Regulars, 1861–1865* (Atlanta: Longstreet Press, 1992); "take a scrub": Mrs. E. F. Neufville in Kollock, "Letters," Part 4, 243; "prepared": Myers, *Children of Pride*, 1096. See also Lucinda H. MacKethan, ed., *Recollections of a Southern Daughter, A Memoir by Cornelia Jones Pond* (Athens: University of Georgia Press, 1998), 63.

32. "a native . . . useful": *Official Records of the Union and Confederate Navies in the War of the Rebellion* (Washington: GPO, 1894–1922), Series 1, Vol. 12, 432–33. The federal manuscript for (summer) 1860 lists one William Bar, twenty-two years old, a laborer and a native of County Clare, Ireland, as a resident of Savannah. He was boarding in the household of James McMahon, a grocer and native of County Meath; the household also included people born in Limerick and Donegal.

33. "the earliest . . . pain": Myers, *Children of Pride*, 845; McPherson, *Battle Cry of Freedom*, 431–32.

34. An account of the event, by Felix Gregory DeFontaine, is reprinted in James M. Merrill, comp., "Personne Goes to Georgia: Five Civil War Letters," *Georgia Historical Quarterly* 43 (June 1959): 202–11; and Frank Moore, ed., *The Rebellion Record: A Diary of American Events . . .* (New York: G. P. Putnam, 1862), 74–75. See also Thigpen, "Cries of the Heart," 634; Bryan, *Confederate Georgia*, 138–39.

35. "low . . . command": Myers, *Children of Pride*, 894; Pemberton in *War of the Rebellion: A Compilation of the Official Records of the Union and Confederate Armies* (Washington: GPO, 1880–1901), Series 1, Vol. 14, 502 (hereinafter ORUCA). See also James M. Clifton, ed., *Life and Labor on Argyle Island* (Savannah, Ga.: Beehive Press, 1978), 333; Mercer Diary, 171, 177–78.

36. "little": Mercer Diary, June 15, 1862, 40; "energetic . . . spade": C. C. Jones Jr., in Myers, *Children of Pride*, 931; chap. 6, Vol. 648, Medical Department Letters Sent and Letters, Orders, and Circulars Received, General Hospital #1, Savannah,

1862–64, 16 (October 7, 1862), War Department Collection of Confederate Records, Record Group 109, National Archives. See also Myers, *Children of Pride*, 857; Savannah CC Minutes, March 26, 1862.

37. *Republican* January 10, 1863; January 3, 1863.

38. "The Slaves": Virginia Matzke Adams, ed., *On the Altar of Freedom: A Black Soldier's Civil War Letters from the Front* (Amherst: University of Massachusetts Press, 1991), 27; Edward William Drummond, *A Confederate Yankee: The Journal of Edward William Drummond, a Confederate Soldier from Maine*, ed. Roger S. Durham (Knoxville: University of Tennessee Press, 2004), 21–22; Edward J. Thomas, *Memoirs of a Southerner, 1840–1923* (Savannah: n.p., 1923), 35.

39. "premium": Clarence L. Mohr, *On the Threshold of Freedom: Masters and Slaves in Civil War Georgia* (Athens: University of Georgia Press, 1986), 182; Records of the Engineering Department, chap. 3, Vol. 7 ½. Register of Letters Received, 1861–1863, War Department Collection of Confederate Records, Record Group 109, National Archives.

40. "I would have": Tony Axon, Liberty County Claim no. 21472, SCC; Penningroth, *Claims of Kinfolk*, 82; Rachel Bromfield, Chatham County claim no. 13361, SCC; Moses Stikes and Binah Butler, Chatham County claim no. 17563, SCC; Johnson, *Black Savannah*, 162; Claim of Jackson B. Sheftall, Claims Disallowed by the Commissioner of Claims, Southern Claims Commission, Records of the U.S. House of Representatives, 1871–1880, Record Group 233, National Archives; Joseph Parsons, "Anthony Odingsells: A Romance of Little Wassaw," *Georgia Historical Quarterly* 55 (Summer 1971): 218–19.

41. "bountiful": MacKethan, *Recollections of a Southern Daughter*, 68; "a…grand": *Republican*, February 22, 1863; "gay": Henrietta J. Wayne to "My Dear Mother," Savannah, January 14, 1863, Harden Family Papers, Correspondence Folder 1862–1863, Duke University Special Collections, William R. Perkins Library, Durham, North Carolina: James David Griffin, "Savannah, Georgia, During the Civil War" (PhD thesis, University of Georgia, 1963), 238–42.

42. For Ehrlich, see CC Minutes, February 25 and April 8, 1863; Theresa Crisp Williams and David Williams, "'The Women Rising': Cotton, Class, and Confederate Georgia's Rioting Women," *Georgia Historical Quarterly* 86 (Spring 2002): 49–83. Ehrlich is listed in the 1860 federal manuscript census as a forty-six-year old "speculator and pedlar," a native of Saxony, Germany, married to a native of Bavaria. The couple's first two of seven children were born in New York City, the youngest five in Bibb County, Georgia. See also Report of Savannah Thomas Holcombe, Mayor of the City of Savannah, for the Year ending September 30, 1863 (Savannah, Ga.: E. J. Purse, 1863), 4–5.

43. "daring": "Department of the South," *New York Times*, May 8, 1864; Williams and Williams, "'The Women Rising,'" 76–77; CC Minutes, April 20, 1864.

44. "miserable": Frank Otto Gattell, "A Yankee Views the Agony of Savannah [John M. Glidden]," *Georgia Historical Quarterly* (December 1959): 429–31; Dan T. Carter, *When the War Was Over: The Failure of Self-Reconstruction in the South, 1865–1867* (Baton Rouge: Louisiana State University Press, 1985), 137; Mary A. De-

Credico, *Patriotism for Profit: Georgia's Urban Entrepreneurs and the Confederate War Effort* (Chapel Hill: University of North Carolina Press, 1990), 115–21; W. T. Sherman, Savannah, Ga. December 31, 1864, in ORUCA,Series 1, Vol. 44, 843; George Ward Nichols, *The Story of the Great March from the Diary of a Staff Officer* (1865; repr., Williamstown, Mass.: Corner House, 1972), 105.

45. *Savannah Daily Herald*, March 18, 1865; Ira Pettibone to W. E. Whiting, February 22, 1865, American Missionary Association Archives, Amistad Research Center, New Orleans, La. (hereinafter AMA Archives); George Crabtree to W. W. Deane, Brunswick, Ga., July 25, 1866, Unregistered Letters Received, Reel 25, Bureau of Refugees, Freedmen, and Abandoned Lands (Georgia) (M798), Record Group 105, National Archives (hereinafter BRFAL-GA [M798]).

46. W. T. Richardson to M. E. Strieby, Savannah, Ga., January 2, 1865, AMA Archives; "General Sherman and the Freedmen" *Freedmen's Record* 1 (March 1865): 33; "Schools in Savannah, Ga," *Freedmen's Record* (May 1865): 72; "Colored Free Schools," *National Freedman* (July 1865) 197–98; Heather A. Williams, *Self-Taught: African American Education in Slavery and Freedom* (Chapel Hill: University of North Carolina Press, 2005).

47. "You": *Republican*, December 13, 1865; *Republican*, December 12, 1865.

48. See, for example, *Republican*, September 5, 1865, where the Republican editor, John Hayes, condemns striking black longshoremen. Hayes titled his news story/editorial, "Insolent Interference of Negroes with Free Labor."

49. "their Fathers": J. M. Simms to "General," enclosure in Davis Tillson to "General," Letters Sent, Correspondence, Office of the Assistant Commissioner of the Bureau of Refugees, Freedmen, and Abandoned Lands, Georgia, entry 626, Freedmen and Southern Society Project A-5161, University of Maryland, College Park.

50. "hottest": Joseph H. Mahaffey, ed., "Carl Schurz's Letters from the South," *Georgia Historical Quarterly* 35 (September 1951): 243. For a biography of Anderson see Myers, *Children of Pride*, 1452. See also Thomas Gamble Jr., *A History of the City Government of Savannah, Georgia, from 1790 to 1901* (Savannah, Ga.: City Council, 1900), 3–25; Greenberg, "Creating Ethnic, Class, and Southern Identity in Nineteenth-Century America," 242–45.

51. Gamble, *History of the City Government of Savannah*, 235–39; F. D. Lee and J. L. Agnew, *Historical Record of the City of Savannah* (Savannah, Ga.: J. H. Estill, 1869), 153–54; William Harden, *Recollections of a Long and Satisfactory Life* (1934; repr. New York: Negro Universities Press, 1968), 122.

52. "the prejudices": quoted in Taylor, *Reminiscences of My Life*, 116; "on . . . on": Dominick O'Byrne, Savannah, February 1, 1866, Unregistered Letters Received, Reel 25, BFRAL-GA (M798). Charges culled from reports of Mayor's Court and Freedmen's Court in *Savannah Republican* and *Savannah Daily News and Herald*. See also Savannah Police Department Register, 1862–69, Vol. 4, Georgia Historical Society, Savannah, Ga.; Carter, *When the War Was Over*, 128–29.

53. "Paris in the South," *New York Times*, September 3, 1866, 8; "worthless": "Report of Edward C. Anderson, Mayor . . . 1867," 15; CC Minutes, July 6, 1865; L. Moody

Simms Jr., "A Comment on Savannah in 1866," *Georgia Historical Quarterly* 50 (December 1966): 459–60.

54. Circular, O. O. Howard, January 17, 1868, Reel 20; Charles Holcombe to C. C. Sibley, Hinesville, March 5, 1868, Reel 20, "Their greater prosperity": J. Murray Hoag to C. C. Sibley, Savannah, Reel 21, Letters Received, BRFAL-GA (M798).

55. Eric Foner, *Reconstruction: America's Unfinished Revolution, 1863–1877* (New York: Harper and Row, 1988), 333–36; *Savannah News and Herald*, January 10, 1868; "A Colored Mass Meeting in Savannah," *New York Times*, February 5, 1868, 8; Extracts from Minute Book of the Georgia Medical Society, January 8, 1868–May 31, 1871, in J. F. Waring Papers, GHS.

56. Alan Conway, *The Reconstruction of Georgia* (Minneapolis: University of Minnesota Press, 1966), 175–76; "the mass": *Savannah Daily News and Herald*, April 21, 1868; "to finish": *Savannah Daily News and Herald*, April 24, 1868; "intimidate": *Freemen's Standard*, April 22, 1868; *Savannah Daily News and Herald*, April 24, 1868.

57. Conway, *Reconstruction in Georgia*, 161; Edmund L. Drago, *Black Politicians and Reconstruction in Georgia: A Splendid Failure* (Athens: University of Georgia Press, 1992), 59.

58. *Savannah Daily News and Herald*, July 29, 1868; J. J. Waring File, Papers of J. F. Waring, GHS; Shryock, *Letters of Richard D. Arnold, M.D.*, 41–42; Folder, Chatham County, Grand Jury Chatham County, "Savannah, City Limits," Georgia State Archives, Atlanta. See also Steven Hahn, *A Nation Under Our Feet: Black Political Struggles in the Rural South from Slavery to the Great Migration* (Cambridge, Mass.: Harvard University Press, 2003), 256; Drago, *Black Politicians*, 49–53.

59. James M. Simms testimony, "Condition of Affairs in Georgia," 40th Congress, 3d sess., House of Representatives, Misc. Docs. No 52, 1869, p. 8; Drago, *Black Politicians*, 76–77.

60. "said they must vote": J. Murray Hoag testimony in "Condition of Affairs in Georgia," 55; *Savannah News and Herald*, November 4, 1868; "Report of Outrages Committed Upon Freedmen, State of Georgia," January 1 to November 15, 1868, Reports, Reel 32, (M798), BRFAL-GA.

61. *Savannah Morning News*, November 6, 1868; E. C. Anderson testimony, "Condition of Affairs in Georgia," 179; Screven testimony, "Condition of Affairs in Georgia," 228.

62. CC Minutes, March 3, 1869; *Savannah Morning News*, April 3, 1869; April 4, 1869; August 13, 1869; August 31, 1869.

63. "At no point": *Savannah Morning News*, September 1, 1869; Myers, *Children of Pride*, 1672–73; "well . . . classes": *Savannah Morning News*, September 9, 1869.

64. "the black element": *Savannah Morning News*, October 2, 1869; *Savannah Morning News*, September 24, 1869; *Savannah Morning News*, September 27, 1869; *Savannah Morning News*, October 11, 1869; *Savannah Morning News*, August 31, 1869; *Savannah Morning News*, September 1, 1869.

65. Conway, *Reconstruction of Georgia*, 188–95; Paul A. Cimbala, *Under the Guardianship of the Nation: The Freedmen's Bureau and the Reconstruction of Geor-*

gia, 1865–1870 (Athens: University of Georgia Press, 1997), 217–28; John E. Reed, "What I Know of the Ku Klux Klan," Part 1, *Uncle Remus's: The Home Magazine* (January 1908): 21–26; Part 2 (February 1908): 60–61; Part 3 (March 1908): 92–95; Part 3 (con't.) (April 1908): 122–23; *Testimony Taken by [U.S. Congress] the Joint Select Committee to Inquire Into the Condition of Affairs in the Late Insurrectionary States*, Georgia testimony, Vols. 1, 2 (Washington, D.C.: Government Printing Office, 1872). See also *Savannah Morning News*, May 7, 1870; *Savannah Morning News*, May 10, 1870.

66. "Strike of the Cotton Stevedores' Employes [*sic*] of Savannah, Ga," *New York Times*, November 7, 1870, 1; *New York Times*, November 23, 1870; Mayor's Report, 1870–71; CC Minutes, December 6, 1871; December 16, 1871; December 26, 1871.

67. Stevens household, Liberty County Ordinary Homestead Exemptions, 1872, Reel 41, Georgia State Archives, Atlanta.

Allison Dorsey

"The great cry of our people is land!"

Black Settlement and Community Development on Ossabaw Island, Georgia, 1865–1900

The great cry of our people is land. If they can be protected
they will get on well enough.... They want to be free-holders,
land holders and to hold office like white men.
—Tunis Campbell, 1871

A SHAKEN Andrew Waters wrote to John W. Magill, superintendent of the Freedmen's Bureau for Ossabaw Island, informing him that, in the face of violent confrontation on December 3, 1866, he had been unsuccessful in arresting a defendant charged with "contempt of authority." Less than pleased, Magill ordered Waters "to arrest Mustapha Shaw and bring him before me ... and this you will not fail to execute at your peril!" The following day Waters, accompanied by John Mungin, reported to Magill's office with a handful of witnesses to lend credence to his tale of woe. Louis, Benjamin, and Thomas Bond, as well as Benjamin Harris and George Savage, had all been pressed into service to help in the arrest of one Mustapha Shaw.

According to their account, when the men arrived at the home of Robert Donegal (Delegal) they were met by Shaw, the brothers Robert and Lee Donegal (Delegal), and Pauldo Brown, who had "armed themselves with three guns." The witnesses said, "Shaw also took a Bowie Knife and pistol, and with the parties above armed defied {said officers} and threatened to kill said officers." Waters and his deputies were driven back by threats of violence and showered in a hail of curses for all blacks on Ossabaw who worked for white men, while Shaw and company made good their escape.[1]

Why were Mustapha Shaw and Andrew Waters, both former members of the U.S. Colored Troops (USCT), on opposing sides of the law on Ossabaw Island within a year of mustering out of the Union Army? Defiant and in possession of his service pistol, Shaw had served with the 33rd Infantry Regiment. Fellow soldier Andrew Waters had mustered out of the 103rd Infantry Regiment in April of that year. Waters, who lived in Savannah, had secured continued government employment by working on behalf of the Bureau of Refugees, Freedmen and Abandoned Lands (henceforth Freedmen's Bureau), whereas Shaw, who resided on Ossabaw Island with Brown and the Delegal brothers, clearly rejected such government service. David Bond, "the Father of Louis, James, Benjamin William & Thomas Bond," and "the Elder of the Baptist Church on said Island," gave testimony suggesting a standing feud, noting that Shaw and company had "repeatedly threatened to kill Louis Bond, Wm McKeever (McKiver), George Savage and other persons on said plantation on Ossabaw Island."[2] The plantation in question was Middle Place, owned by Alexander McDonald. Bond had a long history of association with the land, as he declared himself "the oldest colored man on the Macdonald [sic] place."

The present study seeks to re-create the historic outlines of the Ossabaw community by answering demographic, sociological, and economic questions about island life in the thirty-five years of occupation by black freedmen and women. My research is designed to analyze the process of settlement, community development, and institution building by the freedmen and women who lived on Ossabaw Island, Georgia, beginning in June 1865 through the end of the century.

Part of the Golden Isles situated off the coast of Georgia, Ossabaw is roughly twenty miles south of Savannah. Acquired by John Morel sometime in the 1760s, the twenty-six-thousand-acre island was bequeathed to Morel's sons upon his death in 1776 and divided into three plantations: North End, Middle Place, and South End. A subsequent subdivision of the latter plantation upon the death of John Morel Jr. resulted in the 1802 creation of Buckhead. At the beginning to the Civil War, Bryan McQueen Morel held title to North End, Alexander McDonald was in possession of Middle Place, and George Jones Kollock owned South End. Mary Ann Morel, daughter of John Morel Jr., had inherited Buckhead, giving it to her daughter Mary Rutherford in 1806. William Skrine, who married Mary Rutherford in 1848, worked slaves on the island as did Mary's second husband Joseph T. Simmons, who was in possession of the land during the war.[3]

Close to three hundred enslaved men and women called Ossabaw home in the decade before the war. Morel, McDonald, Kollock, and Simmons each held sixty-plus slaves on Ossabaw, the greatest number belonging to Kollock, who in 1860 held seventy slaves at South End.[4] Sea island cotton and rice flourished in the rich soil of Ossabaw. Slaves also cultivated corn, potatoes, peas, and fruit trees. Hogs and beef cattle were raised on the island as food for enslaved laborers and for sale to the mainland. Planters made supplemental monies selling wood from the abundant oak trees on the island. If his peers followed Kollock's example, slaves on Ossabaw worked under the task system and supplemented their once-weekly food ration with foodstuffs from their gardens.[5] At the close of the war, Middle Place as well other Ossabaw plantations had been confiscated under Sherman's Special Field Order No. 15 and redistributed, in the spring and summer of 1865, to emancipated blacks in ten- to forty-acre allotments. These new landowners were soon to discover that the nation was reluctant to make good on the promise of General Sherman's order. Indeed, these former slaves, including former USCT soldiers who had taken up arms to fight for their freedom, found themselves engaged in another battle on Ossabaw, one to retain their newly acquired property. Having fought to transform the social and political landscape of the nation, these freedmen now found themselves aligned against the federal government, most of the white citizenry, and some fellow blacks as they sought to secure their hard-won freedom, manhood rights, and lands.

By May 1866, a white-owned agricultural firm (Flye, Middleton and Magill, of which Bureau Agent John W. Magill was part owner) operated a three-hundred-acre plantation on the island, growing sea island cotton under a sharecropping system. Plantations were formally restored to their Confederate owners in January 1867, after being wrenched from the hands of the black men and women who had been awarded promissory title to the lands of Ossabaw during the spring and summer of 1865. The armed resistance and violent curses of Mustapha Shaw were but one response to what emancipated blacks understood as an assault on their hard-won freedom.

For African Americans, the goal of the Civil War was freedom — the complete destruction of slavery and a chance to re-create their lives as autonomous people. They sought the freedom to reunite and protect their families and to make their own way in the world. Meeting with Union General William Tecumseh Sherman in January 1865, some twenty black leaders in Savannah made clear their belief that true freedom required access to land, to "turn it and till it by our own labor."[6] Historians have long focused their attention on the bright promise of Special Field Order No. 15, Sherman's response to the urgent request of these leaders, which claimed the sea islands and a swath of the southeastern rice coast for distribution to black freedmen. The greatest hope of freedmen proved to be the briefest of dreams, and much has been written about the federal abandonment of African Americans, spearheaded by President Andrew Johnson and forced upon Freedmen's Bureau commander Oliver O. Howard.[7] Circular 15 revoked the right to land promised in Field Order No. 15, and confiscated properties were soon returned to their Confederate owners. Yet insufficient attention has been paid to the experiences of those freedmen who leapt at the chance to start their lives anew on the Georgia sea islands, and struggled to maintain land ownership.

This investigation of the black community of Ossabaw will help flesh out the story of "first freedom," offering insight into the mind-set of freedmen and women as they exited slavery as evidenced by the nature of community they established on the island. Historian Russell Duncan has argued that entrepreneur and political activist Tunis Campbell played a significant role in black settlement on the Georgia sea islands and that his vision for the freedmen, rooted in a concept of "separatism for strength," guided development in the region. Campbell's experiences with white manipulation of newly emancipated blacks, as well as the incidents of white violence witnessed during the Port Royal experiment, led him to abandon "hopes for a biracial democracy" in the lowcountry.[8] Duncan's study investigates Campbell's work as a bureau agent, justice of the peace, state senator, and black politico in Georgia and provides some detailed discussion about the lives of black settlers on St. Catherine's Island and McIntosh County. Yet the life of black agriculturalists who planted foodstuffs; took advantage of the abundant population of birds, fish, and shellfish; and grew cotton as a cash crop while working to create religious and social institutions on Ossabaw Island were not addressed in Duncan's treatment of the era or the region.

What if any influence did Campbell have on the events that took place on Ossabaw? Did Mustapha and other freedmen of Ossabaw, share

Campbell's black separatist vision? What social networks flourished on the island? Did familial links keep younger islanders on Ossabaw or did market forces lure them to the mainland? What support, if any, did the tiny Baptist church of Ossabaw receive from the First, Second, or Third African Baptist churches of Savannah?

Whites who owned plantations on Ossabaw abandoned them in the face of Union soldiers. Those who had been enslaved on Ossabaw, along with other Georgia sea islands, were alternately relocated to mainland properties or abandoned with the land. Camp followers and refugees joined emancipated men and women who had previously resided on the island and had remained throughout the tumult of the war, as Union forces seized the territory. The community of freedmen on Ossabaw in 1865 thus combined resettled refugees whose lives had been uprooted by the recent conflict and those who had remained in place during the war years and was, of course, a microcosm of a far larger movement of peoples. Following Sherman's edict, the Freedmen's Bureau and the newly emancipated themselves moved quickly to settle freedmen on the islands in the spring and summer of 1865.

Freedmen's Bureau agent Tunis Campbell, for example, oversaw settlement of more than four hundred adults and two hundred children on St. Catherine's and Sapelo Islands.[9] His December 1865 report to the bureau noted the presence of nearly eighty blacks on Ossabaw. Later documents reveal that the black community of Ossabaw grew and thrived, establishing a Baptist church on the island in the three decades before a series of Atlantic hurricanes in the late 1890s forced this agricultural population onto the mainland of Georgia.

In March 1865, Tunis Campbell was appointed as agent of the Freedmen's Bureau for "Burnside, Ausaba, St. Catherines, Sapelo, and Colonel's islands with orders to organize and establish governments on the Islands; protect freedmen and refugees for thirty miles back from the seashore." He held that post until he was dismissed the following March,[10] devoting the bulk of his time and energy to St. Catherine and Sapelo, establishing two schools on St. Catherine that served 250 students and recruiting his son and stepson to work as teachers.[11] The comparatively limited number of freedmen on Ossabaw no doubt encouraged Campbell to focus on the two more populous islands.

The black population of Ossabaw was relatively small and fluctuated appreciably. Freedmen's Bureau Commissioner Captain Alexander P. Ketchum's October 1865 report to the bureau noted the presence of sixty blacks on Ossabaw, ten men and fifty women, a much smaller population than pre–Civil War numbers.[12] The skewed sex ratio may have been a result of the summer 1863 draft of black men from the families on Ossabaw as the Union Army recruited men to form all-black fighting units.[13] Or this sex ratio may reflect the population of female camp followers who were settled on the island while the Union Army made use of their mates as laborers. Certainly, slaves held on Ossabaw took advantage of the chaos of the war to elope to other islands, and some Ossabaw planters hoped to safeguard their human property by relocating or "refugeeing" their slaves to other properties — all of which may have contributed to the limited population on the island.[14]

Campbell's own December 15, 1865, report to the Freedmen's Bureau noted that the death of a sixty-eight-year-old man, and the December 8, 1865, birth of a male child, resulted in a "whole number on this island of 78." This population resided in thirty-two homes shared between the Morel, Lymon, and McDonald "places." None of the bureau reports from the period make mention of Ossabaw Island's fourth plantation, Buckhead owned by the Skrine family.[15] To this population, Campbell distributed bureau-provided rations: one pound of bacon and one pound of hominy, two ounces each of salt and sugar, seven pounds of meal, three and one-quarter pounds of beef, twenty-one boxes of bread, one-quarter keg of vinegar, and one-eighth bottle of soap.[16]

Although it is rich in detail, Campbell's December 1865 report obscures as much as it reveals. None of the freedmen or women were identified by name, and it is impossible to determine the origin of the population Campbell reported as residing on Ossabaw. Were these seventy-eight people refugees who had been relocated to the island, long-term residents who had remained during the course of the war, or a mixture of both?

The Ossabaw Island plantations of McDonald (Middle Place), Kollock (South End), and Morel (North End) were partitioned and distributed to freedmen and women. The distributions, recorded in the Freedmen's Bureau records, appear in the table. What do we know about these men and women who were given title to land on Ossabaw? Most of them have faded into the fabric of the past, but hints survive as to the identity of some.

George J. Kollock purchased South End in February 1849. In correspondence, Kollock identified the eight-hundred-acre Ossabaw property as a "bachelor's retreat," which may account for his wife's reported objection

Ossabaw Island, Special Field Order No. 15 Land Distributions, 1865

RECIPIENT	AMOUNT OF LAND	REMARKS
Middle Place Plantation, owned by Alexander and Georgia McDonald (divided among seven families)		
April 14, 1865		
Frederic Miller, 7 in family	40 acres	
May 1, 1865		
Lisa Adams, 5 in family	30 acres	
Cyprus Bennett, 4 in family	25 acres	
John Timmons, 7 in family	40 acres	"Gone to White Bluff"
Cooper Turner, 5 in family	20 acres	
Isaac White, 5 in family	10 acres	"Gone to Charleston"
June 29, 1865		
Catherine Johnson, 4 in family	10 acres	
South End Plantation, owned by George J. Kollock (divided among eight families, July 31, 1865)		
Cyrus Brown, 2 in family	10 acres	
Moses George, 2 in family	20 acres	
Susan George, 2 in family	10 acres	
John Inman, 4 in family	15 acres	
Bob Kollock, 2 in family	20 acres	
James Mack, 4 in family	20 acres	
Primus Stewart, 3 in family	10 acres	
Mira Woodruff, 4 in family	10 acres	
North End Plantation, owned by Bryan Morel (distributed to one family, August 9, 1865)		
Paul John, 3 in family	15 acres	

Compiled from Bureau of Refugees, Freedmen and Abandoned Lands Records 1865–69, M798 Roll 36.

to the purchase.[17] Spending most of his time tending to plantation matters on the mainland, Kollock had poor luck in maintaining overseers on the island where his slaves raised sea island cotton as well as some corn, rice, and hogs, though he himself kept fairly detailed notes on the property.

His plantation notebooks recorded ownership of, among others, two slaves, "Big" and "Little" Primus, most likely father and son. Big Primus, owned while a boy by Priscilla Houston had been "bequeathed" to "his" Grandfather Boson, for his use until the latter's death. At that point, he was to be sold to "who shall own his Mother Kate at a fair and reasonable valuation." George J. Kollock, one of the executors of Houston's will, acquired Primus three years later in a private sale of slaves from the Houston estate.[18] On May 24, 1865, Kollock charged Big Primus with ferrying white Kollock family members to the mainland. Big Primus returned in four days but, according to Kollock, "ran away" fifteen days later. The following day, as Kollock noted, "Yankees . . . came to Midlands and carried (off) 6 of my negroes," including little Primus.[19] Little Primus returned to the island at the end of ten days, though there is no way to know if he was released from Yankee service or if he eloped to return home. Perhaps his return was in anticipation of the rumored land distribution. There is little doubt that the Primus Stewart awarded Kollock land in July 1865 was one of these two freedmen.

Others who received Kollock land are traceable in the historic record. Mira (Elmira) Woodruff appeared on the 1870 Census at age sixty with her husband, farmer March Woodruff. She and her husband were both born in South Carolina, but resided in the state long before the Civil War, as their forty-year-old daughter Carlotte was Georgia-born. Moses George, who received twenty acres, was married to Susan George, who also received ten acres of Kollock land. Both the Woodruffs and the Georges would pursue their dreams of land ownership off the island.

Yet many who received land leave a less clear historical trail. I found no record of John Inman or of Bob Kollock, both of whom received land on Ossabaw. Bob Kollock, who received part of the Kollock tract, was the only freedman who took the Kollock name.

Lisa Adams and Catherine Johnson, who received land on the McDonald Place, left little trace. Frederic Miller and Cooper Turner, who received McDonald land, and Paul John, who received land on the Morel Place, may have been soldiers, as is the case for Cyrus Brown, who received land on the Kollock place. A Cyrus Brown served in the Twenty-first Regiment of the USCT. He may have been taken up in the "special draft" for the Third South Carolina Volunteers held on Ossabaw Island in June 1863. The Third South Carolina Volunteers were reorganized and became the Twenty-first Regiment, USCT Infantry, South Carolina, in which Brown served. Similarly, a Frederic Miller, Cooper Turner, and Paul John were members of the Eighth, Fifteenth, and Forty-fourth regiments of USCT. Both the Eighth and the Forty-fourth passed through or saw action in the sea island areas of either South Carolina or Georgia, and one Isaac White, given title to McDonald land, was also member of the Thirty-third Regiment, USCT Infantry, South Carolina. Additional research into the pension files of the USCT is necessary to confirm this supposition.[20]

Like the defiant Mustapha Shaw, John Timmons speaks to us from the pages of an arrest warrant. Timmons, who had been granted forty acres of the McDonald Plantation, was arrested and charged by Freedmen's Bureau Superintendent Magill, on April 28, 1866, for conspiring to create disorder. Hired by Flye, Magill, and Middleton to act as "Director or Superintendent" over the black sharecroppers, Timmons instead worked at sowing the seeds of insurrection. The firm accused Timmons of bullying and berating his fellow freedmen, of "endeavoring to hinder the work and injure all concerned." In addition, the black sharecroppers familiar with sea island cotton production argued that Timmons was a fraud who in fact had no familiarity with the crop. For his part, Timmons objected to being denied the right to plant his own cotton crop and condemned as "thoughtless" fellow blacks who had cooperated with the firm. Timmons devoted his energies to disrupting the business of Flye, Magill and Middleton: forcing his adult daughter to withdraw her labor from the fields and roundly protesting to all who cared to listen that white men would ultimately cheat black agriculturalists out of their share of the crop. Resisting the authority of the Freedmen's Bureau and the federal government, Timmons declared whites had "no right to the Island, and that Genl. Tillson nor none else could give that power." Under pain of arrest, he was ultimately forced from Ossabaw and retreated across the waters to White Bluff.[21]

Freedmen given land titles were not the only black residents on the island. By the spring of 1866, the population of Ossabaw Island was rising. The arrest warrants of Timmons and Shaw identify some of the black sharecroppers working on the island for Flye, Magill, and Middleton. Skeet Baker and Prince Brown as well as black patriarch David Bond; his sons Louis, James, Benjamin, William, and Thomas Bond; Benjamin Harris; and William McKiver and George Savage and their families all resided on the island. In addition, William Delancey, William George, James Mack, Robert Mack, and York Thurman and their families continued to live on the island, working for shares of cotton as contracted with George J. Kollock.[22] Widower Amos Johnson lived and farmed on the north end of the island along with his son Abram. Jenney, who had outlived her husband Moses and four of her ten children, continued to make her home on Ossabaw Island with sons Caesar and James, while sons York, Moses Jr., and William and daughter Jeny lived and worked in Savannah.[23]

Of the men and women who received land in the summer of 1865, it appears the vast majority were not "locals," which is to say that they had not lived on the island before the war, and for the most part they did not remain on the island once their land was seized and restored to Confederate owners. James Mack stands as an important exception, inasmuch as he was part of a family network living on Ossabaw before the war, was given land title under Field Order No. 15, and remained on the island to sharecrop after his land was restored to George J. Kollock. As demonstrated in the warrants for the arrest of Mustapha Shaw and John Timmons, some tension existed between those outsiders who secured land on Ossabaw and those local freedmen who did not. Historian Paul Cimbala notes that many freedmen, displaced by the war, returned to the islands in early 1866 to find local plantations already divided among strangers with promissory title.[24] Without means of support, deprived of their portion of the old homestead, and without access to rations, this near-starving population was undoubtedly hostile toward those blacks they recognized only as interlopers. Perhaps lack of access to land on his home island drove Ossabaw native Philip Young to relocate to nearby Skidaway Island along with Jacob Tison and his wife Hagar and their five grown children. In addition, "local" blacks, though they themselves may not have served as soldiers, were well aware of the antagonism southern whites harbored toward former USCT servicemen.[25] Perhaps those who testified against Shaw and sought to distance themselves from those of his ilk were fearful of white retribution. In either case, the intraracial tension between "locals" and other freedmen mirrored the greater tension between black freedmen and the nation, manifest as the progressive forces in the federal government lost ground to recalcitrant conservatives who sought to maintain white supremacy as the order of the day.

President Andrew Johnson's decision to pardon Confederates who begged his favor and Circular No. 15 issued September 12, 1865, designed to restore all lands save those specifically identified as "abandoned," set the stage for the reversal of fortune on Ossabaw Island. The specifics of Circular No. 15 limited the power of the Freedmen's Bureau:

> Abandon(ed) lands are defined in Sec 2 of the Act of Congress, approved July 2, 1864, as lands, the lawful owner whereof shall be voluntarily absent, there from, and engaged either in arms or otherwise in aiding or encouraging the rebellion.
>
> IV. Land will not be regarded as confiscated until it has been condemned, and sold by decree of the U.S. Court for the District in which the property may be found, and the title thereto thus vested in the United States.[26]

Susan Marion Johnston Kollock, wife of George J. Kollock, took the necessary "amnesty oath" in April 1865, thereby securing a pardon and the family's Woodland Plantation. She wrote her son John in June 1865 urging him to encourage his father George to travel to Savannah "to secure his ossobaw [sic] plantation, which will be given up to him the 1st January, provided he has taken the old amnesty oath, or will take the new one, which only differs in that you swore your landed property is not worth over $20,000, you have not yet been in since or under government employ in the Confederate cause. All of which your father can swear to, as he has only done Patrol duty which does not count."[27] While it is difficult to fathom how the combined worth of the Kollocks' Woodland and Ossabaw plantations complete with a thriving live oak timber business did not total twenty thousand dollars or more, it appears he was not an active Confederate solider. Kollock, like Morel and McDonald, regained possession of his Ossabaw Island lands.

The process of restoring lands to southern white owners was fraught with tension on all sides. Black freedmen challenged the decision and resisted the actions of federal actors. Freedmen's Bureau officers themselves struggled with the decision and alternately resisted and complied with President Johnson's commands. Major General Davis Tillson was appointed by a beleaguered Oliver O. Howard in the fall of 1865 to oversee the restoration of Confederate lands along the Georgia sea coast. Howard, along with General Rufus Saxton and Captain Alexander P. Ketchum, had resisted President Johnson's efforts to undo Sherman's promise of land and titles to freedmen. Saxton, in particular, had sidestepped President Johnson's order to restore land to Confederate whites, arguing that land set aside by Sherman's order in the field, establishing a safe haven for black freedmen to become landowners, was exempt from new land policy coming out of the White House. Under Saxton's command, more freedmen were settled on abandoned lands as he actively defied Johnson's authority.[28]

Ketchum, who shared Saxton's vision, also stalled for time and continued to validate black titles and claims to land. In his autobiography, Oliver O. Howard would later express some self-doubt and lamented his decision to implement Johnson's land restoration policy. Yet, faced with direct orders from the president in October 1865 to seize lands from freedmen holding title and restore them to whites, Howard moved to comply. He replaced Saxton with Davis Tillson, who was less progressive in his stance toward blacks. Tunis Campbell reported he was "removed by General Tillson" and that, under Tillson's orders, the leadership schools "I had established on the Islands were broken up, and the people were driven off—unless they work under contracts which were purposely made to cheat the freedmen out of their labor."[29]

General Tillson, of course, remembered his encounter with Campbell and the freedmen of Ossabaw a bit differently.

> Ossabaw, St. Catherine's and Sapelo Islands were under the control of Tunis G. Campbell a colored man from New York City, appointed agent of the Bureau by Gen. Saxton. Well now Campbell, who was afterwards dismissed, is a person of great plausibility, and remarkable cunning. He was found to be cutting wood, selling it to passing steamers, appropriating the proceeds and otherwise managing the Island where he resided for the benefit of himself and a few leaders among the freedmen. Some of the freedmen he employed and whose produce he sold have never received payment. Influenced by Campbell, the freedmen were unwilling to permit the white owners to return to the Islands; even to occupy such portions of their property as had not been assigned to freemen in compliance with General Sherman's S.F.O. No. 15 series of 1865. They insisted that the Government should continue to furnish them with rations in whole or in part representing that they had all the animals, implements, seed and nearly all the food required to enable them to make a crop this year. But as on the Sea Islands and rice fields of the State, they had failed the year previously even when they were fed and assisted by the Government to raise sufficient food for their own support and as there was a great demand for labor and high prices on the coast, I declined to accede to their request.[30]

His quarrels with Campbell aside, Tillson was concerned about the dangers of black dependency and preferred to follow orders with regards to the freedmen. He worked to invalidate promissory titles, restore land to whites, and force blacks on the islands to sign labor contacts with whites in order to reestablish the profitability of the Georgia sea coast.[31] A January 11, 1866, letter from Tillson to Ketchum made his policy clear.

> Upon the application of former owners for the return of said lands, and by order of the President, Maj. Genl Howard, arrange for their immediate restoration. . . . In letter of Nov. 23 I am further instructed through Maj. Stinson "The restoration of lands will be made in the following manner. As soon as the Board of Supervisors is formed for any Island of locality, the

owner of the Estate must make an agreement with the freedmen upon said estate, that shall be satisfactory to the Board of Supervisors."

The order of restoration will then be given upon the owner's signing the obligation and producing proof of title and pardon.[32]

Ketchum, like other pro-freedmen progressives, was forced to comply with this new federal policy. He was removed from the field and reassigned to Washington at the end of February 1866.

Black freedmen who had secured land objected to what they understood as a change in the rules of engagement in the face of Tillson's efforts to invalidate their land titles and to force them to work for white planters. Blacks on Ossabaw had worked to sustain themselves; they could not have survived on the lean rations provided by Campbell. Freedmen hunted, fished, and dug oysters; planted plots of rice and corn; and made improvements in their properties in their six to eight months of ownership. Nevertheless, bureau agents pressured them to relinquish title and sign contracts with white planters or their agents.

In Campbell's wake, John W. Magill was appointed Freedmen's Bureau agent for Ossabaw on April 24, 1866, and he held this position through June 1867. In his capacity as agent, he wrote to the Savannah office to complain that blacks on the island were defiant of his authority. "The freedmen have of late been very slack in the performance of their labor, Etc. and pay no attention to orders of the Bureau, which have been sent to the Social agent. . . . Now is the important time of the season & it is necessary that the freedmen should faithfully & industriously perform their part of the contract, this they are not doing."[33]

In addition to setting their own work schedules, freedmen and women took their liberty of the island when and where they saw fit, and they were apparently not above appropriating the means to do so. A Miss W. Neal Haberscham of Savannah complained that a "certain large six oared built boat painted green and black" had been purloined by Ossabaw freedmen. Captain J. Kearny Smith stressed that should Magill do all he could "to keep order etc. & give the negroes to understand that they must not leave the Island without permission if they do they shall be arrested and locked up."[34]

Clearly out of his element and overwhelmed, Magill requested "an officer of the Bureau," be sent to Ossabaw. His plea generated a visit by First Lieutenant Nelson Bronson, no doubt accompanied by at least a few soldiers, from the Savannah office. Bronson's report to the Savannah office details the firm's operations on the Island.

They have about 300 acres of cotton under good cultivation, mostly, and looking finely although some of it is inferior, owing as Mr. McGill [*sic*], said to bad work on the part of some of the hands. They will probably realize 150 bales. There are about 60 freedmen working under contract and eleven working who are working on their own account. I carefully estimated the crops of corn, cotton and potatoes cultivated by these eleven, and feel confident that they will not realize $50 each. Those working under contract, besides their third of the cotton have over 100 acres of corn on their own account which will average 20 bushels to the acre, perhaps more so that each freedman ought to realize about $200 clear provided he has worked well and lost no time.[35]

Black agriculturists on Ossabaw took advantage of Bronson's presence to express their concerns to what they hoped was a more legitimate face of the Freedmen's Bureau. Most disagreed with Bronson's analysis of their situation, a fact he was forced to admit in his report.

Notwithstanding [the projected profit] which, with the exception of about fifteen, they seemed to manifest a great deal of dissatisfaction, and [say] they could have done better if they had had land and planted on their own account . . . the majority were inclined to be impudent — and intractable, they are not absolutely mutinous but their conduct is such as to intimidate the actions of the Agent of the Bureau; they work when they please, and at such times as they please and the only remedy the planter has is to charge them lost time.[36]

Bronson's commentary gives the lie to claims found in the Timmons affidavit filled by Magill, in which testimony suggested the Ossabaw freedmen were content with their lot: "deponents can cheerfully testify to the good will and kindly feelings prevailing between the Firm, themselves and all others not working with them, that the mules of the firm and the ploughs have worked the cow land of the people, as well those under contract as those who were not, and that all those people have assisted those working with the Firm in return, the only exception is the man Timmons." Undoubtedly, Ossabaw-born Bond, Mungin, and Bowen, all of whom sharecropped for Magill, offered the previous testimony, knowing on which side their bread was buttered.

Lieutenant Bronson quizzed Magill about his less than forceful action as bureau agent, as he reported in his letter to Freedmen's Bureau officer Major W. W. Deane.

I asked Mr. McGill [sic], why he did not enforce his authority as Agent of the Bureau, He said that the few men whom he could depend upon were afraid to arrest the more turbulent ones, that he had no means of sending them to Savannah, and he could only manage them by humoring them. . . . Upon his representing that some of the freedmen were stealing cotton and other property, and that freedmen not living on the Island were frequently in the habit of visiting the Island in boats when they please, and staying sometimes for several days, I issued an order that no boats should land or leave the place exapl [sic] at middle landing and by permission of the Agent of the Bureau. This order they refused to obey. I told them unless they did obey this order, and all other orders from the Agent of the Bureau that I would send down some soldiers and enforce said orders. . . . I think they can be easily managed if the Agent of the Bureau will exercise his authority with firmness and make one or two examples of the worst of them. . . . The present difficulties arise from too much kindness & indulgence on the part of Mr. McGill [sic] which they fail to appreciate or manifest and gratitude for.[37]

Black resistance to the authority of the Freedmen's Bureau coupled with Bronson's law-and-order instructions to Magill led to the December 1866 arrest warrant for Mustapha Shaw; his allies, the Delegals; and Pauldo Brown. Despite this approach, black freedmen across the Georgia sea islands continued to register complaints with the bureau and to resist seizure of their lands.

"Captain Shige" (Abalod Shigg), one of the freedmen involved in the 1865 "seizure" of Savannah River plantations Fairlawn and Whitehall, penned a fiery letter to O. O. Howard in January 1867 (all spelling and emphasis appear as in original).

We your humble Petitioners pray your Honor, to grant us Military Protection . . . against the Military outrages, on Persons, Homes, Papers and Effects contrary to the Constitution and laws of the United States: amendment Art. 4.

Gen Tillson has disregarded the law of the Congress and has *divided* the *Crops* on lands granted by Gen. Sherman's special field order No. 15 at Savannah Jan. 16th 1865.

Gen Tillson has ordered the people of Sappelo, Wilmanton and Argile Islands and other places leave before the Crops of 1866 were gathered in, and without *any, Compensation* for *Improvements* or Warrants, *Leases*, and Crectificates of *Sale* and Transfers . . . to enable him to Restore the lands to their former owners. Marcus Hunter, Andrew Washington and Dainel Willaims have been arrested by Gen. D. Tillson and placed in Barracks in the city of Savannah for giving their Affidavit before Commissioner Stone by orders of Henry S. Fisk United States district attorney: this is an unprecedented *outrage* on all law and order and seemed to be by your orders and disregards of 4 section of the Civil Rights Bill. These affidavits charged General Tillson with driving them off before they have been paid for . . . threatening to have them shot by U.S. soldiers, shut them up in their church on Sunday and carried their minister Rev. King Tatnal on board a U.S. Steamer.

And we your humble Petitioners pray that you order the assistant commissioner for South Carolina and Georgia to hold Courts under the 9th section to determine the validity of all titles to lands. . . .

And your humble Petitioners further pray your Honor to Order "This Commissioner and the Officers of the Bureau to Continue Military Protection over all cases, questions (and stop outrages as now practiced) concerning free enjoyment of Equal Rights and Immunities and no penalty or punishment for any violations of law shall be imposed or Permitted because of Race or Color or Previous conditions of slavery."

Sec. 14 and this is supreme law Art. 6 U.S. Con. "The right of the People to be *Secure* in their Persons, Houses, and Papers and Effects against unreasonable searches and seizures, shall not be violated; 4 art. U.S. Con. Amended.[38]

The letter was signed by Shigg and twenty-four black freedmen. This letter, like the voices of Shaw and Timmons, stands as clear evidence that the freedmen of the sea islands believed themselves entitled to "forty acres and a mule," understood whites (including some associated with the Freedmen's Bureau) to be acting to undermine their liberty, and had clear knowledge of their political rights. Shigg's letter, which referenced the U.S. Constitution, was an attempt to cover himself, and all his black peers, with the rights of citizenship and the power of law.

Despite their best efforts, the black freedmen of Ossabaw Island, like those on St. Catherine's, Sapelo, and Skidaway, those along the Ogeechee Neck, lost their lands as they were restored to their former Confederate owners. Each of the Confederate planters on Ossabaw Island regained formal possession of their land by way of Special Order No. 6, signed by Major-General Davis Tillson, January 19, 1867.

Tunis Campbell jettisoned the dream of Sherman's reservation. Investing one thousand dollars of his own funds, Campbell made a down payment on the Belleville Plantation in Darien, McIntosh County, Georgia, and encouraged freedmen to relocate to this property on the mainland in December 1866, ending his formal affiliation with the Freedmen's Bureau in the Georgia sea islands.[39] The decision to settle in Darien was an intriguing one. Major Robert Gould Shaw, commander of the legendary all-black Massachusetts Fifty-fourth, had, under orders given by Colonel James Montgomery, overseen the burning and destruction of Darien, Georgia, in June 1863, though no military resistance had been offered by citizens of the town. Shaw, who objected to the use of his troops in a manner he deemed dishonorable and immoral, made his objections known to Colonel Montgomery in the moment and later wrote letters of protest to his family and others.[40] It is interesting that Tunis Campbell would in the face of this history seek to relocate to the Darien area.

Cash-poor planter Charles H. Hopkins, who sold his McIntosh County Belleville Plantation to Campbell, facilitated Campbell's relocation to the area. Campbell, who agreed to make periodic payments of five thousand dollars until the property was paid in full, was undeniably a much-needed financial support for Hopkins.[41] While this financial arrangement was temporarily supportive of Campbell's goal to assist freedmen in their struggle for land ownership, there remains the question of what it meant that black freedmen, some of them former colored troops, returned to the site of what whites in McIntosh County understood to be a racial crime of war. The move was nothing if not bold and defiant.

Mustapha Shaw joined Campbell in the move from the islands to the mainland. Shaw, born on the Delegal Plantation, returned to the community of his birth in Harris Neck, McIntosh County. He resided with his wife and four children, in 1870, on a farm valued at $250. He joined other black freedmen who acquired land from the former white plantation owners in the region — purchasing ten acres from his white father, Edward W. Delegal for $1 in 1868. Shaw would later purchase an additional twenty acres of land from a second former slave owner, Charles Spalding.[42]

As lands on Ossabaw were restored to white landowners in January 1867, most of those freedmen who had received promissory title under Field Order No. 15 vacated the island. Isaac White left for Charleston, South Carolina, and under a cloud; John Timmons departed for White Bluff. Primus Stewart, Moses and Susan George, and Elmira and March Woodruff also left the island, settling nearby in White Bluff.

Relocation to White Bluff had benefits for Stewart, the Georges, and the Woodruffs. The three families resettled in close proximity to one another. They appear on the 1870 U.S. Census in the Sixth District in a cluster of dwellings: numbered 1888, 1890, and 1891, respectively. Primus Stewart, age thirty-five, lived alone on his farm valued at $300 and owned an additional $200 worth of personal property. Moses, age thirty, and Susan, thirty-one, lived with their children born in freedom; Mary was five, and John was two. Seniors Elmira and March Woodruff owned $150 in personal property, though there is no indication that they owned their land on White Bluff. They lived with daughter Carlotte and grandson Samuel, age fourteen, Elmira, age six, and Dolly, age one. Elmira Woodruff died within four years of the Census. Her widowed husband March remarried in 1874, taking Grace Jackson as his bride on March 1, 1874.[43]

Like Mustapha Shaw, Stewart and George did become property owners once again; they both owned and paid taxes on their land on White Bluff. Both men also paid their poll taxes in 1875–76 and again in 1878 — an act that secured their voting rights in the state. Primus Stewart paid property tax on $70 in land in 1875–76, and on $75 in land in 1878. He also owned $31.20 in farm equipment that year. Moses George paid property tax on his twenty acres of land in Chatham County in 1878.[44]

Noticeably, no freedmen who remained on Ossabaw after 1867 ever purchased land on the island. John Mungin, who testified against John Timmons, had, at the time of his 1870 deposit to the Freedmen's Savings Bank, relocated from Ossabaw to Skidaway Island. Neither he nor his brother Chas nor sister Sally who remained on Ossabaw became property owners in this period. Several family groupings remained on the island, living in extended kinship clusters not unlike patterns found in slavery. An older Primus Stewart was listed on Ossabaw in Chatham County on the 1880 U.S. Census residing with his wife Elsey (age fifty-six). This Primus Stewart, who lived near a grouping of the Macks, the Bonds, the McKivers, and the Harrises, was, no doubt, George Kollock's "Big" Primus.

James Mack, forty-eight, continued sharecropping on the island along with his wife Dinah, his son Jim Jr. (age twelve), daughter Lizzie (age six), and sons March (age three) and Collins (age one). James's younger brother Bob Mack (age thirty-five), who also signed on to sharecrop with Kollock in 1867, lived nearby with wife Hannah (age thirty), son Jim (age fifteen), and daughters Katy (age ten) and Rachel (age three). The Bond brothers made famous in the Shaw arrest warrant — Louis (age sixty-five), James (age sixty), Thomas (age forty-five), Benjamin (age forty-four), and William (age forty) — and their families also lived in close proximity. A young Louis Bond Jr. (age twenty-two) lived near William and his family — wife Eliza (age twenty-seven) and son Schedrick (age five).

William McKiver and George Savage, two of the others involved in the Mustapha Shaw affair, also remained on Ossabaw. William (age forty-three), his wife Margaret (age forty-eight), and their six children lived next to his brother John McKiver (age forty-five), his wife Rachel (age twenty), and their infant son Freddy. The McKiver men lived immediately adjacent to Louis Bond Sr. and his brother James Bond. George Savage (age fifty-two), his wife Leah (age thirty-nine), and their seven children lived within a stone's throw of the younger Louis Bond and William Bond.[45]

Pauldo Brown, Shaw's former ally, lived but a few paces from William and Ben Bond. At forty, Pauldo lived with his wife Emeline (age forty-eight) and had no children. Despite a wounded leg, he made his living sharecropping, as did the other men on the island. Although we can verify such facts as these, much remains undocumented. We can only speculate as to whether the injury to Brown's leg came as a result of his escape with Shaw or from other causes. In either case, Brown had by 1880 resolved himself to a less rebellious stance and conformed to the status quo.

Further insights into life on Ossabaw beyond work can be gleaned from analyzing the links between various residents on the island. Black men and women set about the business of organizing their lives in freedom, sanctifying their marriages, establishing houses of worship, and educating their children. A handful of ministers maintained a circuit of the region, which included visits to Ossabaw Island. Revs. John Cox and Henry L. Simpson, both of whom served as ministers of the Second African Baptist Church in Savannah, acted as missionaries attending to the spiritual needs of islanders, including performing marriages. John Cox, who had purchased his freedom in 1849, was one of the twenty ministers who met with Sherman in Savannah in January 1865 to outline the needs of the newly freed.[46] He served as minister at Second African Baptist through the war and was deeply engaged in evangelizing freedmen. Cox officiated at the wedding of Catherine Johnson (who had received McDonald land) and Billy Green on the island in the fall of 1867. Rev. Simpson, who served Second African Baptist for a decade (1871–81), formalized the relationship between fifty-one-year-olds Elsey Culbert and Primus Stewart on March 30, 1871. Ordained minister B. O. Butler, who served as a traveling minister for several churches in the region, including the one on Ossabaw, performed the honors for March Woodruff when he took Grace Jackson as his second wife. Twenty-two-year-old Harly Handy, who resided on Ossabaw and worked as a farmer, may have been the son of minister Harly Handy, who served as pastor at the White Bluff Church and performed marriages on Ossabaw Island in the 1860s and 1870s. Minster Handy married couples including John Timmons and Cornelia Adams on October 12, 1866, and Dinah Grate and James Mack on November 2, 1871.[47]

Rev. Hardy Mobley, who had returned to his native Georgia in 1865 as a Congregationalist minister, also served the people of Ossabaw as well as those on neighboring islands and within the city of Savannah. Commissioned by the Union Congregational Church but funded by the American Missionary Association, Mobley, like Campbell, headed south to assist freedmen in their upward climb to acculturation and civilization. Described by historian Joe M. Richardson as a "missionary at large," Mobley aided the poor and the sick, preached at established churches in the area, and offered his services for marriages and burials.[48] Mobley solemnized the marriage of Cyrus Brown and Nancy Ellis in January 1867.

As David Bond's testimony informs us, blacks on Ossabaw had organized a Baptist church by the winter of 1866. Given the prominence of the First and Second African Baptist churches of Savannah and the role John Cox played in bringing "Sherman's reservation" into existence, it is quite logical that the first congregation on the island would identify itself as Baptist — Zion Baptist in particular. At a June 1865 convention in Hilton Head, South Carolina, a group of black Baptist ministers from churches along the southeastern sea coast — the First Baptist Church of Savannah, John Cox's Second Baptist Church, and Ulysses Houston's Third Baptist Church among them — met and organized themselves into the Zion Baptist Association (henceforth ZBA). Rev. Ulysses Houston had also been part of the group that met with Sherman, and he shared the belief in the exclusivity of Sherman's reservation. And Houston, like Tunis Campbell, also worked to aid freedmen, settling a group of emancipated men and women on Skidaway Island in spring of 1865. Ministers Butler and Handy were both members in good standing of Zion Baptist Association churches.[49]

Hinder Me Not Baptist Church of Ossabaw Island, the Baptist church in which David Bond was elder, applied to become a member of the ZBA. "The Committee on the State of the Churches making application for membership recommended the following churches to be in good order for admission viz: Hinder Me Not, Baptist Church, Osabaw [sic]

Island." By this act, Hinder Me Not was voted into the ZBA October 16, 1874, at the Ninth Annual Session of the Zion Baptist Association held at Liberty County, Georgia.⁵⁰ Missionary preacher H. C. Aves and one P. Brown represented the church to the ZBA. Hinder Me Not was a small church. ZBA records for Hinder Me Not published as part of their annual minutes in 1874 and 1878–96 record that the total membership numbers never rose above the high of sixty-eight. In the final year of the church, 1896, total membership had dropped to just twenty-one. Sunday school superintendent and Ossabaw resident T. (Thomas) Bond saw to the spiritual education of nineteen students in 1878, though that number would decline over the decade. The limited number of members and the meager wages of those who continued to live on the island meant that Hinder Me Not was also a very poor church. From a high of $4 to a low of $1.25, the tiny island church struggled to make its associational payments to the ZBA as well as contribute to the minister's widow's fund, and contribute to a fund to support the building of a college for theological studies.⁵¹ Thomas Bond served as a deacon of Hinder Me Not beginning in 1880, was elected evangelist, and became a licentiate in the summer of 1888. Fellow Ossabaw resident Thomas Mack assumed the position of deacon of Hinder Me Not in that same year, a position he would hold for the remaining life of the island church.⁵²

The membership of Hinder Me Not was in decline prior to the storms of 1896 and 1898. Ossabaw residents who frequently traveled to neighboring islands as well as to the mainland may have joined any number of ZBA churches in the region: White Bluff Baptist, Sapelo Island Baptist, St. Simon's Island Baptist, St. Catherine's Island Baptist, Darien Baptist, Harris Neck Baptist, and Ogeechee Baptist churches, to name a few. Movement of the "faithful" caused frequent upheaval in ZBA churches. Congregants complained of new churches accepting members excluded from old ones, ministers wrote to condemn the actions of deacons who "established a new church in a house not 25 feet from the door" of the existing church. The founding of Sweet Field of Eden Baptist Church, located across the river in present-day Pin Point, seems to have been fraught with similar tensions. Members, presumably the elders, of Hinder Me Not wrote a letter of grievance to the ZBA in conjunction with Sweet Field of Eden's application for admission to the association in the summer of 1888. They charged Thomas Bond and Sweet Field of Eden with appropriating property that belonged to the Ossabaw church. "The Committee on Welfare and Grievance," advised "the applying church (Sweet Field of Eden) to return the property claimed by Hinder Me Not church," thus clearing the way for Sweet Field to be admitted to ZBA. The association also honored the new church's "request that Bro. T. Bond, be examined for ordination" as pastor of the new church. In the face of Thomas Bond's departure, Rev. William Anderson assumed the position of acting pastor and governed Hinder Me Not, and Ossabaw native Thomas Mack assumed the position of deacon.[53]

Thomas Bond continues to appear on the list of licentiates for the Zion Baptist Association through 1896, yet he ceased to be affiliated with either Hinder Me Not or Sweet Field of Eden. Instead he appears to have assumed the role of founder and pastor of Beulah Baptist Church in Montgomery a little more than a year after he purchased two and one-half acres on the mainland in January 1887.[54] Ossabaw's Hinder Me Not remained viable and made contributions to the ZBA through the fall of 1896. The membership rolls at Pin Point's Sweet Field of Eden grew steadily; there were twenty-seven members in 1896, thirty-seven in 1897, and forty-five in 1898.

Beyond ZBA minutes, little information survives about the island church, save for its bold defiant name taken from Genesis 24:56: "And he said unto them, Hinder me not, seeing the LORD hath prospered my way; send me away that I may go to my master" (KJV). Freed from slavery by their Lord's hands, black freedmen and women on Ossabaw Island had set out to create a house of worship in which they could give thanks, offer praise, and set their lives on the bright path of righteousness. Far more than would a mere place name, the name of their church beautifully captured the strident energy of the era of its birth.

In seeking to re-create on paper the social network of the island, we must imagine institutions on the island beyond Hinder Me Not Zion Baptist Church. Historians have yet to investigate the First Young Poor and Needy Association, founded by Ossabaw-born Jacob Tison. Notation in the records of the Savannah branch of the Freedmen's savings bank reveal that Tison and Pete Johnson, treasurer and vice president, respectively, maintained an account for what was obviously a charitable society, but to date there is no additional information about the organization.

Similarly, historians are well aware that emancipation across the American South saw freedmen establish churches and simultaneously, or then immediately thereafter, schools for themselves and their children. Did such a church school thrive on Ossabaw Island? The voices of Hardy Mobley and Tunis Campbell report an interest in establishing two schools on Ossabaw. Mobley, via his relationship with the American Missionary Association, facilitated distribution of supplies, "books," and "charts" to Tunis Campbell for use in his proposed schools on St. Catherine's and Ossabaw islands. Campbell did establish a school on St. Catherine's Island, but as of April 1866 he had been unsuccessful in his quest to build a school on Ossabaw before he was relieved of duty.

Only a few of the children on the island were "at school," as noted in the 1880 Census, specifically James Bond's daughter Charity (age twenty) and grandson Jimmy (age ten). The remaining Bond cousins, children of the Bond brothers, had no such identification and may have been involved in helping their parents to farm.[55] More children were listed as "at school" in the Ogeechee District and on St. Catherine's Island. The children of Ossabaw may in fact have been ferried to school on the other side of the river or attended school on one of the neighboring islands.

Though our picture is incomplete, existing data does reveal intriguing glimpses of the island. Mustapha Shaw, John Timmons, and Captain Shigg stand, at least in this retelling, in bold relief in the foreground of the image. Strong, defiant, armed with words of law or weapons of war, these three black men represent freedom and manhood of a particular stripe. If the Civil War itself, the physical conflict, including those black slaves who had taken up arms, had brought freedom to those in bondage, then the fight to hold onto their lands and claim their rights made them men. Were these men inspired or instructed by Tunis Campbell as Russell Duncan suggests? Certainly those who followed Campbell to McIntosh County saw promise in his leadership. Still, in the face of the evidence, I would argue that rather than Campbell's philosophy having influenced freedmen, the defiance and the commitment to black separatism grew from the lived experience of freedmen and women along the Georgia sea coast. As black leaders had suggested to Sherman in Savannah, men and women along the Georgia sea coast were determined to have freedom on their own terms.

Shaw, Timmons, Primus Stewart the younger, Moses George, and March Woodruff rejected the status quo — refusing to resubmit to what they identified as the illegitimate rule of white men — be they businessmen or federal agents. Like their peers who had armed themselves and declared "no white men should live between the two Ogeechees" during the famous Ogeechee uprising of January 1869, a few of the men from Ossabaw rejected what was rapidly becoming the new norm, and refused to sharecrop for whites.[56]

These few who first left the island secured land ownership within a decade of emancipation.

Yet tellingly, of the men and women who had remained on Ossabaw in the first two decades of freedom, few secured land ownership at all. Campbell's observation was correct, the people did cry out for land, and land ownership would have supported the first generation of a rural black middle class in the post–Civil War era. But the reversal of fortunes brought about by the betrayal of the federal government left the vast majority of black freedmen without the opportunity to secure their liberty in the coastal sand of Ossabaw. We can only imagine the sense of satisfaction Mustapha Shaw enjoyed as he, one of the privileged few, who abandoned Ossabaw, farmed his own plot of earth.

Locals who remained on Ossabaw, men and women for whom the sea island cotton fields, oak forests, and tabby houses had always been home, despite the sting of the overseer's lash, stand in the background of our picture. Unable to partake of land distribution, as the federal government reversed its land policy too quickly, they chose to form relationships with returning white land owners or their agents. This choice was rooted not in the promise of land ownership that so animated Mustapha Shaw or Captain Shigg (who in 1885 purchased five acres of the Happy Discovery Tract bordering Pipemaker Creek to the west of the Savannah River), but in the connection to home place, to tradition, and to family.[57] The Bond family knew the island as a place of extended kin, overseen by an elderly patriarch who clearly saw some status in being "the oldest colored man on the MacDonald place." The McKivers and Savages and Macks also stayed, and they, too, reaped the rewards associated with staying in the home place. Their children all knew the culture of the island — learned to hunt and fish and pull oysters from the muddy waters. They learned to speak Gullah and to recite the folk tales and traditions on which their parents had been raised. True, they may not have "owned" Ossabaw, but they certainly occupied and controlled the cultural space. These locals stayed on Ossabaw and sharecropped a full generation beyond emancipation, and when they left they carried their church to the mainland, as much a part of their family history as their names. Ossabaw's Hinder Me Not, which spoke to their hopes for and the promise of independence, gave way to Sweet Field of Eden in Pin Point and was testament to their belief that they had a new, permanent, and blessed home. Once relocated, these former sharecroppers became day laborers, factory workers, and crabbers. A few also became home and land owners — nearly twenty years after their peers who left before the storms. Members of the Bond family purchased land on the mainland as they decamped from the island. Brothers William and Benjamin and nephew Louis Jr. all acquired lots in Block C of the Beaulieu Tract in Pin Point.[58] For them, the dreams of freedom and independence, long postponed, would finally come to fruition, but not on Ossabaw Island.

NOTES

1. Warrant for the Arrest of Mustapha Shaw, Records of the Field Offices of the Bureau of Refugees Freedmen and Abandoned Lands, 1865–1872, Georgia, M1903 Roll 83, National Archives, Atlanta.

2. Ibid.

3. Ann Foskey, *Ossabaw Island*, Images of America Series (Charleston, S.C.: Arcadia Press, 2001), 15. Eric Wills, "Sea Island Strata," *Smithsonian Magazine*, February 2007, http://www.smithsonianmag.com/history-archaeology/sea_island_strata.html.

4. 1860 Federal Census Slave Schedules, Chatham County, Georgia.

5. Dorothy Seay Magoffin, "A Georgia Planter and His Plantation, 1837–1861," *North Carolina Historical Review* (October 1938): 354–77.

6. Eric Foner, *Reconstruction: America's Unfinished Revolution, 1863–1877*, (New York: Harper and Row, 1988), 70.

7. William S. McFeely, *Yankee Stepfather: General O. O. Howard and the Freedmen* (New Haven, Conn.: Yale University Press, 1968), 133–35.

8. Russell Duncan, *Freedom's Shore: Tunis Campbell and the Georgia Freedmen* (Athens: University of Georgia Press, 1986), 21.

9. Duncan, *Freedom's Shore*, 23.

10. Tunis Gulic Campbell, *Sufferings of the Rev. T. G. Campbell and His Family in Georgia* (Ithaca, N.Y.: Cornell University Library Digital Collections), 7. Campbell notes he held his post as "governor" of the islands for two years. This is in conflict with Freedmen Bureau records.

11. Letter from T. G. Campbell to American Missionary Association Secretary, Savannah, Ga., April 11, 1866, American Missionary Association Manuscripts, Georgia, M5064 Roll 1, Amistad Research Center, Dillard University.

12. Paul A. Cimbala, *Under the Guardianship of the Nation: The Freedmen's Bureau and the Reconstruction of Georgia, 1865–1870* (Athens: University of Georgia Press, 1997), 168. Cimbala notes that Ketchum's figures were inaccurate due to the vast territory and the inability of the limited number of agents to cover all the area in Sherman's reservation.

13. Clarence L. Mohr, "Before Sherman: Georgia Blacks and the Union War Effort, 1861–1864," *Journal of Southern History* 45 (August 1979): 350.

14. Clarence L. Mohr, *On the Threshold of Freedom: Masters and Slaves in Civil War Georgia* (Athens: University of Georgia Press, 1986), 99.

15. John W. Magill purchased thirty-seven hundred acres, one-eighth interest of

Buckhead Plantation, from Melissa Skrine in March 1867. He sold the land back to Skrine in January 1868. I would argue that these transactions, documented in Chatham County Deed Books 3 and 4, are a consequence of the volatility of economic relations and confusion over land ownership that mark the period. Unsure of her rights regarding land ownership, and cash poor like most of her peers, Skrine sold her land to Magill, who himself hoped to turn the land to profit by exploiting freedmen as sharecroppers. Once conflict about land ownership for the former Confederates was resolved, Magill was no longer in a position to make the best use of the land. Lymon remains a bit of a mystery; to date, I have found no deeds in the Chatham County records indicating ownership by a Lymon. He may have arranged a rental agreement with one of the owners.

16. Monthly Report of T. Campbell, Agent of Sea Island of St. Catherine's, December 15, 1865, Records of the Field Offices of the Bureau of Refugees, Freedmen and Abandoned Lands, 1865–1872, Georgia, M869 Roll 33, National Archives, Atlanta.

17. Notes of Perry Deane Young. Kollock Papers, Accession No. 2000–123, Box 1, Georgia Historical Society, Savannah, Ga. Kollock retained possession of Woodland Plantation, the family's permanent residence in Habersham County.

18. Folio for Rose Dhu Will. Priscilla Houston, June 17, 1835; Rose Dhu Patrick Houston, et al., George J. Kollock, March 15, 1838, Georgia Historical Society, Savannah, Ga.

19. Diaries of George J. Kollock, May 23–August 9, 1865, Microfilm 1648–06, Georgia Historical Society, Savannah, Ga.

20. National Park Service, Civil War Soldiers and Sailors System, http://www.nps.gov/cww/soldiers.cfm.

21. Affidavit in *The People vs. Timmons*, April 28, 1866, Records of the Field Offices of the Bureau of Refugees, Freedmen and Abandoned Lands, 1865–1872, Georgia, M1903, Roll 83, National Archives, Atlanta.

22. Labor Contract, April 15, 1867, Records of the Field Offices of the Bureau of Refugees, Freedmen and Abandoned Lands, 1865–1872, Georgia, M1908, Roll 83, National Archives, Atlanta.

23. Freedman's Savings Bank Records, Savannah Branch. Records for Amos Johnson and Jenney, www.heritagequestonline.com. Accessed via Delaware County Public Library systems. Nicole Green, Curator of the Old Slave Market Museum in Charleston, S.C., graciously shared her research notes drawn from these records.

24. Cimbala, *Under the Guardianship of the Nation*, 175.

25. Ira Berlin, Joseph Reidy, and Leslie Rowland, eds., *Freedom: A Documentary History of Emancipation, 1861–1867*, Series II, *The Black Military Experience* (Cambridge: Cambridge University Press, 1982), 359. Document 359, Affidavit of the Wife of a Discharged Georgia Black Soldier, details the brutal rape of an ex-soldier's wife on September 25, 1866. I first encountered this document while searching microfilm of Freedmen's Bureau records for information about Ossabaw Island. During the violent gang rape of Rhonda Ann Childs, one of her four white rapists "'damned the Yankee Army,' and Swore they meant to kill every black Son-of-bitch they could find that had ever fought against them." The implication of Mrs. Child's affidavit

was that the family had been singled out for attack because of her husband's previous military service and their financial success after the war.

26. Assistant Adjutant General Circulars 1865–1869, No. 139, Bureau of Refugees, Freedmen and Abandoned Lands, Record Group 105, 17–18, National Archives, Atlanta.

27. Letter from Susan Marion Johnston Kollock to son John F. Kollock, June 25, 1865, Kollock Papers, Box 1, Account No. 2000–123, Georgia Historical Society, Savannah.

28. Cimbala, *Under the Guardianship of the Nation*, 173–74.

29. Campbell, *Sufferings of the Rev. T. G. Campbell*, 8.

30. "Report of Bt. Maj. Gen Davis Tillson, Asst Com Bureau of Refugees of Freedmen and Abandoned Lands for State of Georgia, showing the operations of the Bureau from Sept. 22, 1865–Nov. 1, 1866," Bureau of Refugees, Freedmen and Abandoned Lands, 1865–1869, Georgia, M798 Roll 32, National Archives, Atlanta.

31. Claude Oubre, *Forty Acres and a Mule: The Freedmen's Bureau and Black Land Ownership* (Baton Rouge: Louisiana State University Press 1978), 57–61; Cimbala, *Under the Guardianship of the Nation*, 166–86.

32. Letter from Davis Tillson to Andrew Ketchum, January 11, 1866, Unregistered Documents, Letters A–C 1866, Bureau of Refugees, Freedmen and Abandoned Lands, Georgia, 1865–1869, M798 Roll 32, National Archives, Atlanta.

33. Letter from J. Kearny Smith to W. W. Deane, August 30, 1866, Field Office Records, Letters, Bureau of Refugees, Freedmen and Abandoned Lands, Georgia, 1865–1872, M1903 Roll 77, National Archives, Atlanta.

34. Letter from J. Kearny Smith to J. W. Magill, July 17, 1866, Field Office Records, Bureau of Refugees, Freedmen and Abandoned Lands, Georgia 1865–1872, M1903 Roll 77, National Archives, Atlanta.

35. Letter from Nelson Bronson to W. W. Deane, September 13, 1866, Unregistered Documents, Letters A–C 1866, Bureau of Refugees, Freedmen and Abandoned Lands, Georgia, 1865–1869, M798 Roll 25, National Archives, Atlanta.

36. Ibid.

37. Ibid.

38. Letter to O. O. Howard from Captain Shige, January 16, 1867, Registers and Letters Received by the Commissioner of the Bureau of Refugees, Freedmen and Abandoned Lands, Bureau of Refugees, Freedmen and Abandoned Lands, Georgia, 1865–1872, M752 Roll 44, National Archives, Atlanta.

39. Campbell, *Sufferings of the Rev. T. G. Campbell*, 8; Duncan, *Freedom's Shore*, 31–36. Campbell, his wife Hannah, and son Tunis Jr. were listed in Darien, McIntosh County, on the 1870 Federal Census. They held one thousand dollars in property and shared their home with Hannah Taylor (age sixteen) and T. G. Simpson (age nine).

40. Russell Duncan, ed., *Blue-Eyed Child of Fortune: The Civil War Letters of Colonel Robert Gould Shaw* (Athens: University of Georgia Press, 1992), chap. 13, "The Burning of Darien."

41. Campbell, *Sufferings of the Rev. T. G. Campbell*, 8; Duncan, *Freedom's Shore*, 36.

42. Deed from Edward W. Delegal to Mustapha Shaw, December 22, 1868, McIntosh County Deed Book A 315–316, Recorder's Office, Darien, Georgia. Mustapha Shaw purchased ten acres in the Nephews Hammock region, "bounded on the west by the Eastern branch of the Sapelo river and on all other sides by the DeLegal lands." The deed was formally recorded May 30, 1874. Deed from Charles Spalding to Mustapha Shaw, February 19, 1882. Deed Book A 526–527. Recorder's Office, Darien, Ga.

43. *Marriages of Chatham County Georgia, (Blacks) 1866–1873*, vol. 2 (Savannah: Georgia Historical Society, 1993), 315.

44. Chatham County Georgia Tax Digests, Georgia State Archives, Atlanta, Drawer 61, Roll 7; Drawer 75, Roll 21, 1875–1876. Deeds of sale documenting the land acquisitions of Moses and Susan George and Primus Stewart were found in Chatham County Deed Books 4G, 4R, and 7E held in the recorder's office in Savannah.

45. Schedule 1. Inhabitants in the Islands in the County of Chatham, State of Georgia, June 1880. United States Census Office 1883. Census of Population: 1880, Vol. 1, Statistics of the Population of the United States (Washington, D.C.: U.S. Government Printing Office, 1883).

46. Ira Berlin, Joseph Reidy, and Leslie Rowland, eds., *Freedom: A Documentary History of Emancipation, 1861–1867,* Series 1, *The Wartime Genesis of Free Labor: The Lower South* (Cambridge: Cambridge University Press, 1982), 332.

47. *Marriages of Chatham County*, 223, 221.

48. Joe M. Richardson, "'Labor is rest to me here in this, the Lord's vineyard': Hardy Mobley, Black Missionary during Reconstruction," *Southern Studies* 22 (Spring 1983): 6.

49. Eric Foner, *Freedom's Lawmakers: A Directory of Black Officeholders during Reconstruction*, (Oxford: Oxford University Press, 1993), 109–10.

50. Minutes of the Ninth Annual Session of the Zion Baptist Association, 1874, African American Baptist Annuals, Georgia, Microfilm Roll 1384, Mercer University, Atlanta.

51. Elders of the ZBA first imagined erecting a seminary in the town of Arcadia in Liberty County, Georgia. The organization later voted to support Atlanta Baptist Seminary, which became Morehouse College in Atlanta.

52. Zion Baptist Association Records, 1868–1903, Microfilm 1384, Jack Tarber Library, Mercer University, Macon, Ga.

53. Ibid.

54. The details of the story of why Thomas Bond parted with Sweet Field of Eden after leaving Hinder Me Not are lost. Certainly it is true that many Ossabawians settled in both the Pinpoint and Montgomery area in the late nineteenth and early twentieth centuries and may have wished to bring their church home with them, though careful examination of ZBA records reveals an overlap in the existence of the two churches.

55. Schedule 1. Inhabitants in The Islands in the County of Chatham, State of Georgia, June 1880, United States Census Office 1883. Census of Population: 1880, Vol. 1, *Statistics of the Population of the United States* (Washington, D.C.: U.S. Government Printing Office, 1883).

56. Karen B. Bell, "'The Ogeechee Troubles'": Federal Land Restoration and the 'Lived Realities' of Temporary Proprietors, 1865–1868," *Georgia Historical Quarterly* 85, no. 3 (Fall 2001): 386.

57. Deed of sale from Charles H. J. Sweats to Captain Shigg, January 15, 1885, Chatham County Deed Book 6:178, Recorder's Office, Savannah, Ga.

58. The Bonds acquired adjacent lots. William purchased lot 6 in March and lot 4 in April 1897, Louis Jr. purchased lot 2 in March 1898, and Benjamin purchased lot 3 in March 1899. Deeds to sale found in several books in the Chatham County Courthouse — 6B:25, 7L:162, 7S:314, 7W:54, 7Z:268, 279, 8D:298. Chatham County Courthouse, Savannah, Ga.

Timothy Powell

Summoning the Ancestors

The Flying Africans' Story and
Its Enduring Legacy

THE FLYING Africans' story undoubtedly constitutes one of the most powerful, enduring, and vital examples of the "mysteries of the Gullah and Geechee past." This narrative has been told and embellished for more than two hundred years in the form of communal histories, local legends, children's stories, movies, novels, and television shows. Based on an actual historical event, this remarkable tale of how members of the black communities of coastal Georgia rose up, both in rebellion and in flight, embodies the magical history of this unique region and teaches us a great deal about the curative powers of storytelling.

The historical origins of the flying Africans' story date back to the spring of 1803, to St. Simons Island off the coast of Georgia. Because the "facts" of the event come from archival evidence, much of it written by slave owners and slave dealers, parts of the story remain difficult to recover. What we do know for sure is that in May 1803, a group of Ibo (variations: Ebo, Ibo) slaves arrived at Skidaway Island, just south of Savannah, Georgia, after enduring the nightmare of the Middle Passage. The slave dealer William Mein sold the Ibo to Thomas Spalding and James Couper, both of whom five years earlier had signed the Georgia Constitution, which out-

lawed the importation of Africans. On the short voyage from Skidaway to
St. Simons Island, the Ibo rose in rebellion, leading to the death of the white
overseer and two sailors aboard the *York*. According to archival evidence,
the Ibo did not fly, but instead committed collective suicide by drowning
themselves in Dunbar Creek, at a place now called Ebos Landing.[1]

The black communities of coastal Georgia, however, remember the
same historical event very differently. *Drums and Shadows*, a compendium
of interviews conducted by the Federal Writers' Project (FWP) in the 1930s,
abounds with flying African references that testify to the story's enduring
legacy in the form of oral histories. Interestingly, many black historians
recorded in *Drums and Shadows* recall their relatives witnessing not just
the events that occurred in 1803, but instances of flight that happened years
later, in some cases providing eyewitness accounts. James Moore of Tin
City, Georgia, for example, explained: "I seen folks disappear right before
my eyes. Just go right out of sight. They do say that people brought from
Africa in slavery times could disappear and fly right back to Africa. From
the things I see myself I believe that they could do this."[2] George W. Little,
a root doctor from Brownville, offered both an affirmation of the events at
Ebos Landing and a firsthand observation of contemporary flight: "Take
the story of them people what fly back to Africa. That's all true. You just
had to possess *magic knowledge* to be able to accomplish this. Not long
ago I see a man vanish into thin air by snapping his fingers."[3] The story of
the Ibo uprising was apparently widely known in the black community,
albeit with a very different conclusion. Wallace Quarterman of Darien,
when asked by an FWP interviewer to verify the history of the "Ibos on St.
Simons who walked into the water," replied, "Ain't you heard about them?
... They rise up in the sky and turn themselves into buzzards and fly right
back to Africa." The fieldworkers then asked: "Had Wallace actually seen
this happen[?]" To which Quarterman replied, "Everybody know about
them. . . . I know plenty what did see them, plenty what was right there in
the field with them . . . after they done fly away."[4]

The distinction between suicide and flight may very well depend on
whether the analysis takes into consideration the spiritual dimension of
the story, the realm of the ancestors. The greatest challenge in summoning
the ancestors within the margins of the white page of academic discourse
is overcoming conventions that inhibit the ability to speak of the spirits of
the dead as being active agents in the story. Steven Feierman poignantly
addresses these questions in "Colonizers, Scholars, and the Creation of

Invisible Histories." Writing about public healers in Africa who are powerful enough to have lived in many different historical moments or who exist
outside of historical time, Feierman writes, "Historians read (or hear) these
narratives and conclude that the stories do not describe 'reality.' . . . Since
the narratives are judged by historians to be inadequate, the public healer's
domain becomes invisible."[5] Stories about public healing, like those told
about flying Africans, involve "particular domains of African life which
the conquerors saw as irrational"; thus, "European [and American] sources
hang like a veil between the historian and the African actors of that period. Even if scholars were able to move beyond this veil, actions within the
domain of public healing would appear irrational in terms of the logic of
academic historical narratives."[6] David Schoenbrun, in his article "Conjuring the Modern in Africa: Durability and Rupture in Histories of Public
Healing between the Great Lakes of East Africa," offers a complicated but
highly promising alternative that allows these "invisible histories" to come
into focus. Moving beyond the written, archival records of the colonizers
(or, in this case, the slave owners), Schoenbrun observes that the "missing
narratives are long regional histories of Africa, flawed and compressed and
dependent upon concepts whose explanatory status must be contested."[7]
Recovering the ancestral role in the flying Africans' stories is part of that
contestation. By situating the story in the much broader temporal horizon
of these "long regional histories of Africa," even if they are incomplete and
involve invisible forces considered "irrational" by some scholars, my hope
is that this analysis will reveal how these immensely powerful stories work
as instruments of healing.

Like the oral narratives about African public healers that Feierman
and Schoenbrun discuss, the role of ancestral spirits in the flying Africans'
stories too often are consigned to "invisible histories" or constructed as fig-
ments of the uneducated black imagination. Ancestors almost always play
a centrally important role in the FWP narratives, often flying in the face of
open skepticism from the FWP fieldworkers recording the oral histories. By
utilizing indigenous interpretive paradigms from both Africa and the sea
islands, this analysis respectfully calls upon the ancestors, while remaining acutely aware that it would be improper to reveal certain ceremonial
wisdom in this public forum. More specifically, this analysis focuses on
four different versions of the flying Africans' story — one historical (told
by the slave dealer who sold the flying Africans), one cosmological (told by
the descendant of a slave who witnessed people flying back to Africa), one

fictional (Toni Morrison's novel *Song of Solomon* told in the fullness of cyclical, ancestral time), and, the last, a lived experience by a keeper of the oral tradition of the sea islands (Cornelia Bailey's account of how she flew back to Africa and what the story means to her almost two hundred years after the original event occurred). The sequence of the works — from slavery times to Jim Crow to civil rights and beyond — may appear to conform to a chronologically organized narrative implying a sense of "progress." And yet, once the ancestors are fully acknowledged and integrated into the story, linear time loses its power to bestow or withhold meaning, and "history" instead moves to the rhythms of the ring shout.

What follows does not, however, constitute a definitive version of the flying Africans' story. The slave communities of coastal Georgia were ethnically mixed such that ancestors from many different cultural backgrounds are present in these stories. Although the term "Ibo" is used throughout, it is important to be aware that people from the Niger delta in the Bight of Biafra were an ethnically diverse group who came to be known, in the shorthand of the slave trade, as "Ebo," "Ibo," or "Igbo."[8] This ethnic diversity was, of course, geometrically complicated in speaking of "African American" communities in coastal Georgia. In an effort to be as culturally specific as possible, within the historical parameters of the slave trade and its aftermath, the present study focuses rather narrowly on one particular manifestation of African culture in North America. More specifically, I look at how the Kongo cosmogram can be read as a map of the Atlantic world, conceived so that its borders are not only transnational, connecting Africa to the African American communities of coastal Georgia, but also transtemporal, connecting the world of the living to the realm of the gods and the world of the ancestors. Much has been left out, and I would strongly encourage other scholars to expand this spiritual cartography by studying carefully how ancestors from the cultures of St. Simons, Sapelo, Ibo, Kongo, and so forth, can be included into a fuller expression of the Atlantic world in relation to coastal Georgia.[9]

INVISIBLE ANCESTORS IN SLAVERY TIMES

It's a sad truth, but it is much harder for people to fly in histories derived from archival sources. As the distinguished historian Jill Lepore wrote in an article titled "Just the Facts, Ma'am: Fake Memoirs, Factual Fictions, and the History of History" in the *New Yorker*, "History, the empirical sort based on archival research and practiced in universities," came to be dominated in the twentieth century by "the cult of the fact." Ever since the founding of the American Historical Association [AHA] in 1894, Lepore notes, "Generations of historians have defined themselves by a set of standards that rest on the distinction between truth and invention."[10] The flying Africans' story may trouble the "cult of fact" that Lepore derides, but it also ultimately contests her "distinction between truth and invention" by forcing us to consider whether this dichotomy applies at all in this instance. To reconstruct the cultural epistemology at work in the flying Africans' story, I draw equally upon archival and oral histories to explicate a sense of communal healing that encompasses both living and ancestral spirits.

Perhaps the closest one can come to locating a description of the flying Africans' story in the historical archives is a letter found in the Pierce Butler Papers at the Pennsylvania Historical Society. Butler owned the Hampton Point Plantation on St. Simons Island and was the absentee master of more than five hundred slaves. In the archive, a letter from a slave trader named William Mein to Butler, dated May 24, 1803, recounts the fate of the Ibo slaves purchased by Butler's neighbor on St. Simons, John Couper, and his partner Thomas Spalding:

> We have had a great many Ibo and Angolas — all of which have readily sold about L.E.100 round of his prime. Spalding and Couper bought a whole bay of Ibos and have suffered much by mismanagement of Mr. Couper's overseer Patterson who poor fellow lost his life. The Negroes rose by being confined in a small vessel. Patterson was frightened and in swimming ashore he with two sailors were drowned. The Negroes took to the Marsh and they have lost at least ten or twelve in recovering them besides being subject to an expense [of] ten dollars a head for salvage.[11]

Mein's letter, without question, provides a valuable historical framework for the flying Africans' story. From an academic perspective, its most significant contribution may well be to fix the event in a definite place and time: St. Simons Island in May 1803. To situate the event in a chronological framework proves fundamentally important to gaining academic recognition that the flying African story does, in fact, have a "historical" basis. While this date anchors our story in time, one must be cautious about the kind of causality often associated with chronology as we strive to reconstruct the cultural epistemologies of William Mein, the Ibo, and the African American slaves who later told the story of the flying Africans. In chronological causality, one usually argues that the former event causes latter.[12] Thus, according to Mein's letter, the Ibo's revolt is provoked by the "mismanagement of Mr. Couper's overseer Patterson" and the fact that the slaves were "confined in a small vessel." This uprising, in turn, "causes" Patterson and the two sailors to leap overboard and to drown while "swimming ashore." While these "facts" are an integral part of the story, another logic of causality — based on the relationship between the Ibo and their ancestors — is also fundamentally important.

Appreciating what the root doctor George Little calls the "magic knowledge" that animates the flying Africans' story requires more careful consideration of the multiple meanings made manifest in the phrase, "the Negroes rose," in Mein's letter. That this phrase is followed immediately by "the Negroes took to the Marsh" reveals how linear chronology structures causality, such that Mein's narrative clearly implies that the story ends with the Ibos' death. The oral histories of the black community, on the other hand, focus most intently on what happens immediately after Mein's conclusion, when the Ibo are transformed into powerful ancestral spirits. The different senses of causality are rooted in distinctly different cultural epistemologies, a distinction that will become clearer as we explore more fully the cyclical time of the Kongo cosmogram and the ring shout.

By focusing on the spiritual dimensions of the story, a starkly different narrative begins to take shape. The relatively limited temporal horizon of Mein's chronological narrative gives way to a sense of time in which the ancestors intervene to disrupt the hierarchical power structure of chattel slavery. The Ibo, for example, almost certainly offered prayers, below the decks of the *York*, to summon the ancestral spirits of great warriors to give them strength for the daring revolt. Bruce McCall's research into the Ohafia Ibo's war dance ceremony, in *Dancing Histories: Heurisitic Ethnography with the Ohafia Igbo*, conveys a sense of this dynamic. "Through aesthetically framed enactments of past events and ancestral heroes, the war dance constitutes a collective experience that extends through time, linking the living to their predecessors. . . . The collective community that participates in the creation of the war dance includes the living *and* the dead."[13] Although the claustrophobic space beneath the deck would not allow for a war dance, McCall's expansive definition of "history" as a temporal continuum that "includes the living *and* the dead" moves us considerably closer to a form of storytelling that might be called "spiritual realism" — a new kind of critical narrative where the phrase "the Negroes rose" becomes charged with the presence of ancestral heroes whose wisdom and strength allowed the Ibo, still enchained, to overthrow their guards. By expanding the historical analysis of the story beyond primary documents, like William Mein's letter to Pierce Butler, to include oral histories that fully engage the ancestors as historical agents allows us to appreciate the unique ways that knowledge works in the black communities of coastal Georgia.

STORYTELLING IN AN AGE OF DISTRUST

Just as William Mein undoubtedly tailored his narrative to suit what he believed Pierce Butler wanted to hear, the black historians recorded in *Drums and Shadows* were similarly affected by the race, ideology, and manners of the people who conducted the interviews. The oral histories that would eventually be published in the form of *Drums and Shadows: Survival Studies among the Georgia Coastal Negroes* (1940) must be read with an awareness that African Americans from very small and insulated black communities throughout coastal Georgia were interviewed by "fieldworkers" who, with good reason in most cases, were perceived by the oral historians as outsiders. To the black community, the stories were not just interesting ethnographic "facts" to be objectively recorded, but cherished vessels that contained valuable information about magical powers, medicine, and the ancestors. This rift between those telling the stories and those given the authority to write them down can be mapped along the fault line of how each side perceives the boundary between the world of the living and the realm of the ancestors.

The Federal Writers' Project (FWP) fell under the auspices of the New Deal's Works Projects Administration that employed over six thousand jobless people. The FWP hired novelists, poets, PhD students, journalists, and freelance writers who interviewed American Indians, former slaves, outlaws and desperados, and people reminiscing about baseball in Chicago in a sprawling effort to recover what was known as "regional history." In the specific case of *Drums and Shadows*, fieldworkers of the Savannah Unit of the FWP conducted 139 interviews with members of local black communities in twenty locations over the course of three years. The Savannah Unit was quite unique in its focus, with Melville Herskovits (a distinguished anthropologist of African culture) and Lorenzo Dow Turner (an African American scholar with expertise in the study of sea islands' culture) on the advisory board.[14] Herskovits directed the fieldworkers to focus their interviews on the search for retentions of African culture in the black communities of coastal Georgia. The fieldworkers, hurriedly trained and influenced by a southern culture deeply immersed in the Jim Crow era of segregation, imposed their own views in ways both subtle and explicit.[15] As Jerrold Hirsch documents in *Portrait of America: A Cultural History of the Federal Writers' Project*: "The Georgia FWP writers who worked on *Drums and Shadows* (1940) did not see their search for African survivals as simply part of the argument about whether African cultures had survived and black Americans had a cultural heritage and identity with visible African roots. Rather, they placed the issue of survivals in the context of an evolutionary theory of culture. . . . Cultural materials from an earlier and inferior stage might survive, but with progress they would disappear."[16] This view of their subjects as remnants from an "earlier and inferior stage" of human history led to frequent, if often unstated, clashes with the black historians being interviewed, who saw their African heritage as a "supreme magic power" to be guarded and, in some cases, hidden from patronizing FWP fieldworkers.[17]

This cultural clash can be clearly seen in an interview with Priscilla McCullough of Darien, Georgia, where the fieldworker's biases become clearly evident. The interviewer, for example, describes Miss Priscilla's home as "a queer haphazard little dwelling place that looked like something out of a fairy tale. . . . Even the bizarre exterior had not prepared us for the appearance of the inside of the house. . . . Jumbled closely around Priscilla was a mass of furniture, each article of which was in turn almost hidden by a burden of clothing, dishes, bottles, pictures, and items too numerous to mention."[18] The description of Miss Priscilla's home as "queer," "like something out of a fairytale," "bizarre," and "hidden by a burden" implicitly warns the reader that this oral history cannot be trusted as "fact." The fieldworker continues:

> The story of flying Africans was a familiar one to the old woman and she said that her mother had often told her the following incident which was *supposed to have* taken place on a plantation during slavery times.
>
> "Duh slabes wuz out in duh field wukin. All ub a sudden dey git tuhgedduh an staht tuh moob roun in a ring. Roun dey go fastuhnfastuh. Den one by one dey riz up an take wing lak a bud. Duh obuhseeuh heah duh noise an he come out an he see duh slabes rise up in duh eah an fly back tuh Africa."

["The slave was out in the field working. All of a sudden they get together and start to move round in a ring. Round they go faster and faster.
Then one by one they rise up and take wing like a bird. The overseer hear
the noise and he come out and he see the slaves rise up in the air and fly
back to Africa"].[19]

The fieldworker's phrase "supposed to have . . ." reveals a degree of condescension and distrust that must be factored into how these oral histories are read. The distrust, of course, cuts both ways. Just as stories can be
considered as gifts or as a kind of inheritance in the black community, so
too can they be transformed into shields or carefully contrived disguises.
Miss Priscilla, for example, does not back away from her claim that slaves
could fly. But she protects the all-important spiritual dimensions of the
ring shout — the ceremony being described here — by representing it from
the perspective of the overseer, who is left behind to wonder where this
magical power comes from. In doing so, Miss Priscilla shields the inner
workings of the ring shout.

Equally problematic, to my mind, is the transliteration of the black
historian's speech into the ungrammatical form considered, in the 1930s, to
be an accurate representation of what was then called the "negro dialect":
"Den one by one dey riz up an take wing lak a bud." In all fairness, prominent African American thinkers such as the linguist Lorenzo Dow Turner
and the poet Sterling Brown approved this editorial decision. Charles
Joyner, in his 1986 introduction to the University of Georgia Press's Brown
Thrasher edition of the text, defends the decision by arguing that "scholars
now recognize that coastal blacks of Georgia and South Carolina developed a creole language that played a crucial role in the shaping of a creole
culture. If the Savannah fieldworkers mistakenly considered their informants to be speaking 'dialect,' . . . they nevertheless rendered that speech
so accurately that scholars can reconstruct the grammatical rules of the
creole language as spoken in coastal Georgia."[20] And while Joyner may be
correct that the transcription retains some value to linguists, my concern is
that a more general audience will hear echoes of Uncle Remus in a phrase
like "den dey do dis," thus making it that much easier to dismiss the oral
histories as lacking philosophical sophistication.[21]

The kind of disrespect shown to Priscilla McCullough from a presumably white FWP fieldworker must surely have led to resentment toward
the white folks who were getting paid to collect black folks' history. It is

admittedly difficult to know when precisely the stories turn from honest assessments of the past to carefully contrived evasion or even veiled jokes. One particularly intriguing example may suffice to demonstrate the possibility that some of these stories were used to dupe unsympathetic FWP interviewers. In this instance, the fieldworker interviews London Grayson from White Bluff about root doctors and indigenous medicine. Prince Sneed, described as "an interesting talker," interrupts the conversation to interject a story that his grandmother told him took place on St. Catherine's Island. The slave driver finds two slaves sitting in the shade and says, "What's this?" The slaves then chant: "'Kum buba yali kum buba tambe, Kum kunka yali kum kunka tambe,' quick like. Then they rise off the ground and fly back to Africa. My gran see that with her own eye."[22] This may very well be another historically important account, one that reveals the African phrase that invokes the power to fly. Certainly many creative writers and literary critics have interpreted the passage this way.[23]

It is worth asking, however, if secrets this important to the preservation of a sacred power in the black community would so readily be handed over to an FWP fieldworker. My suspicions stem from a translation of the African phrase used by Mr. Sneed that can be found in *The Bantu Speaking Heritage of the United States* by Winifred Kellersberger Vass:

> A Luba proverb has been preserved in entirety. It is recorded as follows:
>> Kum buba yali kum buba tambe,
>> Kum kunka yali kum kunka tambe.
> This still-current folk-saying, recognized at once by two men from Zaïre to whom it was shown, reads thus in Tshiluba:
>> Ku mbuba yandi, ku mbuba ntambe,
>> Ky nkonku yandi, ku knonku ntambe.
> A free translation of this might be:
>> He is tricky, so I will win by being tricky, too!
>> He asks clever questions, so I will win by using clever questions too![24]

We will never know for sure, but it seems quite plausible that the proverb's cloaked meaning describes not how to fly but how to defeat interrogators, who consider themselves to be "clever," by means of trickery. One can imagine Prince Sneed and his friends, who knew the true meaning of the phrase, telling this story again and again, sharing a belly laugh about how the FWP fieldworkers excitedly scribbled in their notebooks what they believed to be the secret code words that enabled black folks to fly. One might also imagine locals musing on their front porches about how this phrase would fool scholars for years to come, which indeed it has.

Does this mean that all of the flying Africans' stories in *Drums and Shadows* are unreliable? I don't think so. It does suggest, however, that at least some of the oral histories were meticulously constructed to hide culturally sensitive parts of the story, such as the spiritually empowered role played by ancestors. The question then becomes, how does one learn to see the flying Africans' story from within the circle of the ring shout? Can this be written about in a scholarly narrative without disrespecting the communities' right *not to tell* this part of the story?[25] In the following section, I try to approach the spiritual dimension of the stories by listening respectfully to different versions told by scholars, by oral historians from within the community, and by African American novelists who have imaginatively reconstructed the role of the ancestors.

RESTORING THE SPIRITUAL DIMENSION

To imagine what "reality" looks like from within the circle of the ring shout is a formidable challenge. As Sandra Greene, a historian of African studies, pointed out in an article titled "Whispers and Silences: Explorations in African Oral History," it is possible to approach "those things not said, the stories, the unremembered histories, the statements made only in whispers, to be hidden from officialdom and the public."[26] The way to understand "the silence that accompanies an official discourse about the past," Greene argues, is to begin by recognizing that the whispered histories of black communities traumatized by slavery *do exist* in the form of "alternative narratives that refuse to be forgotten."[27] To read stories "hidden from officialdom" proves difficult and, in some cases, impossible work. My goal here is simply to take an initial step that I hope other Americanists may follow by considering how the spiritual dimensions of the flying Africans' story can be made visible by mapping it onto the interpretive paradigm of the Kongo cosmogram, which originated in West Central Africa and took hold in many black communities throughout the Americas, including the coastal region of Georgia.

I want to be careful, however, of a new set of problems associated with the current academic emphasis on globalization. As Steven Feierman notes in "Colonizers, Scholars, and the Creation of Invisible Histories," the call for contemporary scholarship to "demonstrate the powerful effects of the global flow of styles, discourses, and practices" can result in a proliferation of "so many local histories that, taken in the aggregate, they dissolve into a welter of diverse images."[28] Compounding the difficulty, in this instance, is the fact that the many local cultures of coastal Georgia are composed of dozens of local African cultures.

Rather than detailing all of these cultures, I want to focus on one specific cultural philosophy: the Kongo cosmogram. Although one's initial inclination may be to focus on Ibo culture, it is important to bear in mind here that although the events *happened to* the Ibo, the Ibo did not necessarily *create the story* of the flying Africans.[29] The African American community that was left behind after the Ibo flew away is ultimately responsible for the creation and preservation of the many different versions of the story that have been passed down to the present day. As Robert Farris Thompson demonstrates in *Flash of the Spirit: African and Afro-American Art and Philosophy*, the cosmogram can be found throughout the Americas from Rio de Janeiro to Cuba to the southern states in the United States, and traces of Bantu culture can still be seen today throughout the hemisphere.[30] The cosmogram, significantly, has been found in quilts, beads, and pottery in Georgia, many dating back to slavery times.[31] Prince Sneed's phrase *"Kum buba yali kum buba tambe"* is an example of the Bantu language still being used well into the twentieth century.

The origins of the BaKongo or Kongo culture date back to 1350 C.E. A Bantu-speaking culture, the Kongo kingdom rose to power in 1400 in the lower reaches of the Congo River valley. The Portuguese colonized the region in the late fifteenth century, converting many BaKongo to Christianity. This contact with the European slave trade severely complicated BaKongo identity because, in part, their leaders became wealthy from their involvement in the slave trade, while more than a million of their people were sent off to the New World as slaves.[32] According to Michael Gomez, slaves from West Central Africa, where Bantu-speaking cultures are concentrated, made up 26.1 percent of the Africans imported into British North America and Louisiana.[33] Because the BaKongo were victims of the slave trade from early on in its long and ignoble history and because so many were brought to the Americas, the culture had a demonstrable influence on what would become African American identity.

In his highly respected article "Ntangu-Tandu-Kolo: The Bantu-Kongo Concept of Time," the BaKongo philosopher K. K. Bunseki Fu-Kiau provides a simplified drawing, but a complex understanding of how

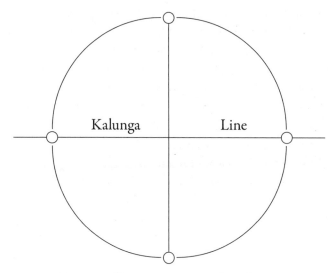

Diagram of Bantu-Kongo cosmological time
(after K. K. Bunseki Fu-Kiau)

the cosmogram functions philosophically, historically, and spiritually.[34] The disks depicted at the cardinal points are known as *dunga* (events) corresponding to the four moments of the sun — sunrise in the east, the zenith in the north, sunset in the west, and midnight in the south — the symbolic meanings of which are allusive. As Robert Farris Thompson explains, "God is imagined at the top, the dead at the bottom, and water in between."[35] The horizontal arm of the cross, known as the *kalunga* line, is associated with the ocean, dividing the world of the living from the world of the dead, which are seen as mirror images of one another. *Kalunga* is also the name of God and thus constitutes an immensely powerful connection between the two events (*dunga*) connected by the horizontal axis — in our case, between coastal Georgia in the west and Africa in the east.

The cosmogram can be used to interpret many different kinds of history. As Bunseki Fu-Kiau explains, the moments of the sun (*dunga*) take on various meanings depending on whether they are read in the context of the "cosmic time" of the universe's creation (*tandu kiayalangana*), the "vital time" of the human life cycle (*Ntangu a zingu/moyo*), the "natural time" of seasonal change (*ntangu yasemuka*), or the "social time" of listening to griots (*Ntangu amvukanana*). Thus, "to speak of time," Bunseki Fu-Kiau notes, "is to talk, discuss, and relate events biologically, ideologically, politically, socially, culturally, philosophically, and economically . . . in the cyclical *dingo-dingo* of time."[36]

In the analysis that follows, William Mein's letter and Miss Priscilla's story are reinterpreted according to the sense of both social time, which Bunseki Fu-Kiau associates with griots or indigenous historians of West Africa, and the vital time of the life/death/spiritual cycle. Before we return to the stories, however, it is worth explaining more fully those parts of the cosmogram that play a particularly important role in the flying Africans' story. The water, for example, represented by the *kalunga* line, takes on an extremely powerful role in the story as points of spiritual transformation. Beyond its association with various points of the sun's journey, Thompson explains that "the whole perspective of the Kongo cosmogram emphasizes that man . . . moves in God's time, not his own."[37] This proves an immense challenge to conventional histories, which are bound by chronological time and do not generally have a working vocabulary to articulate the radical expanse of "God's time," wherein the living, the dead, and the deities are considered integral and dynamic agencies. More positively, this exercise in academic imagination opens a new interpretive horizon for understanding why so many of the black historians recorded in *Drums and Shadows* insist that their ancestors knew how to fly and why these stories have lived on for so long as instruments of healing.

Another crucial point to understand is that the time of the cosmogram does not simply repeat itself, going round and round in a well-worn circle. Instead, Bunseki Fu-Kiau states, the disks symbolizing events (*dunga*) can also be understood as "dams of time" (*n'kama mia ntangu*), which represent moments of profound change or "collisions"; the examples Bunseki Fu-Kiau gives include "births, wars, marriages, funerals." These dams of time (*n'kama*) change the cyclical nature of time: "Only when events (*dunga*) take place can 'things' move and the time line path clear itself. A new cycle of time goes in motion until another collision stops it for a new beginning."[38] By way of mapping William Mein's and Priscilla McCullough's story onto the interpretive framework of the Kongo cosmogram, the analysis focuses on identifying moments that could be said to correspond to events (*dunga*) that bring about the transformations associated with dams of time (*n'kama*). In doing so, we move beyond the linear progression of the chronological narratives to becoming, in Bunseki Fu-Kiau's words, "fully alive" by "living in time and with time," such that the gods and the ancestors appear.[39]

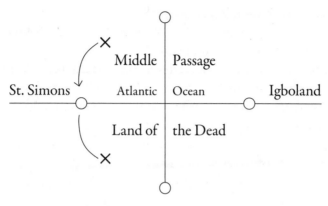

Diagram of William Mein's account of flying Africans'
story on timeline of Bantu-Kongo cosmogram

Given this more complex understanding of how history works within
the circle of the Kongo cosmogram, it becomes possible to revisit the stories
analyzed in the first half of this essay and to gain new insights into events
that, though carefully "hidden from officialdom," nevertheless "refuse to
be forgotten." Here, then, are the text of William Mein's letter and a diagram depicting the narrative in the terms of the Kongo cosmogram.

> We have had a great many Ibo and Angolas — all of which have readily sold
> about L.E.100 round of his prime. Spalding and Couper bought a whole
> bay of Ibos and have suffered much by mismanagement of Mr. Couper's
> overseer Patterson who poor fellow lost his life. The Negroes rose by being
> confined in a small vessel. Patterson was frightened and in swimming
> ashore he with two sailors were drowned. The Negroes took to the Marsh
> and they have lost at least ten or twelve in recovering them besides being
> subject to an expense [of] ten dollars a head for salvage.

Mein's story occupies only a small segment of the cosmogram. The limited temporal scope stems from the narrative's reliance upon chronological
time. More specifically, the account begins when the Ibo enter into the
local slave market — "We have had a great many Ibo . . . all of whom have
readily sold" — and ends when they "took to the Marsh," thus omitting the
spiritual dimensions of the larger story altogether. What I want to do here
is to retell the story in the cosmogram's sense of "being in time and with
time." More specifically, I want to offer a more expansive reading of the

events (*dunga*) that Mein identifies as "the Negroes rose" and "the Negroes took to the Marsh" in addition to two others that remain behind the veil.

Mein, for example, does not discuss the first or second *dunga* that, although not mentioned in the letter, clearly played a role in the events that he describes. The first event, located on the eastern horizon of the cosmogram, can be construed as the capture of "ten or twelve" souls who were transformed from freemen to slaves and thrown into a state of spiritual crisis. This crisis constitutes a dam of time (*n'kama*), wherein the Ibo undergo a transformation of energy that Orlando Patterson calls the "social death" of slavery.[40] The second *dunga*, associated with the highest point in the cosmogram, occurs when the Ibo pray to the ancestors, who empower them to "rise" in revolt, killing the three men manning the *York* and seizing control of the ship. Although Mein himself may very well have believed, on Sunday mornings, that God spoke to Moses in the form of a burning bush, his sense of a spiritual reality almost certainly did not extend to the slaves he bought and sold.

The one *dunga* that Mein does explain quite clearly, located on the western horizon of the cosmogram, is that moment when the Ibo submerge themselves beneath the water or *kalunga* line. Because this event constitutes the endpoint of Mein's linear narration, it fails to acknowledge or explain the moment of rebirth. Instead, Mein's assertion of suicide effectively terminates the threat embodied by the Ibo uprising by creating the impression that the story ends here, with the hierarchical order of slavery restored after the uprising.

To reason within the logic of the Kongo cosmogram, however, reveals a very different interpretation of this moment in the story. As Bunseki Fu-Kiau writes, "The Bantu-Kongo concept of death is very clear. Dying is not the end: '*tufwanga mu soba*' — we die in order to undergo change. Dying is . . . a 'dam of time.' As a dam of time, it [constitutes] . . . a process, it permits life to flow and regenerate (*dikitisa*) its power/energy (*ngolo*)."[41] The moment when the Ibo walk into the water, therefore, does not represent the end of the Ibo's lives but rather a moment of transformation. The *dunga* at the bottom of the cosmogram represents a dam of time that "permits life to flow and regenerate (*dikitisa*) its power/energy (*ngolo*)." In other words, when the Ibo enter the water and cross beneath the *kalunga* line, they do not perish but are transformed into ancestors who continue to take part in the flying Africans' story for centuries to come. The interpretive powers of the Kongo cosmogram thus reveal the spiritual dimension

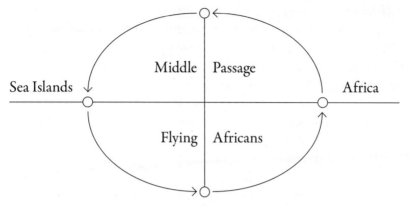

Diagram of the flying Africans' story "fully alive"
(Bunseki Fu-Kiau) with the presence of ancestral spirits

missing from Mein's account of the white owners' financial tragedy. The
flying Africans now appear as a logical extension of the cyclical sequence
of historical events, confirming the ancestors' power to play a dynamic and
curative role in helping to heal the psychological wounds of slavery.

Having seen how William Mein's letter can be reinterpreted in the
fullness of time represented by the Kongo cosmogram, we can now re-
think Priscilla McCullough's story about the relationship between the
ring shout and flying. In doing so, parts of the story carefully calculated to
remain invisible to the condescending FWP fieldworker become available
for analysis:

> The slaves was out in the field working. All of a sudden they get together
> and start to move round in a ring. Round they go faster and faster. Then
> one by one they rise up and take wing and fly like a bird. The overseer hear
> the noise and he come out and he see the slaves rise up the air and fly back
> to Africa.[42]

The counterclockwise motion of the ring shout corresponds to the cyclical
movements of the cosmogram. As Michael Gomez explains, drawing upon
the research of Sterling Stuckey,

> There was a very strong connection, then, between West Central African
> cosmogony and ritual involving circular movement. The latter was an ex-
> pression of the former and was deemed necessary in order to access the

divine. It is Stuckey's view that this visual, physical circumlocution, this expression of the West Central African perspective of the relationship between the living, the dead, and the divine was incorporated into the ring shout, a ceremony in the American South in which participants move counterclockwise in a circle during religious worship.[43]

We are now well beyond the logical confines of William Mein's letter. Miss Priscilla's story, in contrast, begins and ends by recognizing the role of spiritual transformation and ancestral intervention in the flying Africans' story.

Miss Priscilla's "text" must be understood as more than simply a transcription of her words, for the original story to which she refers incorporated the movement of dance and, perhaps, singing intended to summon ancestral spirits. Whereas William Mein's story occupies only a small part of the cosmogram's spiritual map, Miss Priscilla's story moves "in God's time," such that when the slaves "get together and start to move round in a ring" and begin going "round . . . faster and faster," they are able to "rise up and take wing and fly like a bird." The multiple revolutions that occur in the ring shout can be said to symbolize the cosmogram's spiraling movement through time. As Wyatt MacGaffey writes in *Religion and Society in Central Africa: the BaKongo of Lower Zaire*, "The elaborated version of the Kongo cosmology . . . provides for . . . successive cycles in time, generating a spiral rather than a simple repetition."[44] Miss Priscilla's story, seen from this perspective, should be understood not as a lone instance of flying but, instead, as just one cycle of *history* that spirals forward into the future and backward to the deepest antiquity. Here, then, the full spectrum of what "history" means to the black communities of coastal Georgia begins to come into focus. The worlds of the living, the divine, and the dead circumambulate until they become inextricably intertwined. A telling example of what David Schoenbrun calls the "missing narratives" of the "long regional histories of Africa," the flying Africans' story provides a powerful sense of self-worth to slaves and their ancestors in the New World. It is a reflection, not precise but nonetheless powerful, of Africa; as Thomson notes, "Bakongo themselves are aware that their cosmograms reflect an ancient source, and they say that 'every sign has its history.'"[45] Tracing the origins of this sign back to an "ancient source" provided a profound sense of healing that has its roots in what Bunseki Fu-Kiau calls "God's time."

This, then, is why the story has been told again and again over the last two hundred years. A kind of literary enactment of the ring shout, the story of the flying Africans' power emanates from moving "round in a ring" until "one by one [listeners] rise up and take wing and fly like a bird." Despite the fact that the details of the story constantly change, as do the wounds that the stories aim to heal, it is the act of recalling the ancestors in the name of empowering future generations that constitutes the curative powers of the story.

FLYING AS HEALING

Perhaps the most powerful retelling of the flying Africans' story for our own generation is Toni Morrison's novel *Song of Solomon* (1977), which won the National Book Critics Circle Award in 1978.[46] Because the novel explicitly addresses the crossed perceptions of suicide vs. flight, *Song of Solomon* provides a fitting conclusion to the contestation between William Mein's and Miss Priscilla's versions of the flying Africans' story. The novel begins and ends with images of suicide/flight inextricably intertwined, although this dynamic means something entirely different in the opening pages than it does at the novel's conclusion. Only after the protagonist (and the reader) learns to recognize the invisible ancestors and the cyclical history of the ring shout are the secrets of flight finally revealed and a powerful sense of communal healing takes place.

Song of Solomon begins with a failed flight that results in suicide. In the first chapter, a character named Mr. Smith, standing atop a building overlooking Lake Superior and wearing blue silk wings that he believes will enable him to "fly away," leaps to his death. At almost the same moment, the novel's main character, Macon "Milkman" Dead III, is born in the hospital across the street. As Mr. Smith's blue silk wings fail him, Milkman's aunt Pilate sings a blues fragment: "O Sugarman done fly away / Sugarman done gone / Sugarman cut across the sky / Sugarman gone home."[47] Pilate, as we will see in a moment, possesses a powerful link to the ancestors, and the blues fragment provides a crucial reference to the story of the flying Africans, although at the outset of the novel its significance has been forgotten by the black community, too far removed from the South with its direct connection, via the *kalunga* line, to the ancestral forces of Africa.

Morrison symbolically associates Mr. Smith's failed attempt to fly with a psychic and historical wound that cripples Milkman for much of the novel. "Mr. Smith's blue silk wings must have left their mark," Morrison writes, "because when the little boy discovered, at four, the same thing Mr. Smith had learned earlier — that only birds and airplanes could fly — he lost all interest in himself."[48] The historical origin of Macon "Milkman" Dead III's wound can be traced back well before Mr. Smith's suicide. Born "Dead," Milkman's familial name constitutes an unhealed wound that derives from emancipation's unfulfilled promise. "When freedom came," Morrison writes of Milkman's grandfather's symbolic mis-naming, "all the colored people in the state had to register with the Freedmen's Bureau." Milkman's grandfather "went to sign up, but the man behind the desk was drunk. He asked Papa where he was born. Papa said Macon. Then he asked him who owned him, Papa said, 'I'm free.' Well, the Yankee wrote it all down, but in the wrong spaces. . . . In the space for his name the fool wrote, 'Dead' comma 'Macon.'"[49] Thus, at the historical moment (*dunga*) that should constitute the slave's rebirth into the freedom of emancipation, the family is struck "Dead."

Morrison here poignantly attacks the myth of chronological "progress." This cultural myth, propagated by the dominant white society, maintains that America overcomes its past atrocities, (e.g., slavery), by constantly and consistently improving itself, (e.g., emancipation), in its quest for equality. This myth has a dark underside, having also been used by the dominant society to measure the failure of blacks to live up to the implicit promise of the American Dream. Like the FWP fieldworkers' assumptions about the "evolutionary theory of culture" that fixes African American culture as an "earlier and inferior stage" of human civilization, the imposition of a linear time line of "progress" can be read as the infliction of a historical wound that Morrison sets out to heal in the course of the novel. To interpret flying as suicide, Morrison implies, causes lasting damage to the black community's sense of self-esteem — symbolized here by Milkman losing "all interest in himself" when he discovers that he cannot fly.

Submersed in the depths of the Jim Crow era at the novel's outset, the ancestral powers inherent in the flying Africans' story are kept alive by the character of Pilate, Milkman's aunt. If we were to plot her character on the interpretive paradigm of the Kongo cosmogram, Pilate would be situated at the center of the cross. Described as not having a navel, "borned herself," Pilate lives beyond the limits of chronological time.[50] She is in constant contact, for example, with the spirit of her dead father, who repeatedly tells her to "sing." And while it will eventually turn out that "Sing" is the name of her mother — an example of the oral tradition's vagaries — Pilate's misinterpretation of the word nevertheless proves highly significant, for it is this contact with her dead ancestors that leads her to sing repeatedly the blues fragment about a person named "Sugarman" who "done fly away . . . home," which will eventually be the key to Milkman's interpretive quest to recover his ancestral power of flight passed down from the "flying Africans."

With the context of this essay's concerns, the conclusion of *Song of Solomon* can be read as a meaningful example of the curative powers of the flying Africans' story when imbued with the spirits of the ancestors. Although it will take Milkman the entire course of the novel to understand what his grandfather's spirit has been communicating to Pilate, in the closing pages of the novel he makes the redemptive connection. Tellingly, Milkman finds the interpretive secret that unlocks the story's secret powers at the center of a circle, reminiscent of the ring shout described in Miss Priscilla's story. Having finally reached the South, Milkman watches children dancing in a ring and singing verses that "he had heard off and on his whole life. That old blues song Pilate sang all the time." The spiritual implications of the old blues verse finally become clear when Milkman hears the children singing:

> Solomon done fly, Solomon done gone
> Solomon cut across the sky, Solomon gone home.[51]

Realizing, at last, the spiritual connection between his great-grandfather and the Solomon of Pilate's song, Milkman learns that he is descended from "those Africans they brought over here as slaves [who] could fly."[52]

The story, encoded in a blues fragment and dance, heals the psychological wounds, encoded in the name "Dead," that have afflicted his family since slavery times. As he comes into contact with ancestral forces, Milkman gains the power of insight associated with standing at the center of the cosmogram and is able to transform the scar of suicide into the power of flight. He returns north to bring Pilate back to her ancestral home, telling her "My great-granddaddy could fly! Goddamn! . . . Lifted his beautiful black ass up in the sky and flew on home . . . to Africa."[53] In the novel's closing pages, Morrison revisits the theme of suicide/flight, although inverting the dynamic such that when Milkman leaps into a gulch it does not constitute an act of suicide, but the fulfillment of a prophetic promise — "now he knew what [his ancestors] knew: If you surrendered to the air, you could *ride* it."[54]

Here the healing powers associated with "living in God's time" or in direct connection with the ancestors make themselves manifest. Bunseki

Fu-Kiau explains what it means to stand at the center of the cosmogram: "To stand upon this sign, meant that a person was fully capable of governing people, that [they] knew the nature of the world, that [they] mastered the meaning of life and death" and thus lived with the insight of a seer able to perceive both worlds, both halves of the cosmogram.[55] Robert Farris Thompson writes of those authorized to stand at the center of the cosmogram, they "were transformed during initiation, from recovered patients to practicing [healers] and became members of the healing society of Lemba."[56] Thus, in the novel's closing pages, Milkman finally attains the insight associated with standing at the center of the cosmogram — able to understand what his grandfather's ghost had been trying to tell Pilate, that the realms of the living and the ancestors were but two halves of the cosmogram finally brought together by his own knowledge as a healer. In the novel, this healing manifests itself both physically and spiritually. The limp that has plagued Milkman throughout his life is gone. The rage that he feels toward the dominant society, but directs at the women in his own family, finally dissipates such that he comes to appreciate the lessons his aunt Pilate has been trying to teach him by passing down fragments of the oral tradition.

In a larger sense, Morrison's novel helps us to appreciate the cultural legacy of the oral tradition of the black coastal communities of Georgia. The flying African stories teach us to value the remarkable connection that the Gullah and Geechee cultures maintain with western Africa, not just in terms of anthropological evidence but in a deeply spiritual sense. This story has been told again and again for more than two hundred years, to American schoolchildren of all races, because of its healing properties as we all struggle to come to terms with the national psychological scars inflicted by slavery. Rather than seeing African American communities as hapless victims of a horrific moment in American history cloaked by a collective sense of shame, these stories teach us to see the Ibo slaves and their African American descendants as empowered. That power may, finally, be understandable to a wider audience as fiction, but in the end, it does not really matter. The stories live on, calling forth the ancestors, whose powers to heal a nation's wounds cannot be doubted.

CONCLUSION

The flying Africans' story lives on, ever evolving, with its spiritual and healing powers fully intact. Cornelia Bailey's memoir, *God, Dr. Buzzard, and the Bolito Man* (2000), is perhaps the most recent version, although certainly not the last, updated to incorporate modern technology while retaining a deep spiritual link to the ancestral past. Cornelia Bailey, a distinguished keeper of Sapelo Island's oral history, writes in her chapter, "I Flew Back":

> You may not know this but the Africans who came to the Sea Islands believed in flying. They actually *believed* in it. . . . We had song after song about flying, songs like "I'll Fly Away" and the one we sang at church that had the verse, "When I get to Heaven, gonna put on my wings, gonna fly all over God's Heaven." . . . So, I did something my African ancestors on Sapelo dreamed of doing. . . . I *flew* to Africa. I didn't fly like a bird. . . . I flew on the wings of man, but I flew just the same.[57]

Like the flying Africans' story told in *Drums and Shadows* by her uncle Shed Hall — "The overseer he sure thought he catch them when they get to the river. But before he could get to them, they rise up in the air and fly away. They fly right back to Africa" — Cornelia Bailey's personal account of returning to Sierra Leone is a story of redemption and healing.[58]

Immediately upon setting foot on the continent, Bailey feels the pull of the ancestors. On Bunce Island, where slaves were incarcerated before being shipped to North America, Bailey realizes, "I was walking on the ground where many of my people had come from and everywhere I turned, I could feel their presence. It was like a part of them had stayed on that island always. . . . They were restless spirits."[59] Bailey writes of the powerful attachment she felt to this land that she had never before visited, keenly felt at a ring shout performance in Sierra Leone:

> The ring shout is fading away in Africa too but it is still done in a few of the smaller villages on special occasions. Some men and women from one of the outlying villages performed a ring shout dance for us one night. . . . I was watching an ancient part of Africa come alive before my eyes and it gave me a little chill to realize that I had grown up seeing Papa performing a dance that was centuries old.[60]

Here the ancient spiritual connection to Africa, described by Bantu speaking slave descendants as the *kalunga* line, becomes powerfully evident. Just as K. K. Bunseki Fu-Kiau describes those authorized "to stand upon this sign" as achieving a philosophical balance that allows them to see the world of the living and the world of the dead as fully integrated, Bailey realizes a sense of balance between Africa in the east and Sapelo in the west, between the contemporary world in which she lives and the realm of her ancestors.

"They never for a minute let go of their dream of flying back to Africa," Bailey writes. "But what would have seemed odd to them, *very* odd, was that I was on my way back to the New World. I had two homes now, Africa and Sapelo. . . . I knew exactly who I was for the first time."[61]

Here again, the enduring power of the flying Africans' story becomes powerfully evident. Although difficult to fix in relation to historical "facts," the story's constant evolution transcends discrepancies between differing versions, revealing the curative powers of ancestral spirits who are not separated by the distance of chronological time or geographic space but can be summoned by the telling of a story or the dancing of the ring shout. What we learn from listening closely and respectfully to these ancestors is the inherent power of the black community of coastal Georgia to endure a series of historical hardships and to empower present and future generations. It is, as the elders said, a "magical knowledge" that cannot be simply attributed to one local culture either in Africa or in the sea islands. For the hundreds of thousands of high school and college students who have read Toni Morrison's or Cornelia Bailey's modern versions of the story, it offers a profound connection to part of America's past that remained for too long an "invisible history." Rather than thinking of the flying Africans' story in terms of the narrow "distinction between truth and fiction," perhaps what we have discovered in the course of this interpretive journey is that the story can best be understood as a gift from the ancestors, a story to heal old wounds and to keep alive memories that refuse to be forgotten. We thank the elders and ancestors for their generosity in bestowing such a powerful gift upon us.

NOTES

For Jibreel, who has always believed.

Special thanks to Larry Aitken, *miigwech ni we'eh*, for helping me to understand the role that ancestors play in our daily lives. I would also like to thank David Schoenbrun, who taught me how to translate magic into academic prose; John Inscoe, who taught me to love the secret histories of the South; Eve Troutt Powell, Phil Morgan, the audience at the Atlantic World Symposium, and the conference's sponsors. I hope that I have done justice to this magically empowered place. The spirit is theirs; the mistakes are my own.

1. William Mein, Pierce Butler Papers, May 24, 1803, Historical Society of Pennsylvania; Roswell King to Pierce Butler, May 13, 1803, Butler Family Papers, Historical Society of Pennsylvania. See also Malcolm Bell Jr., *Major Butler's Legacy: Five*

Generations of a Slaveholding Family (Athens: University of Georgia Press, 1987); *The Legacy of Ibo Landing: Gullah Roots of African American Culture*, ed. Marquetta L. Goodwine and the Clarity Press Gullah Project (Atlanta: Clarity Press, 1998).

2. Georgia Writers' Project, *Drums and Shadows: Survival Studies among the Georgia Coastal Negroes* (1940; Athens: University of Georgia Press, 1986), 20. I have taken the liberty to translate the broken English of the *Drums and Shadows* text back into a more standard spelling, without changing the grammatical constructions, for reasons that will be explained below.

3. Ibid., 58.

4. Ibid., 150–51.

5. Steven Feierman, "Colonizers, Scholars, and the Creation of Invisible Histories," in *Beyond the Cultural Turn: New Directions in the Study of Society and Culture*, ed. Victoria E. Bonnell and Lynn Hunt (Berkeley: University of California Press, 1999), 190.

6. Ibid., 186.

7. David L. Schoenbrun, "Conjuring the Modern in Africa: Durability and Rupture in Histories of Public Healing between the Great Lakes of East Africa," *American Historical Review* 111, no. 5 (December 2006): 1405.

8. For more on the Ibo, see E. J. Afigbo, *Ropes of Sand: Studies in Igbo History and Culture* (Ibadan: Ibadan University Press in association with Oxford University Press, 1981); Elizabeth Isichei, *Ibo People and the Europeans: The Genesis of a Relationship — to 1906* (London: Faber and Faber, 1973); Emmanuel M. P. Eden, *Towards an Igbo Metaphysics* (Chicago: Loyola University Press, 1985).

9. For a fuller analysis of how the flying African story could be explained from an Ibo point of view, see Michael A. Gomez, *Exchanging Our Country Marks: The Transformation of African Identities in the Colonial and Antebellum South* (Chapel Hill: University of North Carolina Press, 1998), chap. 4; for the BaKongo view, see below in this essay; for a Fulbe view see Nada Elia, "'Kum Buba Yali Kum Buba Tambe, Ameen, Ameen, Ameen': Did Some of the Flying Africans Bow to Allah?" *Callaloo* 26, no. 1 (2003): 182–202.

10. Jill Lepore, "Just the Facts, Ma'am: Fake Memoirs, Factual Fictions, and the History of History," *New Yorker*, March 24, 2008, 79, 80. For more on the relationship between history and fiction, see Wai-Chee Dimock, *Empire for Liberty: Melville and the Poetics of Individualism* (Princeton, N.J.: Princeton University Press, 1989); Simon Schama, *Dead Certainties: Unwarranted Speculations* (New York: Knopf, 1991); Gordon S. Wood, *The Purpose of the Past: Reflections on the Uses of History* (New York: Penguin Press, 2008).

11. Letter from William Mein to Pierce Butler, May 24, 1803, Pierce Butler Papers, Historical Society of Pennsylvania, Philadelphia.

12. For a fuller discussion of the ideological implications of chronological time, see Johannes Fabian, *Time and the Other: How Anthropology Makes its Object* (New York: Columbia University Press, 2002). For a more specific account on how circular time works in an African context see: Jerome S. Handler, "Life Histories of

Enslaved Africans in Barbados," *Slavery and Abolition* 19, no. 1 (1998): 129–44; Vincent Brown, *The Reaper's Garden: Death and Power in the World of Atlantic Slavery* (Cambridge, Mass.: Harvard University Press, 2008).

13. John C. McCall, *Dancing Histories: Heuristic Ethnography with the Ohafia Igbo* (Ann Arbor: University of Michigan Press, 2000), 76.

14. Melville Herskovits, *The Myth of a Negro Past* (New York: Harper and Brothers, 1941); Lorenzo Dow Turner, *Africanisms in the Gullah Dialect* (New York: Arno Press, 1969).

15. Charles Joyner, "Introduction to the Brown Thrasher Edition," in *Drums and Shadows*.

16. Jerrold Hirsch, *Portrait of America: A Cultural History of the Federal Writers' Project* (Chapel Hill: University of North Carolina Press, 2003), 126.

17. Georgia Writers' Project, *Drums and Shadows*, 7.

18. Ibid., 153.

19. Ibid., 154, emphasis added. To hear an actual FWP interview with Wallace Quarterman, go to the Smithsonian Institution's "American Memory" site at http://memory.loc.gov/master/afc/afc9999001/25665a.wav.

20. Joyner, "Introduction," *Drums and Shadows*, xxiv.

21. For connection between Uncle Remus and sea islands' Creole, see Allan B. Austin, *African Muslims in Antebellum America: Transatlantic Stories and Spiritual Struggles* (New York: Routledge, 1997), 112.

22. Georgia Writers' Project, *Drums and Shadows*, 79.

23. The most notable interpretations come from Toni Morrison, *Song of Solomon* (New York: Plume, 1977), and Virginia Hamilton, *The People Could Fly: American Black Folktales* (New York: Knopf, 1985); see also Wendy W. Walters, " 'One of Dese Mornings, Bright and Fair, Take My Wings and Cleave De Air': The legend of the Flying Africans and Diasporic Consciousness," *MELUS* 22, no. 3 (Fall 1997): 3–29.

24. Winifred Kellersberger Vass, *The Bantu Speaking Heritage of the United States* (Los Angeles: Center for Afro-American Studies, University of California, 1979), 70–71. I am indebted to my former student Khalil Johnson, who first discovered this connection. The assertion that it is a deception at the expense of the FWP worker is my own.

25. My sentiment that the oral historian possesses sovereignty over the story comes largely from my work with the Ojibwe Indian Nation in northern Minnesota, especially the guidance of Larry P. Aitken; the theoretical notion of "intellectual sovereignty" comes from Robert Allen Warrior, *Tribal Secrets: Recovering American Indian Intellectual Traditions* (Minneapolis: University of Minnesota Press, 1995). I also want to thank Robert Clinton from the Sandra Day O'Connor College of Law at Arizona State University, who patiently explained what it would take to legally claim sovereignty over stories. There is a great deal more, it seems to me, that could be done with a comparative study between American Indian and African American storytelling in regard to issues of cultural sovereignty.

26. Sandra E. Greene, "Whispers and Silences: Explorations in African Oral History," *Africa Today* 50, no. 2 (Fall/Winter 2003): 41.

27. Ibid., 43.

28. Feierman, "Colonizers," 182.

29. I am indebted to David L. Schoenbrun for helping me to understand this point.

30. Robert Farris Thompson, *Flash of the Spirit: African and Afro-American Art and Philosophy* (New York: Vintage, 1984), 108–13. For more on the Kongo cosmogram's use in the sea islands, see Betty M. Kuyk, *African Voices in the African American Heritage* (Bloomington: University of Indiana Press, 2003); Kenneth L. Brown, "Interwoven Traditions: Archaeology of the Conjurer's Cabin and the African American Cemetery at Jordan and Frogmore Manor Plantations," http://www.nps.gov/history/crdi/conferences/AFR_99-114_KBrown.pdf.

31. See Maude Southwell Wahlman, *Signs and Symbols: African Images in African American Quilts* (Atlanta: Tinwood, 2001); Daniel L. Fountain, "Historians and Historical Archaeology: Slave Sites," *Journal of Interdisciplinary History* 26, no. 1 (Summer 1995): 67–77; Kenneth L. Brown, "Interwoven Traditions: Archaeology of the Conjurer's Cabins and the African American Cemetery at the Jordan and Frogmore Manor Plantations," http://www.nps.gov/history/crdi/conferences/AFR_99-114_KBrown.pdf. What appears to be a mention of the cross at the center of the cosmogram can also be found in *Drums and Shadows*, where Ben Washington remembers, "If you ever see a cross mark in the road, you never walk over it. That's real magic. . . . The cross is a magic sign and have to do with the spirits" (*Drums and Shadows*, 135).

32. For more on BaKongo culture, see Philip D. Curtin, *Atlantic Slave Trade, A Census* (Madison: University of Wisconsin Press, 1969); Wyatt MacGaffey, *Religion and Society in Central Africa: The BaKongo of Lower Zaire* (Chicago: University of Chicago Press, 1986); Anne Hilton, *The Kingdom of Kongo* (New York: Oxford University Press, 1985); Wyatt MacGaffey, ed., *Art and Healing of the Bakongo, Commented by Themselves* (Bloomington: Indiana University Press, 1991); Ronald K. Engard, "Dance and Power in Bafut (Cameroon)," in *Creativity of Power: Cosmology and Action in African Societies*, ed. W. Arens and Ivan Karp (Washington, D.C.: Smithsonian Institution Press, 1989); Gomez, *Exchanging Our Country Marks*.

33. Gomez, *Exchanging Our Country Marks*, 29.

34. The drawings of the cosmogram in this essay were all done by Timothy B. Powell, based on those by K. K. Bunseki Fu-Kiau, "Ntangu-Tandu-Kolo: The Bantu-Kongo Concept of Time," *Time in the Black Experience*, ed. Joseph K. Adjaye (Westport, Conn.: Greenwood Press, 1994).

35. Thompson, *Flash of the Spirit*, 109.

36. Bunseki Fu-Kiau, "Ntangu-Tandu-Kolo," 30.

37. Robert Farris Thompson, "Tendwa kia Nza-n'kongo: The Kongo Cosmogram ('The Four Moments of the Sun,')" in *The Four Moments of the Sun: Kongo Art in Two Worlds*, ed. Robert Farris Thompson and Joseph Cornet (Washington, D.C.: National Gallery of Art, 1981), 44.

38. Bunseki Fu-Kiau, "Ntangu-Tandu-Kolo," 30.

39. Ibid., 25, 30.

40. Orlando Patterson, *Slavery and Social Death: A Comparative Study* (Cambridge, Mass.: Harvard University Press, 1982).

41. Bunseki Fu-Kiau, "Ntangu-Tandu-Kolo," 27.

42. Georgia Writers' Project, *Drums and Shadows*, 154.

43. Gomez, *Exchanging Our Country Marks*, 149.

44. MacGaffey, *Religion and Society*, 96.

45. Thompson, "Tendwa kia Nza-n'kongo," 45. See also Robert Farris Thompson, *Face of the Gods: Art and Altars of Africa and the African Americas* (New York: Museum for African Art, 1993), 48, where Thompson writes, "Kongo cosmograms, documented in seventeenth-century collections of Kongo art now in Copenhagen and Rome, go back for centuries, very likely to the very rise of Kongo civilization."

46. For more on the relationship between *Song of Solomon* and the flying Africans' story, see Elia, *"Kum Buba Yali"*; Walters, "One of Dese Mornings"; Farah Jasmine Griffin, *"Who Set You Flowin'?": The African-American Migration Narrative* (New York: Oxford University Press, 1995); *New Essays on Song of Solomon*, ed. Valerie Smith (New York: Cambridge University Press, 1995); *Toni Morrison's Song of Solomon: A Case Book* (New York: Oxford University Press, 2003). The story of the flying Africans has also been used as a basis for, among others, the following literary works: Julie Dash, *Daughters of the Dust* (New York: Dutton, 1997), and her film of the same name; Robert Hayden, "O Daedalus, Fly Away Home," *Collected Poems*, ed. Frederick Glaysher (New York: Liveright, 1996); Paule Marshall, *Praisesong for the Widow* (New York: Dutton, 1984).

47. Toni Morrison, *Song of Solomon* (New York: Plume, 1978), 6.

48. Ibid., 9.

49. Ibid., 53.

50. Ibid., 244.

51. Ibid., 303.

52. Ibid., 322.

53. Ibid., 328.

54. Ibid., 337.

55. Quoted in Thompson, *Flash of the Spirit*, 110.

56. Ibid., 107. For more on the healing powers of the Lemba society, see John M. Janzen, *Lemba, 1650–1930: A Drum of Affliction in Africa and the New World* (New York: Garland, 1982).

57. Cornelia Bailey with Christena Bledsoe, *God, Dr. Buzzard, and the Bolito Man: A Saltwater Geechee Talks about Life on Sapelo Island* (New York: Doubleday, 2000), 319.

58. Georgia Writers' Project, *Drums and Shadows*, 168.

59. Bailey, *God, Dr. Buzzard*, 316.

60. Ibid., 304.

61. Ibid., 319.

Emory S. Campbell

A Sense of Self and Place

Unmasking My Gullah Cultural Heritage

S O MUCH has been discussed about the unique history of the Gullah culture over recent years that I thought I would use this opportunity to share my story of how I came to have a sense of place and self as a Gullah-Geechee person. My sense of self steadily emerged as outsiders and we Gullahs began to study the mysteries of the Gullah-Geechee culture through research and documentary. Until most recently, Gullah-Geechee people had always been a mystery to outsiders. A composite of this mystery portrayed a close-knit extended family kinship and African-rooted spiritual life anchored in the praise house, as well as African-influenced craft-making and food-gathering practices. Even more striking, our tongues convey a totally unfamiliar language. After encountering outsiders and witnessing their reactions to the mystery, we Gullah-Geechee people wondered about the legitimacy of our own culture.

Evidence of African knowledge, customs, and traditions that have always been exhibited by us Gullahs were either ignored or misunderstood, or they assumed negative connotations. People from the urban regions often described Gullah people as being from the backwoods and the more common term, "country." The origin of most Gullah practices was unknown to us as well as to the wider population. For example, our traditional meals have almost always contained rice. The popular stew of okra, shrimp, and tomatoes is traditionally served over rice. Ironically, the same stew over grits, which we Gullahs considered to be a breakfast of leftovers, is a mainstream delicacy today. Peas and rice — better known as hoppin' John — is a legendary Gullah New Year's Day dish. And our traditional spiritual life includes seeking — a semblance of the "the rights of passage" where solitary deliberation in a secret place in the forest and interpretation of dreams are prerequisites to church membership. In fact, membership in the church depended entirely on interpretations of one's dream. According to Margaret Creel, who expounded on Gullah-Geechee religious practices in her book *A Peculiar People*, the Gullah seeking practice could be linked to a similar religious ritual practiced by the Mende, Timbe, Gola, and other West African Windward coast people that require withdrawal from organized society.[1]

In his book *Souls of Black Folk*, W. E. B. DuBois discusses the first time the Yankees met the enslaved Africans in the sea islands at the beginning of the Civil War in 1861. From the perspective of the northern troops, he said, these Africans were uncouth in appearance and their speech was funny, but they sang with a voice that stirred the soul of mankind. DuBois lamented that those songs of sea island Africans were not recognized or appreciated by early outside visitors, but Gullah people continued to peacefully, albeit esoterically, sing unique spirituals at praise houses until recent years.[2]

Laura Towne, founder of Penn School on St. Helena Island, arriving in 1862 described the praise-house shout that had been developed from African dance tradition as "the most savage thing I've ever seen."[3]

Buddy Sullivan in *Early Days on the Georgia Tidewater*, Judith Carney in *Black Rice*, and Peter Wood in *Black Majority* concluded from their research that rice plantations in South Carolina and Georgia were developed and managed with contributions of enslaved West Africans who may have used knowledge gained from their ancestral Rice Coast.[4]

Conceivably, the most outstanding conundrum for outsiders is still the speech of Gullah people. For generations, linguists have been trying to solve the mystery of the Gullah language with eventual success after acceptance of the fact that its syntax could largely be attributable to African languages and that its vocabulary includes African words.

Lorenzo D. Turner, in 1932 a young black University of Chicago linguist, was attracted to the South Carolina and Georgia sea islands by the strange speech he heard among students at South Carolina State College during a summer teaching stint there. He subsequently interviewed more than a dozen Gullah persons, including one of my uncles. In his book *Africanisms in the Gullah Dialect*, Professor Turner listed hundreds of Gullah terms and first names that he concluded had West African origin. The Gullah language is considered by some linguists to be an English Creole. Indeed, our language contains mostly English words and the pronunciations and intonations are unique, but we also mix in words of African origin such as *biddie* (chicken), *loni* (to stand), and *tote* (to carry).[5]

But at least one scholar who studied the coastal Gullah people during the same period, including Guy Johnson of the University of North Carolina, unlike Turner concluded that there was no evidence of African connections in the Gullah-Geechee culture or language. Thus, the rife of renewed investigation of the mystery of our language origin is relatively recent.[6]

Unaware of the constant investigations of the mysteries of the Gullah-Geechee culture, I grew up like most Gullah-Geechee people with a sense of self and place. I take the liberty here to repeat a famous line of recent times: "This is personal for me," as Democratic presidential candidate Hillary Clinton stated while on the campaign trail. It is easily discernable for one to find that my story is similar to others of Gullah-Geechee ancestry along the South Carolina and Georgia Gullah-Geechee corridor. Here I shall briefly describe how my sense of self and place was formed in my early life.

Not even knowing that Wallace Campbell — my great-great-grandfather, an enslaved African — had ended up on Hilton Head Island from Edisto Island some time around 1820, according to one source, I grew up in the 1940s and 1950s as a fifth-generation Gullah-Geechee person believing that being a Campbell on Hilton Head Island meant the following: I assumed that our tall, lean frame descended from Wallace's genes. We Campbells of Hilton Head Island are tall and most are lean with a distinctive facial feature punctuated by the eyes and nose. So as I grew up observing my father and uncles' extraordinary heights, I assumed that I would too be tall. (My father was six-feet-two and my mother was five-feet-eight.) Adults in my Spanish Wells neighborhood would often tell me how much I looked like my paternal grandfather Solomon, who passed away before I was born.

I grew up thinking that I would be learned, courageous (most people I knew were seafaring), and spiritual (believing in one God, with Dr. Buzzard as a backup). It meant that I would develop a natural taste and affinity for rice dishes; rice was a part of every dinner meal (cooked with the exact amount of water for a dry fluffy consistency), sometime eaten with okra, 'mados (tomatoes), and prawns. I would crave sweet 'tatas (potatoes), watermelon, sugar cane, and benne, among other foods of ancient West African origin. We easily grew these crops. But I also sensed that scholarship would be important because we were encouraged early to learn lessons that would prepare us for the wider world.

It meant that I knew my nineteenth cousin because we shared the same neighborhood of family land. I often use the term "nineteenth cousin" to illustrate how important kinship has been in Gullah traditions of sharing resources. Perhaps the most valuable of these resources is land. I was told that my great-grandfather Phillip was one of the most serious land buyers on Hilton Head Island in the period after Reconstruction. At one point he had accumulated over one hundred acres, but he subsequently sold parcels to other Gullah families. We (my father's and his siblings' family) lived and planted crops on the fifty- to sixty-acre parcel of our ancestral land. It was considered family land, and all family members used it cooperatively under the leadership of my father, the eldest family member.

And I grew up knowing that I would speak two languages — that of my maternal grandmother "Needie," my first babysitter, who spoke only in the Gullah-Geechee language and had retained her basket name as opposed to her legal name Rosa. Her speech included the words oona (you), cooter (turtle), fo-day clean (dawn), buckra (white man), biddie (chicken), loni (to stand alone), fus one (firstborn), Fib (Friday), Mos a man (almost a man, short in stature). And she would speak in Gullah proverbs: Whenever she thought we were trying to do too many things at the same time and doing none of them well, she'd say, "Dog got four foot but can't walk but one road." And she would tell us about ghosts that appeared, particularly near the cemetery. And she would tell of hags, an elderly person (woman), who would leave her body and "ride" you at night while you tried to sleep. This folktale was among the most popular ones repeated among Gullah children for entertainment before television became available.

Then there was the language of my paternal grandmother, Mama Julia, who took pride in speaking only the "Queen's English," did not have a basket name, and called everyone by their legal name. She spoke in terms like "make haste" (hurry up), "fortnight," and "day break" instead of day clean. And she passionately played the piano that sat in the front hallway of her house. Mama Julia struck me as being an avid reader. Her face was very often partially enveloped in what I later learned were month-old issues of the *Beaufort Gazette* newspaper. She and her husband, my paternal grandfather Solomon, had been early post-Reconstruction teachers on Hilton Head Island.

We walked everywhere we went, and as we grew old enough, we rode our marsh tackeys (our breed of horse) through the landscape of age-old, moss-draped live oaks, palmettos, cedars, and pines among other subtropical, coastal plants. This beautifully mixed flora harbored an abundantly mixed fauna of deer, wild turkey, rabbits, raccoons, otter, and a large variety of birds. The earth was real — real dirt and dust on which our bare feet trudged through the warm, wet lumps in spring and piping hot grains in summer.

In my neighborhood, like all the others on the island, there was an ever-present schoolhouse, a standout frame building just across the road from Mama Needie's beyond the sugar cane field, where I would hear the recess bell halt the cheerful noise of children playing, calling them back to study. Two neatly built outhouses surrounded its simple frame bright whitewashed weatherboarding. This same building served as our praise house, where we heard the same bell rung on Sunday, Tuesday, and Thursday evenings calling neighbors for prayer meeting. And I would soon attend both institutions, as did most Gullah-Geechee children. At school our Gullah-Geechee speech was vigorously denounced, and we tried with considerable enthusiasm to learn English. At the praise house, the mourner's bench was our mantra for beginning our "seeking" journey. Seeking required that one visit a secret place in the forest three times a day — *fo day* (dawn), noon, and *fus* dark (dusk) — and through a series of dreams to arrive at an acceptable spiritual life.

Growing up I was able to observe my maternal grandfather, who believed that a witchcraft worker inflicted the epilepsy that he infrequently suffered, carry on an old African handcraft. He constantly knitted cast nets, as demands for his very much-appreciated skill to produce them were constant — mullet net, shrimp net, poor man's net (meaning one that could catch both shrimp and fish if you could only afford one). "Bubba," as we affectionately called him, was not as vocal as Mama Needie, but his Gullah was just as pronounced and he endeared us with his caring ways. To augment the fishnets that Bubba and others made, my father, uncle, and other men built bateaux in their backyards, some of which were fitted with sails while others were moved with oars. These small boats were used to strike for fish, harvest oysters, and travel downstream to Savannah with goods from the field and river. Then Gullah men and women alike would peddle these delicacies door to door in sweet grass baskets toted *pontop* (on top of) their heads up and down city lanes.

Indeed, like my family and hundreds of Gullah-Geechee kinfolks along the South Carolina and Georgia coastline, we have always had a sense of self and place. Still we were all attracted to life on the mainland. Trips to the city brought opportunities for Gullahs and mainland dwellers to meet sometime face to face for the first time. And like DuBois's description of the first Yankee-African meeting of 1861 in the sea islands, Gullahs visiting the mainland often brought similar reactions from city dwellers.

Perhaps I had a chance to visit the mainland earlier than most Gullah children of lowcountry islands because my father worked in Savannah. He and other men were the dredge workers who helped to prepare the Savannah River Port. My mother would alternate taking my eventual twelve siblings and me — during the summer when school was out, each time she made a trip to meet him on his biweekly paydays.

I was six years old when I took my first trip to Savannah. One of our cousins, Charlie Simmons Sr., operated a passenger ferry from Hilton Head to Savannah. Leaving Hilton Head Island soon after "day clean" one Friday morning, the eighteen-mile trip down Broad Creek with a stop at Daufuskie Island took about three hours one way. I remember the comradeship among the all-Gullah crowd. And I remember the men loading the boat with a variety of goods from the farm — watermelon, butter beans, peas, okra, and so on, to be sold at the Savannah market. The ferry would remain docked overnight, allowing its passengers to sell their goods, visit with relatives in the city, and shop. It would retrace the same route back to Hilton Head Island late afternoon the following day.

Savannah was a most fascinating place to me. This first trip was unforgettable because it exposed me to a world beyond anything I had imagined before. There were so many cars! And there were electric lights and indoor bathrooms. And their speech was different from ours on Hilton Head. My cousin Shorty who took me in tow thought my speech was funny. But we got along fine. I remember mimicking the way he would pronounce words. Perhaps this was my first effort to mask my language.

My mother and I spent a week with my father, who lived with our grand-aunt and her family in one of her bedrooms upstairs. I was particularly thrilled to be with both parents, for I saw my father seldom while he worked in Savannah. I would get to know him better when he returned to the island to become our one-room schoolteacher. I was proud to be one of his students from third through fifth grades when he would share with us about his stay as a young man in New York City.

Upon returning from my trip to Savannah, my siblings and cousins posed many curious questions about life there. It would be nearly ten years before my next trip to the mainland when I took an end-of-summer trip, again to Savannah, with two of my younger siblings.

Very often it is our speech with the African Caribbean accent, which was heard in the past more so than in the present day, and our dark complexion that create somewhat of a mystery to the observer. It has been reaction to this mystique (sometimes in the form of ridicule) throughout the history of Gullah-Geechee people that had until recently inspired us Gullahs to effect a mask of our language and particular components of the culture.

Even in these days of cultural diversity, when first-time meetings take place on the mainland (cities), Gullah people tend to secure the mask of their culture through acculturation or assimilation, as some of us will tend to divorce ourselves from rice meals except an occasional Chinese rice dinner. And we permanently switch our language to the King's English. We mask our own cultural traits, as best we can, and adopt the Eurocentricity that has dominated the cultural landscape.

On the sea islands, such as Ossabaw and others, where our culture developed and thrived for generations, masking was not necessary as we had always been (1860s–1960s) the dominant culture in the South Carolina–Georgia coastal region. But whenever outsiders cross the threshold of the coastline, their reaction to their perceived mystiques exhibited by the Gullah culture often result in a repugnance of visitors on the part of the indigenous Gullah-Geechee people. Patrons at the marketplace in Charleston, where basket weavers display their beautiful creations, complain that very few of these Gullah-Geechee women are willing to converse with them. This reticence to speak is the result of the disrespect of the language that was displayed by outsiders over the years. Conversely, admiration and respect for the artistic beauty of the Gullah baskets have engendered a substantial number of prolific basket weavers, and restaurants boast about their delicious bowls of gumbo, rice dishes, and shrimp and grits that satisfy juicy salivary glands.

For me, masking became a very valuable technique for acculturation when I entered high school in Bluffton after Hilton Head was bridged to the mainland in the mid-1950s. Peer pressure was incited most by my Bluffton classmates' ridiculing of my language. Eventually I ceased using Gullah words like *tote* (carry), *cooter* (turtle), *teif* (steal), and *tater* (potato), and I even tried to forget the folktales I had learned growing up. Still I did not succeed, for I believe that my Gullah-Geechee accent caused our senior class advisor to decide to have another person deliver the graduation address, even though I was the valedictorian.

I intensified this masking when I entered Savannah State College. Immediately I recoiled from reactions to my speech. These reactions were not in the form of ridicule, but were presented in curious questions. "Where in the world are you from?" a fellow student would exclaim upon hearing my speech, followed by inquisitions of word translations, my island life, and so on. They readily applied rice as the window to my Gullah-Geechee existence. At the time I had no idea why rice was the staple in our diet or why virtually every mainlander I met associated rice with my speech.

Masking of my Gullah-Geechee existence continued as I moved to Boston after college. I again failed in my attempt to mask my Gullah-Geechee speech, except we, like New Englanders, omit the letter "r" from words. My new acquaintances accepted no explanation of my heritage as a citizen of the United States. They were certain that no U.S. citizen could be so Caribbean or African unless they were born in these places. So when I bade them farewell to return to my native Hilton Head Island several years later, most of them assumed I returned to one of the Caribbean islands.

Personally for me and perhaps for other Gullah persons who practiced cultural masking techniques until recent years, the eureka moment for unmasking my Gullah cultural heritage came after encounters with several scholars from outside the Gullah region. For a number of them, I was a contact for community entry, and I became one of their major informants on Gullah cultural heritage. These contacts reaffirmed my sense of self and place. And, of course, lectures and symposiums on the Gullah-Geechee culture continued to affirm my Gullah heritage.

The 1960s civil rights movement and, perhaps, Martin Luther King's staff retreats at Penn Center on St. Helena Island, South Carolina, inspired a number of black scholars to research the connection between African Americans and the continent of Africa. Again they selected the Georgia–South Carolina coast as their laboratory. These scholars found less resistance from their informants than linguist Turner and others had found thirty years earlier during initial research on our culture.

One of the first research scholars on the Gullah culture that I encountered was J. Herman Blake, then provost of Oaks College at the University of California, Santa Cruz. He visited Daufuskie Island regularly during the 1970s to study the Gullah culture there. During that same period I had begun helping Daufuskie's families cope with problems of isolation from the mainland. Herman and I became good friends, and I learned much from the oral histories he collected from the people. Herman's visits to Daufuskie came on the heel of Pat Conroy's book *The Water Is Wide*, highlighting the unique culture from an outsider's viewpoint.[7]

Later, I came to understand better the importance of our praise houses. Patricia Guthrie published the result of her 1970s research in the book *Catching Sense*, revealing the uniqueness of life on St. Helena Island. She documented five cases that described how praise house leaders effectively judged community disputes. Her work quickened my memory of similar praise house activities when I was growing up on Hilton Head Island.[8]

Arguably the most ironic unmasking efforts of the Gullah-Geechee language were inspired by the Sea Island Language Project conceived by John Gadson, the former executive director of Penn Center in 1976. The project's goal, through a U.S. Department of Labor grant, was to teach English to Gullah-speaking high school graduates to enhance their chances of employment at the developing resorts on Hilton Head Island.

Linguists and laypeople alike predicted that a side effect of this unmasking effort could be the permanent loss of the Gullah language among these students and others. Immediately Claude and Pat Sharpe, two missionary linguists supported by the American Bible Society, rushed to the sea islands and began the Gullah Bible translation project to preserve the language.

In 1982, through the urging of a scholar on Africanisms in American culture, Joseph Holloway, I took a giant step on my unmasking journey when I joined the Bible translation team to translate the New Testament into our language. I was quickly enlightened when I learned that the rudiments of Gullah grammar began in Africa. For the first time in my life I was proud to express myself in Gullah and became a serious translator of English to Gullah. Over the next twenty-four-year period, I was engrossed in the translation until the project was completed in 2005. Today *De Nyew Testament* (*The New Testament in Gullah*) has surpassed sales expectations.[9]

For me, masking of my Gullah-Geechee culture was no longer needed after my contact with Joseph Opala, a former Peace Corps volunteer who shared similarities in our culture with Sierra Leone. My discussion with him on his published pamphlet "The Gullah: Rice, Slavery, and the Sierra Leone–American Connection" culminated in the rebirth of my sense of self and place. I became convinced that there is a clear view that the point of origin of our culture is West Africa.[10]

Eventually, in my capacity as executive director of Penn Center, a Historic Gullah Institution, on St. Helena Island, South Carolina, I hosted a visit in 1988 from President Joseph Momoh of Sierra Leone, West Africa. The main focus of his visit was to highlight the cultural and linguistic link between Gullahs and the people of Sierra Leone. A year later, in response to an invitation of President Momoh, I led a fifteen-member delegation to Sierra Leone. Our ten-day visit was an unforgettable experience in defining the true origin of Gullah people. I was able to compare their cultural features with those of our Gullah culture as we dined on delicious rice dishes, observed the close-knit villages, and listened carefully to the similarity in grammar. I was deeply and proudly touched by the reception from the people of Sierra Leone. It was the most wonderful trip of my life. My Gullah cultural pride grew tremendously during the trip. Upon returning home I vigorously began unveiling my cultural heritage. In essence I began exclaiming through words and deed: call me Gullah because I have been home again.[11]

So, thanks largely to curious academics like those cited earlier, who conducted extensive research of our culture, and my own memory of past traditions, I have become delightfully aware of who I am in relation to my African ancestry. I know that the confidence, with which I now explain the mystique of my Gullah-Geechee culture to my outside friends and colleagues, is partly a consequence of the relationship I forged with academics.

Films and other activities about our culture that have heavily influenced my sense of self and place continuously enhance my unmasking. My trip to Sierra Leone with fifteen fellow Gullah-Geechee colleagues in 1989 that examined the Gullah–Sierra Leone cultural links was documented in the popular film *Family across the Sea* and the popular television series *Gullah-Gullah Island*, starring the Gullah family of Ron and Natalie Daise. And other films, such as *Daughters of the Dust* and *The Will to Survive* have helped abate the mystique of the Gullah culture for outsiders.[12]

At the community level, Gullah-Geechee people are contributing to the unmasking effort. Historic institutions like churches and praise houses, and educational institutions that contribute to the sustenance of our culture are being restored and preserved for regular use. Festivals, family reunions, and tours held throughout Gullah-Geechee land, featuring educational performances of songs, storytelling, and so on, are bringing visibility as well as revenue to the culture. The *Nyew Testament* was published by the American Bible Society in 2005 and has produced sales beyond initial expectations. Restaurants are serving Gullah-Geechee rice dishes and other Gullah-Geechee delicacies to the delight of many outsiders. The art of Jonathan Green highlights the surge of Gullah-Geechee culture–influenced artists, and the Gullah-Geechee basket has become one of the most desired commemorative art objects in the Gullah-Geechee region.

The stretch of coastline from Wilmington, North Carolina, to Jacksonville, Florida, was designated as the Gullah-Geechee Cultural Heritage Corridor by legislation of the U.S. Congress in 2006. A fifteen-member commission for the corridor was recently organized and officers were elected. As a member of the commission, I am elated that implementation of the provisions of the legislation will enhance our effort to preserve our culture.

Unlike when I grew up, I believe there is little reason for contemporary young Gullah-Geechee people to mask their culture. First, the advent of modern development has made the costal region of South Carolina and Georgia readily accessible to outsiders. There is regular contact between Gullah-Geechee people today. Outsiders are much better informed about the Gullah culture than during my youth. Second, these outsiders are regularly becoming residents of the Gullah-Geechee corridor, presenting chances for commingling of cultures. Gullah-Geechee purveyors of traditional Gullah art, Gullah history, and food are fulfilling very well the intellectual thirst and exotic food appetites of immigrants who come to the corridor. Crowds flock to festivals and symposiums on Gullah-Geechee culture. Gullah-Geechee dishes are served in restaurants, and Gullah-influenced artists are among the most popular in art galleries.

Contemporary outsiders are recognizing and understanding Africanisms in the Gullah culture like never before. In these days of promoting cultural diversity, masking is less prevalent than in the past. But the consequences of this cultural mixing could present a stern challenge for us in preserving certain cultural assets. Today's challenge for Gullah-Geechee people is not the deliberate masking of cultural qualities as I have described, but preserving these cultural assets in the face of natural acculturation that may take place. The question is whether we will continue to embrace primarily our Gullah culture or whether we will abandon ours and embrace that of the outsider. I am hoping for the merging of the two worlds, distinguishable, yet whole and unmasked with a sense of self and place.

NOTES

1. Margaret Washington Creel, *A Peculiar People: Slave Religion and Community-Culture among the Gullahs* (New York: New York University Press, 1988), 17.

2. W. E. B. DuBois, *Souls of Black Folk* (Chicago: A. C. McClury, 1903), 20.

3. Laura Towne, *Letters and Diary of Laura M. Towne: Written from the Sea Islands of South Carolina, 1862–1864* (1912; repr., Negro University Press, 1969), 20.

4. Buddy Sullivan, *Early Days on the Georgia Tidewater: The Story of McIntosh County and Sapelo* (Darien, Ga.: McIntosh County Board of Education, 1990); Judith Carney, *Black Rice: The African Origins of Rice Cultivation in the Americas* (Cambridge, Mass.: Harvard University Press, 2001); Peter Wood, *Black Majority: Negroes in Colonial South Carolina from 1670 through the Stono Rebellion* (New York: W. W. Norton, 1974).

5. Lorenzo D. Turner, *Africanisms in the Gullah Dialect* (Ann Arbor: University of Michigan Press, 1949), 40.

6. Guy B. Johnson, *Folk Culture on St. Helena Island* (Chapel Hill: University of North Carolina Press, 1930).

7. Pat Conroy, *The Water Is Wide* (Boston: Houghton, 1972).

8. Patricia Guthrie, *Catching Sense: African American Communities on a South Carolina Sea Island* (Westport, Conn.: Bergin & Garvey, 1996), 101–2.

9. *De Nyew Testament (The New Testament in Gullah)* (New York: American Bible Society, 2005).

10. Joe Opala, *The Gullah: Rice, Slavery and the Sierra Leone–American Connection* (Freetown, Sierra Leone: U.S. Information Service, 1987).

11. Emory S. Campbell, *Gullah Cultural Legacies* (Hilton Head Island, S.C.: Gullah Heritage Consulting Services, LLC, 2002).

12. *Family across the Sea*, videocassette (South Carolina ETV, 1989); *Daughters of the Dust*, K133 DVD (1991; Kino International Corp., 1999).

CONTRIBUTORS

EMORY S. CAMPBELL is a lifelong resident of Hilton Head Island, South Carolina, having grown up there before the island was connected to the mainland. He is executive director emeritus of Penn Center, a distinguished Gullah culture repository on St. Helena Island, South Carolina, and an inaugural member of the Gullah-Geechee Cultural Heritage Corridor Commission. He is the author of *Gullah Cultural Legacies* (2008).

VINCENT CARRETTA is a professor of English at the University of Maryland. He has published studies and authoritative editions of the works of Olaudah Equiano, Ignatius Sancho, Quobna Ottobah Cugoano, Phillis Wheatley, and other eighteenth-century transatlantic authors of African descent. His most recent book is the prize-winning *Equiano, the African: Biography of a Self-Made Man* (University of Georgia Press, 2005). With Ty Reese, Carretta has just completed an edition of the correspondence of the eighteenth-century African missionary Philip Quaque.

ERSKINE CLARKE is professor emeritus of American religious history at Columbia Theological Seminary, Decatur, Georgia. His book *Dwelling Place: A Plantation Epic* (2005) received the Bancroft Prize in American history from Columbia University, New York.

ALLISON DORSEY is an associate professor of history at Swarthmore College. She is the author of *To Build Our Lives Together: Community Formation in Black Atlanta, 1875–1906* (University of Georgia Press, 2004). She is currently working on a biography of black freedman and entrepreneur Mustapha Shaw.

MICHAEL A. GOMEZ is professor of history and Middle Eastern and Islamic studies at New York University. http://history.fas.nyu.edu/object/michaelgomez

JACQUELINE JONES is Mastin Gentry White Professor of Southern History and Walter Prescott Webb Chair in History and Ideas at the University of Texas at Austin. She is the author of, most recently, *Saving Savannah: The City and the Civil War* (2008).

PHILIP MORGAN is Harry C. Black Professor of History, Johns Hopkins University. He is working on the history of the early Caribbean.

TIMOTHY POWELL is a senior research scientist at the University of Pennsylvania Museum of Archaeology and Anthropology. He is currently directing two large grant projects for the American Philosophical Society related to the digitization of Native American images and endangered languages. He is the author of *Ruthless Democracy: A Multicultural Interpretation of the American Renaissance* (2000).

PAUL PRESSLY is an independent scholar who has published articles in the *Georgia Historical Quarterly* and *Annales d'histoire economique et sociale*. He received his DPhil from Oxford University. He is director of the Ossabaw Island Education Alliance and is working on a history of colonial Georgia and the Atlantic world.

THERESA A. SINGLETON is associate professor of anthropology at Syracuse University. She is currently completing an archaeological study of slavery on a Cuban coffee plantation.

BETTY WOOD is reader in American history in the faculty of history at the University of Cambridge and a fellow of Girton College, Cambridge. She writes on the history of slavery, race relations, and gender in the eighteenth- and early nineteenth-century southern United States. Her publications include *Slavery in Colonial Georgia, 1730–1775* (University of Georgia Press, 1984); *Women's Work, Men's Work: The Informal Slave Economies of Lowcountry Georgia* (University of Georgia Press, 1995); *Come Shouting to Zion: African American Protestantism in the American South and British Caribbean to 1830* (1998, with Sylvia R. Frey); and *Slavery in Colonial America, 1619–1776* (2005).

McLane, Julia, 205
Medway conjurer, 131–32, 135, 143–45
Mein, William, 253, 257–58, 259, 266, 267–69, 270, 271
Menendez, Francisco, 21
Mepkin (plantation), 61
Mercer, George A., 200
Methodism movement, 79–80
Methodist Kingswood School (Bristol), 88
Methodist Magazine, 80, 89
Metropolitan Fire Company, 209
Micmacs, 5, 84
Middle Passage: from Africa to Georgia, 30–34, 44n28; and black diaspora back to Africa, 99; kongo cosmogram of flying Africans and, 268–70; memorial honoring Africans of, 3
Milton, John, 97
Misquito Indians, 5
Mobley, Hardy, 245
Mohammed of Sapelo, 5
Momoh, President, 290
Montgomery, James, 240
Montgomery Guards, 196
Moore, James, 254
Moore, Matthew, 85
Moorish Science Temple, 10, 122
Morel, John, Jr., 225, 226, 234
Morel, Mary Ann, 225–26
Morgan, Philip, 3, 4, 13, 48
Morning News, 214
Morrison, Toni, 256, 271–74, 276
Mosa (enslaved person), 28, 95
Mossman, James, 92, 93
Mpongwe people (Africa), 139
Mungin, John, 241
Musgrove, Mary, 21–22
Muslims. *See* African Muslims

Nancy (merchant sloop), 92, 93, 95
A Narrative of the Lord's Wonderful Dealings with John Marrant, a Black.

See Marrant's *A Narrative of the Lord's Wonderful Dealings with John Marrant, a Black . . .*
narratives. *See* autobiographical narratives; oral narratives
Nassau, Robert Hamill, 141
National Book Critics Circle Award, 271
National Park Service, 3
Nation of Islam, 122
Native Americans: comparing slave-made pottery with that of, 158–59; contact between slave population and, 5, 20–25; cultural sovereignty of oral tradition of, 278n25; Marrant's life among, 82; slavery practiced among, 21–22
naval impressment practice, 15
Ned (enslaved person), 132
Needle Woman's Society, 195
Nelson (enslaved person), 5
New Britannia (slaving vessel), 34
Newton, John, 87
New York Times, 209
New Yorker, 256
North Newport Baptist Church, 138
"Ntangu-Tandu-Kolo: The Bantu-Kongo Concept of Time" (Fu-Kiau), 264
"nucleated plantation village," 168–69
De Nyew Testament (*The New Testament in Gullah*), 289

Oaks College (UC Santa Cruz), 289
O'Byrne, Dominick, 209
Odingsells, Anthony, 203
Oglethorpe, James, 15, 18, 20–21, 50
Oglethorpe Light Club, 209
Oglethorpe Light Infantry, 196
Ojibwe Indian Nation, 278n25
Okra (enslaved person), 9, 164
Okra's house, 9, 164
"Old King," 115
Olwell, Robert, 48

RACE IN THE ATLANTIC WORLD, 1700–1900

*The Hanging of Angélique: The Untold Story of
Canadian Slavery and the Burning of Old Montréal*
by Afua Cooper

Christian Ritual and the Creation of British Slave Societies, 1650–1780
by Nicholas M. Beasley

*African American Life in the Georgia Lowcountry:
The Atlantic World and the Gullah Geechee*
Edited by Philip Morgan

*The Horrible Gift of Freedom: Atlantic Slavery
and the Representation of Emancipation*
by Marcus Wood

*The Life and Letters of Philip Quaque,
the First African Anglican Missionary*
edited by Vincent Carretta and Ty M. Reese

*In Search of Brightest Africa: Reimagining the
Dark Continent in American Culture, 1884–1936*
by Jeannette Eileen Jones

*Contentious Liberties: American Abolitionists in
Post-emancipation Jamaica, 1834–1866*
by Gale L. Kenny

*We Are the Revolutionists: German-Speaking Immigrants
and American Abolitionists after 1848*
by Mischa Honeck

The American Dreams of John B. Prentis, Slave Trader
by Kari J. Winter

*Missing Links: The African and American Worlds
of R. L. Garner, Primate Collector*
by Jeremy Rich

Almost Free: A Story about Family and Race in Antebellum Virginia
by Eva Sheppard Wolf